THE FREEDOM-OF-THOUGHT STRUGGLE IN THE OLD SOUTH

hARPER TORChBOOKS

A reference-list of Harper Torchbooks, classified
by subjects, is printed at the end of this volume.

Orton, near Wilmington, North Carolina

From a photograph by Ernest Graham, by courtesy of J. Laurence Sprunt

CLEMENT EATON

THE FREEDOM-OF-THOUGHT STRUGGLE IN THE OLD SOUTH

Harper Torchbooks ▼ The Academy Library
Harper & Row, Publishers
New York, Evanston, and London

To My *Alma Maters,*
the University of North Carolina
and Harvard University

PREFACE TO THE TORCHBOOK EDITION

RECENT EVENTS have shown that a supposedly democratic nation can be complacent for a long time to great social and political evils within its bosom. Then, a time of maturation comes; a revolution of opinion emerges; a dramatic struggle takes place between the forces of conservatism and liberalism. In the Old South such a struggle arose in the 1830's and continued until the Civil War. It was a conflict between the ideas of the Age of the American Enlightenment and the new spirit of economic exploitation generated by the westward movement. In this contest between liberals and conservatives—fought over the gradual removal of human bondage, civil liberties, adoption of a democratic system of education, and freedom from religious orthodoxy—the liberals were defeated on almost all fronts. Their epitaph is recorded in a letter written in 1857 by ex-Senator William C. Preston of South Carolina, who had been visiting in Virginia, where he read a defense of slavery by Thornton Stringfellow, a Baptist minister of the state. Preston urged his correspondent, a prominent political leader of the South Carolina up country, to read the Stringfellow book, which he described as "vastly the best work I have ever read on the subject, especially the *Scriptural*. It has wrought a change in my views which have been worrying me all my life."[1] Thus this admirable representative of the Old South, a man of culture and thought, who had been president of South Carolina College as well as a Whig Senator, described a change that had come over the Southern mind—the culmination of a struggle which is portrayed in *Freedom of Thought in the Old South*.

Under a slightly modified title, this new edition contains a study of certain aspects of the subject not considered in the original work. A chapter on censorship of the mails has been added, based on an article that I published in 1943 in the

---

[1] William C. Preston to Waddy Thompson, August 10, 1857, MS. In William C. Preston Papers, South Caroliniana Library, Columbia.

American Historical Review. I wish that I could have included also a pertinent study of the suppression of civil liberties presented in my article, "Mob Violence in the Old South," (*Mississippi Valley Historical Review,* December, 1942), but space did not permit. Two other new chapters treat those political leaders of the Old South who displayed independence of mind and often moral courage by opposing popular measures that they regarded as harmful. This theme is developed particularly in Chapter XIV, an expanded version of my article, "Southern Senators and the Right of Instruction, 1789–1860," published in the *Journal of Southern History* (August, 1952). The concluding chapter, written this year, portrays the role of the American nationalists in the pre-war South—those leaders who transcended the sectional view in politics, and by so doing incurred obloquy, social ostracism, and at times the ominous threat of mobs.

In order to save space for the new material, the preface of the original 1940 edition has been omitted, as well as the much longer preface of the 1951 edition (Peter Smith) in which I outlined some of the changes I would have made then if the opportunity of rewriting the book had been given to me. I stated then, as I reaffirm in this latest edition, that though I would make textual changes if I could rewrite this story of the suppression of civil liberties in the Old South, I should not alter my principal conclusions, for I believe that they are as valid today as when I first published them. When I published *Freedom of Thought* I followed the usage of American writers of the time in not capitalizing the word "Negro." This I have changed, and some minor factual errors have also been corrected.

Rereading *Freedom of Thought* in the light of recent events I am impressed with the remarkable parallel in attitudes toward social change between the society of the Old South and that of Mississippi and Alabama today. The Old South went to war rather than risk any basic change in its social order. Recently Mississippi and Alabama as well as other parts of the South have violently resisted any significant change in race relationships; both the old and the new societies have suppressed freedom of speech and forced their moderate citizens to acquiescence or to silence. The president of the Southern Historical Association in his presidential address at Asheville, North Carolina, in 1963, spoke of "the closed society" of Mississippi, where time has stood still for a hundred years with regard to race relationships and where dissent is not tolerated.[2] Yet after he had thus scathingly denounced the people of Mississippi he was allowed to return to his chair of history in the University of Mississippi, which he could not have done in the period before the Civil War. Hardly a day passes in the United States—in the world—that we do not see fresh examples of the violation of the dignity of man by the suppression of his freedom of thought and speech and by the display of prejudice. Indeed, freedom of thought and speech is today both a timely and timeless subject.

June, 1964

C. E.

---

[2] James W. Silver, "Mississippi: The Closed Society," *Journal of Southern History*, XXX (February, 1964), 3–34. (This article has been incorporated into a book by Professor Silver, published under the same title by Harcourt, Brace & World, 1964.)

Contents

LIST OF ILLUSTRATIONS

*Plates II through VIII will be found in
a group following page 214.*

Orton was the home of rice planters on the Cape Fear River,
near Wilmington, North Carolina. "The lower central
portion of Orton house was the original colonial home of
'King' Roger Moore, [with walls] from 18 inches to 24
inches thick.—Around 1840 a second story and the columns
were added by Dr. Frederick Hill who owned Orton in
those years. About 1910 my father, James Sprunt, added
the two wings. . . . Rice was the main crop in pre-Civil
War times, in fact on up to about 1900. . . . Orton was attacked by a landing force from Cornwallis' expedition and
used by the Northern forces as a smallpox hospital after the
fall of Fort Fisher."

(J. Laurence Sprunt to the writer, October 5, 1939)

Frontispiece

George Mason (1725-1792) was one of the liberal aristocrats
who made a contribution to the culture of the South. He
was a large slaveowner, a tobacco planter, a speculator in
Western lands, a justice of the peace, a vestryman of Pohick
Episcopal Church, an active agitator of the American Revo-
lution, one of the most important framers of the Virginia
Constitution of 1776, and a delegate to the Constitutional
Convention in Philadelphia. His liberal ideas were ex-
pressed in the Virginia Declaration of Rights, the Virginia
Constitution, and the "Objections of Hon. George Mason
to the Proposed Federal Constitution; Assigned as His
Reasons for not Signing the Same."

PLATE I

Gunston Hall, the home of George Mason, on the Potomac
River, was completed in 1758. The architect and builder
of this Georgian house was William Buckland, a skilled
craftsman brought from England under indenture. Gunston
Hall was a brick story-and-a-half house possessing two
small but distinctive porticos; one, pentagonal in shape,
faced a formal garden sloping down to the Potomac River;

[ix]

the other, on the opposite side of the house, was supported by four Doric columns and had a vista through a long avenue of cherry trees. The grounds contain some of the most magnificent boxwoods in America. The principal rooms of Gunston Hall were paneled, and the window and door frames were exquisitely carved in Chinese Chippendale style.

Berry Hill, the home of the Bruces at Halifax, Virginia, built about 1843, illustrates the great enthusiasm for the Greek revival style of architecture that pervaded the ante-bellum South. In the modern South brains and culture have been drained from the country and concentrated in the cities and towns. But in the days "befo' the war," the rural roads of the South led the traveler by many charming homes, such as Berry Hill, where the true aristocrats lived. To the writer such a social revolution seems to be, next to the abolition of slavery, the most profound difference between "the Old South" and "the New South."

"A Cotton Plantation on the Mississippi." The invention of the cotton gin by the Connecticut Yankee, Eli Whitney, in 1793, made profitable the growing of short staple or green seed cotton in the interior of the Lower South. The Upper South, unsuited to the growing of cotton except in western Tennessee and eastern North Carolina, continued to raise tobacco, wheat and corn, and to sell its surplus slaves to the cotton and sugar planters of the Gulf states. The leadership in the production of cotton passed from the Atlantic seaboard states to the Gulf region by 1830.

Cooleemee, near Mocksville, North Carolina, was built in 1854 by Major Peter W. Hairston. "It is of an Anglo-Grecian style of architecture and is made of brick-stucco. Much of the woodwork and materials were brought from Philadelphia by boat to Fayetteville, North Carolina, and from there by wagons! . . . The plans [for building Cooleemee] were taken from an English publication called *The Archi-*

tect and reprinted in an old *Godey's Lady's Book* of 1850. The name Cooleemee is supposed to have been the name of an Indian village, the home of a little Creek Indian whom Gen. Pearson [a former owner of the estate] captured in the Creek Indian Wars in Florida and brought home with him. . . . The Hairstons as a family owned a great many slaves. My husband's great-grandmother was said to have owned more slaves than any other woman in the South. There were about 300 slaves on the Cooleemee Plantation."

(Mrs. Peter W. Hairston to the writer, October 1, 1939)

PLATE IV a

The Grand Stairway at Cooleemee is of a spiral design built around a square hall, which forms the intersection of a Maltese cross.

PLATE IV b

Dixon H. Lewis (1802-1848), Senator from Alabama, lived in the delightful village of Lownesboro in the Black Belt of Alabama. He weighed four hundred and thirty pounds, a circumstance which forced him always to engage two seats in the stagecoach that transported him to Washington. Furthermore, the Senate had a special chair constructed for him, the fattest Senator that has ever appeared among that august body of legislators. It is now owned by the University of Alabama at Tuscaloosa. Dixon Lewis was the most devoted Calhoun leader in the Lower South. Nevertheless, he wrote: "Calhoun is now my principal associate, and he is too intelligent, too industrious, too intent in the struggle of politics to suit me except as an occasional companion. There is no *relaxation* with him. On the contrary, when I seek relaxation with him, he screws me only the higher in some sort of excitement."

(To R. K. Crallé, Washington, March 20, 1840)

PLATE V a

Doctor Thomas Cooper (1759-1839) was born in England, and emigrated to Pennsylvania in 1794. Here he became an ardent Jeffersonian and as a result of his criticism of the Adams administration and of the Sedition Act in 1800, he was fined four hundred dollars and imprisoned for six months. In 1820 he was chosen president of South Carolina College at Columbia, a position he held until 1834 despite his heterodox religious opinions.

PLATE V b

James Louis Petigru (1789-1863) has been properly called Charleston's greatest private citizen. Although he was one of the most brilliant lawyers of South Carolina, he never held high political office. In a civilization strongly affected by the Romantic Movement, Petigru was a realist, whose sparkling wit deflated popular illusions and pricked the glamour of the heroes of the moment. He reminds one of Chief Justice John Marshall, thoroughly Southern in the geniality and simplicity of his personality, but out of sympathy with the political trends of his section. In 1832 he led the Unionist party in South Carolina against the Nullifiers and in 1860 he vigorously protested against secession.

PLATE VI a

Henry A. Wise (1806-1876), Congressman, Minister to Brazil, and Governor of Virginia at the time of the John Brown Raid, was a vivid type of the Southern fire-eater. In physical appearance he was tall and very thin, with a large mobile mouth, and a sallow, emaciated face illuminated by great flashing eyes. His nature was extraordinarily combative, so that he took extreme positions out of sheer defiance. When he entered Congress as a very youthful member, John Quincy Adams referred to him as the successor of John Randolph of Roanoke, because of his "tartness, his bitterness, his malignity, and his inconsistencies" (*Memoirs,* IX, 88). In season and out, Wise attacked the abolitionists with a torrent of words, bitter, sardonic, eloquent, until, at times, his voice lost its ringing quality and broke into "a childish treble." He insisted on the most rigid application of the "Gag Resolution," and when Representative Slade of Vermont undertook to criticize the slave system of the South, he led the Southern members in an exodus from the hall of Congress. But level-headed Southerners distrusted the leadership, as James Louis Petigru wrote, of "an orator like Wise who speaks from Monday morning till Saturday night." (To Cary, August 22, 1861, Petigru Papers in Library of Congress)

John Hampden Pleasants (1797-1846) was one of the most forceful and courageous editors of the Old South. As editor of the Richmond *Whig,* which he founded in 1824, he was the leading exponent of Whig doctrines in Virginia. He had the courage to criticize the institution of Southern slavery. His death came as the result of a duel fought over the charge by a rival editor that he had abolitionist sympathies.

Cassius Marcellus Clay (1810-1903) edited the *True American.* an antislavery newspaper that was suppressed by a mob in 1845. He attempted to organize the nonslaveholders of Kentucky into a movement to rid the state of slavery. His truculent career was punctuated by duels, fights with the bowie knife, several murders, and a participation in the Mexican War. He joined the Republican party in 1856, and was sent by Lincoln as Minister to Russia.

"Fort Hill," Calhoun's home, near Pendleton, South Carolina, remodeled after 1826, was located in the extreme northwest portion of the state, far from the exclusive aristocracy of Charleston.

CHAPTER I

ARISTOCRATS WITH LIBERAL VIEWS

THE SOUTHERN section of the United States was the home of a small but powerful aristocracy at the close of the eighteenth century. From three main ingredients it was composed: merchants, planters, and lawyers. With few exceptions the ruling families were developed on the native soil from middle-class origins.[1] They attained, nonetheless, a genuine aristocratic temper that defied the leveling influence of the frontier. The conditions of a slave plantation, the example of a royal "governor's set," the sense of social stratification brought over from England, were conducive to the emergence of a capable native aristocracy.[2] The country squires from the Sweet-scented tobacco parishes and the rice country developed the requisite substratum of wealth, a sense of dignity, the habit of leadership, and refined tastes, that make an aristocrat. The tremendous responsibilities of managing large slave plantations, of acting as justices of the peace, and of serving as vestrymen in the Episcopal Church were a crucible in which forceful yet superbly controlled characters were formed. Before the Revolution the common people looked up to this group as superior men, "gentlemen." Whenever "King" Carter, the owner of three hundred thousand acres of land and seven hundred slaves, rode in his coach to church, he would find all the congregation awaiting his arrival before they entered. The psychology of the common people toward the governing classes was not fundamentally changed until the coming of the Jacksonian movement.

[1] T. J. Wertenbaker, *Patrician and Plebeian in Virginia* (Charlottesville, Va., 1910), and P. A. Bruce, *Social Life in Virginia in the Seventeenth Century* (Lynchburg, Va., 1902), present somewhat conflicting points of view on this subject. See also A. H. Hirsch, *The Huguenots of Colonial South Carolina* (Durham, N. C., 1928).

[2] A. M. Schlesinger, *New Viewpoints in American History* (New York, 1922), chap. iv, "The Decline of Aristocracy in America."

The Southern aristocracy of the early Republic was relatively small in numbers as compared to the whole body of white people. The best economic test of aristocracy at this period was the ownership of slaves. The South Carolina Tidewater area contained the greatest concentration of slaveholdings, yet in 1790 there were only one hundred and forty-two families in the state who could be counted as great slaveholders, and about three hundred who owned between fifty and one hundred slaves.[3] In Maryland there were only twenty, and in North Carolina only twelve, individuals listed in the census of 1790 as owning over one hundred slaves. Some of the wealthy slave masters were Ralph Izard of South Carolina with six hundred and four slaves, George Mason with over three hundred, Washington with one hundred and eighty-eight, Charles Carroll of Maryland with three hundred and sixteen, and Willie Jones of North Carolina with one hundred and twenty. In Maryland there existed certain great landlords, like Charles Carroll and Daniel Dulany, who, besides their slaves, secured many tenants from Europe to cultivate their lordly acres. Although most of the aristocrats of this period dwelt in the Tidewater, there were some masterful individuals, such as Judge Richard Henderson and Colonel Edmund Fanning of the North Carolina back country, John Sevier in Tennessee, and John Adair in Kentucky, who undoubtedly belonged to the aristocracy.[4] The merchant-aristocrat of the South almost invariably acquired great estates in the country like the Galloways of Maryland, who owned Tulip Hill.[5] The most picturesque of these merchant-aristocrats was Christopher Gadsden, who owned a thousand-foot wharf in Charleston. Although he led the mechanics of Charleston in the agitation

[3] *Heads of Families at the First Census of the United States Taken in the Year 1790* (Washington, D. C., 1908), IV, North Carolina, South Carolina, Maryland, Virginia, *passim*. The Virginia returns are lost, but state lists for about half of the counties are preserved. In this incomplete enumeration, the writer counted only twenty owners of a hundred slaves or more.

[4] For frontier criticisms of such aristocrats, see W. K. Boyd (ed.), *Some Eighteenth Century Tracts Concerning North Carolina* (Raleigh, N. C., 1927).

[5] Several generations of Galloways lived at Tulip Hill, and their papers, preserved in the Library of Congress, illuminate the life of the Southern aristocracy.

against the British rule, he believed in a democracy under aristocratic leadership. When he died in 1805, he ordered that
his grave should be leveled and unmarked, "disliking ostenta-
tion of any kind."[6]

An aristocracy necessarily implies the existence of a large
body of plebeians. The census of 1790 indicates that approximately two thirds of the white population of the South did
not belong to slaveholding families. Nevertheless, this large
body of commoners were prevented from playing a dominant
role in politics by the property qualifications on voting, their
lack of education, the difficulty of communication, and, above
all, by their own attitude toward government. They were
accustomed to follow aristocratic leadership. Consequently, it
was the tradition for the leading families to provide the political representatives of the county and the state. The history
of the Virginia Lees illustrates how an aristocracy of public
service perpetuated itself. The direct descendants of Richard
Lee, the immigrant, to the time of Robert E. Lee included
fifty-four males who lived to maturity, of whom thirty-seven
were engaged in public service, holding seventy-two offices.
This imposing record included two signers of the Declaration,
three governors, six members of the council, fifteen military
officers, two diplomats, three members of the Continental Congress, and three United States Congressmen.[7] Even more notable than the Lees in producing political leaders were the Randolph and Carter families. Money was seldom the object of
these well-born gentlemen in accepting public office. The love
of honor, the tradition of the family, and *noblesse oblige* were
the dominant motives.

The aristocratic temper was powerfully stimulated by the
practice of the wealthy planters of sending their sons to Europe
for an education. Colonel William Byrd II, for example, min-
gled with a gay set of aristocrats in England, counting as his
friends the Duke of Argyle, the Marquis of Halifax, the Earl

[6] Mrs. St. Julien Ravenel, *Charleston: The Place and the People* (New York,
1927), p. 400.
[7] Douglas Southall Freeman, *R. E. Lee: A Biography* (4 vols.; New York, 1934),
I, 165.

of Orrery, Lord Oxford, Lord Egmont, the Lady Betty Crom-
well. Their portraits he brought back with him to hang on
the walls of Westover, as trophies of his social conquests.[8] The
South Carolina planters, especially, appreciated the need of an
education in Europe, while their wealth from the rice trade and
from commerce, and their convenient communications with
England through the port of Charleston facilitated the vogue
of sending their sons to Eton, Oxford, and the Middle Temple.
Prior to the year 1860 more than three hundred and fifty
Americans were admitted to the Inns of Court in London.
Of this group, two hundred and twenty-five were from the
South or intimately connected with that section. South Carolina sent eighty-nine youths, Virginia, seventy-six, in contrast
to the thirty from Massachusetts and the forty from New
York.[9] The Pinckneys, the Rutledges, the Laurens', the Mid-
dletons, the Manigaults, the Izards—hardly a prominent man
of the second half of the eighteenth century in South Carolina
can be omitted—had been educated in England. The letters
of Peter Manigault, whose grandfather had been a victualer
and distiller, show his profound interest while a student of
the Inner Temple in the fashionable life of London, its
theaters, and coffeehouses.[10] Charles Carroll of Maryland,
the Catholic, had been sent to France for his education. A
British actor, John Bernard, met the latter in 1798, and his
description of Carroll gives the portrait of an ideal eighteenth-
century aristocrat: "From the refinement of his manners, a
stranger would have surmised that he had passed all his days
in the *salons* of Paris. He had all that suavity and softness,
in combination with dignity, which bespeak the perfection of
good taste. This attested the character of his society. Ease may
be natural to a man, but elegance—the union of propriety
with ease—must be acquired; the art of respecting one's com-

[8] Dixon Wecter, *The Saga of American Society: A Record of Social Aspiration,
1607-1937* (New York, 1937), p. 26; see also R. C. Beatty, *William Byrd of Westover* (Boston, 1932), chaps. ii and iii.

[9] J. G. deR. Hamilton, "Southern Members of the Inns of Court," *North Carolina Historical Review*, X, 274 (Oct., 1933).

[10] See *South Carolina Historical and Genealogical Magazine*, XV, 113-123 (July,
1914); XXXI, 171-183, 269-282 (July and Oct., 1930).

pany as well as one's self necessarily implies that one's company is worth respecting."[11]

Beautiful homes in the Georgian style exhibited the taste of these aristocrats. Westover, Shirley, Stratford, Chantilly, Corotoman, Marmion, Rosegill, Mt. Airy, Sabine Hall, Mount Vernon, Belvoir, Greenway Court, Bewdly, Tulip Hill, Middleton Place, Drayton Hall, Montpellier, and Monticello were noble estates, whose owners lived like English country gentlemen. The pride of some of these eighteenth-century aristocrats overreached itself, as in the case of Mann Page, who built Rosewell on a branch of the York River. The son-in-law of "King" Carter, educated at Eton and Oxford, Mann Page, was a great landed proprietor, owning over twenty-seven thousand acres of land. He built Rosewell with lavish magnificence, disdainful of the debt he incurred. Its thirty-five rooms made it probably the largest house built in the South in the eighteenth century. When he died, however, his son had to petition the Virginia legislature to break the entail on the estate in order to pay for the folly of the builder of Rosewell.[12]

A sample of the cultivated life lived by many of these country gentlemen is given in the Journal of Philip Fithian, a tutor at Nomini Hall.[13] Robert Carter, the proprietor, was on the governor's council and owned sixty thousand acres of land and six hundred Negroes. He drove along the dusty Virginia roads in a pea-green and black coach imported from England at a cost of £130 sterling, and he drank from imported silver goblets. "Councillor" Carter had a library of over fifteen hundred books and a large collection of musical instruments. One of his neighbors, Colonel John Tayloe, was distinguished by his formal garden adorned with four beau-

[11] Allan Nevins (ed.), *American Social History as Recorded by British Travellers* (New York, 1923), pp. 28-29. Something of the restraint of the Southern aristocrat was revealed in a letter of Carroll to his son, advising "Avoid parade and useless expense" (letter of Aug. 13, 1800, Charles Carroll Papers, MSS in Library of Congress).

[12] William Meade, *Old Churches, Ministers and Families of Virginia* (Philadelphia, 1872), I, 331-333.

[13] See Philip Vickers Fithian, *Journal, 1773-74* (Princeton, 1900). A large collection of the letter books and papers of "Councillor" Carter are preserved in the Library of Congress.

tiful marble statutes and by his famed racer, "Yorick," who won a prize of £500. Fithian observed the Virginia love of the stately dances of that period, their ceremonious manners, their regard for class distinctions, and he trained himself to fit into this society by reading the letters of Lord Chesterfield. Some of the finest private libraries in America were accumulated by these Southern planters, notably the splendid library of Sir John Randolph, the five hundred and thirty-five volumes of Hayes near Edenton, the four thousand volumes at Westover, and the seven thousand volumes at Monticello.[14]

But a majority of the planters did not possess stately mansions or live in refined luxury. Their homes were usually modest frame or log structures that were inadequate for their large families.[15] Even the home of "King" Roger Moore, a masterful rice planter of the Cape Fear River, was a small story and a half house, whose thick brick walls were capable of repelling attacks of pirates or Indians. To a Scotch lady of quality, Miss Janet Schaw, who visited in the Cape Fear region on the eve of the Revolution, the society of the rice planters seemed rather uncouth. She was invited to a ball in Wilmington, at which the dances, ceremonies, and costumes appeared laughable, reminding her of a Dutch picture. ". . . but there was no object on which my own ridicule fixed," she wrote, "equal to myself and the figure I made, dressed out in all my British airs with a high head and a hoop and trudging thro' the unpaved streets in embroidered shoes by the light of a lanthorn carried by a black wench half naked."[16] She observed the incongruity of the conduct of Mrs. Cornelius Harnett, the wife of a prominent Revolutionary leader. This extraordinary lady lived on the beautiful plantation of Hilton,

[14] Stephen B. Weeks, "Libraries and Literature in North Carolina in the Eighteenth Century," *Annual Report of the American Historical Association, 1895,* pp. 171-261.

[15] See Washington's observations on his Southern tour (J. C. Fitzpatrick, ed., *The Diaries of George Washington, 1748-1799,* Boston, 1925, IV, 195).

[16] Evangeline Walker Andrews and Charles McLean Andrews (eds.), *Journal of a Lady of Quality; Being the Narrative of a Journey from Scotland to the West Indies, North Carolina, and Portugal in the years 1774 to 1776* (New Haven, Conn., 1934), p. 154.

but she did not deign it beneath her dignity "to make minced pies, cheese-cakes, tarts and little biskets," which she sent to Wilmington along with poultry and eggs to be sold strictly for cash.[17] One of the magnates of the region, who drew large revenues from making tar and turpentine, Miss Schaw found living in a house not much better than one of his negro huts, so that "it appeared droll enough to eat out of China and be served in plate in such a parlour."[18] Furthermore, this insignificant house was furnished with a splendid library, fine mathematical instruments, globes, and telescopes.

The social changes brought about by the American Revolution did not seriously interrupt the continuity of the aristocratic tradition. A few large estates owned by Loyalists were confiscated, such as the property of Sir James Wright in Georgia which was valued at one hundred and sixty thousand dollars, the Fairfax lands in Virginia, and the Dulany estate in Maryland.[19] Some aristocratic Tories, like Doctor Alexander Garden of Charleston (after whom the gardenia was named), retired permanently to England. Notwithstanding, the majority of Southern squires continued to own their great estates and to pursue the calm pattern of daily life inherited from colonial days. Although the abolition of primogeniture and entail, completed in the Southern States by 1791, struck a blow at aristocracy, it was not a very dangerous blow. Prior to the Revolution, many estates were not entailed, and the practice of willing all the lands to the eldest son was an exception. Entails had become burdensome on exhausted tobacco lands, a fact which resulted in many petitions to the Virginia legislature to dock them.[20] The prevalence of the aristocratic spirit following the Revolution, moreover, was exhibited in the rise of the Order of the Cincinnati and in the high property quali-

[17] *Ibid.*, pp. 178-179.   [18] *Ibid.*, pp. 184-185.

[19] J. F. Jameson, *The American Revolution Considered as a Social Movement* (Princeton, 1926), p. 53.

[20] L. H. Gipson, *The British Empire Before the American Revolution* (Caldwell, Idaho, 1936), II, 50-51, cites the conclusions of Dr. Clarence Keim in an unpublished doctoral thesis, "Influence of Primogeniture and Entail on the Development of Virginia."

fications placed on officeholding.[21] Aristocratic control was also maintained by the under-representation of the back country.[22] In South Carolina the planters of the low country arranged representation so that a minority of large slaveholders could check the action of a majority of yeoman farmers. Thus arose the principle of the concurrent majority, which Calhoun sought to apply to the nation.

The Southern aristocrats presented a striking paradox, in their combination of the habits and tastes of patricians with the possession of liberal views concerning religion, slavery, and politics. They had recently been members of a spacious empire, a connection that tended to broaden their vision and make them more cosmopolitan than the generation which succeeded them.[23] The tobacco trade was also a direct link between the planters and the luxuries, the social ideas, and the philosophy of the European world. It is not surprising, therefore, that Chastellux found many amateur philosophers among the homespun aristocracy of the South. Over a bowl of punch he and Jefferson discussed the poems of Ossian far into the night, and this cultivated nobleman discovered that he and his host agreed famously in their tastes and thoughts.[24]

The Southerners of this period shared in the European movement of the Enlightenment. They were enthusiastic disciples of "the great Mr. Locke" who exalted Reason as the basis of society.[25] This appeal to reason constituted the centralizing principle of Southern liberalism. The freethinking and deism of the Southern planters was an outgrowth of the

[21] E. E. Hume, "Light-Horse Harry and His Fellow Members of the Cincinnati," *William and Mary College Quarterly* (Second Series), XV, 271-281 (July, 1935).

[22] See C. H. Ambler, *Sectionalism in Virginia from 1776 to 1861* (Chicago, 1910), p. 94, and W. A. Schaper, *Sectionalism and Representation in South Carolina* (Washington, D. C., 1901).

[23] The effect of membership in the British Empire on the minds of the colonials has not properly been appreciated.

[24] Marquis de Chastellux, *Travels in North-America in the Years 1780, 1781, and 1782* (Dublin, Ireland, 1787), II, 45.

[25] For the influence of Locke on American thought, see Merle Curti, "The Great Mr. Locke: America's Philosopher, 1783-1861," *Huntington Library Bulletin* (April, 1937), No. XI, pp. 107-151.

faith in reason. The opposition to slavery, philosophically, sprang from the same root. Finally, the natural rights theory that supported democracy and freedom of thought was a product of eighteenth-century rationalism. In contrast to a modern distrust of reason, the leading minds of Jefferson's generation believed in the certainty of fundamental principles of nature, which could be deduced by the human reason and stated in resounding documents like the Virginia Bill of Rights, the Declaration of Independence, and *The Rights of Man*. Reason was a term that applied both to the fixed, orderly design of the universe, and to the intelligence of man that grasped the immutable laws of the Deity. It is true, however, that a few realists among the planters, like John Taylor of Caroline, brutally stated the economic substratum of political opinions.[26] Even Jefferson shrewdly managed not to shut his eyes to the economic determination of opinions, while at the same time he was the greatest exponent in his period of the appeal to reason.[27]

The leading men of Jefferson's generation emancipated their minds from the shackles of religious orthodoxy through the instrument of deism. Just as the aristocrats imported their Georgian architecture and their Madeira wine from England, so were they influenced by the intellectual currents that stirred the mother country. English deism arose from the discovery of Newton's master laws of nature and from the materialistic psychology of Locke.[28] Reason and Nature were the two shibboleths applied to religion. Unlike the followers of the French type of deism, which Voltaire popularized in his old age, the English deists were only mildly revolutionary. A great many of them did not discard the revelation of the Bible; they believed in the rational worship of the Supreme Being, who ruled the universe by natural laws. As Gustav Koch has penetrat-

[26] John Taylor, *An Inquiry into the Principles and Policy of the Government of the United States* (Fredericksburg, Va., 1814).

[27] See his famous letter to Mazzei, April 24, 1796, and Charles A. Beard, *Economic Origins of Jeffersonian Democracy* (New York, 1915), chap. xiv.

[28] For a good discussion of the deistic movement in Europe, see H. M. Morais, *Deism in Eighteenth Century America* (New York, 1934), chap. ii.

ingly observed, the deistic movement of the eighteenth century was "an attitude of mind rather than a specific creed."[29] It may be compared to the scientific temper of our age.

Deism in the South appealed especially to the aristocrats. When Joseph Caldwell, a graduate of Princeton, entered upon his duties as presiding professor at the University of North Carolina in 1797, he wrote a gloomy letter to a friend in New Jersey describing the religious condition of the state. "In North Carolina and particularly in the part east of Chapel Hill," he observed, "every one believes that the way of rising to respectability is to disavow as often, and as publicly as possible the leading doctrines of the Scriptures. They are bugbears, very well fitted to scare the ignorant and weak into obedience to the law; but the laws of morality and honor are sufficient to regulate the conduct of men of letters and cultivated reasons. One reason why religion is as scouted from the most influential part of society, is that it is taught only by ranters, with whom it seems to consist only in the powers of their throats and the wildness and madness of their gesticulations and distortions."[30] This lamentable state of religion was partly due to the Revolutionary War, which had disorganized churches and had contributed to a wave of religious indifference. In Virginia the ninety-one clergymen of the Episcopal Church at the beginning of the Revolution had been reduced to twenty-eight at the conclusion of peace.[31] Also, the political sympathies of the Jeffersonians with the French Republic tended to stimulate an interest in the skeptical works of Voltaire, Volney, and the Encyclopedia.[32]

[29] G. A. Koch, *Republican Religion: The American Revolution and the Cult of Reason* (New York, 1933), Preface, p. xiv.

[30] Kemp Battle, *History of the University of North Carolina* (2 vols.; Raleigh, N. C., 1907), I, 113.

[31] Meade, *op. cit.*, I, 17. Many of the Virginia clergy prior to the Revolution had weakened the reverence for religion by their mundane and often scandalous lives.

[32] "The works of Voltaire and his royal patron, Frederick of Prussia, of Rousseau, of Helvetius, Bolingbroke, Hume, Gibbon, and Paine were found in the libraries of our principal families, however small these libraries were" (a pamphlet by William Hooper, *Fifty Years Since: Address before the University of North Carolina Alumni*, Raleigh, N. C., 1859, p. 39).

Although deism was an upper-class religion, it expanded into the frontier and across the mountains to Kentucky. Even in the remote backwoods of North Carolina there existed among the Scotch-Irish a debating society which questioned the revelation of the Bible and established a circulating library replete with skeptical books.[33] To combat deism, and especially the vogue of Tom Paine's *The Age of Reason,* Rev. Samuel McCorkle of the back country of North Carolina published a vigorous polemic in which he examined the conflicting claims of deism and revelation. This work was an able and intelligent attack on the main contention of the deists, the sufficiency of reason. McCorkle displayed an acquaintance with a wide range of deistic and skeptical writers, Tindal, Pope, Gibbon, Bullinger, Bolingbroke, Hume, and Paine. He asked the pertinent question, "if human reason be a sufficient and universal principle, why have not all ages been *ages of reason?*" Since men have always had access to "the deist's Bible, the book of Creation . . . in the name of God, where have the deists been and what have they been doing?"[34] The distribution of Tom Paine's *The Age of Reason* was even aided by the famous "Parson" Weems, whom Bishop Meade found selling the heretical book under the portico of the tavern at Fairfax Courthouse, as well as the antidote, the reply of the Bishop of Llandaff.[35]

The existence of skepticism, as distinguished from irreligion, in the Southern back country is an extremely interesting phenomenon. John Basil Lamar has related an anecdote of a skeptical blacksmith located in one of the mountain passes of the Appalachians. This picturesque character had a hobby of perusing heretical books, for the purpose of shocking and overawing the ignorant backwoodsmen by quoting Tom Paine and making mysterious references to Volney and Taylor's *Diegesis.* The Methodist ministers had preached bitterly

[33] W. H. Foote, *Sketches of North Carolina: Historical and Biographical* (New York, 1846), p. 248.

[34] Samuel E. McCorkle, *Four Discourses on the General First Principles of Deism and Revelation Contrasted* (Salisbury, N. C., 1797), p. 31.

[35] Meade, *op. cit.,* II, 235.

against him, a fact which led him to whip all preachers of that persuasion who journeyed through the pass. Finally he was converted from his atheism by an unusually agile and muscular reverend, "who beat the hell out of him."[36] Another example of the frontier deist was Elihu Embree, who had the double distinction of being a pioneer in the iron industry of eastern Tennessee, and of founding the first newspaper in the United States devoted exclusively to antislavery. He was converted from deism to the Quaker faith in 1812.[37]

When Amos Kendall arrived in Kentucky to become a tutor in the family of Henry Clay, his pious soul was shocked at the prevalence of skepticism in the Bluegrass country. On one occasion he was obliged to listen to a long conversation at the home of his employer in which religion and religious men were ridiculed.[38] Finding it futile to attempt reasoning with infidels, he deemed it best to preserve a prudent silence. His partner in the editing of the Georgetown *Patriot* was an infidel. One of the great landowners of Kentucky at this period, Senator Humphrey Marshall, openly expressed his scorn for revealed religion and for the rule of the multitude.

The Southern deists and skeptics were isolated individuals and unorganized. They did not form deistical or skeptical societies, like the Society of Ancient Druids in Newburgh on the Hudson, or the Universal Society of Philadelphia, or the Deistical Society of New York City. They produced no ardent propagandist, like the blind Elihu Palmer, nor an organ of deistic opinion, such as *The Temple of Reason,* edited in New York by Dennis Driscol. They did not even publish an important skeptical book, like *Reason, the Only Oracle of Man,* written by Ethan Allen, the famous leader of "the Green Mountain Boys." The deists and skeptics of the South were

[36] M. L. Rutherford, *The South in History and Literature* (Athens, Ga., 1906), pp. 309-316.
[37] B. H. Murphy (ed.), *The Emancipator (Complete), Published by Elihu Embree, Jonesborough, Tennessee, 1820* (Nashville, Tenn., 1932), p. vi.
[38] William Stickney (ed.), *Autobiography of Amos Kendall* (Boston, 1872), pp. 119, 140.

passive, content to dabble in skeptical works, to read Tom
Paine, Voltaire, and Volney as a fashionable pastime.[39] Indeed,
it was regarded as a badge of distinction and of aristocracy to
have the reputation of being a freethinker.[40] Willie Jones, virtual dictator of North Carolina following the Revolution, belonged to this class—a man described by William E. Dodd
as "a wealthy planter who lived like a prince but who talked
and voted like a Jacobin."[41] He stipulated in his will that no
priest should insult his body by mumbling religious words
over it.[42]

The strongholds of deistic and skeptical opinion in the
South were found in college communities. At the close of the
eighteenth century the faculty and trustees of the University
of North Carolina were tainted with skepticism and infidelity.
Colonel William R. Davie, one of the founders of the institution, a polished and aristocratic gentleman, entertained continental ideas of dancing and of polite society conjoined with
the skepticism prevalent among the educated classes. In 1795
the presiding professor, Dr. David Ker, educated at Trinity
College, Dublin, became a violent republican and an outspoken
infidel. His writings were burned by his wife lest they should
contaminate others. When Caldwell became president in 1800
he found that Harris, a leading professor, was shaky on
the Christian doctrines and inclined to infidelity, and that
Davies, an instructor, was an infidel. Another member of
the faculty was Delvaux, a French ex-monk; still another,
Richards, had been a strolling actor (ungodly profession!)
and a deserter from the British navy. The climax of this
motley group was Professor Samuel Allen Holmes, an an-
archist, who openly avowed that what is called virtue and

[39] H. M. Jones, *America and French Culture, 1750-1848* (Chapel Hill, 1927),
chaps. x and xi.

[40] W. L. Grissom, *History of Methodism in North Carolina* (Nashville, Tenn.,
1905), I, 309; and E. W. Caruthers, *Life of David Caldwell* (Greensboro, N. C.,
1842), p. 263.

[41] W. E. Dodd, "The Role of Nathaniel Macon in Southern History," *American
Historical Review,* VII, 665 (July, 1922).

[42] *Dictionary of American Biography,* X, 211.

integrity are "deceptions and injurious pretenses." In 1799 he urged the students to resist authority, and thus provoked a riot, during which some of the instructors were beaten.[43]

Williamsburg was described by Bishop Meade as a seat of infidelity at the turn of the century. One of the first free-thinkers of the Old Dominion was the highly cultured Sir John Randolph of Williamsburg, whom the clergy maligned as "Deist, Heretic, Schismatic." In his will, however, he affirmed his faith in a Supreme Being and in Christ, but made a scathing attack on the clergy and theologians who had sown dissension by their artificial doctrines.[44] Governor Fauquier had also contributed to the vogue of skepticism. Jefferson's law professor at William and Mary, George Wythe, was a religious liberal. Bishop Madison, the president of the college from 1777 to 1812, was a very tolerant churchman who was suspected of being a freethinker.[45] General Winfield Scott, who was a student at William and Mary in 1805, declared that most of the bright boys of that day affected to regard religion as a base superstition and that Bishop Madison contributed to this prevalent evil by denouncing Hume, Voltaire, Godwin, and Helvetius in such a manner as to arouse the curiosity of his students.[46]

At the University of Georgia an irreligious atmosphere prevailed during the early stages of its growth. President Meigs, who directed the young institution from 1801 to 1811, was a scientist imported from Yale. His scientific zeal led him to calculate the exact depth of Hell. By using the formula for falling bodies and applying it to the nine days' fall of Lucifer and the perverse angels, he estimated that Hell was 1,832,308,-363 miles deep.[47] The spirit of tolerance at Athens was more profoundly influenced by the religious indifference characteristic of frontier conditions than by the prevalence of skepticism.

[43] Battle, op. cit., I, 156.
[44] Part of Sir John Randolph's Will, William and Mary College Quarterly (Second Series), IV, 286-288 (Oct., 1924).   [45] Meade, op. cit., I, 28-29.
[46] Memoirs of Lieut.-General Scott, LL.D. Written by Himself (New York, 1864), I, 9-10.
[47] E. M. Coulter, College Life in the Old South (New York, 1928), p. 21.

The growth of liberal ideas at Transylvania University in Kentucky, on the other hand, was genuinely alarming to the orthodox. In 1818 Horace Holley, a graduate of Yale, and a liberal minister of Boston, was elected president of the university. A handsome, brilliant man, a superb orator, he aspired to make Transylvania University the focus of intellectual life in the West.[48] So great was his success in building up the university that the enrollment during his presidency increased from ninety to four hundred and eighteen students. Among those who came to study law was Jefferson Davis. Holley opposed the doctrine of the depravity of human nature, upheld the Unitarian faith, and sought to overcome the sectarian spirit by preaching a religion of love and catholic tolerance. Furthermore, his genial manner of living, which included card playing and dancing, was a rebuke to the narrow ascetic spirit of evangelical religion.[49]

The founder of the University of Virginia was also a freethinker. Jefferson had too much culture and too philosophical a mind to adopt the crude conceptions of religion held by the masses. He believed that the religious teachings of Christ were the most sublime the world had produced, but that the priests and preachers had corrupted pristine Christianity by mixing the philosophy of Plato with it.[50] In order to free Christianity from its accretion of superstitions and Platonic dogmas, he culled from the New Testament those teachings of Christ which he believed to be authentic and entitled them "The Philosophy of Jesus." A disciple of Joseph Priestley, whose work, *The Corruptions of Christianity,* he had read over and over, Jefferson was really a Unitarian, although he did not proclaim this belief in public. In 1798 or 1799 he translated twenty chapters of Volney's *Ruins,* a French skeptical work

[48] E. G. Swem (ed.), *Letters on the Condition of Kentucky in 1825* (New York, 1916), pp. 42-43; Robert Peter, *Transylvania University, Its Origin, Rise, Decline, and Fall* (Louisville, Ky., 1896), p. 116.

[49] Robert Davidson, *History of the Presbyterian Church in the State of Kentucky* (New York, 1847), p. 305.

[50] Jefferson to John Adams, Aug. 22, 1813 (P. L. Ford, ed., *The Works of Thomas Jefferson,* New York, 1905, XI, 323-334).

that the devout placed in the same class as Tom Paine's *The Age of Reason,* but commissioned Joel Barlow to finish it and take the responsibility of the publishing.[51] Jefferson believed that reason should be the purifier of religion, which had been "muffled up in mysteries."[52]

The philosophical spirit that lay back of deism predisposed many of the Southern aristocrats to favor the eradication of slavery. Chastellux observed that mixed motives were involved in the spreading emancipation sentiment in Virginia following the Revolution. "The philosophers and the young men, who are almost all educated in the principles of a sound philosophy, regard nothing but justice, and the rights of humanity," he observed.[53] On the other hand, the more materialistic members of the planter class were guided by economic considerations, such as the declining profitableness of slavery on exhausted tobacco plantations. The American Revolution, moreover, gave a powerful fillip toward liberalizing the Southern aristocracy by popularizing the theory of natural or inherent rights.

The invention of the cotton gin in 1793 is held responsible for crushing this nascent humanitarianism. Nevertheless, the large number of wills of emancipation which Catterall has collected show that the doctrine of natural rights continued after the Revolution to exert an influence toward emancipation. The will of George Smith, written in 1830, is a typical example: "Whereas I, George Smith, of Powhatan County, (Va.) being fully convinced that slavery in all its forms, is contrary to good policy, that it is inconsistent with republican principles; that it is a violation of our bill of rights, which declares, *that all men are by nature equally free;* and above all, that it is repugnant to the spirit of the gospel, which enjoins universal

[51] Gilbert Chinard, *Volney et l'Amérique* (Baltimore, 1923), pp. 110-118.

[52] An unpublished letter of Jefferson to Mr. Vanderkemp, July 9, 1820 (Papers of Thomas Jefferson, Vol. 218, MSS in Library of Congress). See also the correspondence of Jefferson with William Short, in which he discusses Christianity and Greek philosophy. In a letter of April 13, 1820, he writes of the "Eastern hyperbolism" of Jesus (MSS in the Library of William and Mary College).

[53] Chastellux, *op. cit.,* II, 197-198.

love and benevolence. . . ."[54] Doubtless many a sensitive Southerner felt qualms of conscience in holding black men in bondage. A North Carolina planter, Sterling Ruffin, wrote to his son that he was averse to farming with slaves, because he could not discipline them properly, feeling that slavery was a violation of "the natural rights of a being who is as much entitled to the enjoyment of liberty as myself."[55]

Scarcely one of the great Virginians of the Revolutionary generation (Washington, Jefferson, Madison, Patrick Henry, George Wythe, professor of law at William and Mary College) failed to put himself on record as favoring emancipation.[56] Notable cases of large slaveholders in Virginia who emancipated their slaves are those of "Councillor" Carter of Nomini Hall, Robert Pleasants, General Horatio Gates of Traveller's Rest, George Washington, and John Randolph of Roanoke.[57] An excellent specimen of their liberal views is found in the papers of George Mason, the aristocratic owner of Gunston Hall and, at the time of his death in 1792, the master of three hundred slaves. He described slavery as a slow poison contaminating the minds and morals of the slaveowners and constituting an infernal school of tyranny for future legislators. "Taught to regard a part of our own Species in the most abject & contemptible Degree below us," he wrote, "we lose that Idea of the Dignity of Man, which the Hand of Nature had planted in us, for great and useful purposes."[58]

When the Mason manuscripts expressing such sentiments

[54] H. T. Catterall, *Judicial Cases Concerning American Slavery and the Negro* (Washington, D. C., 1926), I, 317.

[55] J. G. deR. Hamilton (ed.), *The Papers of Thomas Ruffin* (Raleigh, N. C., 1920), I, 80.

[56] These condemnations of slavery by the great men of the Revolutionary generation were gathered later into a pamphlet by a North Carolina antislavery man, Daniel R. Goodloe, *The Southern Platform; or Manual of Southern Sentiment on the Subject of Slavery* (Boston, 1858).

[57] In 1794 Robert Carter emancipated some of his slaves, sent for the *History of Josephus* and *Utopia* from his library at Nomini Hall, and requested his friends to discontinue addressing him as "Honorable" (Letter Book of Robert Carter, 1786-1796, pp. 4-5, 15, MS in Library of Congress).

[58] "Extracts from the Virginia Charters with Some Remarks on Them," 1773 (George Mason Papers, 1766-88: Bancroft Transcripts, pp. 85-89, MSS in New York Public Library).

were sent to the historian, George Bancroft, in 1857 by Senator J. M. Mason, the latter stipulated that no one else be allowed to copy anything from them regarding the institution of slavery. Senator Mason apologized for the liberal views of his grandfather by pointing out the influences that predisposed the men of the post-Revolutionary generation to condemn slavery: the cruelties of the slave trade, the struggle for liberty against England, and the absence of the great Southern staples of cotton and sugar. Nevertheless, Senator Mason wrote to the historian that if George Mason were living in his own day, he would be the first to prevent such free expressions from falling into "profane or depraved hands."[59]

In 1796 St. George Tucker published a very significant antislavery pamphlet. An influential man in Virginia at the time, a professor of law at William and Mary, and one of the judges of the General Court, he taught his boys that slavery was at variance with the Bill of Rights and that it was their duty to support a plan for the eradication of the evil. Moreover, he sought to influence the Virginia legislature to action on the subject by publishing his antislavery lectures. His proposal of emancipation was that all female slaves born after the adoption of the plan should be free, but that they should serve their masters until twenty-five years of age. At the same time, he opposed granting civil rights to the freedmen. He warned his fellow citizens that every day a plan of emancipation was postponed the problem became more difficult.[60] It is indicative of the liberal attitude of the intellectual leaders of Virginia toward slavery that in 1791 William and Mary College conferred a degree of LL.D. on Granville Sharp, a noted abolition agitator of England.[61]

A pupil of George Wythe, Henry Clay, carried the liberal ideas of his mentor into the Bluegrass region of Kentucky.

[59] J. M. Mason to George Bancroft, Selma, near Winchester, Va., June 1, 1857 (George Mason Papers, New York Public Library).

[60] St. George Tucker, *A Dissertation on Slavery with a Proposal for the Gradual Abolition of It in the State of Virginia* (Philadelphia, 1796), pp. 10, 30, 77, 91, 98.

[61] W. F. Poole, *Anti-Slavery Opinions before the Year 1800* (Cincinnati, 1873), p. 73.

The frontier spirit of that state was hostile to an institution that denied the Rights of Man. David Rice, the father of Presbyterianism in the West, led a movement to exclude slavery from the state in 1792, while the convention was drawing up the first constitution of Kentucky. His pamphlet, *Slavery Inconsistent with Justice and Good Policy,* was a realistic document that foretold the evil effects which negro bondage would have on a growing young commonwealth.[62] The opponents of slavery were defeated at this time, but seven years later they made another gallant effort to erase its stain from the state. Clay, "a beardless boy" of twenty-one years, wrote a series of articles for the *Kentucky Gazette,* urging the adoption of a plan of gradual emancipation. The momentous subject was discussed freely in the newspapers. In fact, one of the emancipation candidates for election to the constitutional convention of 1799 was the editor, John Bradford, a gambling and drinking partner of Clay. A slaveholders' clique, raising "the whine of interest," overwhelmed the idealistic reformers, and only one antislavery candidate from all of Kentucky was elected.[63]

In Maryland two great aristocrats, Charles Carroll of Carrollton and William Pinckney, championed the cause of the slave. In the legislature of 1789 the proposal of Charles Carroll to consider a plan of emancipation was voted down.[64] In the same session William Pinkney made a brilliant speech attacking the institution of slavery during which he pointed out the incongruity of talking like philosophers, of "perpetually sermonizing it with liberty for our text," and yet holding men in bondage. He declared that the reverence for liberty, which sustained democratic institutions, would be destroyed by the practice of slaveholding.[65] This speech was resurrected by the

[62] David Rice, *Slavery Inconsistent with Justice and Good Policy; Proved by a Speech Delivered in the Convention Held at Danville, Kentucky* (Philadelphia, 1792).

[63] Bernard Mayo, *Henry Clay, Spokesman of the New West* (Cambridge, Mass., 1937), pp. 78-80, 120-121; I. E. McDougle, *Slavery in Kentucky, 1792-1865* (Lancaster, Pa., 1918), chap. v; and Asa E. Martin, *The Anti-Slavery Movement in Kentucky Prior to 1850* (Louisville, Ky., 1918), chaps. i and ii.

[64] J. R. Brackett, *The Negro in Maryland* (Baltimore, 1889), pp. 53-54.

[65] *Speech of William Pinkney, Esq., in the House of Delegates of Maryland at Their Session in November, 1789* (Philadelphia, 1790), pp. 8-9.

Quakers in 1820 and published to show the inconsistency of Pinkney's speech on the Missouri Compromise.[66] Another Marylander, Dr. George Buchanan, bitterly condemned American slavery in an oration before the Maryland Abolition Society, July 4, 1791, in which he also pointed out the mockery of professing the Rights of Man and retaining slavery. Buchanan's pamphlet, with its vivid references to slave revolt, especially in Santo Domingo, would have been classed as an incendiary document in the South after 1830.[67] A copy of this speech was found in George Washington's library, now preserved in the Boston Athenaeum. Finally, a Maryland Quaker, John Parrish, in 1806 published a pamphlet entitled *Remarks on the Slavery of the Black People,* in which he took the position that slavery violated the Declaration of Independence, the Federal Constitution, and the Golden Rule.[68]

A true picture of the Southern mind contemplating slavery cannot be obtained by examining only the opinions of the most enlightened leaders. Much closer to the rank and file of slaveowners were Nathaniel Macon and John Taylor of Caroline, who frankly expressed their skepticism of the expediency of emancipation. "Negro Slavery," Taylor declared, "is a misfortune to agriculture, incapable of removal, and only within the reach of palliation."[69] Jefferson's criticism of slavery, he observed, was refuted by the profusion of splendid characters produced by the slave states. Instead of slavery evoking furious passions in the masters, the opposite was true; the slaves called forth benevolent and paternal feelings in the superior race.

Such a conservative attitude on race relations was even more marked in South Carolina and Georgia. A few Carolina aristocrats, like Henry Laurens and his son John, expressed dis-

[66] *Dictionary of American Biography,* XIV, 627.

[67] George Buchanan, M.D., *An Oration Upon the Moral and Political Evil of Slavery* (Baltimore, 1793), reprinted in an appendix of Poole, *op. cit.,* pp. 12, 13, 17.

[68] M. S. Locke, *Anti-Slavery in America from the Introduction of African Slaves to the Prohibition of the Slave Trade, 1619-1808* (Boston, 1901), pp. 175-176.

[69] John Taylor, *Arator: Being a Series of Agricultural Essays, Practical and Political* (Georgetown, 1813), pp. 62, 69, 73.

approval of slavery, but even the former did not emancipate his slaves by his will.[70] Some of the more farsighted leaders of this region, like Gabriel Manigault, opposed the dominant sentiment of their neighbors in favor of the African slave trade.[71] Shortly after the serious slave plot of Denmark Vesey, a Revolutionary patriot, Thomas Pinckney, published a pamphlet in which he proposed a policy gradually to substitute white labor for slave labor in Charleston. In the course of his argument he declared that slavery was generally admitted in the Southern States to be "an evil entailed."[72] But in this region of malarial rice fields, where the Negroes enjoyed an immunity from the poison of the mosquito, the planters were more convinced of the necessity of black slavery than the inhabitants of the cooler and more salubrious climate of the Upper South.[73]

One of the most effective causes for the liberalism of the Southern aristocrats was the vogue of the natural rights philosophy. This political theory viewed society as a collection of individuals, loosely bound together by a social compact, each citizen a little sovereign in his sphere. In entering the social compact the individual reserved certain natural rights, such as the freedom of the press, the freedom of speech, and the freedom of conscience, which could never be taken from him.[74] Such a theory, which tended to reduce government to a minimum of power, was suited to that rural Utopia praised by Nathaniel Macon, where no man lived so close to his neighbor that he could hear his dogs barking. These Southern agrarians believed that government, whether it be the state government or the distant Federal government, but especially the latter, should be severely restrained from invading the per-

[70] D. P. Wallace, *Life of Henry Laurens* (New York, 1915), pp. 444-456. In his early career Henry Laurens had increased his fortune by importing slaves for sale.

[71] Duncan Clinch Heyward, *Seed from Madagascar* (Chapel Hill, 1937), p. 66.

[72] Achates, *Reflections Occasioned by the Late Disturbances in Charleston* (Charleston, S. C., 1822), p. 24.

[73] Duc de la Rochefoucault Liancourt, *Travels through the United States of North America* (London, 1799), I, 598-599.

[74] See B. F. Wright, *American Interpretations of Natural Law* (Cambridge, Mass., 1931).

sonal liberties of country gentlemen, thus allowing a lush development of individuality. Said John Randolph of Roanoke: "The principles of free Government in this country . . . have more to fear from over legislation than from any other cause. Yes, Sir—they have more to fear from armies of Legislators and from armies of Judges than from any other, or from all other, causes."[75]

Following the American Revolution, a great gap arose between the democratic theory of the Tidewater aristocrats and the *status quo* in the Southern States. This discrepancy was due to the fact that the natural rights philosophy dominated their theory, but colonial precedents and economic interests determined their practice. The paradox of the republican aristocrat was illustrated in the life of George Mason of Gunston Hall. This great planter's lineage, wealth, elegant taste placed him in the forefront of the aristocrats of the Northern Neck of Virginia. Moreover, his nature was essentially aristocratic, seasoned, as Jefferson observed, by "a dash of biting cynicism." His letters and his will show that he had a low opinion of the actual working of the democratic process. With ironic contempt he described the inefficiency and stupidity of the Virginia Assembly of 1786, "doing little but making one week & the next week unmaking laws, except indeed going thro' several of the acts in the new code and spoiling some of them."[76] Hating demagogues and political deals, he believed that the business of government should be undertaken by public-spirited and cultured leaders, like Richard Henry Lee or Edmund Randolph, who would brush aside the thousand ridiculous and impracticable proposals made by lesser men.[77] The Virginia Constitution of 1776, which Mason drew up, was far from being a democratic document.

[75] W. C. Bruce, *John Randolph of Roanoke, 1773-1833* (New York, 1922), I, 622.

[76] George Mason to William Fitzhugh, Feb. 26, 1786 (MS in Gunston Hall, Lorton, Va.).

[77] Helen Hill, *George Mason, Constitutionalist* (Cambridge, Mass., 1938), pp. 135-136.

The democratic side of Mason was revealed in his authorship of the Virginia Declaration of Rights. This celebrated
document was really an amalgam of the natural rights philoso-
ophy, of the ideas of John Locke, and of principles derived
directly from English constitutional development. Perhaps
also the influence of the American frontier and the dynamics
of the Revolutionary movement contributed to its formula-
tion. Adopted June 15, 1776, it preceded by two weeks the
Declaration of Independence of Jefferson, and also the bill
of rights of other states, which closely imitated it. Today
it appears extreme, and even doctrinaire, in its assertion of
the rights of the individual against the authority of the state,
yet it was written by a Virginia planter of "copious understanding," who was practical and businesslike. Mason possessed the capacity for philosophic detachment that enabled
him to rise above the viewpoint of his own class and to think in
terms of the welfare of the whole people.[78] In the Virginia
Declaration of Rights he was primarily concerned in preventing government from invading the inherent natural rights of
citizens, guaranteeing to them freedom from arbitrary arrest,
the freedom of the press, religious toleration, etc. This doctrine of natural rights afforded liberals of the eighteenth and
early nineteenth centuries with their main arguments for the
toleration of free speech, freedom of conscience and of opinion.

Jefferson and Madison were the most outstanding advocates
of freedom of thought in the Upper South, while Dr. Thomas
Cooper was the leading exponent in the Lower South. Jefferson's statute of religious toleration, passed by the Virginia legislature in 1786, his advocacy of the freedom of the press, Madison's great services in the cause of religious freedom, are too

[78] In the Constitutional Convention of 1787, Mason declared: "We ought to
attend to the rights of every class of the people. He had often wondered at the
indifference of the superior classes of society to this dictate of humanity & policy,
considering that however affluent their circumstances, or elevated their situations,
might be, the course of a few years, not only might but certainly would, distribute their posterity throughout the lowest classes of Society" (Gaillard Hunt, ed.,
*The Journal of the Debates in the Convention Which Framed the Constitution of
the United States, May-September, 1787, as Recorded by James Madison*, New York,
1908, I, 40-41).

well known to bear repetition in this study.[79] Dr. Thomas
Cooper, President of South Carolina College from 1820 to
1834, was a more extreme advocate of free speech and liberal
opinions in the South than either Jefferson or Madison. He
followed the typical pattern of the eighteenth-century liberal
with his exaggerated faith in the supremacy of reason over
the minds of men. Although the portly, baldheaded doctor
practically claimed omniscience, he seems not to have explored
the emotional side of people, their deep-seated prejudices.
Seventy years of experience did not teach him to let sleeping
dogs lie. He poked them with his cane and went out of his
way to stir up the orthodox and shock the conservatives to
a fury. It is one of the mysteries of Southern history that he
was able to hold his position in South Carolina College so
long.[80]

Dr. Cooper gave the South its boldest charter of free speech
in a pamphlet entitled *The Right of Free Discussion.* Ap-
pended to the second edition (1829) of his *Lectures on the
Elements of Political Science,* it was used as a text in his classes.
The irrepressible doctor admitted no limitations to the rights
of discussion. All opinions, political, theological, moral,
philosophical, should be tolerated. A man's belief is not an
act of will, but is the effect of evidence presented to his mind,
so ran his argument. Even mischievous opinions should be
allowed to be expressed or published, for reason and free discussion will destroy their errors. The only motive for fettering
the human mind is the design of those in authority to protect
their vested interests.[81] A few years later, however, Dr. Cooper
did not believe in tolerating abolition petitions.[82]

[79] For a good summary, see Virginius Dabney, *Liberalism in the South* (Chapel
Hill, 1932), chap. ii.

[80] Dumas Malone believes that the political views of Dr. Cooper, free trade,
States' rights, opposition to abolitionists, explain the tolerance of South Carolinians
toward his unorthodox religious beliefs (*The Public Life of Thomas Cooper, 1783-
1839,* New Haven, Conn., 1926, pp. 360-361).

[81] Thomas Cooper, *Lectures on the Elements of Political Economy* (Columbia,
S. C., 1831), pp. 1-17, at the end of the book; see also his admirable letter to
Mahlon Dickerson, Feb. 13, 1826 (*American Historical Review,* VI, 727, July,
1901).

[82] Cooper to James H. Hammond, Jan. 8, 1836 (James H. Hammond Papers,
V, MSS in Library of Congress).

The tolerant atmosphere of North Carolina at the beginning of the nineteenth century was indicated by the case of Jacob Henry. Despite the fact that he was a Jew, he was elected to the legislature from Carteret County for a second term in 1809. When his right to resume his seat in the legislature was challenged, he made an eloquent speech in defense of religious liberty. Deriving his arguments from Thomas Jefferson, he maintained that government should concern itself with the actions of men and not with their speculative opinions. The Bill of Rights in the state constitution, he declared, annulled any provisions in that document inconsistent with the freedom of religion and of speech. The legislature accepted his argument, and he was allowed to serve as legislator.[83] But in 1835 a constitutional convention definitely disqualified Jews from holding office. Not until 1868 was Jewish emancipation from such religious restrictions accomplished in North Carolina.

A turning point came in Southern liberalism shortly after the death of Jefferson in 1826—a change preceded by a profound economic revolution. The old Tidewater aristocracy, mellowed by age, sank in importance as exhausted tobacco fields and rice plantations became less productive. Cotton was enthroned as king on the rich black loam of Alabama, Mississippi, and Louisiana.[84] "Cotton capitalism" became a strident, aggressive force in politics and the intellectual life of the section. A new political philosophy arose that discarded much of the idealism of Jefferson.[85] In 1829 Thomas Cooper was teaching to his classes a doctrine that repudiated the theory of natural rights—"Rights are what society acknowledges and sanctions, and they are nothing else."[86] The transition to a different political philosophy was clearly revealed during the

[83] Leon Hühner, "The Struggle for Religious Liberty in North Carolina, with Special Reference to the Jews," *Publications of the American Jewish Historical Society* (1907), No. 16, pp. 49-51.

[84] See a humorous account of the tyranny of cotton by a traveler in 1827 (U. B. Phillips, *Plantation and Frontier, 1649-1863*, Cleveland, Ohio, 1910, I, 283-289).

[85] William E. Dodd has described this revolution in political theory in Chapter III of *The Cotton Kingdom: A Chronicle of the Old South* (New Haven, Conn., 1919).

[86] Malone, *Public Life of Thomas Cooper*, p. 290.

debates in the Virginia Constitutional Convention of 1829-30, when the older leaders spoke against manhood suffrage and in favor of giving slave property rights a privileged position.[87]

The conservative reaction in political theory of the South, however, was countered in 1828 by the election of Andrew Jackson to the Presidency. His inauguration symbolized the rise of the common man to power, and it was the votes of the South and West that won the victory. So powerful a dissolvent of old traditions was this force that die-hards like Beverley Tucker bemoaned the passing of political control from the hands of Southern gentlemen. In a letter to William Gilmore Simms he declared that Virginia was "sunk in the slough of democracy, which has no sense of honor."[88] The rise of the common man was reflected in the changing style of dress. James Monroe was the last President to wear the knee breeches and silk stockings of the eighteenth-century aristocrat. A generation later, in 1860-61, three of the most important Southern states were led by men of distinctly plebeian origins. The governor of Virginia was "Honest John" Letcher, son of a Methodist butcher, the governor of Georgia was Joseph E. Brown from the red hills, while Mississippi boasted of the uncouth J. J. Pettus. This chief executive sat in his office with his spittoon, while the "sovereigns" of Mississippi walked freely through his door and acted in every respect as if they were in a public house, save in ordering drinks.[89]

The rise of the common man to political power in the South was a serious threat to freedom of thought and of speech. The essence of preserving freedom of thought and of speech is the protection of minority rights—the safeguarding of the right to express opinions odious to the majority. The

[87] S. M. Hamilton (ed.), *The Writings of James Monroe* (New York, 1903), VII, 224-225; G. Hunt (ed.), *Writings of James Madison* (New York, 1910), IX, 358-364. Younger members of the convention, like Abel Upshur and Benjamin W. Leigh, derided the doctrine of majority rule, the rule of numbers, as a mere abstraction (*Proceedings and Debates of the Virginia State Convention, 1829-1830*, Richmond, 1830, pp. 53, 66-67).

[88] W. P. Trent, *William Gilmore Simms* (Boston, 1892), p. 186.

[89] W. H. Russell, *My Diary North and South* (Boston, 1863), p. 299.

masses can seldom endure any divergence from the majority opinion on matters of deep emotional content. Lord Acton has observed that toleration is secured with more difficulty in a government controlled by the masses than in an aristocracy. "For there is a reserve of latent power in the masses," he points out, "which if it is called into play the minority can seldom resist. But from the absolute will of an entire people, there is no appeal, no redemption, no refuge, but tyranny."[90] The cardinal doctrine of liberals, held by them from the time of Milton to the recent days of Justice Holmes, that error of opinion can be eradicated only by truth, and not by force, is unsatisfactory to the multitude, impatient for immediate results.[91] Since the common man is easily swayed by propaganda and the skilful manipulation of pressure groups, the laws and the courts are less important in suppressing free thought than is the power of social disapproval or ostracism.[92]

The synthesis of the two conflicting forces, Jacksonian democracy and the repudiation of eighteenth-century liberalism, was attained in connection with the slavery question. The Jacksonian democrats made no effort to disturb the vast complex of property rights involved in the institution of slavery. Although they murmured at times against the inequality of slave taxation compared with the taxation of other property, they accepted it. Furthermore, they co-operated in the censorship of belated Jeffersonians who criticized slavery. The great Whig planters, on the other hand, became the most tolerant, the moderating, group in the South. Supporting this point of view were some highly cultivated Democrats, like Joel R. Poinsett, who had schooled themselves in calm, dispassionate reflection.[93] Aristocrat and plebeian alike, however, wished to

[90] Lord J. E. E. D. Acton, *History of Freedom and Other Essays* (London, 1907), p. 11.
[91] See Zechariah Chafee, *Freedom of Speech* (New York, 1920), pp. 46-56; and Alfred Lief (ed.), *The Dissenting Opinions of Mr. Justice Holmes* (New York, 1929).
[92] Harwood L. Childs, *Pressure Groups and Propaganda* (Philadelphia, 1935); Howard K. Beale, *Are American Teachers Free?* (New York, 1936).
[93] Poinsett to Edward Coles, March 28, 1851 (Joel R. Poinsett Papers, XVI, 191, MSS in Pennsylvania Historical Society Library).

keep the land of Dixie a white man's country.[94] The turning
point in the Southern attitude to slavery came about the year
1831. In that year occurred both the shock of the Nat Turner
rebellion, and the irritation caused by appearance of the abolitionist newspaper, the *Liberator*. In the autumn of that yeaɪ
the famous debate on emancipation in the legislature of Virginia began, and shortly afterwards Thomas Dew published
his classical defense of slavery—one of the first big guns in
the proslavery argument that held slavery to be a positive
good.[95]

In the religious life of the South, a reaction from liberalism
had also taken place. The conversion of the South from its
deistic and skeptical ways was wrought in part by a success-
sion of waves of evangelism. Moreover, skepticism had already
been discredited in the South by the excesses of the French
Revolution.[96] One of the mightiest weapons in the arsenal
of the orthodox was to point with horror at French infidelity.
Hoary-headed deists recanted their errors of young manhood.
Edmund Randolph, a deist, and the son of a deist, was converted by the piety of his wife, and solaced his last years with
Wesley's sermons.[97] The freethinking "Councillor" Carter had
become a devout Baptist and a financial mainstay of the preachers at the close of the eighteenth century, although he was
also interested in the doctrines of Swedenborg.[98] The profane skeptic, John Randolph of Roanoke, surrendered in 1817,
and was reconciled to orthodox Christianity. Even Jefferson
concealed his religious views from the public in his old age.
When his grandson at South Carolina College wrote to him
for his opinion of the great freethinkers, Lord Bolingbroke

[94] U. B. Phillips, "The Central Theme of Southern History," *American Historical Review*, XXXIV, 30-43 (Oct., 1928).

[95] The significance of Dew's work has probably been overemphasized by Dodd,
The Cotton Kingdom, pp. 49-53.

[96] C. D. Hazen, *Contemporary American Opinion of the French Revolution*
(Baltimore, 1897), pp. 266-272; McCorkle, *op. cit.*, pp. 52-56.

[97] Morais, *op. cit.*, pp. 118-119.

[98] Asa Hunt to Carter, Aug. 12, 1788; J. J. Wilmer to Carter, Jan. 2, 1797;
Carter to James Maund, May 18, 1795 (3 vols. of religious writings by Carter,
MSS in Library of Congress).

and Thomas Paine, Jefferson replied with a letter of praise. He, however, requested that his sentiments should not be made public, for he recoiled from the bitter intolerance that might arise. In 1847 Henry Clay, who had been a doubter in his early days, buffeted by tremendous personal sorrows, joined the Episcopal Church.[99]

The Jeffersonian phase of Southern history affords a valuable yardstick to measure the later recession of tolerance below the Potomac. Its liberal ideas were largely those of a small group of cultivated and aristocratic leaders who were under the spell of eighteenth-century Reason. These Southern gentlemen, clad in knee breeches and silk stockings, were more cosmopolitan in spirit than the succeeding generation. Many of them had been educated in England, or like Jefferson and John Randolph of Roanoke, had established contacts with the intelligentsia of Europe. The Revolution had shaken them out of petty concerns and the routine of plantation life into a world of spacious ideas, where was caught a glimpse of the dignity of man. Also economic conditions at the close of the eighteenth century favored liberalism, especially the declining profitableness of slavery. Nor were the high-mettled planters of the Tidewater subjected to the tirade of abuse and insults from the abolitionists that affected the mental poise of their children and grandchildren. To these colonial-bred aristocrats one must look for the catholic point of view which makes for tolerance. The liberal principles which they transmitted, however, began to lose popular favor even before the death of Jefferson. Why the great traditions of the Jeffersonian epoch broke down in the first half of the nineteenth century is the theme of the succeeding chapters.

[99] G. G. Van Deusen, *The Life of Henry Clay* (Boston, 1937), p. 383.

Chapter II

PLANTATION LIFE AS A MOULDER OF OPINION

THE DISINTEGRATION of the great traditions of the Tidewater aristocracy was accomplished by both external and internal forces. In the decades from 1790 to 1860 the impact of ideas radiating from Europe and from the urban centers of the North profoundly modified the cultural history of the South. At the same time, the myriad plastic influences of geography and of economic factors were ceaselessly operating to disturb old patterns of life and modes of thought peculiar to the colonial-bred Southerners.[1] Since the spacious land of Dixie included many diverse geographic regions and twelve million people in 1860, the social fabric was bound to become variegated. Indeed, there was not one South but many Souths.[2] The moulding effect of the Southern terrain on the inhabitants of each of these regions is a subject for unending contemplation. The purpose of this chapter is to select only those salient forces of environment and society that had a bearing on Southern liberalism.

The complex aspect of society below the Potomac has been obscured by the romantic tradition of the plantation. Francis Pendleton Gaines has shown in his study of *The Southern Plantation* how a stereotype has been created by exaggerating certain real features of Southern society and by ascribing to the whole section the characteristics of privileged regions. Extremely attractive are the traditions of the splendid days "befo' the war," and they have undoubtedly furnished a romantic compensation for the generation of poverty-stricken Southerners who survived Appomattox. As long as one recognizes

[1] For the influence of geography, see the admirable study of Rupert Vance, *Human Geography of the South* (Chapel Hill, 1932).

[2] This idea is suggested in Frederick Jackson Turner's *The United States, 1830-1850: The Nation and Its Sections* (New York, 1935), chap. v; see also H. W. Odum, *Southern Regions of the United States* (Chapel Hill, 1936).

that these traditions apply only to the privileged life of the
aristocracy, that the vast majority of people did not live in
spacious white homes fronted by Grecian columns, and were
not waited on by a throng of black servants, such charming
vignettes have a valid place in the gallery of American civilization.

Large areas of the South were ill adapted to an economy of
big plantations, especially the mountainous sections, the pine
barrens, and considerable portions of the Piedmont. Partly on
this account, partly because of clashes over internal improvements and over the apportionment of representation, a strong
feeling of sectionalism arose within practically all the Southern
states, traces of which still remain.[3] The breach between the
coastal plain and the back country was further widened by the
diverse strains in their population. The Piedmont and the Great
Valley had been settled by a large element of Germans and
Scotch-Irish, who brought with them somewhat of the free-
state atmosphere of Pennsylvania. The hedonistic "Tuckahoe"
of Tidewater Virginia was a very different person from the
"Cohee" of the West; even his pronunciation of the King's
English was different. Piedmont society was also affected by
a strong tincture of Quakers, centered in Guilford County,
North Carolina. In the placid villages of Wachovia were settled the Moravians with their peculiar customs. Yankee farmers had migrated into northern Virginia to take up abandoned
tobacco lands, and a thriving colony of antislavery Germans
had settled in Texas. The Creoles of Louisiana contributed a
picturesque but languorous element to Southern society. In
the mountains and the pine barrens lived a race of people who
looked sullenly upon the fortunate planters of the seaboard.
Out of such heterogeneous groups might have come a rich diversity of opinion. But the partial unification of the Tidewater
and the Piedmont by the expansion of slavery and the plantation system into those areas tended to prevent the growth of
powerful and articulate minorities. The desire to control the

[3] See A. R. Newsome, *The Presidential Election of 1824 in North Carolina*
(Chapel Hill, 1939), chap. i.

Negro, to keep the South a white man's country, operated to unite all classes and discourage bold and radical thinking.

In the Bluegrass region of Kentucky, in the Nashville lime-stone basin, on the alluvial soils of Louisiana, in the Black Belt of Alabama and Mississippi, in the fertile valleys, in towns like Natchez and Charleston, a genuine aristocratic spirit flour-ished. A glimpse into the tastes of Southern gentlemen might be obtained by an inventory of some boxes containing the per-sonal effects of Joel R. Poinsett. Poinsett was one of the most cultivated men in America, famed for his "breakfasts," to which the most brilliant and witty people of Charleston were invited, and for his introduction of the poinsettia into this country from Mexico. There were cases of claret and Bur-gundy, boxes of books, vases, candelabra. "In one of the Boxes," wrote a friend supervising the packing, "is a curious mixture—Fame supporting the candles—and your Honor's silver Stirrups—the Branch Candlesticks & your white beaver Hat—a pr. large Plated Candlesticks & a new pr. of Pantaloons with some odd silver chains."[4] On the broad porticoes, made fragrant by the magnolia blossoms, the aristocrats sat in the cool of the evening and engaged in carefree conversation. Their stables contained blooded racing and saddle horses, their smokehouses were filled with hams, they were surrounded by servants to answer every whim.

An example of plantation magnificence was Berry Hill, near Halifax, Virginia. About 1843 Berry Hill was built or remodeled in the form of a Doric temple with eight large white columns supporting the pediment of the porch. The main edifice was flanked by two miniature Doric temples, one used as an office, the other as a school. Within the hall a grand stairway was constructed that afforded a romantic set-ting for Southern belles to display their hoop skirts. Mantels of Carrara marble embellished with caryatids, crystal chande-liers, massive silver, and aristocratic portraits gave a tone of courtly elegance to the interior.[5] This charming home of the

---

[4] Jos. Johnson to Poinsett, March 30, 1825 (Joel R. Poinsett Papers, II, MSS).
[5] One object of former grandeur which has escaped the wreck of time is a large silver wash basin, now used as a punch bowl.

Greek revival style was an expression of the personality of the proprietor, James Coles Bruce, a highly cultivated man, who had studied at Harvard and had traveled widely. His elegant taste was based on a love of grandeur restrained by classic simplicity. From his father he had inherited in 1837 a fortune that amounted to about two million dollars, which he increased to four millions by the time the Civil War broke out.[6] In politics a Whig, in religion an Episcopalian, the father of nine boys, he combined the practice and study of agriculture with a taste for classical learning and literature. He preserved sufficient detachment and wisdom to criticize slavery and to uphold the Union cause in the Virginia Secession Convention. Such a type represented the ideal of a Southern country gentleman of the ante-bellum period.

The extreme minority position of the large slaveholders in the South, compared with their great political influence, is one of the most striking aspects of Southern ante-bellum society. In 1860 those planters who possessed fifty or more slaves numbered slightly less than eleven thousand individuals, comprising about three fourths of one per cent of the total free population. The whole South on the eve of the rebellion could muster only two thousand, three hundred and fifty-eight slaveholders who owned so many as a hundred slaves.[7] Great proprietors, like Samuel Hairston of Pittsylvania, Virginia, who owned nearly seventeen hundred slaves, Wade Hampton, Nathaniel Heyward of Charleston, who left at his death in 1851 fourteen rice plantations and over two thousand slaves, Howell Cobb of Georgia, William B. Goulden, and Joseph Davis, the brother of the President of the Confederacy, were the millionaires of their section.[8]

Indeed, the large slaveholders were really cotton capitalists,

[6] Kathleen Bruce, "Materials for Virginia Agricultural History," *Agricultural History*, IV, 13 (Jan., 1930).

[7] L. C. Gray, *History of Agriculture in the Southern United States to 1860* (Washington, D. C., 1933), I, 483. At the same time nearly one hundred thousand middle-class planters owned from ten to fifty slaves each.

[8] *De Bow's Review*, XIV, 70-71 (Jan., 1853). For an insight into the wealth of sugar planters, see J. Carlyle Sitterson, "Magnolia Plantation, 1852-1862, a Decade of a Louisiana Sugar Estate," *Mississippi Valley Historical Review*, XXV, 197-210 (Sept., 1938). In 1861 Magnolia plantation sold $148,500 worth of sugar.

as Professor Schlesinger has termed them, interested in controlling politics and the press to preserve their slave property.[9]
Four billion dollars at a liberal estimate were invested by
Southerners in black slaves.[10] This property, held in opposition to the opinion of the civilized world, tended to make
them eminently conservative. A feeling of bitterness arose in
them as they envisaged profits from their peculiar institution
flowing into Northern coffers through the unjust operation of
the tariff laws. This conviction of the unfairness of the opera-
tions of the Federal government was accentuated by the fact
that the planters were in a state of chronic debt, and that although the value of their cotton, rice, and sugar crops was
more than two hundred million dollars in 1860, less than thirty
million of this sum was deposited in Southern banks.[11]

Another concomitant of the ownership of slave property
in nineteenth-century America was the development of a pronounced sensitivity on the part of Southerners to criticism.
The romantic vogue that prevailed in the South and the pro-
vincialism of the people may have exaggerated this failing.
But the real cause for the Southerner's violent resentment of
outside criticism lay deeper. Slavery was an institution that
needed an apology. Was it not likely that many of the most
vociferous advocates of the rightfulness of slavery had troubled
consciences? When *Uncle Tom's Cabin* appeared, the editor
of the *Southern Literary Messenger* sought a reviewer who
stood pre-eminent in the mastery of vitriolic invective. He
first appealed to John M. Daniel to perform this patriotic task,
but the latter was engaged in a political campaign and was not
available. He then turned to George Frederick Holmes with
the request that the review be written according to the following recipe: "I would have the review as hot as hell-fire, blast-
ing and searing the reputation of the vile wretch in petticoats

---

[9] A. M. Schlesinger, *Political and Social History of the United States, 1829-1925*
(New York, 1925), p. 91.

[10] "A Declaration of the Immediate Causes Which Induce and Justify the Secession of the State of Mississippi from the Federal Union" (H. V. Ames, *State Documents on Federal Relations,* Philadelphia, 1906, No. VI, p. 80).

[11] Dodd, *The Cotton Kingdom,* p. 29.

who could write such a volume."[12] This counsel-for-the-defense attitude, this loss of critical faculty, unfortunately, marred the work of the Southern novelists and historians of the period as well as the reviewers.

Plantation life, based on reluctant Negro labor, was characterized by routine and a certain indolence, factors which also contributed to the conservatism of the planters. Like people living in the tropics who lose the feeling of the passing of time, so Southerners dwelling in a balmy climate lacked the vivid time sense of the hustling Yankees, whose recurring winters warned of the transitoriness of life. The tendency of Southerners to procrastination, nonetheless, did not prevent some of the more energetic planters from undertaking bold experiments in agriculture, such as John Taylor of Caroline, Edmund Ruffin, Fielding Lewis, James H. Hammond, Jethro V. Jones, and Dr. N. B. Cloud.[13] John Taylor wrote to James Mercer Garnett that he would rather be president of the Virginia Agricultural Society than President of the United States.[14] Dixon H. Lewis, the four hundred and thirty pound Senator from Alabama, was actuated by motives of regional patriotism in experimenting with new crops and in seeking to break up the rigid adherence of the Lower South to staple agriculture.[15]

In the social pyramid of the South the businessmen occupied a position close to the apex, perhaps slightly lower than that of the planters and great politicians. This small group was too weak to correct the bias of plantation society by opposing a one-sided economy. At the Southern commercial conventions, held at frequent intervals from 1837 to 1859, businessmen rubbed shoulders with politicians in urging the emancipation of the South from economic vassalage to the

[12] John R. Thompson to Holmes, Sept. 11, 1852 (George Frederick Holmes MSS in Library of Congress).

[13] See Kathleen Bruce, "Virginian Agricultural Decline to 1860: A Fallacy," *Agricultural History*, VI, 3-13 (Jan., 1932).

[14] John Taylor to James Mercer Garnett, Jan. 28, 1818 (MS in Duke University Library).

[15] Lewis to Jessie Buel, Jan. 18, 1838 (Dixon H. Lewis Letters, MSS in Pennsylvania Historical Society Library).

North.[16] Nevertheless, between 1810 and 1850 the Southern States suffered a great decline in the relative rank of their manufactures within the nation.

The evolution of the thinking of industrialists like William Gregg and Joseph R. Anderson about Southern problems illustrates both the potentialities and the failures of Southern businessmen in opposing the main trends of their section. In a pamphlet entitled *Essays on Domestic Industry* (1845) Gregg urged the South to turn to manufacturing and pointed out the supply of cheap labor to be obtained from the service of the poor whites. He gave practical expression to his views by building the model cotton mill village of Graniteville, South Carolina. At first he accepted the ideas of his section about the protective tariff, but gradually he became a declared protectionist. Nevertheless, he followed the leadership of the planters in supporting slavery and secession. Indeed, he strengthened the case for slavery, by arguing that slavery gave to capital "a positive control over labor," and that in case of strikes in the mills, the blacks could be used as strikebreakers.[17] Joseph R. Anderson, proprietor of the famous Tredegar Iron Works that built cannon for the Confederacy, also disagreed with the slavocracy in respect to the protective tariff, but he, too, accepted slavery as a valuable aid to manufacturing, and he was an ardent Secessionist.[18] Surrounded by planters, and subjected to the pressure of Southern nationalism, the industrialists of the Old South, with the exception of a few magnates like James Guthrie of Louisville, Kentucky, succumbed to the emotional currents of their section.

Glimpses of the life of these privileged classes should be balanced by the accounts of travelers who did not stop in the homes of the wealthy planters. Having escaped the seduction of the exclusive aristocracy, they described a South of log

[16] See Herbert Wender, *Southern Commercial Conventions, 1837-1859* (Baltimore, 1930).

[17] Broadus Mitchell, *William Gregg, Factory Master of the Old South* (Chapel Hill, 1928), p. 143.

[18] Kathleen Bruce, *Virginia Iron Manufacture in the Slave Era* (New York, 1931), pp. 264-267.

cabins, zigzag rail fences, and the silence broken by an occasional *oof! oof!* of a hog, or the barking of a hound, or the
loud guffaw of a negro. Even the cultivated fields were dis-
figured with stumps or girdled trees that rose "like great,
naked, death-poles."[19] A traveler who rode in a sulky through
North Carolina in 1837 was depressed by the miles of turpentine forests, the poverty-stricken aspect of the country, and the
ignorance of the people. Everywhere, to his disgust, he was
served ham and eggs, inedible corn pone, and coffee that
looked like soot.[20] Women of the lower class could be seen
in poke bonnets, smoking pipes, dipping snuff, going barefooted. In the yards little black pickaninnies sported with a
complete absence of clothing, as though they were in the
Garden of Eden.

These families of the plain people, despite their slight acquaintance with money, practiced the code of hospitality that
had been adopted in the spacious homes of the aristocrats. The
Northern novelist, J. K. Paulding, gives a refreshing picture
of the hospitality of the nonchalant Virginian that belied the
sour report on Southern hospitality later made by Olmsted.
Avoiding snug, clean, newly painted houses, he would seek
an old rusty mansion. "If I saw a broken pane stuffed with
a petticoat," he wrote, "then I was sure of a welcome."[21] A
similar experience was encountered by a Northern youth,
Henry Watson, who went to Alabama in 1834 to become a
tutor. To a friend in Connecticut he wrote: "Stop where I
will, I am invited to dinner and to stay the night or a week
or so."[22] The ante-bellum Southerner did not have the keen
money sense that the Yankee possessed.

In the land of Dixie on the eve of the Civil War, nearly

[19] James Stirling, *Letters from the Slave States* (London, 1857), Letter XXV.
[20] W. H. Wills, "A Southern Sulky Ride in 1837 from North Carolina to
Alabama," *Publications of the Southern Historical Association*, VI, 473 (Nov., 1902).
[21] J. K. Paulding, *Letters from the South* (New York, 1817), II, 125. For a
later point of view, see F. L. Olmsted, *The Cotton Kingdom: A Traveller's Observations of Cotton and Slavery in the American Slave States* (New York, 1861),
pp. 311-324.
[22] Henry Watson to Julius Reed, Feb. 12, 1834 (Henry Watson Papers, MSS
in Duke University Library).

six of the eight million whites did not belong to slave-owning families.[23] A small proportion of this slaveless population of the South consisted of shiftless poor whites, but the great bulk of them might properly be called yeoman farmers. In the latter class also must be included the lesser slaveholders, who worked side by side with their slaves in the fields.[24] The yeomanry of the South was composed of various types of individuals. Many of them were respectable God-fearing farmers, not unlike the small farmers of the North. The farmers of German extraction in the Great Valley lived on "bacon, potatoe, and bonny claber," eschewing expensive education for their children, but using them for the thrifty cultivation of the soil.[25] These small farmers, who constituted the majority of the white population of the Old South, must not be confused with the "poor whites," a class who are described in a later chapter.[26]

The artisan class and the factory workers were a submerged group. The cotton mill at Graniteville, South Carolina, paid its female hands three to four dollars a week and its male employees four to five dollars, yet it disbursed large dividends to its stockholders.[27] Toward the close of the ante-bellum period, the mechanics and nonslaveholders were beginning to show some signs of class consciousness. The artisans bitterly protested against slaves being employed in the skilled trades, and they tried ineffectually to ban them from these trades by law.[28] Furthermore, they resented the fact that slaves under twelve and over fifty years of age paid no tax at all, and that even

[23] U. B. Phillips, *Life and Labor in the Old South* (Boston, 1929), p. 339. Phillips reaches this conclusion by estimating the average family as five persons.

[24] In the Old South a stigma was attached to menial labor, but not to manual labor, by the institution of slavery (R. R. Russel, "The General Effects of Slavery upon Southern Economic Progress," *Journal of Southern History*, IV, 38, Feb., 1938).

[25] B. Faux, *Memorable Days in America* (1823), reprinted in R. G. Thwaites, *Early Western Travels, 1748-1846* (Cleveland, Ohio, 1905), XI, 153-154.

[26] See W. T. Couch (ed.), *Culture in the South* (Chapel Hill, 1934), chap. xx, "The Tradition of the 'Poor Whites.'"

[27] Mitchell, *William Gregg*, pp. 60-63, 102. Skilled artisans in the South, on the other hand, frequently made good wages.

[28] Phillips, *Plantation and Frontier*, II, 360-368.

the prime adult slaves paid only a poll tax of fifty cents, while in North Carolina the tools and implements of mechanics were taxed ten dollars per thousand. This glaring injustice was exposed by Moses Bledsoe of Raleigh, who introduced a resolution in the state senate providing for the ad valorem taxation of all property.[29] When his proposal was defeated in the legislature, he organized the Raleigh Workingmen's Association to agitate for this reform. In 1860 the Whig party in North Carolina adopted a plank in its platform advocating ad valorem taxation, but it went down to ignominious defeat. The same issue was brought forward by the representatives of western Virginia in the Convention of 1861. Cassius Marcellus Clay of Kentucky and Hinton Rowan Helper, the author of *The Impending Crisis* (1857), sought unavailingly to awaken the class consciousness of the mechanics and nonslaveholders.[30]

All classes of Southern society were profoundly influenced by the isolation of plantation and farm. Olmsted has left graphic pen pictures of the lonely homes of the planters, which he described as "these isolated plantation patriarchates."[31] In 1854 he rode by stagecoach from Raleigh to Fayetteville. The driver, with the adroitness of a Roman charioteer, guided the team out into the open fields to avoid deep ruts, old stumps, and fallen trees. He belabored the emaciated horses, swore strange piney-woods oaths at them, but all his efforts resulted only in the overturning of the coach. The traveler in the Old South would traverse miles and miles of country without seeing two dwellings within sight of each other, and villages marked on the map with high-sounding classical names would turn out to be a few ramshackle, unpainted houses at a crossroad. It took Calhoun nearly three weeks to journey from

[29] W. K. Boyd, "North Carolina on the Eve of Secession," *Annual Report of the American Historical Association, 1910,* pp. 174-175; see also the *National Era,* Dec. 22, 1859.

[30] Clay received only five thousand votes in 1850 when he ran for governor as "the Peoples Candidate" (*Progress of the Age,* Lexington, Ky., April 19, 1851).

[31] Frederick Law Olmsted, *A Journey in the Seaboard Slave States, with Remarks on Their Economy* (New York, 1856), p. 87; for an insight into Olmsted's personality and prejudices, see Broadus Mitchell, *Frederick Law Olmsted: A Critic of the Old South* (Baltimore, 1924).

Washington to his home, Fort Hill, over the almost impassable roads.[32] In truth, large parts of the South were still in a semifrontier condition on the eve of the Civil War.

Lack of railroad facilities emphasized the isolation of the land of Dixie. In 1850 the slave states had only one third as many miles of completed railroads as the North possessed, but within a decade the mileage of Southern railroads was equal to one half that of the Northern States.[33] Although there was a line between Washington, Richmond, and Wilmington by 1840, the Piedmont was not penetrated until the decade of the fifties. This tardiness was due partly to the opposition of the aristocratic East and partly to the absorption of Southern capital in "cotton capitalism." The western part of Virginia that later detached itself from the mother state was isolated from the eastern half because of a lack of railroad connections. The Baltimore and Ohio Railroad tried again and again to secure the privilege of extending a line down the Shenandoah Valley along the Kanawha River to the Ohio, but permission was repeatedly refused.[34] The famous Danville connection between Danville, Virginia, and Greensboro, North Carolina, which was needed to give the Confederacy a third line going south from Richmond, was not completed until 1863. This sector, known as the Piedmont Railway, was built only when military necessity forced it, on account of eastern opposition to chartering a western railroad that would carry trade into a neighboring state.[35] In the Lower South, Charleston had been a pioneer in building the Hamburg Railroad, opened in 1833, whose one hundred and thirty-six miles of track made it at the time the longest railroad in the United States. The splendid inland waterways of the Lower South, however, were not conducive

[32] John C. Calhoun to L. W. Tazewell, April 14, 1829 (Calhoun MSS in Library of Congress).

[33] *The Census of 1860: Mortality and Miscellaneous Statistics*, p. 333.

[34] See Governor's Message, Dec. 6, 1847, in *Journal of House of Delegates, Session 1847-48*, pp. 180-190, for an attitude of narrow sectionalism in regard to the extension of the Baltimore and Ohio Railroad into Virginia.

[35] See an account of the dramatic struggle to build the Piedmont Railroad by C. K. Brown in *North Carolina Historical Review*, III, 198-222 (April, 1926).

to the construction of many railways.[36] There was a notable era of railroad building in the Southern States after 1855, but by this time the pattern of ante-bellum society had apparently become fixed.

Along with this inadequacy of transportation during the greater part of the ante-bellum period went a corresponding lack of city life. North Carolina's largest city, Wilmington, had a population in 1850 of 7,264 people, of whom 3,683 were negroes. Richmond contained 15,274 whites, but the whole great state of Virginia had only seven towns with a population above five thousand. Montgomery boasted a population of 6,511 whites, Charleston, 20,012 whites and 22,973 blacks. The two largest towns in Mississippi, Natchez and Vicksburg, had populations of less than three thousand white people. The metropolis of the South was New Orleans, with a total population of 116,375. Most of the villages of the South were merely political and trading centers, the rendezvous for the country people who would flock to town on court days, talk politics, and swap horses. These meetings of the squires and yeoman farmers at the courthouse took the place of the New England lyceum.

The isolation of the ante-bellum South made for conservatism in husbandry and the arts. In 1860 Edmund Ruffin conducted an extensive survey of agriculture in eastern North Carolina and carefully noted the effect that isolation had on the habits of the people. He found in Perquimans County that wheat was harvested in the same manner as in the days of the patriarch Jacob, with the sickle. Near the Mattamuskeet Swamp, a region of rich soils, the inhabitants lived secluded from the world, the roads being almost impassable. Their agricultural opinions and practices belonged to colonial times, and they were convinced that they owned the richest lands in the world and tilled them in the best possible manner.[37] Yet

[36] See U. B. Phillips, *Transportation in the Eastern Cotton Belt* (New York, 1908).

[37] Edmund Ruffin, *Agricultural Sketches of Lower North Carolina* (Raleigh, N. C., 1861), pp. 85, 228; see also G. W. Featherstonhaugh, *Excursion Through the Slave States* (New York, 1844), p. 61.

the antiquated agricultural implements used in the South were the result of the incorrigibly careless nature of the negro field hand more than the factor of isolation. Olmsted was told by a Southern planter, "Such hoes as you use at the North would not last a Negro a day."[38]

News percolated into the back country slowly along the few railways and the miserable roads. When Olmsted reached Asheville, North Carolina, and inquired for a recent paper, the clerk handed him the Asheville *News* with articles copied from the New York papers that he had read a month before.[39] He found hazy ideas of geography among the natives, such as the naïve supposition that coffee grew in New York State. Bishop Whipple narrates in his Southern Diary an anecdote of a cracker's amazement at seeing an umbrella. "Sall, by golly, did you ever seed an umberilla?" asked the cracker. "No, John, law du tell." "Well its got a top for all the world like a May apple, its as green as pizen and shoves up and down, oh golly."[40] The poor whites of the ante-bellum South bore a remarkable resemblance to the Connecticut bumpkins of the eighteenth century, who had been denied the privileges of education and of a normal intercourse with society.[41] Indeed, the most deplorable effect of isolation on the ante-bellum South was that it prevented the education of the masses.

Life on the lonely plantations of the South, nevertheless, often bred a sturdy individualism and a respect for the personalities of others that was favorable to the development of free thought and free speech. During the Civil War, Robert Toombs, acting as a sovereign over his Georgia plantation, defied the Confederate government to interfere with his natural rights and force him to plant food crops instead of cotton.[42]

[38] Olmsted, *Seaboard Slave States,* p. 666.

[39] Olmsted, *A Journey in the Back Country,* p. 251.

[40] L. B. Shippee (ed.), *Bishop Whipple's Southern Diary 1843-1844* (Minneapolis, 1937), pp. 36-37.

[41] See descriptions by Madam Knight (G. P. Winship, ed., *The Journal of Madam Knight,* New York, 1935, pp. 41-44).

[42] U. B. Phillips, *The Life of Robert Toombs* (New York, 1913), p. 247.

James Mason, Confederate Ambassador to the Court of St. James, converted rural individualism into a refreshing freedom from convention. Mrs. Chesnut drew a vivid picture of him appearing in British society: "He will say chaw for chew, and he will call himself Jeems, and he will wear a dress coat to breakfast. Over here, whatever a Mason does is right in his own eyes. He is above law. Somebody asked him how he pronounced his wife's maiden name; she was a Miss Chew from Philadelphia."[43] Moreover, an independent spirit, a contempt for servility, distinguished even the lower classes. The juxtaposition of black slaves and freemen in the same society contributed to this result.

The proud planters who had dominated the nation through the Virginia dynasty were profoundly depressed in the decades of the 1820's and 1830's by the decadence of their section. One cause of this decline was emigration to the rich cotton lands of the Southwest and to the free territory north of the Ohio. This movement carried away many bold and dissatisfied spirits who protested against slavery, for example, the North Carolina Quakers who settled in Indiana and Ohio. Along with the tide went some representatives of the old aristocracy, like Colonel Thomas Dabney, who left Elmington, Virginia, in 1835, carrying his slaves with him, to settle in the flourishing young state of Mississippi.[44] J. G. Baldwin has vividly described in *Flush Times in Alabama and Mississippi* the invasion of the cotton states on the Gulf by Virginians, who contributed a large share of the lawyers, judges, and gentlemen to that undeveloped section.[45] The strength of this tide of immigration is measured by the fact that in 1850 over thirty per cent of native Virginians and nearly thirty-four per cent of North Carolinians were living in other states. Of those who had abandoned the old states of Virginia and North Carolina,

---

[43] Mary Boykin Chesnut, *A Diary from Dixie* (New York, 1929), p. 116.

[44] See Susan D. Smedes, *Memorials of a Southern Planter* (Baltimore, 1887).

[45] J. G. Baldwin, *Flush Times in Alabama and Mississippi* (New York, 1853), pp. 72-105.

approximately two thirds had settled in slave territory and one third in the free states, especially Indiana and Ohio.[46]

This loss in population of the older South was due to the exhaustion of the soils of the Tidewater, the lure of the West, and the poor means of communication. The cream of the fertility of the Tidewater soils had been skimmed away by a wasteful frontier system of agriculture and by the cultivation of tobacco without regard to rotation of crops. Edmund Ruffin, the noted agriculturist, estimated that nine tenths of the land of Tidewater Virginia (and for thirty miles above the fall line) failed to produce as much as ten bushels of Indian corn per acre, although that crop was best suited to the soil.[47] Joel Poinsett pointed out that the reason why so many natives of South Carolina were deserting the state, was that the West possessed waterways and means of transportation that made its crops more valuable. South Carolina was rapidly losing its relative position in the Union, partly because of the distressing shortsightedness of the people of Charleston and the Tidewater, who took the stand that the improvement of the interior of the state was no concern of theirs.[48] But the agricultural decline of the Upper South was halted in the decade of the 1830's by the work of Edmund Ruffin, who popularized the use of marl, by the introduction of Peruvian guano, by the adoption of more diversified farming, and by the activity of agricultural societies.[49] Avery Craven finds that the most prosperous era of agriculture for the Upper South was the decade 1850-60.[50]

Nevertheless, the relative stagnation of the older South, in comparison with the rapidly growing Northern States, was one of the factors that rendered Southerners abnormally sensi-

[46] Estimated from *The Census of 1850*, p. xxxvi; at the same time twenty-eight per cent of the natives of Massachusetts were living in other states.

[47] Edmund Ruffin, *An Essay on Calcareous Manures* (Petersburg, Va., 1842), p. 21.

[48] Draft of a Speech on the Extension of the R. R. to Greenville Delivered in Charleston, Nov., 1846 (Joel R. Poinsett Papers, XX, 129).

[49] Bruce, "Virginian Agricultural Decline to 1860: A Fallacy," pp. 8-13.

[50] A. O. Craven, *Soil Exhaustion as a Factor in the Agricultural History of Virginia and Maryland, 1606-1860* (Urbana, Ill., 1926), p. 122.

tive to criticism. In 1852 the Virginia Agricultural Society issued an address which exposed the inferiority of Virginia agriculture to that of the Northern States. A quotation from it
reflects the wounded pride of Virginians: "And thus we, who
once swayed the councils of the Union, find our power gone,
and our influence on the wane, at a time when both are of
vital importance to our prosperity, if not to our safety. As
other States accumulate the means of material greatness, and
glide past us on the road to wealth and empire, we slight the
warnings of dull statistics, and drive lazily along the fields of
ancient customs, or stop the *plough* to speed the *politician*—
should we not, in too many cases, say with more propriety,
the *demagogue!*"[51] This address was at first suppressed, in
order not to furnish a gratuitous weapon to Northern critics,
but later was printed. Likewise the humiliating comparisons
of prosperity between the North and the South made by Daniel Reaves Goodloe, Henry Ruffner, and Hinton Rowan
Helper were received with closed minds by most Southerners.

The sensitiveness of Southerners to criticism was exaggerated by the existence of a well-developed vein of romanticism
in their society. The vogue of romanticism was not peculiar
to the Southern States of this period, but it attained a more
luxuriant growth below the Potomac than elsewhere in America.[52] The romantic temper in the South, based on the desire
to escape from reality, was not due primarily to the institution
of slavery. Rather, it was an outgrowth of an agrarian civilization emerging from the conquest of the wilderness. The
Southern States as a whole were not free from the shadow of
the frontier. The taste for the romantic tale, with its melodramatic plot and its focus on the strange and unusual, was a
natural concomitant. The homes of the planters were set back
from the road behind great avenues of trees, and brooding si-

[51] Olmsted, *Seaboard Slave States,* p. 169; Professor Avery Craven (*The Repressible Conflict, 1830-1861,* Baton Rouge, La., 1939) has pointed out that much
of the backwardness of the South, which the abolitionists attributed to slavery, was
due rather to the presence of the Negro.

[52] For an analysis of the term "romanticism," see Irving Babbitt, *Rousseau and
Romanticism* (Boston, 1919).

lence rested upon them. The unvarying routine of life on the
great plantations, the monotony of the small village, stimulated the extroverts to frequent traveling and visiting, while
the introverts tended to seek refuge in romance and cavalier
poetry. Furthermore, the chivalric spirit in the South escaped
the withering influence of rapid industrialization which affected Northern society. Mark Twain's observation that Sir
Walter Scott had run the Southern people mad with his medieval romances contained much truth.[53]

Although the Southern people would probably have developed romantic tendencies regardless of the existence of slavery,
this dominant institution fostered such a movement. Slavery
freed the favored planting class from drudgery and, especially,
gave the young men the leisure to indulge romantic fancies.
Tyrone Power lamented the fact that he saw many aristocratic,
intelligent-looking young men, the sons of planters, lounging
about in the most hopeless idleness.[54] In the Tidewater region
the myth of the cavalier origin of the best families contributed
to the romantic delusion. Southerners of the upper class found
a certain satisfaction in comparing their civilization based on
black dependents, with medieval manors, knights on caracol-
ing horses, and humble serfs. Slavery nourished a quixotic
pride in the ruling class, and it deflected Southern literature
from dealing realistically with social problems. The idealizing
trend of Southern fiction after 1830 was in part a reaction from
abolitionist criticism.[55]

So powerful was the trend to romantic writing that William Gilmore Simms, who was by nature a realist, could not
escape its influence. His romantic tales, however, are shot
through with veins of realism. His Captain Porgy, whom Van
Doren has called "the most truly comic character ever pro-

[53] Samuel L. Clemens, *Life on the Mississippi* (New York, 1903), pp. 308-309.
[54] Tyrone Power, *Impressions of America during the Years 1833, 1834, and
1835* (Philadelphia, 1836), p. 65.
[55] See Vernon L. Parrington, *The Romantic Revolution in America, 1800-1860*
(New York, 1927), pp. 35-46, 93-103. The proslavery dialectic, on the other hand,
followed Aristotle in being pragmatic and based on experience. See W. S. Jenkins,
Pro-Slavery Thought in the Old South (Chapel Hill, 1935), pp. 64-65.

duced by this school of American romance,"[56] and his Indians of the Southern frontier, much more natural than Cooper's, show his gifts as a realistic writer. Likewise, William Alexander Caruthers indulged in one novel of realistic criticism of Southern life, *The Kentuckian in New-York* (1834), and then turned to romanticizing the land of Dixie.[57]

The dominance of the romantic temper in Southern poetry is admirably illustrated in the life and verse of Philip Pendleton Cooke. Cooke's poetry flowed from a traditional well. Proud of his Virginia ancestry, he was filled with the desire to transmit "the unsullied position of our house" to the next generation. At a time when the old aristocracy of Virginia was threatened with economic insecurity he wrote, "It is lamentable to see the old families of the land, the first in gentility & caste, *reduced;* to see their descendants gradually sinking by marriage & association into humbler classes, and to see *mine* thus would break my heart."[58] It was natural, therefore, that he should nourish his fancy on Froissart's *Chronicles* and on Sir Walter Scott's works. In 1843 he was writing ballads founded on Froissart's *Chronicles,* reading the novels of Disraeli, and composing a romance of his own.[59] "Florence Vane," his best known poem, is written in the pure romantic style. The theme of unrequited love, the trysting place, a "ruin lone and hoary," a dreamlike maiden, and the use of the pathetic fallacy contributed ingredients of sentimental unreality.

Mirabeau Buonaparte Lamar was another attractive figure in the school of Southern cavalier poets extinguished by the Civil War. Reared on a plantation near Milledgeville, Georgia, the youthful Lamar hated the monotony of the plantation and dreamed of heroic exploits on distant arenas. The daughters of the planters, who so carefully preserved the whiteness of

[56] Carl Van Doren, *The American Novel* (New York, 1921), p. 63.

[57] See Theodore Hunt, *Le Roman Américain, 1830-1850* (Paris, 1937), pp. 51-55.

[58] Philip Pendleton Cooke to his father, John R. Cooke, Dec. 29, 1840 (John Esten Cooke MSS in Duke University Library).

[59] Cooke to his father, April 26 and Aug. 10, 1843 (*ibid.*).

their complexions from the rays of a semitropic sun, Tabitha, Sally, Fanny, and Irene were transformed by the magic of his verse into "the rose of Sharon," "the Blue-eyed Queen," "the belle of the Brazos," and "the Lily in the Vale." Often he wrote cavalier compliments in the albums of these maidens. When his young wife died, he nursed his sorrow, declaring there was bliss in the tears shed for the loved. "To forget is guilt, and not to weep is worse than ingratitude."[60] After a series of bitter disappointments, this knight of King Arthur departed for Texas, fought gallantly in the war for independence, and was elected President of the Lone Star Republic. Because he wrote poetry, his opponents called him a dreamer, but there was a hard realistic side to his nature, as exhibited in his demand that no leniency be shown to the captured Santa Anna, and in his ruthless policy toward the Indians.

The flowering of the romantic genius in the South occurred in the ornate style of oratory that won popular favor. The English traveler, Lieutenant Francis Hall, classified the various brands of Southern orators: the Political Spouters descanting upon liberty, the rights of man, and the freedom of the seas; the Fourth of July Orators; the Orators of the Human Race; and the tobacco-spitting Stump Orators.[61] The Nashville Convention that met in 1850 to concert measures of defense against the aggressions of the North displayed the frequent divorcement of Southern oratory from realistic action. The delegates assembled in the largest church in the city and were surrounded by Southern belles and matrons, "like borders of flowers [that is a gallant delegate's figure of speech] enclosing them on each side."[62] The delegates were inspired by the occasion and audience to unfurl their most elegant figures of speech, their most graceful gestures, and their richest tones of forensic eloquence; "at one moment, the audience would be

[60] Philip Graham, *The Life and Poems of Mirabeau B. Lamar* (Chapel Hill, 1938), p. 32.

[61] Lieutenant Francis Hall, *Travels in Canada and the United States* (London, 1819), pp. 303-305.

[62] J. H. Ingraham, *The Sunny South or the Southerner at Home* (Philadelphia, 1860), pp. 131, 133, 135.

startled with the thunders of rock-beating surges; and at another, soothed by the soft zephyrs of a summer sea." One of the fire-eaters who spoke in the convention was Francis Pickens of South Carolina, who had a face like one of the old Roman emperors and whose oratory was described as being worthy of the Forum. "His rhetoric was profusely ornamented with figures and metaphors like an exquisite mosaic." But one of the most violent delegates present, Beverley Tucker of Virginia, imitated the vituperative style of John Randolph "and was sometimes forgetful that ladies were present." A potent cause for the widespread Southern interest in the hustings was the allure of oratory, and doubtless many young men were led into politics that they might enjoy a forum for their eloquent voices. Whenever William Lowndes Yancey, the orator of secession, arose to speak in the villages of the Deep South, it was as if an enchanter had waved his magic wand and temporarily deprived the audience of their reason.[63]

Although the main current of Southern literature flowed in the direction of romanticism, there was a school of realists who cannot be neglected. These men exploited a rich vein of humor, drawing realistic pictures of crackers, scamps, gander pullings, practical joking, horse trading, militia musters, country dances, etc. Such stories first appeared in local newspapers, but their popularity induced publishers to bring them out in book form. Some of this outwardly realistic literature was so exaggerated and imaginative that it bordered on the romantic, for example, Thorpe's "The Big Bear of Arkansas," and the David Crockett stories. These authors were, with few exceptions, newspapermen who wrote to entertain their subscribers by using local material.[64] It is interesting to note that

[63] It seems to the writer that the technique of the camp meeting was often employed by Southern orators. See a description of the effect of Yancey's speech during a protracted political meeting at Uniontown, Alabama, in 1856. At the conclusion of his speech several thousand of his audience sprang to their feet as one man; yells, shouts, cries filled the air; men announced their change of votes, as if they had been converted by an evangelist (John Witherspoon DuBose's manuscript life of W. L. Yancey, chap. viii, p. 316, in State Capitol at Montgomery).

[64] F. J. Meine, *Tall Tales of the Southwest: An Anthology of Southern and Southwestern Humor, 1830-1860* (New York, 1937), p. xxvii.

several of the most successful exploiters of the comic aspects
of Southern society were born in the North, William Tappan
Thompson, George Washington Harris, and Thomas Bangs
Thorpe. The pioneer in this type of writing, though, was that
versatile Southerner, Augustus Baldwin Longstreet, whose
Georgia Scenes made a great hit with the Southern public. A
wealthy Mississippi planter of critical mind, Joseph B. Cobb,
also followed the lead of Longstreet in turning away from
the imitation of Byron and Sir Walter Scott to produce some
humorous *genre* writing in his work entitled *Mississippi
Scenes*.[65] Such writers, neglected by the students of American
literature until recently, afford both a breath of realism and
a comic relief from the high-flown oratory of the period, the
romantic novels, the notions of Southern honor, and the artificial attitude toward women.

Besides literature, other important manifestations of the romantic spirit in the South were the prevalence of the duel,
the development of the notion of "Southern honor" in politics,
and the chivalric attitude toward women. The fateful development of the notion of "Southern honor" in politics must
be left to a later chapter. The duel was popularized among
the Southern gentry by the French officers who aided the
Americans to win their independence.[66] Challenges were sent
only to gentlemen; men not considered in this category were
caned or horsewhipped.[67] It was considered cowardly in most
Southern communities to decline a challenge or to resort to
the courts for protection from slander and insult. "I was educated to believe," wrote the famous Charleston physician,
Marion Sims, "that duels inspired the proprieties of society
and protected the honor of women."[68] Some of the most

[65] George T. Buckley, "Joseph B. Cobb: Mississippi Essayist and Critic," *American Literature*, X, 166-178 (May, 1938).

[66] D. R. Fox, "Culture in Knapsacks," *Quarterly Journal*, XI, 42 (Jan., 1930).

[67] For the rules of dueling, see John Lyde Wilson, *The Code of Honor; or Rules
for the Government of Principals and Seconds in Duelling* (Charleston, S. C., 1858).
The professed purpose of this pamphlet was to prevent unnecessary duels.

[68] E. L. Green, *A History of the University of South Carolina* (Columbia, S. C.,
1916), p. 244; see also Governor Henry A. Wise's justification of the duel (John
S. Wise, "The Fire-Eaters," *Saturday Evening Post*, CLXXVII, 6, June 2, 1906).

prominent statesmen of the South supported "the code of honor," both by precept and example, like Henry Clay, John Randolph of Roanoke, Andrew Jackson, Henry S. Foote, Alexander Stephens, and W. L. Yancey. Nevertheless, the frequent laws passed by Southern legislatures against the practice, the numerous sermons against the institution, the antidueling associations in the South, lead to the suspicion that the majority of the people were not in favor of this relic of feudal days.[69]

The romantic attitude toward women held by the upperclass Southerner drew a false line of exaggeration between the sexes. An instance of this artificiality was related to the writer by a descendant of one of the upper plantation group. Her grandfather, Charles Bruce, a graduate of Harvard, met the yeoman farmers of his neighborhood on a perfect plane of equality. At the village store he would spend hours, cracking jokes, discussing crops, and talking politics with them. But the line was instantly drawn when the feminine members of the family were concerned. He would not think of inviting these plain countrymen to his house or introduce them to his wife and daughters.

Woman was a being made of finer clay than man, according to this chivalric ideal, but she was confined to a narrow sphere of activity by iron bands of convention. Even during the early part of the Civil War, there was a prejudice against women performing the actual duties of nursing soldiers in the hospitals. It was fitting that these angelic creatures should hold the fevered brow, but they must not do the dirty work of dressing wounds and caring for the diseased. Wrote Kate Cumming, who brushed aside such prejudices: "There is scarcely a day passes that I do not hear some derogatory re-

[69] A collection of pamphlets on dueling was made by the late Professor Yates Snowden of the University of South Carolina, among which is an interesting *Sermon upon Duelling together with the Constitution of the Grahamville Association for Suppression of Duelling* by Rev. Wigfall, who declared that dueling should not be called by a flattering name but by the harsh term "murder." See also a pamphlet in the De Renne Library, Wormsloe, Ga., by William Jay, *An Essay on Duelling,* for which a gold medal was awarded by the Savannah Anti-Duelling Association in 1829.

marks about the ladies who are in the hospitals, until I think, if there is any credit due them at all, it is for the moral courage they have in braving public opinion."[70]

How far the notions of chivalry penetrated into the lower strata of Southern society it is difficult to ascertain. Whipple observed some country girls near Memphis whose manners were calculated to dispel illusions of romance. When Henry Clay was traveling through this region, he attended a country dance, and, wishing to be agreeable, said to one of the girls, "Will you dance?" "Well, I will, horse," she replied, causing the statesman to blush.[71] Furthermore, the many capable Southern mistresses who supervised house servants, administered medicines to sick slaves, and reared large families of healthy children, as well as the vast majority of the farmer wives, who worked from morning till night milking cows, spinning and weaving, making sausages and lard, and rocking the cradle, belied the romantic stereotype of the fragile Southern lady with lily hands.[72]

The cult of chivalry, while it imposed limitations on the intellectual life of the South, produced at the same time some fine fruits in manners and behavior. In no other Southerner did romantic ideals show to greater advantage than in James Johnston Pettigrew, a young lawyer of Charleston. When a plague of yellow fever ravaged Charleston, young Pettigrew refused to look after his own safety but remained in the pestilent city to care for the sick.[73] In the South Carolina legislature shortly afterwards he led a gallant fight against the reopening of the African slave trade. The outbreak of the war in Italy for independence gave him an opportunity to abandon his law practice, in which he was not vitally interested, to

[70] Francis B. Simkins and James W. Patton, *The Women of the Confederacy* (Richmond, 1936), p. 89.   [71] Whipple, *Southern Diary*, p. 130.

[72] It is interesting to note that one of the first women to publish a newspaper in the United States was a Southerner, Sarah Hillhouse, who started the *Monitor* in Washington County, Georgia, in 1806. A volume of this rare publication is preserved in the University of North Carolina Library.

[73] Ben Allston to J. J. Pettigrew, Oct. 1, 1858 (Pettigrew Papers, XIII, 1857-61, MSS in archives of the North Carolina Historical Association).

sail for Turin *"pour entrer dans l'armée piémontaise et me
battre pour la Saint Liberté des Italiennes."*[74] His friends made
a great fuss over his going, but he declared, what is life to
a young man without adventures? His witty and realistic
law partner, James Louis Petigru, wrote: "Johnston is gone to
fight for Italian Liberty—but it's doubtful, exceedingly doubtful, if he will get the chance; as he does not mean to fight on
foot."[75] Two days after his arrival in Turin a suspension of
hostilities took place which hurled him to earth. His Italian
adventure thus ending in a fiasco, he traveled in Spain and
wrote a vivacious book, *Spain and the Spaniards.*

Returning to Charleston, he became active in training and
parading the militia of the city before the admiring gaze of
fair Southern belles. Although he was not one of the fire-
eaters, he immediately volunteered when South Carolina seceded and was appointed a colonel by Governor Pickens.
Once more his cool-headed law partner and relative made fun
of his romantic enthusiasms: "Your cousin Johnston giving in
to the general sentiment and being put at the head of a Regiment of Volunteers is no longer a pale inmate of St. Michaels'
Alley where he used to pore over dusty books in a foreign
tongue; but bestrides a gallant steed with gay trappings and
bright shoulder knots."[76] As a young officer he refused to eat
the delicacies sent him by fond relatives and admirers, because his men could not share them.[77] Pettigrew was sent by
Governor Pickens to demand the return of Major Anderson
from Fort Sumter to his original base, and this encounter with
the Union commander was characterized by the knightly
courtesy of Richard the Lion-heart and Saladin. With almost
medieval humility he hastened to Virginia when hostilities
threatened and offered himself as a private in the ranks. The
glorious moment in his life was experienced as he led a divi-

[74] Pettigrew to William Carson, Turin, July, 1859 (Pettigrew Papers, XIII).

[75] James Louis Petigru to Willie [Carson], June 8, 1858 [1859?] (James Louis
Petigru Papers, MSS in Library of Congress).

[76] J. L. Petigru to Willie, March 2, 1861 (James Louis Petigru Papers).

[77] L. Porcher to Pettigrew, Jan. 12, 1861 (Pettigrew Papers, XIII).

sion of North Carolina troops in the heroic but futile charge ordered by Lee at Gettysburg. A few weeks after his command was shattered, he died in Virginia, and in the account of his last hours, one is again reminded of the humility of the medieval crusader. When the clergyman asked if he were a communicant of the Holy Sacrament, he replied in the negative, but added, "Not from a want of faith nor want of disposition, but a sense of unworthiness. I feared to incur the guilt of presumption."[78] Thus perished a true romantic of the Old South, who exhibited the virtues and defects of romanticism as understood in his day.

The society that produced a type like Johnston Pettigrew was more interested in the refined gentleman than the scholar. With all his admirable qualities, the typical Southern aristocrat of 1850 was not a man of distinguished culture or literary tastes. Remote from the stimulating contacts of city life, he pursued the quiet tenor of his way, harvesting his crops, attending to the welfare of his slaves, and taking a vigorous interest in politics. In 1828 Jesse Burton Harrison, a Virginian of rare culture, delivered *A Discourse on the Prospects of Letters and Taste in Virginia* at Hampden-Sydney College, in which he characterized the aristocracy as follows: "In making an estimate of the condition of learning here before the Revolution, I feel warranted in saying, that while the lower orders were scarcely at all instructed, the richer class was vastly better educated in proportion to the light and spirit of the age, than the present generation are, acknowledging a great advancement since in Europe."[79] The decline of the Tidewater and the rise of the Cotton Kingdom tended to dilute the inherited culture of colonial days. Howison, the most candid of the Virginia historians, wrote of his native state: "It is a melancholy truth that her people have never been a *reading people*. In the mass, they have shown an in-

---

[78] MS Letter from J. P. B. Wilmer (James Johnston Pettigrew Scrap Book, in archives of North Carolina Historical Commission).

[79] J. B. Harrison, *A Discourse on the Prospects of Letters and Taste in Virginia* (Cambridge, Mass., 1828), p. 18.

difference to polite letters and to education in general, depressing to the mind that wishes to see them respectable and happy."[80] In the place of William Byrd II with his magnificent library, there was living at Westover from 1829 to the close of the Civil War, John A. Selden, admirable gentleman, planter, and justice of the peace. In the Westover Journal of Selden, which faithfully records the daily events of his life, 1858-1862, he mentions books only once, to note the fact that he had paid two dollars for two novels, *Wandering Seer* and *What Will He Do With It?*[81]

In the newer parts of the South, there was less interest in books than in Virginia and the Carolinas. As late as the decade of the fifties, a large proportion of the Alabama and Mississippi planters lived in log houses. These homes of the cotton planters contained numerous guns, pistols, powderhorns, and on the porches, saddles, bridles, and whips; but they lacked some of the ordinary refinements to be found in Northern homes, good reading lamps, pianos, thermometers, and recent books. The talk of the inhabitants was constantly on the subjects of cotton, Negroes, and land. In the rich Black Belt, however, some cultured Virginians and Carolinians had settled. Beautiful old homes in the classical renaissance style were built, like Clifton, Thorn Hill, Rosemount, Tulip Hill, Gaineswood, and Bluff Hall.[82] The aristocrats who lived in them engaged in fox hunts, enjoyed the fashionable society of Pass Christian on the Gulf, White Sulphur Springs, or Saratoga and Newport, wrote amateur poetry, and read the romances of Scott. But their culture was primarily derived from social intercourse, the art of good conversation, and the observation of the world, rather than from books or scholarship.

Francis Lieber was an intelligent observer of the state of culture in the South from 1835 to 1855. During those years he was marooned at Columbia, teaching in South Carolina Col-

[80] R. R. Howison, *History of Virginia* (Richmond, 1848), II, 464.

[81] J. S. Bassett, *The Westover Journal of John A. Selden, 1858-1862* (Northampton, Mass., 1921), p. 283.

[82] Carl Carmer, *Stars Fell on Alabama* (New York, 1934), pp. 93-105.

lege and writing his great book on *Civil Liberty*. His journal and letters to friends in the North were severe in their strictures on Southern culture. On November 20, 1839, he wrote in his journal: "Now, I have not one, not even one, here who sympathizes with me, still less one from whom I could derive stirring knowledge in my sphere. My book, as it is before the public, I have been obliged to spin solitarily out of my brain, as the spider spins its cobweb, without one cheering conversation, one word of friendly advice—in utter mental isolation."[83]

Lieber failed to make the distinction between the scholar, of whom there were comparatively few in the ante-bellum South, and the cultured gentlemen, who were much more numerous. He longed for comradeship with his Northern friends, Sumner, Longfellow, Ticknor, Prescott, who were professional writers and scholars. His nostalgia for the social contacts, books, and intellectual stimulus of the North was expressed in a proposed epitaph for himself: "There lies a man who died of the South."[84] Those in authority in South Carolina assuredly did not appreciate such a scholar, for they refused to make him president of South Carolina College in 1855. The objections urged against him were that he spent his vacations in the North, he was too national, he was a foreigner, he was not an advocate of slavery, and he was religiously unorthodox. In a trenchant sentence, Lieber drew a picture of the limitations of the South Carolina mind: "What a man I would be had I become a Methodist!"[85]

This picture of an intellectual desert in South Carolina was hardly fair to the state. Lieber himself contradicted his sweeping indictment by recording in his journal his fruitful conversation with Legaré, Professor Nott, W. C. Preston, Bishop Elliot, and James L. Petigru. Certainly Langdon Cheves, Joel Poinsett, Calhoun, Robert Barnwell Rhett, and W. H. Trescott

[83] Thomas S. Perry, *The Life and Letters of Francis Lieber* (Boston, 1882), p. 141.

[84] Lieber to Samuel B. Ruggles, Columbia, S. C., April 8, 1849 (Correspondence of Francis Lieber with Samuel B. Ruggles, MSS in Library of Congress).

[85] Lieber to Ruggles, Christmas Eve, 1854 (Lieber Correspondence, MSS).

were men of stimulating intellects. Joseph LeConte, the noted scientist, disagreed radically with Lieber's estimate. "My life in Columbia," he wrote, "was perhaps the most pleasant in my whole career. The society was the most refined and cultivated I have ever known. . . . Three institutions of learning, the South Carolina College, the Theological Seminary, and the Military Academy (Arsenal) formed the nucleus about which gathered many intellectual men and women. Such men as Dr. Thornwell, Dr. Palmer, William C. Preston, and Wade Hampton, are rare in any community. My intellectual activity was powerfully stimulated, and I wrote many articles."[86]

Moreover, some of the planters provided libraries for the use of their sons that showed discriminating taste. John Witherspoon DuBose listed the following books in the family library of Cedar Grove, near Demopolis, Alabama: a full set of Sir Walter Scott's novels, poems of Byron, works of Emerson, Thornwell's *Discourses on Truth,* Locke's Essay on Human Understanding, *Eloquence of the United States* (five volumes), Shakespeare's complete plays, speeches of Curran and Grattan, works of Fielding, Milton, Heber, Pollock, Rollin's *Ancient History,* Gibbon's *Decline and Fall of the Roman Empire,* Plutarch, Madison's *Journal of the Federal Convention,* and *National Portraits.*[87] One of the most attractive private libraries in the South was owned by a wealthy merchant of Savannah, A. A. Smets. He had collected eight thousand volumes, including some rare illuminated manuscripts of the Middle Ages. In his library were the works of the best poets, novelists, historians, and biographers, all bound in the most elegant manner.[88] Another fine ante-bellum library, owned by Mitchell King of Charleston, included many Italian authors, Pulci, Boiardo, Poggio, Varchi, and a large collection of French

[86] W. D. Armes (ed.), *The Autobiography of Joseph LeConte* (New York, 1903), p. 172.

[87] "List of Library books of DuBose family at Cedar Grove" (John Witherspoon DuBose Papers, MSS in Alabama State Library).

[88] *De Bow's Review,* XIII, 97-98 (July, 1852).

books, including such skeptical writers as D'Alembert, Volney, and Voltaire.[89] The library of Dr. M. W. Phillips of Log Hall, in Mississippi, contained a complete set of Audubon's *Birds of America,* works of Calhoun, Webster's speeches, lives of Jefferson, Jackson, and other statesmen, and sumptuous editions of Shakespeare, Byron, and Sir Walter Scott.[90]

That the Southern aristocrat of 1850 was not a patron of letters or literary men is indicated by the fact that the South, in contrast with New England and the Middle States, produced few literary men of note. John Esten Cooke, the most gifted Virginia novelist of ante-bellum days, wavered between law and literature. He would make a heroic resolution to eschew literature, but his innate love for writing would overcome his vow. Although the *Southern Literary Messenger* accepted dozens of his articles, it paid nothing for them, and the aspiring young writer had to dine on crackers and tea.[91] Even patriotic Southern writers, like William Gilmore Simms, sent their best work to Northern publishers, who paid them liberally. Literary magazine after magazine started up a brief existence in the South only to expire from want of patronage.[92] Professor Trent called Charleston "the graveyard of magazines." Yet it should be noted that intelligent Southerners did subscribe to the superior English and Scotch magazines; for example, among the Pickens Papers for 1845, there is a bill for thirty-two dollars for subscriptions to the *London Quar-*

[89] Catalogue of the Library of Mitchell King (MS in Library of the College of Charleston).

[90] *Publications of the Mississippi Historical Association* (Oxford, Miss., 1909), X, 307.

[91] Cooke wrote in 1852, apropos of contributing to the *Messenger:* "If he [Thompson, the editor] expects me to write for him forever, he's mistaken—without some remuneration" (quoted from J. O. Beaty, *John Esten Cooke, Virginian,* New York, 1922, p. 28).

[92] Calvin Wiley, editor of the *Southern Weekly Post,* explained the literary sterility of the South on the bases: (1) the attempt had never been made to build up a first-class paper in the South with adequate capital; (2) the contributions printed in these papers were "wishey-washey imitations of fashionable literature"; (3) another prime cause was the agitation and fear produced by the abolition movement (*Southern Weekly Post,* Nov. 3, 1855). See also F. L. Mott, *A History of American Magazines, 1741-1850* (Cambridge, Mass., 1938).

terly Review, the *Edinburgh Review,* the *Westminster Review* and the *Foreign Quarterly Review.*[93] The diaries of B. F. Perry and the fire-eater, Edmund Ruffin, show that they were avid readers of the English and Scotch periodicals.

The attitude of the Southern aristocrat to the native literary man was shown in the treatment of William Gilmore Simms and Henry Timrod. Simms struggled in vain for social recognition and appreciation of his merits until he turned from literature to polemics.[94] His depression was described by D. F. Jamison of Orangeburg in a letter to George Frederick Holmes: "He says he has labored for the wind—that his works are not appreciated, as he reasonably expected they would be —especially in South Carolina for whose people he has written everything. I am sorry to admit that the last charge is too true. His more labored compositions and his occasional contributions to the periodical press, all sell at the North and what is more to him, excite attention and call forth praise or blame, while at home they do not sell and come and go unnoticed."[95] Simms compared the literary man residing in the South to a blooded race horse locked up in the stable, and declared that his true policy would be to live in one of the great Northern cities.[96] In 1857 he reached the nadir of his disillusionment. He confessed to Holmes that his labors in trying to build up a literature and run a periodical in the South had been vain and fruitless. "I am sick of the labor," he wrote, "—of drawing water in a sieve—."[97] Timrod found so little market for his literary abilities that when the Civil War came, he was forced to enlist as a private, because he was too poor to buy a Confederate officer's uniform.[98]

[93] Bill of Leonard Scott and Co., Sept. 18, 1845, to Samuel Pickens, Greensboro, Ala. (Pickens Papers, MSS in Alabama State Library).

[94] Trent, *William Gilmore Simms,* pp. 102-104, 128-129. See also Montrose J. Moses, *The Literature of the South* (New York, 1910), pp. 163-291.

[95] D. F. Jamison to George Frederick Holmes, May 26, 1852 (G. F. Holmes MSS in Library of Congress).

[96] Simms to Holmes, Sept. 15, 1853 (G. F. Holmes MSS).

[97] Simms to Holmes, June 17, 1857 (W. G. Simms MSS in Library of Congress).

[98] G. P. Voigt, "Timrod in the Light of Newly Revealed Letters," *South Atlantic Quarterly,* XXXVII, 263-269 (July, 1938).

The Southern disapprobation of literature as a profession
was reflected in the advice of John R. Thompson, editor of
the foremost literary magazine of his section, the *Southern
Literary Messenger,* to the young men of Washington College. He declared: "Indeed anyone who should choose the
making of books as a means of support in this day, with his
eyes open to the bankruptcy of thousands before him might
well, in my judgment, be made the subject of a commission
of lunacy."[99] However futile it might be to hope to earn a
living from literature, he recommended the cultivation of
letters as providing relaxation from severer toil and as offer-
ing "a wreath of fadeless verdure." Thompson demonstrated
in his own life the frustration of a literary career in the South.
On December 2, 1851, he wrote to Rufus Griswold that the
Messenger was nearly bankrupt, that he had spent his patri-
mony in trying to keep it alive, and that he had followed
"the will-of-the-wisp, literary fame, into a morass."[100] Undoubtedly one of the most fundamental causes for this failure
to support Southern literary men was economic; the chronic
dearth of ready money among the literate classes to spend for
such luxuries as newspapers, magazines, and books.

Between 1790 and 1850 a striking change had taken place
in the quality of the leaders produced by the South. The
Southern plantations of the eighteenth century had bred such
liberals as George Mason, George Washington, Thomas Jeffer-
son, Charles Carroll, James Madison, James Monroe, John
Randolph of Roanoke, Christopher Gadsden, and Willie Jones.
In 1850 their places were occupied by men of smaller stature,
Calhoun, Rhett, Yancey, Jefferson Davis, John Slidell, Senator
Wigfall, David Yulee, Roger Pryor, and Henry A. Wise.
These men who led the South to disaster lacked the philo-
sophical spirit that had sustained the eighteenth-century aris-

---

[99] John R. Thompson, *An Address on Education and Literature in Virginia*
(Richmond, 1850), pp. 33-34. A pamphlet.

[100] John R. Thompson Papers (MSS in the University of Virginia Library); see
also a letter of Augustin L. Taveau, a South Carolina rice planter, to Thompson,
May 16, 1850, describing his failure to interest the Charleston aristocrats in the
Messenger (Taveau MSS in Duke University Library).

tocrat. It is true that they were devoted to the South, but they were warped by strong sectional prejudices, they lacked a catholic point of view, and they had lost the magic glow of republicanism. Many of the representative men of the South at this time were duelists or supporters of the code of honor. Their breadth of vision was limited by their vested interests in slavery and a devotion to the romantic, so that they did not appreciate the fine flower of tolerance.

The rise of the common man, furthermore, was a potent factor in the decline of tolerance. The vast majority of the Southern people in 1850 were hard-working farmers, whose reading was limited to the Bible and an occasional newspaper. Confined to a narrow world by the lack of education and difficult means of communication, they were provincial and conservative in outlook, but hardly more so than the country people of New England or Pennsylvania. The aristocratic culture of the Virginia and Carolina Tidewater, restricted as it was to a small class, was not extensive enough to leaven the vast, inchoate regions of the Cotton Kingdom. The yeoman farmers, who constituted the backbone of their section, had the vote, and they served on juries. Converted by waves of evangelism, they were dominated by a strong puritanical feeling. On the slavery question, disregarding their real economic interests, they were ruled by emotion. In truth, they imparted a fervent flavor of intolerance to all racial and sectional issues. Their want of education rendered them susceptible to the religious exhorters as well as to the florid orator of the planter class. The society of the Cotton and Tobacco kingdoms was still raw, still reminiscent of the frontier. Such an environment was not favorable to the preservation of freedom of thought; for freedom of thought, Lord Acton has observed, is "the delicate fruit of a mature civilization."

CHAPTER III

A DARK CLOUD OF ILLITERACY

A BRILLIANT Northern journalist ascribed much of the intolerance displayed toward antislavery men in the South to the widespread illiteracy of that section.[1] So natural is such a conclusion that few persons would be disposed to question it. Nevertheless, it is not sufficient simply to show a co-existence of intolerance and an extraordinary state of illiteracy in the Southern States. It must be ascertained what role the illiterates played in determining the laws and social atmosphere of that section. Within the classification of "illiterates," moreover, those persons should be included who could barely read and sign their names, yet who were, to all practical purposes, as ignorant as the completely unschooled. Horace Mann declared that the statistics of illiteracy during this period should be increased by one third in recognition of this fact.[2] Did these unlettered people of the South vote in large numbers? Were they kept illiterate that they might not question the *status quo?* Did the planters and their silver-tongued orators use them as pawns in the game of politics? Were the illiterates necessarily unintelligent and incapable of voting wisely?

Until the Federal census of 1840 no official statistics of illiteracy in the Southern States could be had. But even the illiteracy returns of this census were shown by Dr. Henry Ruffner, President of Washington College at Lexington, Virginia, to be grossly inaccurate. In a report to the Virginia legislature (1841), he pointed out that in four large counties of the state, not dis-

[1] Horace Greeley in the New York *Daily Tribune,* Jan. 30, 1856.

[2] A. D. Mayo, "The Organization and Development of the American Common School in the Atlantic and Central States of the South, 1830-1860," *Report of the Commissioner of Education, United States Bureau of Education, 1899-1900* (Washington, D. C., 1901), I, 436.

tinguished for intelligence, the census takers returned no illiterates and that in not a few other counties the number of illiterates given was incredibly small, as eight in Rockbridge, eight in Ohio, and sixteen in Powhatan. In Cabell County one fourth of the adults were returned as completely illiterate, but in the wilder county of Logan only one out of thirty-two adults. Discarding the census statistics, Ruffner estimated that more than one third of the adult white population of Virginia was in a state of abject ignorance.[3]

Prior to 1840, therefore, the investigator is compelled to rely on fortuitous evidence. For Virginia, the message of Governor Campbell to the legislature in 1839 contains some data which afford a basis for estimating illiteracy during this early period. He maintained that the extent of illiteracy had remained about the same during the twenty preceding years. As proof of this statement, he used statistics of those who could not sign the marriage register in ninety-three counties of the state. In 1818 four thousand, six hundred and eighty-two applied for marriage licenses, of which number eleven hundred and twenty-seven could not write their names; in 1837 four thousand, six hundred and fourteen applied of whom one thousand and forty-eight could not write their names.[4] Some data for western North Carolina were furnished by a contested election (1831) in one of the Congressional districts. Out of one hundred and eleven voters who gave testimony, twenty-eight made their mark; in other words, one fourth could not write their names.[5] *Niles' Weekly Register* in July, 1829, contained an item which told of conditions in Wake County, where Raleigh is located. In one community of this county, out of one hundred and fourteen families,

[3] Henry Ruffner, "Proposed Plan for the Organization and Support of Common Schools in Virginia," *Report of the Commissioner of Education, United States Bureau of Education, 1899-1900,* I, 395-396.

[4] *Journal of the House of Delegates of the Commonwealth of Virginia, 1839* (Richmond, 1839), p. 9.

[5] Report of the Directors of the Literary Fund, Jan. 14, 1839 (C. L. Coon, *Documentary History of Public Education in North Carolina,* 2 vols.; Raleigh, N. C., 1908, II, 833).

forty-nine were found that did not possess a Bible—in twelve of them, not an individual could read.[6]

In the Deep South the illiteracy of the people and the neglect of education were perhaps more distressing than in the Upper South. A Committee on Education of the Louisiana legislature reported, March 22, 1831, that there were approximately nine thousand white children in the state between the ages of ten and fifteen years but that "not one third of that number received any instruction whatever."[7] Georgia was one of the earliest states to found a state university and had academies for the well-to-do, but it woefully neglected the education of the masses. Not until 1877 did the state finally establish free public schools. Liberal laws permitting counties to tax property for school purposes, which had been enacted in the late 1830's, were repealed in 1840. Governor George W. Crawford declared in 1845 that not half of the counties applied for their proportion of the state funds for free schooling.[8] As late as 1859 Gabriel DuVal, Superintendent of Education of the State of Alabama, reported to the governor that nearly one half of the children of the state were not attending any school and were growing up in ignorance.[9]

The census of 1850 seemed to indicate that the Southern States were even retrograding in literacy. The returns from Virginia, for example, showed the presence of seventy-seven thousand and five adult white illiterates as compared with fifty-eight thousand, seven hundred and eighty-seven in the previous census. This increase could probably be explained in part by the more careful and accurate enumeration of the census takers of 1850. According to their report the Southern States had an illiteracy ratio among the native white popula-

[6] Niles' Weekly Register, XXXVI, 302 (July 4, 1829).

[7] Journal of the House of Representatives of the State of Louisiana, Tenth Legislature (New Orleans, 1831), p. 144.

[8] Charles William Dabney, Universal Education in the South (Chapel Hill, 1936), I, 248-250.

[9] Report of Gabriel B. DuVal, Superintendent of Education of the State of Alabama, Made to the Governor for the Year 1858 (Montgomery, Ala., 1859), pp. 4-5. A pamphlet in Gov. Lewis Parsons's Papers in the Department of History and Archives, Montgomery, Ala.

tion over twenty years of age of 20.30 per cent, the Middle States 3 per cent, and New England .42 per cent. Superintendent De Bow pointed out that so excellent was the New England school system that only one person over twenty years of age in four hundred of the native white population could not read and write, as compared with one in twelve for the slaveholding states, and one in forty for the free states as a whole.[10]

Many reasons have been advanced to explain this widespread illiteracy of the South. The aristocratic attitude, inherited from England, that it was not necessary to educate the masses, changed slowly in sections of the older South like Virginia and South Carolina. Certainly the isolation characteristic of Southern life with its scattered homes and indescribably bad roads did much to hinder the diffusion of education. Fully as important as these factors was the reluctance of the people to tax themselves. Governor Swain in his message to the legislature of North Carolina in 1835 said that the legislature was in the habit of imposing taxes on the people amounting to less than one hundred thousand dollars annually. Of this sum, half was spent in rewarding the legislators for their services, while the remainder was employed in paying the administrative officers of the state government.[11] It required a long period of agitation before the people of the Southern States, as well as their Northern neighbors, would tax themselves for education.

The individualism of the Southern people was also a hindrance to the establishment of a comprehensive system of public education. It was regarded as the duty of the individual and not of the state to see that his children were educated. When Governor Gilmer of Georgia wrote letters to the most distinguished men of his state for their opinions on public

[10] J. D. B. De Bow, *Compendium of the Seventh Census* (Washington, D. C., 1854), p. 153. At the same time it should be pointed out that the large immigrant population of New England had a higher ratio of illiteracy than the native whites of the South.

[11] Gov. Swain's message to the legislature of North Carolina, 1835 (Coon, *op. cit.*, II, 714).

education, he stated his own position in the words: "The policy of making appropriations by the Government to effect objects which are within the means of individuals has always appeared to me to be extremely questionable."[12] Joseph Henry Lumpkin, later to become Chief Justice of the Supreme Court of Georgia, replied that he opposed scattering the state educational funds of twenty thousand dollars for common schools, but that they should be used in developing the university. The most promising youths from each county should be sent to the university; and "soon every foreigner will be dislodged from our academies."[13]

The mental attitude of the various classes of Southern society toward education was admirably analyzed by Joseph Caldwell, President of the University of North Carolina, in a series of *Letters on Popular Education* published in 1832. He pointed out that so invincible was the aversion of North Carolinians to taxation, even to provide for the education of poor children, that any proposal to establish a public school system supported solely by taxation would be doomed to failure. He also described the position of many of the illiterate or semi-illiterate as proud of their ignorance of "book learning." From another angle, he portrayed the attitude of the rural communities toward "book learning" by showing their contemptuous disparagement of the profession of teaching school. With bitter satire he described the unfit type of men who had been recruited by the profession in North Carolina: "Is a man constitutionally and habitually indolent, a burden upon all from whom he can extract a support? Then there is a way of shaking him off, let us make him a schoolmaster. To teach a school is in the opinion of many little else than sitting still and doing nothing. Has any man wasted all his property, or ended in debt by indiscretion and misconduct? The business of schoolkeeping stands wide-open for his recep-

[12] G. R. Gilmer to J. H. Lumpkin, Wm. Cumming, Henry Jackson, and John Wingfield, April 8, 1830 (Letter Book of the Governors of Georgia, 1829-31, pp. 108-112, MSS).

[13] Joseph Henry Lumpkin to Gov. Gilmer, Oct. 8, 1830 (Miscellaneous MSS in Department of Archives and History of Georgia).

tion and here he sinks to the bottom, for want of capacity to support himself."[14] At the same time Caldwell recognized the great importance of economic factors, the business depression in the state caused by lack of markets and of internal improvements, and the failure to keep informed of what other states, such as Connecticut, were doing in the way of educational reform.

The contrast between the conditions favoring education in the North and the retarding factors in the South is brought out vividly by comparing the density of population in a state like Massachusetts, which had one hundred and twenty-seven inhabitants to the square mile, and Southern states, like Virginia and North Carolina, which had respectively only fourteen and twelve white inhabitants to the square mile.[15] The coming of the Irish immigrants to New England during this period increased the illiteracy of that section, but among the *native* whites the percentage of illiteracy was less than one half of one per cent.[16] Nevertheless, the struggle for the adoption of free public schools in the North was an extremely bitter one. Henry Barnard, the distinguished educational leader, was threatened with a load of buckshot by an irate Rhode Islander, if the former was ever caught again on his land advocating "such heresy as the partial confiscation of one man's property to educate another man's child."[17]

It was the policy of writers under the influence of the abolitionists to saddle all the blame for illiteracy upon the planters.[18] Yet the indifference of the lower classes was fully as responsible as the selfishness of the aristocracy. Olmsted copied in 1853 some reports of county superintendents in Virginia to the Directors of the Literary Fund which are illuminating. The Superintendent of Nansemond County wrote: "A

[14] Joseph Caldwell, *Letters on Popular Education* (Hillsborough, N. C., 1832), a pamphlet in Library of University of North Carolina; reprinted in Coon, *op. cit.*, II, 560.

[15] J. D. B. De Bow, *The Industrial Resources of the South and West* (New Orleans, 1853), II, 473.

[16] Turner, *The United States, 1830-1850*, p. 81.

[17] Schlesinger, *Political and Social History of the United States, 1829-1925*, p. 72.

[18] See J. R. Gilmore, *Among the Pines* (New York, 1862), p. 175.

majority of the school commissioners find difficulty in getting indigent children to attend school regularly, *principally owing to the schools not being located near them.*" The Superintendent of Rappahannock County wrote: "*as there are many indigent children, whose parents cannot be prevailed upon to send them to school,* they generally enter all the indigent children who will attend school." The Superintendent of Southampton County reported: "*the irregular attendance of the poor children still continues to be one of the greatest difficulties they labor under in judiciously applying the funds allotted them.*"[19] Moncure Daniel Conway tells in his *Autobiography* of a quixotic effort he made in 1850 to arouse an enthusiasm in Virginia for public schools. He printed and distributed at his own expense a pamphlet entitled *Free Schools in Virginia,* but it had no effect.[20] Referring to this failure, he observed: "But the social, physical and financial condition of Virginia was little comprehended by me, in my nineteenth year. There was little or no longing for education among the poor whites—probably more among the negroes. I was expecting echoes where there were no hills."[21] William Gregg encountered great difficulty in getting the mill workers to send their children to his free school at Graniteville, South Carolina. Out of eight hundred people at his factory, he could secure only sixty children to attend his school, and then, only after he had called in the minister to lecture their parents on the subject.[22]

Something of this apathy toward education on the part of the lower classes was undoubtedly due to physical illness and to a false sense of pride. Travelers in the ante-bellum South often referred to the sallow, unhealthy appearance of the "poor

[19] Olmsted, *Seaboard Slave States,* pp. 294-295.

[20] Moncure D. Conway, *Free Schools in Virginia* (Fredericksburg, Va., 1850).

[21] M. D. Conway, *Autobiography, Memories and Experiences* (2 vols.; Boston, 1904), I, 85.

[22] *De Bow's Review,* XI, 136 (Aug., 1851). Gregg wrote: "We are nearly ready to despair of success in the matter, for even penal laws against the neglect of education would fail to bring many of our country people to send their children to school, notwithstanding it could be done without a cent of expense" (*ibid.,* XI, 135).

whites" and to their addiction to eating clay.[23] These "clay-eaters," "sand-hillers," and "crackers" were in many cases the victims of hookworm, which sapped their energy and deprived them of ambition.[24] In the lowland regions and in river valleys malaria and the ague wrought great havoc in the health of the poorer classes, who remained in their habitations throughout the year.[25] Furthermore, many destitute farmers were deterred from sending their children to such public schools as were provided because of their repugnance to make the required declaration of poverty. The mountain whites who looked upon all outsiders as "furriners," preferred to remain in ignorance and to cling to their more primitive ways of life.[26]

The educational needs of the upper classes were fairly well met by the private academies and old field schools. A group of neighbors would form a board of trustees for the proposed school and apply to the legislature for an act of incorporation.[27] They would then build a log or frame schoolhouse and hire a teacher, frequently a Northerner who had recently graduated from college. Some of these academies attained a wide and well-deserved reputation for training eminent men. The celebrated academy at Willington, South Carolina, presided over by Moses Waddell, numbered among its pupils William H. Crawford, John C. Calhoun, George McDuffie, Augustus Baldwin Longstreet, J. L. Petigru, and Hugh Swin-

[23] Fredrika Bremer, *The Homes of the New World: Impressions of America* (New York, 1853), I, 365-367.

[24] When the Rockefeller Commission began its fight to eliminate hookworm from the South in 1909, it found during the first year that two fifths of the persons it examined had the disease. In one school thirty-eight of the forty pupils were infected, while forty-five of their brothers and sisters were prevented from attending school on account of the disease. By 1914 over three hundred and eighty thousand Southerners had been treated during the campaign to eradicate hookworm (Mark Sullivan, *Our Times, The United States, 1900-1925,* New York, 1930, III, 329-331).

[25] Frances Trollope, *Domestic Manners of the Americans* (New York, 1901), pp. 28-29.

[26] Horace Kephart, *Our Southern Highlanders* (New York, 1921), chaps. i, ix, x.

[27] See the bills incorporating Flea Hill Academy and Tick Creek Academy (*Acts of the General Assembly of the State of North Carolina,* Raleigh, N. C., 1832, chaps. xxi and cxx).

ton Legaré.[28]   The academy of Zion-Parnassus in Rowan
County, North Carolina, had the distinction of training forty-
five ministers as well as some of the most prominent political
leaders of the state.[29]   In 1850 the South led the nation in the
number of academies it possessed; New England had about
one thousand academies, the Middle States nearly twenty-one
hundred, and the Southern States more than twenty-seven hundred.[30]   The academy movement, with its concentration on the
education of the superior classes, was really a deterrent to
the founding of a vigorous public school system.[31]

In addition to the academies, the wealthiest planters employed tutors or sent their sons North to be educated.   The
number of Southern boys educated in this exclusive manner
during the ante-bellum period, however, was negligible as
compared with those sent to academies and old field schools.
A young Northerner who went to Alabama in 1831 to find
a job as tutor, discovered that very few private tutors were
employed in that state and salaries were never more than
three hundred dollars.[32]   A common practice among the rich
was to send their sons to a fashionable Northern school.   When
Frederick Porcher arrived at Captain Partridge's Academy at
Norwich, Connecticut, he found twenty other South Carolina
boys there.[33]   Just prior to the Civil War, Randolph Shotwell
was sent from North Carolina to Tuscarora Academy in Pennsylvania, where his ardent sectional prejudices were supported
by a number of Southern schoolmates.   It was fashionable,

[28] W. M. Meigs, *The Life of John Caldwell Calhoun* (2 vols.; New York, 1917),
I, 63-66.

[29] J. F. Hurley and J. G. Eagan, *The Prophet of Zion-Parnassus* (Richmond,
1934), p. 84.

[30] De Bow, *Compendium of the Seventh Census*, pp. 142-143.

[31] For a defense of this aristocratic system, see Twelve Southerners, *I'll Take
My Stand: The South and the Agrarian Tradition* (New York, 1930), pp. 92-121.

[32] Henry Watson to Julius Reed, Jan. 8, 1831 (Watson MSS in Duke University
Library). In 1847 James H. Hammond was seeking a tutor for his children at his
plantation, Silver Bluff, on the Savannah River. He offered five hundred dollars
a year and the use of a horse to a tutor who would teach his children the classics,
French, mathematics, and English (Hammond to Lewis R. Gibbes, Dec. 3, 1847,
Lewis R. Gibbes Papers, III, MSS in Library of Congress).

[33] Frederick A. Porcher Reminiscences, p. 195 (MS in Library of the College
of Charleston).

he observed, for well-to-do planters to send their sons to Northern schools, "chiefly because the expense was a great deal heavier and the thing sounded better in talking to their neighbors."[34] From a selfish point of view, the upper classes, who could send their sons to exclusive Northern schools, or at least to private academies and old field schools in the South, had little incentive to support a movement to educate the common people by voting taxes for that end.

From 1840 to 1860, however, the Southern States were slowly awakening to the need of free public schools.[35] One of the most eloquent and influential voices for popular education during these years was that of Henry A. Wise, Congressman from the Accomac district of Virginia. In 1844, shortly after his retirement from Congress to become Minister to Brazil, he delivered an earnest speech to his constituents advising them to tax themselves to educate every child at public cost. He showed that more than one fourth of the adult whites in Accomac district (consisting of twelve counties) could not read and write, and that the number of illiterate adults exceeded even the number of voters in the district (four thousand three hundred and seventy-nine). The main defect of the existent system, he indicated, was the taint of charity which inhered in the payment of the tuition of poor children only by the state. "There should be no distinction between the children of a republic," he said. "They are not in the school sense the children of their parents, but the state is parens patriae, and they should all be regarded as sons and daughters of Mother Commonwealth."[36] He proposed that the counties should not wait for state action, but that each county should levy taxes sufficient to educate every child within its limits.

[34] J. G. deR. Hamilton, *The Papers of Randolph Abbott Shotwell* (Raleigh, N. C., 1929), I, 11.

[35] See Edgar W. Knight, *Public School Education in North Carolina* (Boston, 1916), and W. A. Maddox, *The Free School Idea in Virginia Before the Civil War* (New York, 1918).

[36] *Report of the Commissioner of Education for the Year 1899-1900*, I, 399; see also B. H. Wise, *The Life of Henry A. Wise of Virginia, 1806-1876* (New York, 1899), pp. 105-107.

The political leaders, most influential in the movement for free public schools, were men who had arisen from the ranks of the common people, such as Governor Joseph E. Brown, Christopher G. Memminger, Albert Gallatin Brown, and Andrew Johnson. Nevertheless, some notable aristocratic leaders championed free schools, like Archibald DeBow Murphey in North Carolina, Henry A. Wise in Virginia, Robert J. Breckinridge in Kentucky, and William Lowndes Yancey in Alabama. Governor Joseph E. Brown made a powerful but belated effort to arouse the people of Georgia from their apathy toward the education of the masses. In his message to the legislature of November 3, 1858, he exhorted: "Let it be a Common School, not a Poor School System. Let the children of the richest and poorest parents in the State, meet in the schoolroom on the terms of perfect equality of right. Let there be no aristocracy there but an aristocracy of color and conduct."[37] He proposed that one hundred and forty young men of poor parents annually should be given a college education at the expense of the state, in return for which they should teach in the Georgia schools. Skilfully appealing to the powerful religious emotions of the Georgia electorate, he declared that the most important reason for adopting a common school system was "that every person in the State be enabled to read for himself or herself the Holy Bible, and to comprehend the great principles of Christianity, in the eternal truths of which I am a firm, though humble believer."[38] In the aristocratic state of South Carolina, Christopher G. Memminger, who had spent part of his childhood in an orphanage, secured the adoption of a good system of free schools for Charleston in 1856, but as for the rest of the state, the education of the common people was badly neglected.[39] The former tailor, Andrew Johnson, was the first

[37] Executive Minutes of the State of Georgia, Nov. 7, 1855, to Dec. 26, 1859, p. 478 (MS in Georgia Department of Archives and History).

[38] Ibid., p. 475.

[39] H. D. Capers, The Life and Times of C. G. Memminger (Richmond, 1893), pp. 112-114.

governor of Tennessee who had the will and courage to force
a bill through the legislature (1854) taxing the property of
the state for free common schools. The representatives of East
Tennessee voted unanimously for the education bill, but West
Tennessee, with its large slaveholding interests, unanimously
opposed it.[40]

The new gospel of taxation for free schools was also advocated by education conventions, such as the Clarksburg and
Lexington conventions in western Virginia, in which Dr.
Henry Ruffner and Governor McDowell took a prominent
part. The meager result of this agitation, however, was the
passing of a bill in 1846, permitting counties to establish free
common schools by local taxation. Few of the districts of
western Virginia had the resolution to tax themselves for this
purpose, the exceptions being Ohio, Jefferson, and Kanawha
counties. Eastern Virginia was slightly more alive to the need
for free education, as shown by the fact that seven counties
and three towns adopted a system of free public schools. Samuel Janney, seeking to explain the failure of his own county
[a western one] and others to adopt a rational scheme of education, concluded: "The chief causes of its rejection in the
other counties were the apathy and prejudice of the laboring
classes whom it was intended to benefit and the jealousy of
the slaveholders."[41] In Albemarle County, where the University of Virginia was located, both William Fitzhugh Gordon,
an aristocratic planter who had aided in the founding of the
University, and Thomas Jefferson Randolph, a grandson of
Jefferson, opposed the adoption of a more liberal free school
system. On the other hand, the famous Professor W. H.
McGuffey, originally from Ohio, took the stump for free
schools, but the measure was voted down by the taxpayers.[42]

Faced by the depressing record presented by the census of

[40] Dabney, *op. cit.*, I, 294.
[41] S. M. Janney, "Virginia: Her Past, Present, and Future," an article in the
Reports of the United States Department of Agriculture, 1865, p. 40.
[42] Armistead C. Gordon, *William Fitzhugh Gordon* (New York, 1909), pp.
382-383.

1850, newspapers and individuals made an earnest appeal to the people for the cause of popular education. A memorial to the legislature from Halifax County urging the adoption of a system of public schools, assigned three causes for the backwardness of Virginia in education: (1) the scattered population, (2) the burden of taxation, and (3) the unwillingness of ignorant parents to send their children to school.[43] Education conventions were held at Richmond in 1856 and 1857, dominated by the personality of Governor Wise. Shortly after he assumed office Wise outlined a comprehensive system of public education. Severely condemning the existing system of educating indigent children for only fifty-three days a year at a cost of $2.57 per capita, he declared that in a republic equal educational advantages should be given to all children. The poor children should have the opportunity "to taste of the more delicate food of the mind" rather than merely the coarser husks which the miserable elementary schools provided.[44] He therefore proposed the creation of three hundred and seventy-five academies and twenty colleges. The state would thus meet an imperative need of training teachers for the common schools. As a result of such stimulus to education, the census of 1860 disclosed the fact that although the number of illiterates in Virginia had remained constant, school attendance had more than doubled.[45]

In the Southern cities, where population was concentrated, creditable public school systems were established before the Civil War. In New Orleans, Glendy Burke, a prominent merchant, was the invigorating personality behind the movement to establish free common schools. By 1851 De Bow boasted: "already 5,000 scholars are receiving the daily benefits of one of the most perfect systems of public schools in America."[46] Charleston not only had excellent public schools but also a city college with a low tuition fee and numerous free scholar-

[43] Richmond *Whig*, April 4, 1854.

[44] Wise to Rev. W. A. Smith of Randolph-Macon College, Dec. 9, 1856 (Letter Book of Governor Henry A. Wise, 1850-60, pp. 1-10, MS in Virginia State Library).

[45] *The Eighth Census of the United States: Mortality and Miscellaneous Statistics* (Washington, D. C., 1866), pp. 507-508.

[46] *De Bow's Review*, XI, 219 (Aug., 1851).

ships.[47] Memphis, with a large proletariat, had a public school
system in 1860, consisting of twenty-one schools with an enrollment of sixteen hundred and eighty-two and an average
daily attendance of seven hundred and ninety-eight students.[48]
Before 1840 Louisville had a well-managed system of free
public schools, in the founding of which New England men
had a prominent role.[49]

North Carolina had the greatest educational awakening
of any of the Southern States. This progress was due partly
to the more democratic constitution of its society and partly
to the personality of a noble educational leader, Calvin H.
Wiley, a Whig representative from the Piedmont county of
Guilford. In 1852 he secured the passage of a bill creating
a state superintendent of education in a legislature controlled
by a Democratic majority. He himself was chosen for the
new position, and under his regime the public school system
was enormously expanded. By 1860 North Carolina was the
leading state in the South in developing a common school
system. Illiteracy had decreased from 29.2 per cent of the
adult white population in 1850 to 23.5 per cent in 1860.[50] So
dominating was North Carolina's leadership in free education
in the South that on the eve of secession, the superintendent
was applied to by various Southern states for copies of the
common school laws and for plans and suggestions, and he
was invited by the state of Georgia to visit it for the purpose
of organizing its system of education.[51] This promising struc-
ture was shattered by the Civil War.

Nothing is more tragic in the history of the Old South than
this destruction of the free schools. The day after the North

[47] J. H. Easterby, *A History of the College of Charleston, Founded 1770*
(Charleston, S. C., 1935), p. 102. In 1920 tuition fees were waived for residents
of Charleston.

[48] Gerald Capers, *The Biography of a River Town: Memphis, Its Heroic Age*
(Chapel Hill, 1939), pp. 122-123.

[49] See James Freeman Clarke, *Autobiography, Diary and Correspondence* (Boston, 1892), pp. 66, 131-132.

[50] S. B. Weeks, "Calvin Henderson Wiley and the Organization of the Common
Schools of North Carolina," *Report of the Commissioner of Education for the
Year 1896-97* (Washington, D. C., 1898), II, 1423.

[51] *Ibid.*, II, 1452.

Carolina Convention passed the secession ordinance, Calvin Wiley wrote to former Governor William A. Graham, a member of the convention, beseeching the continuance of the school system. "A great and glorious revolution seemed to be rapidly going on," he wrote, "and in ten years if we had been permitted to pursue our career every citizen could have lifted up his head as a member of a rich, happy and powerful Commonwealth."[52] But he feared, as events proved, that the fond hopes of years would be destroyed by the recklessness of the hour.

Likewise, the enlightenment of the adult population of the South, through the rapid expansion of public libraries and newspapers, was rudely interrupted by the Civil War. In 1850 the per capita circulation of newspapers and periodicals among the white population of the South was eight copies annually, which was less than one third of the per capita circulation in the North.[53] Within a decade, however, the per capita circulation among the Southern whites had more than doubled—a per capita circulation of nineteen newspapers and periodicals annually. At the same time the per capita circulation in Northern states containing metropolitan areas, such as Massachusetts, New York, and Pennsylvania, was ninety, eighty-four, and forty-one respectively. The decisive factor in the per capita circulation throughout the country was the degree of concentration of population. Predominantly rural states in the North did not make appreciably better records in this respect than did Southern states. Connecticut, for example, had a per capita circulation of newspapers and periodicals of twenty-one; New Jersey, twenty; Maine, thirteen; New Hampshire, three; as compared with Virginia's twenty-five; Georgia's twenty-three; Alabama's fourteen; Tennessee's thirteen; Louisiana's forty-seven; and North Carolina's seven.[54]

[52] Calvin H. Wiley to W. A. Graham, May 21, 1861 (William A. Graham Papers, MSS in archives of North Carolina Historical Commission).

[53] De Bow, *Compendium of the Seventh Census,* p. 158.

[54] *The Census of 1860: Mortality and Miscellaneous Statistics,* p. 322. Averages computed by the author.

Much more striking than the increase of newspapers below the Potomac was the accumulation of books in the public libraries of the South. The number of volumes in Southern libraries other than private was 561,188 in 1850, a figure that was increased fivefold before the guns of Fort Sumter stayed Southerners from collecting books. During this last decade the Federal census recorded that the three public libraries of Georgia had expanded to two hundred and eighty-eight; the sixteen libraries of South Carolina had multiplied to one hundred and ninety-three; the four in North Carolina to two hundred and sixty-three; the four in Alabama to three hundred and sixty-one; the twenty-one in Virginia to thirteen hundred and fifty.[55] This phenomenal increase of library facilities for the common man must not be interpreted too sanguinely, for in 1860 the number of volumes available to the public in Southern libraries did not average more than a single volume for every two or three white persons. South Carolina was an outstanding exception, possessing one and one half volumes per white person, which was equivalent to the ratio in Massachusetts.

The low level of education among the Southern masses during the ante-bellum period was a more serious social problem than a similar state of illiteracy had presented in the time of Jefferson and Madison. The illiterates and semi-illiterates in this later period formed a substantial fraction of the voters and jurymen. The Directors of the Literary Fund in North Carolina made a report to the legislature in 1839 on common schools, in which they estimated the number of illiterate voters for the state at more than one eighth of the total number of voters.[56] They cited the case of the contested Congressional election in western North Carolina in 1831, in which twenty-eight of the one hundred and eleven voters made their mark in giving testimony, or about one fourth of the voters. In the bitter campaign of 1839 over the issue of free schools in North

[55] De Bow, *Compendium of the Seventh Census*, p. 159, and *The Census of 1860: Mortality and Miscellaneous Statistics*, p. 505. [56] Coon, *op. cit.*, II, 833.

Carolina, the arguments of the progressives were directed largely to convincing the illiterate voters that "book learning" was a good thing and a paying investment. The uncultured sheriff of Stokes County, for example, issued a vigorous appeal for schools. "But I am aware," he said, "that there are certain individuals in the community who are endeavoring to excite alarm among you, and 'bugology' you and frighten you from voting for the school system, by telling you if you do, you will smell a polecat—that it is intended to tax the poor for the benefit of the rich—that you will be taxed higher than all creation can pay, and finally within a few years you will be 'distinguished' like Jackson 'distinguished' the national debt."[57] The type of country audience to which this style of address would appeal is patent. Likewise Dr. Henry Ruffner gave as his reason for not suggesting compulsory education to the Virginia electorate his fear of antagonizing illiterate voters. "We do not propose," he wrote, "to compel parents by legal penalties to send their children to school, but we offer such inducements as must ultimately prevail with all. We abstain as far as possible from coercive measures, because we remember that the ignorant and blindly parsimonious have votes at elections, and we wish not unnecessarily to array their political power against the means of removing ignorance from their children."[58]

In 1845 the Richmond *Whig* connected illiterate voters with staunch support of the Democratic party in Virginia. The editor derived great satisfaction from noting that the banner counties in illiteracy also carried Polk's banner higher in the air than any others. These eminent districts constituted the celebrated "Tenth Legion," consisting of the counties of Page, Shenandoah, and Rockingham, which lay in the rich limestone valley of Virginia, and were inhabited by a large proportion of prosperous German farmers. Accomac, the bailiwick of Henry A. Wise, was also presented as a banner section

[57] *Ibid.*, II, 901.
[58] *Report of the Commissioner of Education, 1899-1900*, I, 395.

of Democracy and illiteracy. This county was a part of the eastern shore of Virginia that had been settled by old English stock.[59] Certain characteristics of Southern oratory arose from the need of appealing to the large class of illiterate voters.

Some artful politicians stole a march on their rivals by affecting democratic manners and old clothes to appeal to their constituents. In this manner Franklin E. Plummer built up a political machine in the poor white districts of Mississippi. He did not resort to any conventional tactics of kissing dirty babies, but he pleased mothers and fathers in the log cabins by taking their children upon his lap and searching for red bugs, lice, and other vermin.[60] When Powhatan Ellis, one of his political rivals, lost his portmanteau, Plummer advertised for it in local papers, describing its contents as consisting of various effeminate luxuries. He knew the psychology of the illiterate voters.

Governor James H. Adams of South Carolina found that the use of money in buying the votes of the sand-hillers was an important factor in elections. During a bitter campaign for election to the state senate, the price of a sand-hill vote was quoted as high as fifty dollars. He was fond of relating an anecdote about one of these poor whites to whom he offered ten dollars for his vote. "He had on his head an old straw hat, which looked as if half of it had been eaten up by the cows. He was a long, pale-faced, gangling sandlapper, with a calico hunting shirt in tatters, barefooted, and a ragged pair of pantaloons which came only halfway between his knees and ankles."[61] He had already sold his vote to one party, but he was willing to sell it to Adams for fifty dollars. This high sum he demanded because his *honor* was involved. It is no wonder that in the Richland district of South Carolina both

[59] Richmond *Whig*, Sept. 2, 1845. The Richmond *Enquirer*, Sept. 4, 1856, retorted by pointing to certain illiterate Whig counties.

[60] P. H. Buck, "The Poor Whites of the Ante-Bellum South," *American Historical Review*, XXXI, 52-54 (Oct., 1925).

[61] Ex-Gov. B. F. Perry, *Reminiscences of Public Men* (Philadelphia, 1883), pp. 154-155.

sides kept "pens" for these illiterate voters who would sell their votes.

One of the most successful vote-pollers in Alabama toward the close of the ante-bellum period was Congressman W. R. W. Cobb. A favorite device which he used to catch the votes of the ignorant farmers and villagers was to sing demagogue songs. At the end of a stump speech he would sing with a stentorian voice a composition called "The Homestead Bill." The song began, "Uncle Sam is rich enough to give us all a farm." He would accompany this masterpiece of demagoguery by winking at individuals in the audience, and by chewing an onion and a piece of cornbread. By such methods he defeated in 1849 the highly cultured and brilliant Jere Clemens for Congress. Mrs. Clement C. Clay contributed to a political victory for her husband by wearing a pea-green sunbonnet, such as the farmers' daughters wore.[62] James Farrow of Spartanburg, South Carolina, who ran as a candidate for the legislature in 1858, found that he was handicapped by being the only college man among the candidates. One of his competitors, on the other hand, had a strong claim for the suffrage of the people, in that he "used to wear copperas breeches as he would tell in his Speeches."[63]

What was the effect of these illiterate voters on the development of an intolerant spirit in the South? Was Horace Greeley right in ascribing so much weight to illiteracy as a factor in Southern decisions?

The rise of the common man to political power, as symbolized by the election of the uneducated Andrew Jackson to the Presidency, was undoubtedly a threat to freedom of thought and expression. After this upheaval the party organization, party workers, and party slogans brought out the vote.[64] In the newer parts of the South especially, there arose a flamboyant democracy. The subservience of the politicians in Alabama

[62] Mrs. Clement C. Clay, Jr., *A Belle of the Fifties* (New York, 1905), pp. 21-22.

[63] Jas. Farrow to Johnston Pettigrew, Oct. 24, 1858 (Pettigrew Papers, XIII, MSS).

[64] C. R. Fish, *The Rise of the Common Man, 1830-1850* (New York, 1927), pp. 164-166.

to popular whims was vividly described by Henry Watson. The candidates for office, he reported, would consider it madness to attempt to lead public opinion—"All went for Jackson in the election, the Old Hero right or wrong."[65] The people of Alabama and Mississippi in this youthful phase of their history regarded themselves as "sovereigns." To them the question of literacy was irrelevant in testing a man's fitness to vote.

In 1836 the Virginia legislature passed a most intolerant law abridging freedom of speech and press. It was carried to enactment by a Democratic legislature, of whose personnel the editor of the Richmond *Whig* wrote: "The country we believe has never been so sick of any legislature, or with such good reason. There were many men of talent in it, but about forty of its members were the most stupid legislators we have ever seen here in the experience of thirteen years. They never could have gotten into the General Assembly, except upon the new qualification which has come into fashion of late years— the loudest shouter for General Jackson."[66] Although partisan bias probably entered into this judgment, nevertheless it reflects accurately the disdain of the Whig aristocrats for the less cultured representatives of the common man.

Bishop Whipple, who traveled through the Lower South in 1843-44, noted the effects of illiteracy on politics. He declared that "the backwoods people are easily gulled and made the dupes of for the benefit of designing men, and when they have once made up their mind about a man or measure no argument can change them. This gives to Georgia elections the character of a drama."[67] He observed that the Georgia crackers, by which term he seems to have included the yeoman farmers, looked on "book larning" as superfluous. Although many of these illiterates or semi-illiterates were stupid and comically ignorant, others were sharp-witted and very intelligent. Whipple has preserved some specimens of the crackers' political arguments in favor of chosen candidates which indicate how frequently their decisions were based on prejudice.

[65] Henry Watson to his father, Aug. 7, 1834 (Watson MSS).
[66] Richmond *Whig*, March 26, 1836.   [67] Whipple, *Southern Diary*, p. 52.

He was told by a gentleman that some of the members of the Georgia legislature needed only long ears and a tail to classify them openly as asses. After visiting the Louisiana legislature in session, he commented: "There are some fine talented men, men that would well represent any people in such a body, but the mass are somewhat sorry specimens of a people governing themselves. I saw some men who I am sure were never burdened with an extra stock of ideas & whose personal appearance was a little of the Dick Swiveller order. Dickens would have at once noted down the amount of tobacco juice on the floor and the smell of smoke in the room."[68] Whipple also pointed out that numbers of illiterate men served on Southern juries, and on this account, the verdicts of the juries were no more liable to be based on reason and justice than if they had been decided by a throw of the dice.[69]

In the older states of the South the political power of the common man was somewhat curbed by the maintenance of aristocratic control. Not until 1850 did Virginia adopt complete manhood suffrage, and not until 1857 did North Carolina remove the property qualification on voting for state senators. Indeed, up to 1850 the governor of Virginia was chosen by the legislature and not by popular vote.[70] Furthermore, the viva voce method of voting and the privilege of plural voting, by which a planter could cast a vote in each county where his property lay, strengthened the hands of the planters. The aristocratic control of South Carolina was even more pronounced. During the period, 1778-1865, of the sixty-three different South Carolinians who held the offices of governor and United States Senator, only two of this number— George McDuffie and William Smith—appear to have been of

[68] *Ibid.,* pp. 107-108.

[69] *Ibid.,* pp. 44-45. Such harsh judgments were made by a man who liked Southern people and who understood their attitude toward slavery.

[70] See Julian A. C. Chandler, *The History of Suffrage in Virginia* (Baltimore, 1901), pp. 21-53; J. S. Bassett, "Suffrage in the State of North Carolina," *American Historical Association Report of 1895,* pp. 271-285, and J. H. Carr, "Manhood Suffrage in North Carolina," *Historical Papers of the Trinity College Historical Society* (Durham, N. C., 1915), Series XI, p. 47.

humble birth, and only five belonged to the Methodist and
Baptist churches.[71] South Carolina remained the only state in
the Union where Presidential electors were chosen, not by the
people, but by the legislature. The Jacksonian movement did
not at first overthrow the control of the planter aristocracy
within the borders of the older states of the South.[72] The dominance of the upper classes in politics was indicated by the
small percentage of Southerners, only one third of the adult
white males, who voted in the exciting Presidential contest of
1832.[73]

By the decade of the 1850's, however, the common man
in the South had progressed perceptibly toward political
power. This notable advance from the earlier aristocratic system was registered in the much larger proportion of adult males
who voted. In the Presidential election of 1852 at least forty-
seven per cent of the adult white males of the Lower South and
sixty-six per cent of the same group in the Upper South actually exercised the suffrage. Such evidence of growing political democracy in the South should be compared with the record of industrial states, like Massachusetts, where forty-seven
per cent of the adult males voted, of Pennsylvania, where sixty-
seven per cent voted, and of New York, where sixty-two per
cent went to the polls.[74] Further evidence of the growing political power of the common man was furnished by the liber-
alization of state constitutions. By amendments or by consti-

[71] Francis Butler Simkins, *The Tillman Movement in South Carolina* (Durham,
N. C., 1926), p. 4.

[72] Schlesinger, *New Viewpoints in American History*, p. 91.

[73] This figure is an estimate, derived from the *Compendium of the Sixth Census,*
p. 374, and A. C. McLaughlin and A. B. Hart, *Cyclopedia of American Government* (New York, 1914), III, 22. In the Presidential election of 1824 only 36,036
votes were cast in North Carolina, which had a white population of 419,200 in
1820 (Newsome, *The Presidential Election of 1824 in North Carolina,* p. 156).

[74] These percentages were computed from data in De Bow's *Compendium of the
Seventh Census,* p. 50. In arriving at the ratios no account was taken of the non-
voting foreign element, which would undoubtedly cause the percentages of states
like Massachusetts to appear less democratic than was actually the case. For purposes of comparison it is interesting to note that studies of nonvoting in twentieth-
century America, show that not more than fifty per cent of those entitled to vote
go to the polls. See C. E. Merriam and H. F. Gosnell, *Non-Voting, Causes and
Methods of Control* (Chicago, 1914).

tutional conventions that thoroughly revised the old constitutions, as in Virginia and Maryland in 1850, the poorer slaveless population was given fairer representation, the last vestiges
of property qualifications were removed, and popular elections
were substituted for the former legislative or executive appointment.[75] Such a democratic upsurge increased the weight
of the illiterates in determining the policies of the South.

Illiteracy in the Southern States, Frederick Jackson Turner
has shown in his posthumous work, *The United States, 1830-
1850,* had a bearing on the composition of political parties.
The map of illiteracy was darkest in the areas of poor soils,
the pine barrens of Georgia, the mountain counties, large regions of North Carolina, and of Tidewater Virginia. On the
other hand, in the districts of dense Negro population, the
Black Belt of Alabama and Mississippi, the alluvial soils of the
Mississippi Valley, the Charleston district, the Nashville and
Lexington limestone basins, the white Southerners made the
best record for literacy and education. The areas of large slave
plantations and of a higher rate of literacy for the whites usually voted the Whig ticket, while the Democrats were dominant in the regions of poor soils, of large white ratios of population, and of outstanding illiteracy.[76] This generalization is
less reliable in relation to the Upper South. In North Carolina,
the mountainous and Piedmont sections were the strongholds
of Whig sentiment, while the regions of large plantations supported the Democratic party. This allegiance of western
North Carolina to the Whig party was due primarily to the
Whig program of internal improvements and to the influence
of magnetic leaders.[77] In Virginia a study of the election of
1840 shows that many small farmers in the Piedmont and
Tidewater voted the Whig ticket. The Virginia cities, more-

[75] See Fletcher Green, *Constitutional Development in the South Atlantic States,
1776-1860* (Chapel Hill, 1930), chap. vii, "The Reform Movement of the Fifties."
[76] See map in U. B. Phillips, *State Rights in Georgia* (Washington, D. C.,
1902), p. 151.
[77] See B. A. Konkle, *John Motley Morehead and the Development of North
Carolina* (Philadelphia, 1922).

over, were swept by the Whigs.[78] In East Tennessee, where slavery maintained only a feeble foothold, the Whigs had a strong following under "Parson" Brownlow and Thomas R. R. Nelson.

The Whigs were distinctly the "broadcloth" element of society in the deep South, and their leaders in the Upper South were in most instances men of dignified and aristocratic bearing.[79] Varina Howell wrote her first impression of her future husband, Jefferson Davis: "Would you believe it, he is refined and cultivated, and yet he is a Democrat!"[80] Opposed to the agitation of slavery by the extremists of both sides, they frowned upon rabble rousing, bitter sectional attacks, and the ceaseless endeavor of politicians to stir up the uneducated classes to intolerance against antislavery men. The moderating influence of the Whig leaders was due partly to the culture and restraint of the aristocrat, but more directly to a belief that violent attacks on antislavery men and on Northern abolitionists would disrupt the Union.

The poor white voters who supported the Democratic party, on the other hand, were more bitterly hostile to abolitionists and antislavery men than the owners of hundreds of slaves. Fanatical devotees of a "white America," they were easy victims for the politicians who agitated the slavery question. The mobs that drove antislavery men out of the South contained numbers of these ignorant and propertyless men.[81] Some of these voters were yeomen "on the make," who hoped to acquire slaves. Others were ignorant hillbillies or piney-woods folks who went to the polls because of a free drink or the instigation of demagogues and politicians.

Yet the more enlightened classes, with a large property interest at stake, were chiefly responsible for the inception of

[78] Bruce, *Virginia Iron Manufacture in the Slave Era*, pp. 260-261.
[79] See Arthur C. Cole, *The Whig Party of the South* (Washington, D. C., 1912), and for the portrait of a dignified Whig leader, Konkle, *op. cit.*
[80] *Jefferson Davis, Ex-President of the Confederate States of America, a Memoir by his Wife* (New York, 1890), I, 192.
[81] See W. G. Hawkins, *Memoir of Lunsford Lane, or Another Helper from North Carolina* (Boston, 1863).

the policy of silence enforced in the Southern States. The intolerant attitude toward any criticism of slavery in the South was fixed during the decade of the 1830's. At this time the common man was becoming political-minded, but aristocratic control was still powerful enough to dominate the government and the temper of society. Prominent leaders like John C. Calhoun, a Yale graduate, urged the South to a stern intolerance in dealing with antislavery men. Individuals of the upper class served on vigilance committees and secured the passage of repressive laws. A North Carolina blacksmith, John Stafford, pointed out that mobs and illegal tribunals were encouraged by members of the governor's council and by influential editors in the state.[82] The rise of the common man as a political and social power intensified the atmosphere of intolerance. Such concurrence of the illiterate and of the educated classes of the South in a policy of repression indicates that factors other than illiteracy played a dominant role in closing the Southern mind on the slavery question.

[82] Hamilton (ed.), *The Papers of Thomas Ruffin*, III, 66-67.

CHAPTER IV

THE FEAR OF SERVILE INSURRECTION

WITH A KEEN eye for telling detail, Frederick Law Olmsted observed during his visit to Richmond in 1853 an armed sentinel standing by the door of the Capitol. This military figure, he was informed, belonged to the Public Guard of Virginia, a little army of a hundred men enlisted under a law passed after the Gabriel revolt of 1800. To the highly sensitive Northern traveler this disciplined guard was a symbol of the fear of servile insurrection that perturbed the tranquility of Southern society.[1]

Whether there existed a genuine fear of slave revolt below the Potomac is a question that directly impinges on the freedom of the press and of public speaking. The champion of a free press in the Southern States was continually confronted with the argument that the slaves might be stirred to revolt if radical criticism of slavery should be allowed. No adequate investigation has ever been made to ascertain the effect of the fear of servile insurrection upon the Southern mind. The term "the black terror" is a melodramatic one if applied to the normal state of Southern feeling, but an accurate phrase when applied to the times of abnormal fright which occurred at intervals in the Southern States.[2]

The fear of servile insurrection was kept alive in the South by a series of actual revolts and by intermittent rumors of others. The horrible massacre perpetrated by the blacks in Santo Domingo left an unforgettable impression on the Southern

[1] Olmsted, *Seaboard Slave States*, pp. 20-21. Mrs. Basil Hall made a similar observation (*The Aristocratic Journey, Being the Outspoken Letters of Mrs. Basil Hall, Written during a Fourteen Months' Sojourn in America, 1827-1828*, New York, 1931, p. 197).

[2] In 1925 John Spencer Bassett, a pioneer in the critical writing of Southern history, suggested to the writer the need of a study of "the black terror," as he called it.

people.[3] Over ten thousand *émigrés* from that island fled to the Southern States, bringing with them new elements of fear of slave uprisings.[4] The outbreak in the West Indies was followed in 1800 by the discovery of a serious plot to kill the inhabitants of Richmond. The city was saved by an accident, the fact that the roads were blocked by swollen streams on the appointed night when "General" Gabriel and his followers started.[5] The alarm caused by this event led to a move by the legislature to colonize emancipated slaves and free Negroes on the Western frontier or in a territory outside of the United States.[6]

The Denmark Vesey plot of 1822 revealed the danger of allowing slaves to be taught to read and write. Vesey had been captured in Africa and brought to America as a boy. By a strange boon of fortune he won a prize of fifteen hundred dollars through a lottery ticket—with which he bought his freedom. He acquired a knowledge of reading and writing, and evidence was brought out in court that he had collected newspaper articles on antislavery, including some of the speeches on the Missouri Compromise.[7] It was believed also that Vesey and his accomplices were in communication with the blacks of Santo Domingo. The leaders of the conspiracy, besides Vesey, were intelligent house slaves and free Negroes, Peter Poyas, Monday Gell, and Gullah Jack, who provided the negroes with invincible charms. A majority of the conspirators belonged to the African Church, and Vesey quoted Scripture

[3] Louis Schade, *Appeal to the Common Sense and Patriotism of the People of the United States or Helperism Annihilated* (Washington, D. C., 1860), pp. 8-24.

[4] Jones, *America and French Culture*, p. 134. Among the Gabriel Manigault Papers in the archives of the South Carolina Historical Society there is an account of Santo Domingo refugees who fled to Charleston, by General Caradeuc, who came to Charleston from Santo Domingo in 1797, bringing with him thirty of his slaves.

[5] T. W. Higginson, *Travellers and Outlaws* (Boston, 1889), pp. 185-214, and Howison, *op. cit.*, II, 390.

[6] Hamilton, *Writings of James Monroe*, III, 216-218, 292-295.

[7] *An Account of the Late Intended Insurrection of the Blacks of the City of Charleston. Published by the Authority of the Corporation of Charleston* (Charleston, S. C., 1822), Appendix (1). See also E. C. Holland, *A Refutation of the Calumnies Circulated against the Southern and Western States* (Charleston, S. C., 1822).

to influence them.[8] The plot was disclosed by a slave and subsequently was frustrated by the city authorities on the night
selected for the uprising. So alarmed were the Charlestonians
that a special court of prominent citizens sat through the sultry
days of June and July listening to the voluminous evidence.
Over one hundred and thirty Negroes were arrested, of whom
thirty-five were executed. The editor of the *Western Carolinian* observed that "not a whisper of all this was echoed in
the Charleston papers."[9]

In 1829 Georgia and Virginia were disturbed by rumors of
slave plots. Disastrous fires in Augusta and Savannah had
aroused the suspicions of the whites. Accordingly, Governor
Forsyth sent an urgent appeal to the Secretary of War for
arms to protect the people of the state in case of a slave revolt.[10] Although he himself was skeptical of the danger of a
servile insurrection in Georgia, he declared that prudence as
well as due consideration for public apprehension excited by
the recent calamities dictated preparation for an emergency.[11]
Virginia fears of insurrection occurred at a time when elections for delegates to a constitutional convention were ap-
proaching.[12] In order to quiet the nerves of the people, the
governor sent arms and ammunition to those counties where
plots had been reported. These weapons of defense were dispatched through the disaffected region without any guard, in a
watermelon cart driven by a negro.[13] In his subsequent message to the legislature, he declared that the excitement over

[8] Lionel H. Kennedy and Thomas Parker (Presiding Magistrates), *An Official
Report of the Trials of Sundry Negroes Charged with an Attempt to Raise an Insurrection* (Charleston, S. C., 1822), pp. 17, 19.

[9] *Western Carolinian*, Salisbury, N. C., July 16, 1822. The writer has searched
the files of the Charleston *Courier* and the *Southern Patriot*, June-July, 1822, and
finds that they did not report the trials, but issued laconic notices of the executions
of the convicted slaves.

[10] John Forsyth to Secretary of War John H. Eaton, May 6, 1829 (Letter Book
of the Governors of Georgia, 1821-29, MS in Department of Archives and History
of the State of Georgia).

[11] Forsyth to William W. Montgomery, Major General of Militia at Augusta,
May 6, 1829 (*ibid.*).

[12] H. W. Flournoy, *Calendar of Virginia State Papers* (Richmond, 1892), X,
569.

[13] Richmond *Constitutional Whig*, Aug. 4, 1829.

slave revolt had been produced by misrepresentations and exaggerations.[14]

In the lonely quiet of the night, August 21, 1831, Nat Turner began a servile revolt that sent a thrill of terror through the Southern States. Sixty-one inhabitants of the peaceful Virginia county of Southampton were massacred. Although the Southampton insurrection was quickly suppressed, the latent danger of the slave system was poignantly revealed. The most frightening fact was this: the revolt was not due to cruel treatment, for Nat had received throughout his life kind consideration from his masters, and the rebel leader had been a faithful and industrious slave. But his was a complex personality. He was the son of a wild African woman and a runaway slave who had not been captured. His mother had led him to believe that he was a prophet, that he had the power of healing. Consequently, he adopted an air of reserve and mystery in his relations with his fellow slaves. Nat was, in truth, a mystic who saw visions of white and black angels engaged in battle and blood flowing in streams. At the same time he possessed a highly observant and restless mind, which impelled him to experiment with making paper and gunpowder, and to learn to read. Thomas R. Gray, who interviewed him in prison and wrote down his "Confessions," believed that the savage outbreak was due to "the gloomy fanaticism" of the Negro.[15] This primitive fanaticism was an unfathomable quality in the Negro character, which might at any time furnish a spark to the tinder of revolt. It was curiously ironic also, that Nat had been profoundly affected by reading the prophecies of vengeance in the Book of Revelation. The insurrection was made more terrifying by the fact that, maddened by apple brandy, the slaves committed fiendish murders.

The Nat Turner insurrection affords some of the best evi-

[14] *Journal of the House of Delegates of the Commonwealth of Virginia, 1829-30* (Richmond, 1829), Doc. I, p. 2.

[15] Thomas R. Gray, *The Confession, Trial and Execution of Nat Turner* (Baltimore, 1831), a pamphlet in the Virginia State Library, the chief source for this discussion of Nat Turner. See also an excellent account of the revolt by W. S. Drewry, *The Southampton Insurrection* (Washington, D. C., 1900).

dence to indicate the potentialities of fear in the slave system. John Hampden Pleasants, editor of the Richmond *Whig,* hastened to the scene of the massacre and sent to his paper an account of the terror which agitated the people. "On the route from Petersburg," he wrote, "we found the whole country thoroughly alarmed; every man armed, the dwellings all deserted by the white inhabitants, and the farms most generally left in the possession of the blacks."[16] All Virginia was agog with military preparations, and volunteer companies sprang up like mushrooms. As late as November 21 Governor Floyd received pressing demands for arms. He noted in his diary: "I could not have believed there was half the fear amongst the people of the lower county in respect to their slaves. Before I leave this Government I will have contrived to have a law passed gradually abolishing slavery in this state, or at all events to begin the work by prohibiting slavery on the west side of the Blue Ridge mountains."[17] A committee of citizens of Southampton County addressed a letter to President Jackson, August 29, in which they described the excitement as being so great that were the justices to pronounce a slave innocent, mob action would probably be the consequence.[18] Some of the prisoners were shot without trial, and their heads were stuck on poles, a grim warning to those who should conspire to gain their liberty.

The Nat Turner revolt started a wave of contagious fear in other Southern states. The commander of the militia of Gates County, North Carolina, sent an urgent request to Governor Montfort Stokes, declaring "the town of Murfreesboro in the county of Hertford is hourly expected to be the next scene of bloodshed."[19] George W. Mordecai, a Jewish lawyer and bank president of Raleigh, wrote that the people of Raleigh had been frightened by extremely exaggerated accounts of the Southampton insurrection, but that the alarm had sub-

[16] Richmond *Constitutional Whig,* Aug. 29, 1831.

[17] C. H. Ambler, *The Life and Diary of John Floyd* (Richmond, 1918), p. 170.

[18] Drewry, *op. cit.,* pp. 84-85.

[19] J. D. Pipkin to Gov. Montfort Stokes, Aug. 23, 1831 (Executive Papers of North Carolina, LXII, 2, MSS in archives of North Carolina Historical Commission).

sided quickly.[20] Governor Stokes wrote to the governor of South Carolina, who had requested information, that in the southeastern counties ten or twelve slaves had been convicted of conspiracy, and most of them executed. He feared that some of these were innocent, for in places where the excitement had subsided, the prisoners were all acquitted.[21] The most unfortunate consequence of this hysteria, affecting whole communities, was that the methods of the Spanish Inquisition were applied to extort incriminating evidence from the slaves. This fact was revealed in a case where the governor pardoned a slave named Jerry, who had been advised by his master to confess "in order to save him from the severe and cruel torture to which other slaves had been subjected."[22]

Governor A. B. Roman of Louisiana called a special session of the legislature to consider preventive measures against slave plots and insurrections. In his message to the legislature of November 14, 1831, he declared that despite vague rumors to the contrary, the slaves in Louisiana had not been affected by the spirit of insubordination prevailing in the Upper South and that the evils to be feared from slave revolt could only be very partial and momentary. Nevertheless, Louisiana had received through the domestic slave trade many Negroes who might be considered as the scum of that population. Virginia had condemned slaves who had participated in insurrection and crime to transportation, and they had been sold in Louisiana despite the laws of the state. To prevent insurrectionary plots from such sources, he proposed the total prohibition of the importation of slaves into Louisiana for a certain number of years.[23] Another solution to the problem of preventing slave insurrection was suggested by Robert Carter Nicholas, a prominent planter of Donaldson, Louisiana, who proposed

[20] G. W. Mordecai to J. Mordecai, Sept. 2, 1831 (Mordecai MSS in University of North Carolina Library).

[21] Montfort Stokes to Gov. James Hamilton, Nov. 18, 1831 (Letter Book of Gov. Montfort Stokes, pp. 70-71).

[22] Proclamation of Pardon, Dec. 5, 1831 (Letter Book of Gov. Montfort Stokes, 1830-32).

[23] *Journal of the House of Representatives of the State of Louisiana, Tenth Legislature, Extra Session, Message of Governor*, pp. 2-4.

a patrol of Federal gunboats between Francisville and New Orleans. "The late occurrences in Virginia," he wrote, "have awakened a deep solicitude here as to the perils of our own situation."[24]

The Southern newspapers did much to spread "the black terror." John Hampden Pleasants, returning from an investigation of the Southampton insurrection, found that there was a great deal of exaggeration in the newspapers accumulated on his desk.[25] A distrust of Southern newspapers was also expressed by George Badger, a leader of the Whig party in North Carolina. In the middle of October, 1831, five justices of the peace applied to the governor of North Carolina to issue a commission of Oyer and Terminer in order to try several slaves charged with plotting insurrection. Badger advised the governor to give no information to the newspapers in regard to the plot, for any reference to a supposed conspiracy, he said, would be made the foundation of the most gross and exaggerated reports, which might uselessly alarm the whites, and lead to the inflicting of cruel and undeserved punishment on the slaves. "Such is the imprudence and inconsideration of editors," he wrote, "that this application will be soon blazoned forth in their papers and magnified into actual rebellion and murder. It is therefore respectfully suggested that no notice whatever ought to be taken of the matter in the public prints, or if possible, elsewhere.[26] The *Carolina Observer* of Fayetteville described the tremendous excitement that prevailed in the state after the Nat Turner revolt as due to the most extravagant reports.[27] The *Southern Recorder* of Milledgeville, Georgia, advocated the punishment of those who originated such alarming rumors.[28]

In the summer of 1835 there occurred one of the most serious outbreaks of popular fear over servile insurrection that

[24] Robert Carter Nicholas to Nicholas Trist, Oct. 22, 1831 (Nicholas Trist Papers, Vol. VIII, MSS in Library of Congress).

[25] Alexandria *Gazette*, Sept. 6, 1831.

[26] G. E. Badger to Gov. Stokes, Louisburg, Oct. 14, 1831 (Letter Book of Gov. Stokes, 1830-31, p. 63).

[27] *Carolina Observer*, Sept. 14, 1831.   [28] *Southern Recorder*, Oct. 6, 1831.

the South ever witnessed. Virgil Stewart's hair-raising story of an extensive conspiracy organized by the outlaw, John A. Murrell, to stir up an insurrection among the slaves had recently been published.[29] Despite its incredible melodramatic revelations, Stewart's pamphlet made a profound impression on the communities of the Lower South. He was hailed as a hero, public gatherings received him with great honor, lavish gifts were bestowed upon him, and he sold thousands of copies of his book.[30] When critical-minded Southerners expressed doubt of his dime-novel narrative, Stewart represented himself as a martyr to the implacable enmity of the secret adherents of the "Mystic Clan," and declared that his life was in constant danger.[31] Not since the day of Cotton Mather's *Memorable Providences* (1689) had a book been published in this country that had produced such a wave of fear and popular frenzy.

The spark that ignited this inflammable tinder originated in the fears of a lady of Beattie's Bluff, Mississippi, a few days before July 4, 1835. She grew alarmed over the insolent behavior of her house slaves, whom she observed holding secret conversations with each other. When several of her maids were examined by gentlemen of the community, the suspicions of a servile plot were confirmed.[32] The neighborhood was then alarmed, strong patrols were established, "a matter which had been entirely neglected heretofore," and a fearful frenzy gathered momentum. The storm center was the area embraced by Madison and Hinds counties, where the Negro population was fifty times more numerous than the white. So great was the fear generated that women and children were

[29] A. Q. Walton (pseudonym), *Hist. of the Detection, Conviction, Life and Designs of John A. Murel* (Athens, Tenn., 1835).

[30] Henry S. Foote, *Casket of Reminiscences* (Washington, D. C., 1874), p. 251.

[31] See a card from Virgil A. Stewart "To the Public," July 23, 1835, replying to the attacks of Judge Matthew Clanton of Yalobusha County, Miss. (*Mississippian*, Jackson, Miss., July 31, 1835).

[32] Thomas Shackelford, *Proceedings of the Citizens of Madison County, Mississippi, at Livingston, in July, 1835, in Relation to the Trial and Punishment of Several Individuals Implicated in a Contemplated Insurrection in This State* (Jackson, Miss., 1836), pp. 3-4. A pamphlet in the Rare Book Room, Library of Congress.

collected in central places at night and guarded by armed detachments, while other squads of armed men moved through the country to detect the earliest approach of the imagined insurrectionists. Henry S. Foote, at that time a lawyer of Clinton, Hinds County, and later governor of Mississippi, described this demoralizing fear: "Never was there an instance of more extraordinary or even maddening excitement amid a refined, intelligent and virtue loving people than that which I had the pain to witness in the counties of central Mississippi in the summer of 1835."[33]

During this hallucination of the Mississippians, the courts were ignored, men who urged moderate counsels were in danger of their lives, and mob violence reigned supreme. Virgil Stewart's fabrication had asserted that the Murrell gang planned a servile insurrection on December 25, but it was believed that the revelations of Stewart had caused the conspirators to hasten their preparation and set July 4 as the date. Consequently, the people of Livingston did not resort to the slow operation of the civil power to protect themselves in this grave peril. A vigilance committee was immediately organized which tried and hanged five white men and more than a dozen Negroes. Two of the executed men, Cotton and Saunders, were Thompsonian doctors, popularly called "steam doctors," a body of men whom Virgil Stewart declared to be emissaries of Murrell. Cotton signed a confession that he belonged to the grand council of Murrell and that the notorious outlaw planned a servile insurrection reaching from Maryland to Louisiana. It is significant that nearly all the accused were men of Northern birth. Evidence which the mob desired, was extorted from the Negroes by unmerciful whippings. The vigilance committee of Livingston later justified their summary procedure by declaring that no jail in the county was sufficient to contain more than six or eight persons, and these insecurely, "besides, immediate example, and its consequent terror, without hope from the law's delay or evasion seemed,

---

[33] Foote, *Casket of Reminiscences,* p. 25.

as in truth it was, indispensable to safety."[34] The vigilance committee was preferable to the courts because it was freed from the limitation of legal procedure which excluded slave evidence against white men.

That the central counties of Mississippi were suffering from a phobia in regard to servile insurrection is indicated by letters received at the governor's office. George Wyche of Fleetwood, Hinds County, wrote to Governor Runnels, July 8, 1835: "An excitement to an un-[illegible] extent prevails in Madison in our neighborhood and will soon spread over the State. All law is put down and the government of the county is in the hands of the mob, whose minds are in a state of feverish excitement. I pray you to issue a proclamation exhorting to peace and moderation and submission to the Civil Power. The danger from the slaves vanished at the detection of the conspiracy and another danger has taken place more formidable than that."[35] In response to such frantic appeals Governor Runnels issued a proclamation summoning the police boards of each county to organize efficient patrols to apprehend "a band of lawless, base, villainous whitemen traversing the country endeavoring to get up an insurrection among our slaves."[36]

One of the most remarkable cases of sadism exhibited by the mob was the attack on Patrick Sharkey, a justice of the peace and a wealthy planter of Hinds County. In an appeal to Governor Runnels he begged him to issue a proclamation ordering all illegal tribunals to disperse; he described the disturbed condition of the country in the words: "It is acknowledged on all hands that the danger of insurrection is over. No person that we can learn stands in any further fear of Negroes. But the lawless passions of men seem to have

[34] H. R. Howard (comp.), *The History of Virgil A. Stewart and His Adventure in Capturing and Exposing the Great Western Land Pirate* (New York: Harper and Brothers, 1836), p. 223.

[35] George Wyche to Gov. Runnels, July 8, 1835 (Executive Papers of Mississippi).

[36] Proclamation of Hiram G. Runnels, July 13, 1835 *(ibid.)*.

broken loose and unless there is a stop put to the shedding of blood, confusion and revolution must shortly reign over the land."[37] Shortly after this letter was written, the mob attacked his house and wounded him, but he managed to kill one of the regulating band and escape in the dark. He was later captured and in imminent peril of being hung, brought before a vigilance committee. He was saved, however, by the shrewdness of his cousin, Judge William Sharkey, who made a speech before the committee. The judge scrupulously refrained from calling in question the authority of the committee and he admitted the powerlessness of the courts in time of great peril, but he showed the absurdity of the charges made against his kinsman and appealed to the intelligence and self-respect of the committee.[38] Later Patrick Sharkey brought suit against the invaders and recovered $10,000 damages.

Although the South was untroubled by any actual insurrections of the slaves after 1831, it was racked at intervals by dark rumors and imagined plots. In the autumn of 1856 it suffered one of the worst panics of fear concerning slave insurrection that it had experienced. In that year the Southern people were disturbed by the prospect of a Republican victory electing Frémont as President. The discovery of most of the actual or supposed plots, however, came after the election. The height of the alarm was reached in December, for it was believed that the rising of the slaves was set for the Christmas holidays. The striking characteristic of this panic was that it spread in concentric circles all over the Southern States, plots being detected in Mississippi, Louisiana, Missouri, Arkansas, South Carolina, Tennessee, Kentucky, and Virginia.[39] The British consul at Richmond reported to his government that the wide diffusion of the plot of servile insurrection and the

---

[37] James B. Kilborn and Patrick Sharkey to Gov. Runnels, July 7, 1835 (ibid.).

[38] Henry S. Foote, The Bench and Bar of the South and the Southwest (St. Louis, Mo., 1876), pp. 67-68.

[39] See Harvey Wish, "The Slave Insurrection Panic of 1856," Journal of Southern History, V, 222 (May, 1939). He concludes: "It seems probable, however, that a large number of actual slave plots did exist in 1856."

implication of whites in it indicated that the movement had been planned in the North.[40] This stampede of fear led to the arrest of a number of Negroes, who were severely whipped to secure confessions. The Memphis *Eagle and Enquirer* estimated that during the excitement not less than forty Negroes were hung for plotting insurrection.[41]

The factor which made the insurrectionary scare of 1856 so intense was the belief that abolition agents had instigated the slaves to revolt. The Savannah *Daily Republican* explained the reports of slave plots all over the South as due to the widespread activities of white instigators.[42] Johnson J. Hooper, editor of the *Daily Montgomery Mail,* believed that the numerous reports of insurrection extending over such a wide area in the South indicated that these plots had been instigated by an organized band of white cutthroats.[43] The same suspicion of abolitionists disaffecting the slaves was expressed by Barksdale, editor of the Jackson *Daily Mississippian.* In an editorial on "Servile Insurrections," he declared: "The conspiracies detected among slaves in Tennessee, Kentucky, South Carolina, and Texas show that the vile emissaries of abolition, working like moles under the ground, have been secretly breathing the poison of insubordination into their minds."[44] These newspapers advocated summary punishment of such meddling white men.

Other leading Southern editors explained the hysteria of 1856 on the basis of the excitement of the Frémont campaign. The conservative New Orleans *Picayune* offered this explanation: "But from various quarters in many states there are evidences of a very unsettled state of mind among the servile population—a vague impression among them that a critical change in their condition is at hand, to be effected by a power-

[40] Laura A. White, "The South in the 1850's as Seen by British Consuls," *Journal of Southern History,* I, 43-44 (Feb., 1935).
[41] Memphis *Eagle and Enquirer,* Dec. 30, 1856.
[42] Savannah *Daily Republican,* Dec. 19, 1856.
[43] *Daily Montgomery Mail,* Dec. 11, 1856.
[44] *Daily Mississippian,* Dec. 19, 1856.

ful party, which temporarily defeated at the polls, is ready to give them help of arms and troops when they shall undertake to rise on their own account . . . in places remote from each other all the disclosures obtained have fixed upon the same day, December 24th or the Christmas holidays—the same notion prevails in Kentucky, Arkansas, Tennessee, as well as Mississippi, Louisiana and Texas."[45] The New Orleans *Bulletin* pointed out that masters had indulged their slaves unwisely in permitting them to hang on the outskirts of political assemblies and listen to the harangues of politicians.[46]

During the popular hysteria that prevailed in some sections of the South at this time an old slave, named Beverley, was condemned to death in New Kent County, Virginia, for plotting insurrection. After the people had recovered their senses, one of the trial justices urged Governor Wise to commute the death sentence to transportation. He stated that he had never seen slaves more obedient than before "the rumors" and that he had not observed the least reason to justify the belief that they contemplated insurrection. He had sentenced Beverley because he could not discredit the witness against him.[47] Another plea for clemency was made by a lawyer, John P. Pierce, whose letter affords a remarkable analysis of the origin of the black terror in his neighborhood. Referring to the intemperate speeches during the Presidential campaign which probably were overheard by the slaves, he asserted: "From such remarks and discussions, the slaves who are imitative beings, were led and induced to have, among themselves, conversations and to make remarks which were possibly misunderstood, and which induced the suspicious whites of weak and unsteady nerves to imagine that they were standing on a volcano, almost ready to burst forth with fury and destruction, that they were on the eve of a servile war, and momentarily expecting to hear the cries, groans, and shrieks of women and

[45] *Daily Picayune*, Dec. 24, 1856.

[46] Extract printed in Mobile *Daily Advertizer*, Dec. 25, 1856.

[47] W. H. Macon to Wise, New Kent County, Jan. 20, 1857 (Executive Papers of Virginia, MSS).

children who were being murdered by the hands of slaves—
this feeling constantly stirred up by the tremulous and timid
portion of society was fanned into a flame, and by the powerful principle of sympathetic affection, ultimately pervaded all
classes of society, and to some extent affected every member
of the community. Such was evident to every man who attended our last court. Intense anxiety, deep solicitude, and
an eager desire for revenge, because of imagined wrongs,
seemed to be the feelings of a large portion of the people who
were at our last court."[48]

The John Brown raid of October 16, 1859, sent a thrill of
terror through the Southern States. The professed purpose of
John Brown was to free the Negroes from their masters, organize them into troops to fight for their liberty, and establish
a Negro republic in western Virginia. Not a single slave rallied
to the cause of the Northern fanatic, and the first man killed
in the raid at Harper's Ferry was a free Negro who was shot
because he refused to halt when ordered.[49] Nevertheless, a
panic of fear swept the South, caused chiefly by a dread of
the abolitionists tampering with the slaves.[50] Governor Wise
rushed troops to the scene of the projected insurrection, issued
proclamations, and magnified the danger which threatened
Virginia. Charlestown, where Brown was imprisoned, bore
resemblance to a military post with its militia on duty varying
in numbers from several hundred to sixteen hundred. A joint
committee of the legislature added to the alarm by stating as
a result of its investigations that evidence indicated the existence of a widespread plot not merely against Virginia but
against the peace and security of the Southern States.[51] So
deeply aroused were the Virginians that all strangers coming

[48] John P. Pierce to Wise, New Kent County, Jan. 21, 1857 (ibid.).
[49] O. G. Villard, John Brown, 1800-1859 (Boston, 1910), pp. 433, 468-469.
[50] Source materials for the study of this phase of the John Brown raid are
deposited in the State Library at Richmond, Executive Papers, Oct.-Dec., 1859,
In Re John Brown; in the telegrams and letters of the Edwin Tatham Collection,
Library of Congress; and in the archives of the Pennsylvania Historical Society.
[51] Report of the Joint Committee of the General Assembly of Virginia on the
Harper's Ferry Outrages, Jan. 26, 1860, Doc. No. XXXI.

from the North were objects of suspicion, and the violence of the mob was frequently exerted against them.[52]

One other serious fright started in Texas in July, 1860, just after a series of mysterious fires had occurred. A long drought had affected the nerves of the people, and the memory of John Brown's invasion was fresh in their minds.[53] A lurid design was reported to have been discovered among the slaves to rise up on election day, August 6. Abolition preachers of the Northern Methodist Church who had formerly been expelled were accused of engineering the plot. Charles Pryor, a citizen of high standing in Dallas, in a letter to Major John Marshall, editor of the Austin *State Gazette,* gave details of the plot and of the alarm of the people and concluded his letter with the following admonition: "You had better issue extras containing these facts, and warn the country of the dangers that threaten it. We are expecting the worst, and do not know what an hour may bring forth. Do the best you can for us. We have no printing press and can do nothing in that line."[54] To this appeal Major Marshall responded nobly in his newspaper.

General Sam Houston and his friends made the charge that the accounts of servile plots in Texas were created or published for political effect. John Marshall replied with spirit to these accusations, declaring that he had published nothing but information furnished by reliable correspondents or extracted from respectable papers, including the accounts of the burning of Dallas and Henderson. The Committees of Safety which had been organized to deal with the emergency, he pointed out, had been composed of members of both parties. Marshall expressed his view of the danger of servile insurrection as follows: "We do not believe that the great majority of Southern slaves would countenance or join in an insurrec-

[52] Diary of Edmund Ruffin, pp. 100-102; Flournoy, *Calendar of Virginia State Papers,* XI, 72-93; John G. Rosengarten, "John Brown's Raid; How I Got Into It, and How I Got Out of It," *Atlantic Monthly,* XV, 711-717 (June, 1865).

[53] Sarah R. Espy, Private Journal, Aug. 31, 1860 (MS in Capitol at Montgomery, Ala.); also Austin *State Gazette,* July 28, Aug. 25, and Sept. 22, 1860.

[54] Austin *State Gazette,* Aug. 7, 1860.

tion against their masters, but there are wicked characters in all populations and so among our Negroes there could be found wretches who, aided and advised by Kansas ruffians would perform any deed of blood or outrage. The North is crowded with people and many of the abolition leaders are anxious to repeat in Texas the bloody scenes of Kansas."[55] As late as October 27, 1860, Marshall was publishing lurid extracts of Negro insurrections. He was also replying to critics of opposing papers which predicted that the agitation about abolition plots would die out after the election.[56]

Melodramatic accounts of the plots in Texas were spread broadcast by Southern newspapers. The Natchez *Daily Free Trader* flaunted an article entitled "Abolition Diabolism in Texas."[57] The New Orleans *Daily Delta* printed accounts of the Texas terror nearly every day from July 31 to the end of August. The Columbus *Daily Sun* published a letter from a correspondent in Texas who wrote that the only two topics of conversation in his community were "the contemplated Negro insurrection and the Presidential election."[58] The slave panic spread far north to Princess Anne and Norfolk counties, Virginia, where twenty-one frightened negroes were arrested. The prisoners were later discharged by the courts, but the justices who had displayed firmness in resisting the crowd were severely condemned by a Committee of Safety.[59]

That a considerable number of Southern newspapers published these alarming accounts of servile insurrections for political effect seems probable. Parson Brownlow made this charge in the autumn of 1860. "These unfounded rumors," he asserted, "were started by Breckinridge men for effect. . . . These tales were originated by scheming politicians, and were a part of their vile plan 'to nerve the Southern arm' and 'fire the Southern mind.' "[60] The *Hinds County Gazette* in the black belt of Alabama branded these rumors as "fabrics manu-

[55] *Ibid.*, Aug. 25, 1860.   [56] *Ibid.*, Sept. 5, 1860.
[57] Natchez *Daily Free Trader*, Aug. 5, 1860.
[58] Columbus, Ga., *Daily Sun*, Aug. 20, 1860.
[59] *Southern Argus* (Norfolk, Va.), Oct. 12, Dec. 1, 1860.
[60] *Brownlow's Knoxville Whig*, Nov. 17, 1860.

factured for political consumption."[61] Nevertheless, it was a Breckinridge paper that made one of the most vigorous protests in the Old South against the dissemination of alarming rumors. The *Daily Avalanche* observed that time invariably proved that the constant reports of servile insurrection were unfounded. In every community there were panic-makers. They aroused suspicions of the loyalty of the slaves, in which previously the masters had undoubting confidence. The newspapers seized upon these groundless rumors and published them. "We respectfully submit," declared the editor, "that it is the duty of southern editors to be entirely satisfied of their truth, before they publish flaming accounts of contemplated insurrections."[62]

The slaves were remarkably peaceful and tractable during the Civil War despite the provocation to rebel. The fear of servile insurrection, nevertheless, haunted the minds of some Southerners. A Virginia justice of the peace, having examined some suspicious slaves in May, 1861, became convinced that an insurrection was "on foot" among the slaves of Shirley and in Charles City County. He had elicited from negro testimony the allegation that, since the election of Lincoln, the blacks had been holding singing and praying meetings at which insurrection was discussed. Thinking it prudent, however, not to create any excitement by giving publicity to the evidence, he had dismissed the suspected slaves with a severe charge and thirty lashes each. To Hill Carter, the master of Shirley, he wrote a letter of warning, in which he ascribed the rebellious disposition of the slaves to the intemperate discussion of the objects of the Black Republican party by the whites in the newspapers, on the stump, and in the family circle.[63]

In the spring of 1861 the river counties of Mississippi were frightened by the discovery of a plot of the Negroes to kill their masters on July 4. Great excitement followed, several

[61] *Hinds County Gazette*, Nov. 7, 1860.
[62] Memphis *Daily Avalanche*, Dec. 10, 1860.
[63] W. Eppes to Hill Carter, May 25, 1861 (Miscellaneous Papers of the Governor of Virginia, MSS in the Virginia State Library).

Negroes were hanged, and the people of Jefferson County opposed any more volunteer companies leaving the county. Governor Pettus received letters urging him to keep at home as many of the militia companies as possible on account of the danger of Negro uprisings.[64] A volunteer who was the father of five young children was so alarmed by the news of a servile plot in his county that he wrote Governor Pettus for permission to secure a substitute that he might stay and defend his family.

"A plot has been discovered," he wrote, "and already three Negroes have gone the way of all flesh or rather paid the penalty by the forfeiture of their lives. We have five white men and one Negro in our jail who will doubtless pull hemp, there are others who we have not yet succeeded in arresting. In a population of 650 voters surrounded by 1,000 slaves, with one company already in the field of over one hundred men, 'Charley Clark's Rifles' and three other companies mustered into service awaiting your call. Has set me to thinking where I could be of the most service to my Country *at home* or *in the army* you will see that nothing but eternal Vigilance will keep down the enemy at home as well as our frontier and costs [*sic*]. The plans as developed are of the most diabolical character, the white males were all to be destroyed—such of the females as suited their fancy were to be preserved as *Wifes* and they were to march up the river to meet 'Mr. Linkim' bearing off as booty such things as they could carry."[65]

A more convincing type of evidence indicating this fear of insurrection is found in the pencilled notes of a lynch court held near Natchez in 1862. As each trembling slave gave his testimony it was written down by one of the planters on scraps of paper now in the possession of an old resident of Natchez.[66] This illegal court, held in the woods, discovered,

[64] H. O. W. Hines to Gov. John J. Pettus, May 14, 1861; J. G. Randle to Gov. Pettus, June 15, 1861, asking for arms to form a Home Guard (Executive Papers of the State of Mississippi).

[65] J. D. L. Davenport to Gov. Jn. J. Pettus, May 14, 1861 (*ibid.*).

[66] Testimony of Slaves Implicated in a Plot of Insurrection in Adams County, Miss., in 1862 (MSS in possession of Mrs. Lemuel P. Conner, of Natchez, Miss.).

or thought it had detected, a plot among the slaves of Adams County to rise in rebellion when the Federal army reached Natchez. According to the testimony of certain slaves, the plot originated shortly after General Butler had occupied New Orleans by Colonel Mosby's slave, Orange, who could read. The testimony extorted from the negroes revealed that some of the conspirators had guns, that they had been talking frequently of freedom, that they had communicated with lurking runaway slaves and with a white man painted like a Negro. The plot as uncovered by the testimony of the scared Negroes was a melodramatic one, the killing of the masters with axes and hoes, and the apportioning of the beautiful white girls among the black leaders. The Negroes were hanged in the woods, and as a terrifying warning their bodies were left swaying in the wind for many months.

The feminine "intellectual," Julia LeGrand, noted in her journal, December 31, 1862, the fears of servile revolt entertained by some people in New Orleans. The Negroes of that city had developed secret voodoo societies, at the meetings of which they danced around a huge snake representing the Devil. These organizations had been broken up by the police, but they had stirred up vague feelings of uneasiness among the populace. The rumor of a Negro insurrection on New Year's Day had sent patrols marching all over the city. Julia LeGrand, however, saw the humor in the situation. "I feel no fear," she wrote in her diary, December 31, "but many are in great alarm. Fires are frequent—it is feared that incendiaries are at work. . . . The bells rang out and the streets resounded with cries. I awoke from sleep and said, 'Perhaps the moment has come.' . . . Mrs. Norton has a hatchet, a tomahawk, and a vial of some kind of spirits with which she intends to blind all invaders."[67]

The poor whites were especially susceptible to rumors of slave plots and revolts. Olmsted gives a vivid transcript of a conversation which shows this susceptibility. "Where I used

[67] Kate Mason Rowland and Mrs. Morris L. Croxall (eds.), *The Journal of Julia LeGrand, New Orleans, 1862-1863* (Richmond, 1911), pp. 58-59.

to live [Alabama]," said an ignorant farmer to Olmsted, "I remember when I was a boy—must ha' been about twenty years ago—folks was dreadful frightened about the niggers. I remember they built pens in the woods where they could hide, and Christmas time they went and got into the pens 'fraid the niggers was risin'."

"I remember the same time where we was in South Carolina," said his wife, "we had all our things put up in bags, so we could tote 'em if we heerd they was comin our way."[68] A striking analogy to the panics excited by rumors of insurrection was presented by the Indian scares that affected frontier communities from time to time.[69]

The more enlightened members of Southern communities, having observed so many times the baselessness of rumors of servile insurrection, had become more or less inured. DePuy Van Buren tells of an old Southern major living on a plantation near Vicksburg named Ridge House who treated rumors of insurrection cavalierly. After a late party of merrymaking and eggnog, during the Christmas holidays, the guests and family of Ridge House were awakened late at night by a loud "haloo" of a messenger who reported a slave insurrection. The major told the members of his household that they might arm and prepare for the Negroes if they wished, but that he needed his rest and would return to bed. All the occupants of the house, feeling safe because of the coolness with which the major treated the rumor, followed his example and forgot the cause of alarm, except Cousin Jerry, who jumped up in his nightshirt at intervals, tormented by dreams of muskets, bowie knives, pitchforks, and scythes wielded by vicious slaves, and periodically cried out, "There! the niggers are coming!" But the Negroes never came.[70]

When an analysis is made of the ideas of Southern leaders in regard to the dangers of servile insurrection, the fact be-

[68] Olmsted, *A Journey in the Back Country*, p. 203.

[69] See M. M. Quaife, "The Panic of 1862 in Wisconsin," *Wisconsin Magazine of History*, IV, 166-195 (Dec., 1920).

[70] DePuy Van Buren, *Jottings of a Year's Sojourn in the South* (Battle Creek, Mich., 1859), pp. 121-122.

comes clear that there was no consistent opinion. During the famous debate on emancipation in the Virginia legislature of 1831-32 caused by the Nat Turner revolt, Charles Faulkner confuted the argument that slave insurrections rarely happened and that Virginia might not have another for half a century by pointing out that no one knew the day when, and the place where, an insurrection might occur and that no vigilance of the police could prevent such a calamity.[71] Another young speaker in favor of emancipation gave a dramatic portrayal of the intimate danger of household slavery: "Was it this [the Nat Turner insurrection] that induced distant counties where the very name of Southampton was strange, to arm and equip for a struggle? No, Sir, it was the suspicion that a Nat Turner might be in every family, that the same bloody deed could be acted over at any time and in any place, that the materials for it were spread through the land and always ready for a like explosion."[72] Outside the legislature the brilliant Jesse Burton Harrison discussed the dangers that lurked in the slave system. He rejected the idea of a successful servile revolt, but he declared that partial uprisings, like the Southampton revolt, could occur at any time, and a contemptible handful of slaves could strike alarm in the heart of the state.[73] The leaders in the opposite camp, on the other hand, like Thomas R. Dew, and the able pamphleteer, "Appomattox," tended to minimize the dangers of servile revolt.[74]

Daniel Reaves Goodloe, a North Carolina antislavery man who became the editor of the *National Era* in Washington, wrote some sensible observations on insurrection scares in his unpublished autobiography. He was a young fellow seventeen years old when the Southampton insurrection occurred.

[71] *The Speech of Charles James Faulkner on the Policy of the State with Respect to Her Slave Population* (Richmond, 1832), p. 21.
[72] *The Speech of James McDowell on the Slave Question* (Richmond, 1832), p. 29.
[73] Jesse Burton Harrison, *Review of the Slave Question by a Virginian* (Richmond, 1833), p. 22. A pamphlet.
[74] *The Letter of Appomattox to the People of Virginia* (Richmond, 1832), p. 45; *The Pro-Slavery Argument* (Charleston, S. C., 1852), pp. 462, 481.

Militia companies sprang up like mushrooms in his section of the state, and young Goodloe volunteered for one of the companies. He received his first taste of military service while marching about the country "to suppress imaginary combinations of insurgent Negroes." Later in life he expressed the opinion that there never was a time when the Negroes were so far removed from the purpose of revolting. They were ten times more scared than the whites.[75]

Several Northerners who settled in the South and became prominent leaders discounted the danger of servile insurrection in letters to relatives at the North. Shortly after the great alarm in Mississippi in 1835, John A. Quitman wrote to his brother that it was "like most other excitements about Negro insurrections, more that of indignation than of fear." The danger from insurrectionary movements in the South was remote.[76] Sergeant Prentiss reassured his mother and sisters from Vicksburg, September 19, 1835, that after the excitement growing out of the insurrection of the slaves had subsided, not the slightest danger was anticipated. He declared that the severe measures which had been pursued would prevent a recurrence of Negro insurrection, at least for a long period of time.[77] Henry Watson, living near Greensboro, Alabama, was not at all alarmed during the excitement of 1835. He wrote: "I would as freely sleep with my door wide open now as ever, and here, as in Connecticut." He noted how tales of insurrection originated without the least foundation and spread, frightening distant communities.[78]

Although the rumors of slave plots caused uneasiness, intelligent Southerners were apt to discount them. During the slave panic of December, 1856, Edmund Ruffin jotted down in

[75] MSS of D. R. Goodloe in the Library of the University of North Carolina.

[76] J. F. H. Claiborne, *Life and Correspondence of John A. Quitman* (New York, 1880), I, 138-139; see also Charles S. Sydnor, *Slavery in Mississippi* (New York, 1933), p. 251.

[77] *A Memoir of S. S. Prentiss Edited by His Brother* (New York, 1856), I, 162; for a similar reassuring conclusion, see Joseph B. Cobb, *Mississippi Scenes; or Sketches of Southern and Western Life and Adventure* (Philadelphia, 1851), pp. 160-161.

[78] Henry Watson to Julius Reed, Aug. 23, 1835 (Henry Watson Papers, MSS in Duke University Library).

his diary the effect these rumors had on the Virginia community in which he lived. "The reports of Negro plots of designed insurrection," he wrote, "have in this neighborhood also induced proper measures of vigilance, though there are few persons who feel any alarm. Patrols, composed of respectable men, have been out every night—and have found nothing whatever to give any indication of misconduct on the part of the slaves."[79] On Sunday, December 28, he went to church and noted in his diary that he had heard nothing said by any of the neighbors about the rumors of Negro plots. "As usual," commented Ruffin, "all was unfounded and absurd rumor—except at the Tennessee Iron Works. There, there was probably some plot, instigated by Northern abolition agents—and whether justly or unjustly, and certainly illegally many of the Negroes have been put to death."[80]

The conclusions of travelers in the South on the danger of servile insurrection likewise did not agree. Foreign travelers with an antislavery bias reported that Southerners greatly feared an insurrection. James Silk Buckingham, the English reformer, traveled through the Southern States in 1842 and wrote an extensive account of what he saw. He reported that there was a general fear of servile revolt in the South, especially in Louisiana. The horror of abolitionists that Southerners entertained, the harsh slave codes, and the cruel examples made of slaves who plotted insurrection indicated a fear of the slaves.[81] The English actress, Fanny Kemble, wrote in her *Journal of a Residence on a Georgian Plantation in 1838-1839* that Southern men were apt to deny the fact that they lived under an habitual sense of danger, but every Southern woman to whom she spoke on the subject had admitted that they lived in terror of their slaves.[82] Alexis de Tocqueville noted "the tacit forebodings of insurrection" in the

[79] MS Diary of Edmund Ruffin in the Library of Congress, Dec. 25, 1856.

[80] *Ibid.*, Dec. 28, 1856.

[81] James Silk Buckingham, *The Slave States of America* (London, 1842), I, 63, 131, 183, 375, 377; II, 431-433.

[82] Frances Anne Kemble, *Journal of a Residence on a Georgian Plantation in 1838-1839* (New York, 1863), pp. 295-296. See also Harriet Martineau, *Society in America* (London, 1837), II, 330, 344.

South.[83] James Stirling, who traveled through that section during the summer and autumn of 1856, when the insurrection panic was raging, believed that the danger of servile re-revolt was a real one, but he observed that slaveholders in general affected to make light of it.[84] The traveling actor, Tasistro, found the slaves happy and contented in the Lower South, but he was impressed by the strict precautions taken to prevent insurrections.[85]

W. H. Russell, correspondent of the London *Times* in 1860-61, pointed out that many planters reposed trust in their own slaves but were suspicious of those of their neighbors. Of the slaves of the White House Plantation on the Pee Dee River, he wrote: "Their fidelity is undoubted. The house breathes an air of security. The doors and windows are unlocked. There is but one gun, a fowling-piece, on the premises. No planter hereabouts has any dread of his slaves. But I have seen, within the short time I have been in this part of the world, several dreadful accounts of murder and violence in which masters suffered at the hands of their slaves. There is something suspicious in the constant never ending statement that 'we are not afraid of our slaves.' The curfew and the night patrol in the streets, the prisons and the watch-houses, and the police regulations, prove that strict supervision, at all events, is needed and necessary."[86]

Olmsted, perhaps the most capable observer who traveled in the prewar South, reported that Southerners did not fear any successful general uprising of the slaves. "So far as I could ascertain, there are but few districts in which, ordinarily, insurrection is much or constantly, at present apprehended. Yet there is no part of the South where the slave population is felt to be quite safe from a contagion of insurrectionary excitement. Any great event having the slightest bearing upon the question of emancipation is known to produce an 'un-

[83] Alexis de Tocqueville, *Democracy in America* (New York, 1900), I, 381.

[84] James Stirling, *Letters from the Slave States* (London, 1857), p. 298.

[85] Louis F. Tasistro, *Random Shots and Southern Breezes* (New York, 1843), II, 13.

[86] Russell, *My Diary North and South*, pp. 131-132.

wholesome excitement,' even in parts of the country where
the slave population is, and has least reason not to be, pecu-
liarly contented with its condition."[87] Olmsted was impressed
by the fact that in areas of the densest slave population the
white race posted the weakest guard. Often in a region containing hundreds of black slaves there would be only a few
scattered overseer families, miles apart, totally inadequate to
control an insurrection.

The testimony of the negro himself as to the Southern
fear of insurrections emphasized the point that the slaveholders realized the wrong of slavery.[88] Frederick Douglass,
who spent his early life as a slave in Maryland, observed that
slave masters became acute students of human nature. Their
safety depended upon vigilance over so much intellect surrounding them. Realizing the injustice of slavery, the slaveholders were constantly looking for the first signs of insubordination.[89] Douglass was undoubtedly a dangerous slave. He secretly taught his fellow slaves to read and write and then organized a runaway plot among them. Instead of becoming
an insurrectionary leader, he escaped as a fugitive to the North,
where he edited the antislavery journal, the *North Star*. This
brilliant mulatto furnishes an excellent example of the way
in which dangerous slaves were withdrawn from the Southern
social system. The negro historian, Williams, maintained that
the underground railroad was the safety valve to the institution of slavery. "As soon as leaders arose among the slaves
refusing to endure the yoke," he wrote, "they came North.
Had they remained, the direful scenes of San Domingo would
have been enacted, and the hot vengeful breath of massacre
would have swept the South as a tornado and blanched the
cheek of the civilized world."[90]

Perhaps the most objective and reliable source for study-

[87] Olmsted, *A Journey in the Back Country*, pp. 376-377, 474-475.
[88] Booker T. Washington, *The Story of the Negro* (New York, 1909), I, 180.
[89] Frederick Douglass, *My Bondage and My Freedom* (New York, 1855), pp.
376-377.
[90] George W. Williams, *History of the Negro Race in America* (New York,
1883), II, 59.

ing the Southern fear of servile revolt is the slave code. Practically all of the severe laws regulating the slaves were passed after the crises of revolts or conspiracies. By 1835 the black code of the South was substantially complete. Thereafter it was modified or strengthened only in details. The perfected slave code contained many Draconic regulations indicating fear of insurrection. Death was the penalty for rebelling or plotting an insurrection. Slaves could not stray from their plantations without written passes, nor were they permitted to assemble for dancing or sociable objects without a white man's being present. Slaves could not own firearms, horses, horns, drums, nor could they administer medicine to a white person. Whiskey was denied to them by law, for it might incite them to insurrection or crimes of violence. Black preachers were prohibited from haranguing their colored brethren unless a white person should be present. Negroes could not be taught to read and write, save in Maryland, Tennessee, and Kentucky. All owners of slaves were required to keep white persons on their plantations. Various laws were passed to get rid of the free Negro, who was regarded as an instigator of slave crime and a potential leader of insurrection.[91] The patrol system was a striking evidence of the dangers which Southerners apprehended from their dark servants. Like all disciplinary institutions of the ante-bellum South, the patrol tended to be administered loosely, and then to be rejuvenated by popular fear. In time of supposed servile plots the patrol was strongly manned and was active every night. The legislatures of the Southern States were constantly amending and patching the patrol system.[92]

Some of the Southern States had immigration laws that were designed to exclude all Negroes that might instigate the slaves to revolution. In 1795 the General Assembly of North Carolina prohibited any person emigrating from the West

[91] See J. E. Hurd, *The Law of Freedom and Bondage in the United States* (2 vols.; Boston, 1862).

[92] See chapter on "The Patrol System," in H. M. Henry, *The Police Control of the Slave in South Carolina* (Emory, Va., 1914), pp. 28-52.

Indies to bring his slaves into the state.[93] Shortly after the excitement caused by the seditious Walker pamphlet the North Carolina legislature passed a law requiring all ships carrying Negro stewards or mariners to go into quarantine during their stay in North Carolina ports. No native Negroes, either slave or free, were permitted to have communication with free Negroes on board, nor were the latter permitted to come ashore.[94] A similar law was enacted in South Carolina in 1835. Such legislation was regarded as so outrageous at the North that in 1844 the government of Massachusetts sent Samuel Hoar to Charleston in order to test the constitutionality of the South Carolina act. The legislature, however, requested the governor to expel him from the soil of the state. Resolutions were passed upholding this law as necessary to public safety. Only Christopher Memminger voted against these resolutions.[95] The brilliant Carolina lawyer, James Louis Petigru, declared that it was "a mere figment" to contend that Hoar's mission was dangerous to public tranquillity.[96]

The harsh features of the slave code were frequently tempered in practice. Olmsted observed that the slaves on a large rice plantation in Georgia were permitted to purchase firearms and ammunition and keep them in their cabins, in violation of the law. The doors of the master's house were never locked nor the windows closed, although his wife and daughters resided with him and his house was miles distant from any other white family.[97] Another example of careless disregard of legislation for the protection of society was the non-enforcement of the laws against the residence of free Negroes. According to Russell, from one fourth to one third of the free

[93] François-Xavier Martin, *The Public Acts of the General Assembly of North Carolina* (Newbern, N. C., 1804), II, 54-79.

[94] *Acts of General Assembly of North Carolina, Session, 1830-1831*, chap. xxx.

[95] Capers, *The Life and Times of C. G. Memminger*, p. 190.

[96] J. P. Carson, *Life, Letters, and Speeches of James Louis Petigru* (Washington, D. C., 1920), p. 240.

[97] Olmsted, *Seaboard Slave States*, p. 447; see also Lady Emmeline Stuart Wortley, *Travels in the United States, etc., during 1849 and 1850* (New York, 1851), pp. 117-118.

colored population of Virginia were unlawful residents.[98] Henry Howe has preserved the remark of a Virginia judge on the softening of Southern laws by custom. "These laws, and every other having the appearance of rigor towards the slave, are nearly dead letters upon our statute books," he observed, "unless during times of excitement, or since the efforts of the abolitionists have reanimated them. I have, until lately, scarcely known an instance in which they have been enforced."[99] Ulrich Bonnell Phillips has pointed out this custom in the Southern States to legislate with a view of possible emergencies.[100] In normal times these stern laws remained unenforced. Rather, they were regarded, like pistols, as instruments to be used in crises, and then to be laid away and forgotten until danger again arose.

It is not the function of this chapter to assess the danger of servile revolt in the South but to uncover the state of opinion in regard to it. The writer believes, from a study of various types of evidence, that the Southern people suffered at times and in certain sections from a pathological fear of their slaves, not at all justified by actual danger. The evidence points to the fact that the Southern people overemphasized the potentialities of danger in the slave system. It is true that they did not anticipate any successful revolt of the slaves, but they believed that much harm and bloodshed could result from sporadic outbreaks. The stringent slave codes, the patrol system, the efforts to get rid of the free Negro, the prevalence of alarming rumors, the savage severity with which Negroes accused of plotting insurrection were punished, the flimsy evidence of the existence of plots which was credited, all indicate a certain current of uneasiness in Southern society, a feeling that stern precautions should be taken against possible slave revolt.

This fear of servile insurrection was not constant but grew

[98] J. R. Russell, *The Free Negro in Virginia* (Baltimore, 1913), p. 175.

[99] Henry Howe, *Historical Collections of Virginia* (Charleston, S. C., 1845), p. 157.

[100] Phillips, *American Negro Slavery*, p. 484; also *The South in the Building of the Nation* (Richmond, 1909), IV, 200. The pistol simile was used by Phillips.

so intense at certain times as to amount to a panic or hallucination and then subsided until another stimulus was provided. The period from 1793 to 1801 was one of these storm centers of fear; the years from 1829 to 1832 mark another; in 1835 the Lower South was affected by a hysteria with respect to servile insurrection; while the swift half-decade before the Civil War was in general a time of disquiet and apprehension. Moreover, the Southern press was alarmist in tone, especially during the campaign years of 1856 and 1860. After the discovery of the incendiary pamphlet of David Walker there was always the suspicion that some abolitionist might disaffect the normally contented slaves, or that inflammatory literature might fall into the hands of some brooding Nat Turner. This fear of servile insurrection cannot be dismissed in assessing the causes for the atrophy of the great traditions of Jeffersonian liberalism.

CHAPTER V

THE LAW AND THE COURTS

THE ABOLITIONIST crusade of the North was an important influence in turning the South away from the liberal principles
of Jefferson. The Southern answer to this outside pressure
was the enactment of a series of laws, beginning in 1830, which
abridged the freedom of speech and of the press. They registered the emotions of a rural folk as they contemplated a new
danger of servile insurrections, and as they reacted with hot
resentment against the attacks of abolitionists. Men and women
who knew nothing of Southern slavery from direct contact
and experience undertook to enlighten the North and de-
nounce the South in regard to the peculiar institution. Their
technique was the denunciatory style of the Great Revival
that swept western New York and Ohio in the later 1820's.
The greatest of these abolition evangelists, Theodore D. Weld,
may be taken as an example of the more respectable pam-
phleteers. In 1839 he published a handbook entitled *Slavery
As It Is,* which had an enormous sale and influence. His material he gathered from searching the files of Southern newspapers in the New York Commercial Reading Room. These
selected morsels of crime and abnormality were presented as
a mirror of Southern slavery. His purpose was to shock the
North from its lethargy by his terrible tract which represented
the South as a demoniac land. Harriet Beecher Stowe told
Angelina Grimké Weld "how she kept that book [*Slavery
As It Is*] in her work basket by day, and slept with it under
her pillow by night, till its facts crystallized into Uncle Tom's
Cabin."[1] The master of the lurid and denunciatory style, however, was William Lloyd Garrison, editor of the *Liberator.*

[1] Gilbert H. Barnes, *The Antislavery Impulse, 1830-1844* (New York, 1933),
p. 231.

His observations of Southern slavery were confined to a brief sojourn in Maryland, forty-nine days of which were spent in a Baltimore jail.

It was inevitable that the gross caricatures of Southern society by the abolitionists should arouse the intolerance of the Southern people, who possessed a pride fully equal to that of the sixteenth-century Castilian. A man who would fight a duel with his fellow Southerner if his honor was impugned in the slightest degree could hardly be expected mildly to turn the other cheek when his compatriots were called murderers, robbers, and whoremongers by the abolitionists. Even if his personal safety and his economic interests had not been involved, such abusive language demanded a curb.

The accumulative effect of this scourging upon the Southern mind and manners was unquestionably great, although it is incapable of measurement. The newspapers below Mason and Dixon's line extensively advertised the abolitionists by printing extracts from the *Liberator* and the *Emancipator*. The writings of the abolitionists did infinite damage in driving Southerners from the poise necessary to deal with the Negro problem with an open mind. By castigating slaveholders for committing an appalling sin, they adopted the surest method of winning support in the North, but at the same time of arousing bitter intolerance below Mason and Dixon's line. The publications of the abolitionists, moreover, were regarded in the South as firebrands hurled by fanatics into peaceful and unoffending communities to encourage servile insurrection.

Many of the slaves could read the emotional propaganda of the abolitionists. It was an ominous fact that both Denmark Vesey and Nat Turner were influenced by the printed page, and that the runaway slave, Frederick Douglass, had been deeply stirred by a schoolbook, *The Columbian Orator*, to hate slavery. The estimate of Carter Woodson, the Negro historian, that ten per cent of the adult Negroes could read in 1860 is undoubtedly a great exaggeration.[2] Innumerable cases, however, occurred of intelligent house slaves learning to read by stealth or being taught by an indulgent master. Moncure Conway relates how he was bribed by a gaudy necktie to give his father's slave, Peter Humstead, lessons in reading and writing in the cellar.[3] Grant Thorburn noted during a trip through Virginia in 1848 that the laws forbidding the teaching of slaves to read and write were largely ignored.[4] In the Deep South, especially in the cities, there was a considerable number of Negroes who could read and write. One of the most interesting of these literate Negroes was a slave in Georgia, named London, who wrote a manuscript of the Bible in Arabic characters as well as a book of hymns in that exotic script.[5] A collection of poetry composed by Louisiana Negroes, containing about a dozen authors, was made by Armand Lanusse in 1845 and published under the title, *Les Cenelles, Choix de Poésies Indigènes.*[6] In North Carolina, John Chavis, a Negro, was conducting a famous school for white children as late as 1833, teaching the sons of Chief Justice Henderson, and the future Senator, Willie P. Mangum, and Governor Manly. His correspondence with Mangum shows that he took a lively interest in politics, being a Whig with conservative prejudices and bitterly opposed to abolitionists.[7] Another remarkable literate Negro was George Horton, a poet of Chapel Hill. In 1853 he wrote to Horace Greeley asking for a bounty of one hundred and seventy-five dollars to buy his freedom from "these loathsome fetters." Claiming to be the only poet in slavery, he wished his freedom in order

[2] Carter Woodson, *The Education of the Negro Prior to 1861* (New York, 1915), p. 228. See also his volume, *The Mind of the Negro as Reflected in Letters* (Washington, D. C., 1926), p. 29.

[3] Conway, *Autobiography,* I, 21.

[4] Grant Thorburn, *Notes on Virginia* (New York, 1848), p. 8.

[5] W. B. Hodgson, *The Gospels Written in the Negro Patois of English, with Arabic Characters by a Mandingo Slave in Georgia* (n.p., 1857). A pamphlet in the collection of Mr. Arthur B. Spingarn, of New York City.

[6] Armand Lanusse, *Les Cenelles, Choix de Poésies Indigènes* (New Orleans, 1845).

[7] John Chavis to Willie P. Mangum, March 24, 1826, July 30, 1833, April 4, 1836 (Willie P. Mangum MSS in Library of Congress).

to facilitate his work as a poet.[8] Harriet Martineau was told frequently during her travels in the South that the abolitionists of Boston and New York were in the habit of sending incendiary tracts among the slaves. "Mr. Madison made the charge," she wrote, "so did Mr. Clay, so did Mr. Calhoun, so did every slaveholder and merchant with whom I conversed."[9]

The David Walker pamphlet of 1829 was the first of these incendiary publications that caused a drastic regulation of freedom of speech and of the press.[10] This seditious document, entitled *Walker's Appeal in Four Articles Together with a Preamble to the Colored Citizens of the World, But in Particular and Very Expressly to Those of the United States of America*, was written by a free Negro from North Carolina who had emigrated to Boston.[11] In this work he directly incited the slaves to acts of violence to free themselves.[12] The governor of North Carolina was informed of its appearance at Wilmington by a magistrate who described its contents as "treating in most inflammatory terms of the condition of the slaves in the Southern States exaggerating their sufferings, magnifying their physical strength and underrating the power of the whites, containing also an open appeal to their natural love of liberty; and throughout expressing sentiments totally subversive of all subordination in our slaves."[13]

The mayor of Savannah, alarmed by the appearance of

[8] George M. Horton to Horace Greeley, Sept. 11, 1853 (David Swain MSS in archives of the North Carolina Historical Commission).

[9] Martineau, *Society in America*, I, 167.

[10] For an extended study of the effects of the pamphlet, see Clement Eaton, "A Dangerous Pamphlet in the Old South," *Journal of Southern History*, II, 1-12 (Aug., 1936).

[11] The only copy of the first edition of this pamphlet (1829) that is known to the writer is in the private collection of Mr. Arthur B. Spingarn. Mr. Spingarn's copy was found in a building in New York City where William Lloyd Garrison died, and bears the autograph of Francis Jackson Garrison.

[12] *Walker's Appeal in Four Articles Together with a Preamble to the Colored Citizens of the World, But in Particular and Very Expressly to Those of the United States of America* (Boston, 1830), p. 23. The second edition was more inflammatory than the first one.

[13] James F. McRae to Gov. Owen, Aug. 7, 1830 (Letter Book of the Governors of North Carolina, 1829-30, pp. 218-219, MSS in archives of the North Carolina Historical Commission).

the pamphlet in his city, wrote the mayor of Boston requesting the arrest and punishment of Walker. In reply, Mayor Otis stated that Walker was a dealer in old clothes, that he was the true author of the pamphlet, and that he had announced his intention to circulate his pamphlet by the mails, at his own expense if he could not otherwise secure financial aid. The significant part of Otis's letter was that while he and the respectable people of Boston condemned Walker's project, the latter had not violated any Massachusetts law and could not therefore be arrested.[14] Consequently, this Negro abolitionist was allowed to publish at least two other editions of his work, which were sent to Southern ports and distributed among the blacks.[15]

On December 21, 1829, the governor of Georgia sent a copy of the incendiary pamphlet to the legislature, in order to secure the adoption of restrictive legislation. He stated that sixty copies had been seized by the police of Savannah, and that they had been brought to that city by the white steward of a ship and delivered to a Negro preacher for distribution.[16] The legislature responded to his recommendations by passing some severe laws in regard to the colored population. Vessels carrying Negro sailors that entered Georgia ports must go into quarantine for forty days, and Negro sailors of such vessels who stepped on shore were subject to imprisonment.[17] Also, anyone found guilty of introducing into the state or circulating any publication for the purpose of exciting a revolt among the slaves was liable to the penalty of death. If a person were convicted of teaching a slave to read or write, he should be fined or sentenced to jail, and slaves were prohibited from being employed in printing offices.[18]

[14] *Niles' Weekly Register*, XXXVIII, 87 (March 27, 1830).

[15] In the Spingarn collection there are two different printings of the 1830 edition with minor variations.

[16] *Journal of the House of Representatives of the State of Georgia, 1829-30* (Milledgeville, Ga.. 1830), pp. 353-354.

[17] See an article by Philip M. Hamer, "Great Britain, the United States, and the Negro Seamen Acts, 1822-1848," *Journal of Southern History*, I, 12-13 (Feb., 1935).

[18] *Acts of the General Assembly of the State of Georgia, 1829* (Milledgeville, Ga., 1830), pp. 168-175.

While Georgia was being agitated by the Walker pamphlet, the mayor of Richmond found a copy of the dreaded publication in the home of a free Negro. He turned it over to Governor Giles, who brought the matter to the attention of the legislature.[19] The Virginia legislature thereupon held a secret session to discuss proper measures to prevent its circulation. Despite great opposition, a law was passed by the lower house making it criminal to write, print, or circulate among slaves seditious writings. The teaching of slaves to read and write, whether in Sunday schools or by private instruction, was also strictly forbidden. These acts, which passed the House of Delegates by the close vote of eighty-one to eighty, were rejected in the Senate.[20]

Thomas Ritchie, the powerful editor of the Richmond *Enquirer,* expressed his belief that a systematic design had been formed to distribute incendiary pamphlets clandestinely among the slaves. He called attention to the fact that the House of Delegates had considered the Walker pamphlet behind closed doors, and that the Georgia legislature had already passed severe laws to avert danger from the source of incendiary writings.[21] However, John Hampden Pleasants, editor of the rival *Whig,* ridiculed the ostentatious secrecy of the legislature in considering the incendiary pamphlet. *Niles' Weekly Register* also commented disparagingly on the proceedings of the Virginia legislature: "How much is it to be regretted, that a Negro dealer in old clothes, should thus excite two states to legislative action."[22]

In North Carolina, Governor Owen received letters from Wilmington, Fayetteville, and Newbern describing the excitement and fear of insurrection caused by the Walker pamphlet.[23] When the legislature met in the autumn of 1830, he

[19] Message of Gov. Wm. B. Giles to the Virginia legislature, Feb. 16, 1830, in *Journal of the House of Delegates of the Commonwealth of Virginia, 1829-30* (Richmond, 1829), p. 172.

[20] *Niles' Weekly Register,* XXXVIII, 87 (March 27, 1830).

[21] Editorial, "The Pamphlet," Richmond *Enquirer,* Jan. 28, 1830.

[22] *Niles' Weekly Register,* XXXVIII, 4 (Feb. 27, 1830).

[23] L. D. Henry to Gov. Owen, Sept. 3, 1830 (Executive Papers); J. Burgwyn to Gov. Owen, Nov. 15, 1830 (Letter Book, pp. 247-249).

sent a copy of the Walker pamphlet to the members. In his message he declared that this inflammatory production had been discovered in Virginia, South Carolina, Georgia, and Louisiana, as well as in North Carolina. He believed that a systematic attempt was being made by reckless persons in the North to sow sedition among the slaves, "distorting the peaceful doctrines of the Bible," and that free blacks were being used as agents in distributing these seditious publications.[24]

The legislature went into secret session to consider measures to avert dangerous consequences from the dreaded pamphlet. The Joint Committee on Slaves and Free Persons of Color reported on December 1 that they were satisfied an extensive conspiracy existed to disaffect the slaves.[25] Accordingly, the General Assembly passed a bill December 9, 1830, to prevent the teaching of slaves to read and write and to stop the circulation of seditious publications. Persons convicted of writing or circulating publications, "the evident tendency whereof would be to excite insurrection, conspiracy, or resistance in the slaves or free Negroes" should for the first offense be imprisoned for not less than a year and be put in the pillory and whipped, at the discretion of the court, but for the second offense should suffer death without benefit of clergy.[26]

Such repressive laws were not placed on the statute books without considerable opposition. The bill to prevent the teaching of slaves to read and write was passed in the Senate by a vote of thirty-six "ayes" to twenty-two "noes," eighteen of the "noes" coming from the Piedmont and western counties.[27] A decisive factor in securing the passage of both the education and the incendiary bills was the excitement that resulted from David Walker's *Appeal*. Among the Executive Papers

[24] *Journals of the Senate and House of Commons of the General Assembly of the State of North Carolina, 1830-31* (Raleigh, N. C., 1831), p. 161.

[25] Coon, *op. cit.*, I, 178.

[26] *Laws of North Carolina, Enacted by a General Assembly begun and held at Raleigh on the Fifteenth Day of November in the year of our Lord one thousand eight hundred and thirty, and in the fifty-fifth year of the Independence of the said State* (Raleigh, N. C., n.d.).

[27] Derived from table of votes on the bill, Coon, *op. cit.*, I, 480-481.

of North Carolina is a letter from Bryan Trailand of Laurel Hill, asking to borrow the Walker pamphlet. He had been assailed for his vote on the law prohibiting the teaching of slaves to read and write. He had often spoken of this pamphlet and wished to make his statements good. Having been criticized in the last electioneering campaign, he desired to show some of the people that their ideas on slavery were founded on "false philanthropy."[28]

The significance of the Walker pamphlet has been overshadowed by the attention which has been given to the more spectacular Nat Turner insurrection that followed a year later. The Walker pamphlet represented virtually the first impact of incendiary literature on the Southern States. That this publication with its doctrine of servile revolt and its instigation to commit illegal acts deserved suppression hardly admits of a doubt. The laws which Georgia, North Carolina, Mississippi, and Louisiana enacted to cope with the situation occasioned by the obnoxious pamphlet were extremely severe. Whether these harsh laws were the achievement of a powerful minority of proslavery men, cleverly utilizing the latent fear of servile insurrection, or the expression of the popular will is difficult to ascertain. Professor John Spencer Bassett attributed the passage of these laws in North Carolina to the activity of a determined proslavery group.[29] It was indeed unfortunate that Southern legislation in respect to antislavery publications was enacted during periods of excitement following such incidents as the Walker pamphlet and the Southampton insurrection. Once such laws were placed on the statute books they were left intact and received the silent acquiescence of the masses.

The violent shock of the Nat Turner insurrection of 1831 started another wave of legislation restraining the freedom of the press and of speech. Governor Floyd attributed the in-

[28] Bryan Trailand to Gov. Stokes, Sept. 3, 1831 (Executive Papers).
[29] J. S. Bassett, *Slavery in the State of North Carolina* (Baltimore, 1899), pp. 98-101.

surrection to incendiary publications of the abolitionists, especially to the recently founded *Liberator*.[30] In a letter to the
governor of South Carolina, he affirmed that black preachers
had read from the pulpit the inflammatory publications of
Walker and Garrison, and that Yankee pedlars and traders
had been instruments of inciting the slaves.[31] The Virginia
legislature of 1831-32 enacted laws which prohibited Negroes
from preaching to their own color, and made illegal the printing or circulation of any pamphlet or other writing "advising
persons of colour in this commonwealth to commit insurrection or rebellion."[32] Likewise, other Southern states like North
Carolina, Alabama, and Tennessee, passed laws at this time
limiting the freedom of Negroes to preach and to assemble.

Not until 1836, on the other hand, did the most intolerant
period of Southern lawmaking begin. The abolition societies
in the North had just initiated an active campaign to deluge the
Southern States with emotional propaganda. A comparatively
enormous output of pamphlets and newspapers was issued in
the two years 1835 and 1836.[33] This campaign of pamphlets
was designed to reach the white slaveholders but not to circulate among the slaves. Consequently, they were sent to influential people throughout the South, Congressmen, clergymen, governors, etc.[34] Southern resentment, as well as fear,
was stirred by the discovery of a large sack of such pamphlets
in the Charleston post-office in May, 1835. A mob destroyed
this material, and throughout the South anti-abolition meet-

---

[30] *Journal of the Virginia House of Delegates, 1831-32* (Richmond, Va., 1832),
p. 10, and Ambler, *Life and Diary of John Floyd*, p. 161. Garrison emphatically
denied any such design, and pointed out that his paper did not have a single
subscriber below the Potomac.

[31] John Floyd to James Hamilton, Jr., Nov. 19, 1831 (Papers of John Floyd,
1823-32, MSS in Library of Congress).

[32] *Acts of the General Assembly of the Commonwealth of Virginia, 1831-32*
(Richmond, 1832), chap. xxii, sec. 7.

[33] *Annual Report of the American Anti-Slavery Society* (New York, 1835), pp.
48-53; also letter from Lewis Tappan, Aug. 19, 1835 (*Niles' Weekly Register*,
XLIX, 21, Sept. 12, 1835).

[34] *Fourth Annual Report of the Massachusetts Anti-Slavery Society* (Boston, Jan.
20, 1836), pp. 15-17.

ings were held, and legislatures called on the Northern States to suppress their abolition presses. Undoubtedly some of this zeal to suppress "the fanatics" was motivated by political considerations, namely, to defeat Van Buren for President.

To meet this menace of incendiary publications, the Virginia legislature passed in 1836 the most intolerant law that was ever placed on its statute books. It provided severe punishment for any member or agent of an abolition society who should come into the state and maintain "that the owners of slaves have no property in the same, or advocate or advise the abolition of slavery." Likewise, any person who should print or circulate a book, pamphlet, or newspaper for the purpose of persuading slaves to rebel or denying the right of masters to property in their slaves and inculcating the duty of resistance to such right, should be deemed guilty of felony. To enforce these provisions postmasters and justices of the peace were given inquisitorial power over the mails, and offenders against these laws could be arrested by any free white person.[35]

This statute was vigorously assailed by the editor of the Richmond *Whig,* who declared that it violated some of the great constitutional safeguards of the liberty of speech and of the press. "It is far worse," he said, "than Lynching and Lynch's law, and a reflection on the legislation of the state that such deformed crudities are submitted in the shape of bills."[36] It seems clear that such legislation went beyond what was demanded by public safety and gravely encroached upon the liberty of speech and of the press. This law, which seriously interfered with the free transmission of the mail, never came before the Supreme Court to test its constitutionality and afforded a striking example of the nonassertion of Federal power.

[35] *Acts of the General Assembly of the Commonwealth of Virginia, 1835-36* (Richmond, 1836), chap. lxvi, p. 44. In 1848 the statute was broadened to include any free person denying that masters had a right of property in their slaves (*Acts of the General Assembly of the Commonwealth of Virginia, 1847-48*, Richmond, 1848, chap. x, sec. 25). [36] Richmond *Whig,* April 1, 1836.

The governor of Georgia in his message to the legislature, November 3, 1835, discussed the question whether force or reason should be used in controlling the writers and distributors of incendiary publications. He concluded: "Should, however, the abolitionists be permitted to proceed without molestation or only have to encounter the weapons of reason and argument, have we not reason to fear, that their untiring efforts may succeed in misleading the majority of a people who have no direct interest in the great question at issue, and finally produce interference with the constitutional rights of the slaveholders."[37] The abolitionists in his eyes were monsters urged on by a reckless and bloodthirsty spirit. The Southern people had unalterably made up their minds about the preservation of slavery. "It is a subject with which we cannot suffer a Stranger to intermeddle," he declared. It was a clear duty of the Northern States therefore to suppress the abolitionists and their incendiary publications.

The legislation of the states of the Upper South, with one striking exception, reveals the same general rigor. Maryland had a very severe law, enacted in 1836, that trenched upon the liberty of speech and of the press. It was declared "a high offence against the supremacy of this State" for a person to write or circulate any publication, having a tendency to create discontent among, and stir up to insurrection, the people of color of the state. The penalty for violating this provision was confinement in the penitentiary for not less than ten nor more than twenty years.[38] In 1842 the legislature increased the stringency of laws relating to seditious publications, by making it a felony for any free Negro to call for or receive any abolition newspaper or pamphlet at the post-office. The grand juries were required to summon all postmasters before them when they deemed it proper to examine them in regard

[37] Message of Gov. Wilson Lumpkin, Nov. 3, 1835 (Minutes of the Executive Department of the State of Georgia, 1834-39, pp. 115-116, MSS in Atlanta).

[38] Acts of the General Assembly of Maryland (Annapolis, 1836), chap. 325, secs. 1, 2.

to incendiary publications.[39] The Tennessee law, also passed in 1836, was practically identical with that of Maryland. Neither Maryland nor Tennessee, however, prohibited the teaching of Negroes to read and write.[40]

The legislation of Kentucky presented a notable exception to the stern laws of the other border states. Kentucky had no legislation prohibiting the teaching of Negroes to read and write, nor until 1860 did she have any laws infringing the freedom of the press or of speech. On March 3, 1860, the General Assembly finally passed a law prohibiting the writing or circulation of publications, "with intent to advise or incite negroes in this state to rebel or make insurrection, or inculcating resistance to the rights of property of masters in their slaves."[41] The mildness of Kentucky's laws may explain, in part, the prevalence of so much mob violence there in the decade 1850-60. It may seem strange that Kentucky, being so near a dangerous abolition center, Ohio, did not have stringent laws against incendiary publications at an earlier date. Several reasons contribute to explain this anomaly: the presence of remarkable leaders, like Henry and Cassius Marcellus Clay, who threw the weight of their magnetic personalities on the side of liberalism; the influence of the neighboring free-soil states; and the relatively small proportion of slaves in Kentucky, constituting about one fifth of the population in 1850.

The laws of the Lower South infringing the liberty of speech and of the press differed scarcely at all from those of the Upper South, except that they carried with them savage penalties. The Louisiana law, for example, enacted in 1830, placed extreme penalties on anyone who published, or spoke from the bar, the bench, the stage, or the pulpit, any language that had a tendency to produce discontent among the free colored population or excite insubordination among the

[39] *Laws of the General Assembly of Maryland* (Annapolis, 1842), chap. 272, secs. 1, 3.
[40] *Session Laws of Tennessee, 1835-36* (Nashville, Tenn., 1836), chap. xliv.
[41] *The Revised Statutes of Kentucky with Amendments to 1860* (Cincinnati, 1860), II, 764.

slaves.[42] This law practically suppressed criticism of slavery and constituted a dangerous invasion of constitutional liberty.

Most of the states of the Cotton Kingdom, Georgia, Alabama, Mississippi, and Louisiana, passed severe laws early—around the year 1830—and thereafter did not find it necessary to modify or strengthen them. The Upper South, on the other hand, was continually repairing the old laws in the direction of greater strictness. The volatile state of South Carolina also followed this latter procedure. Not until 1859 was the copestone placed on her edifice of legislation suppressing free speech. In that year she made it a crime, punishable at the discretion of the jury, to subscribe to or receive a newspaper, book, or pamphlet "calculated to disaffect any slave or slaves in this state," or to write or speak on slavery to that effect.[43] The Western border states passed laws prohibiting the writing or circulation of seditious publications relatively late, and were very much influenced by the Virginia law of 1836. The Arkansas law of 1850, for example, made it a penal crime to "maintain that owners have not right of property in their slaves."[44]

When the legislation of the border states is compared with that of the Lower South, it becomes clear that, so far as legal enactment was concerned, both sections were equally intolerant. The severe code of border states like Virginia and Maryland was affected by the fact that they lay close to the literary frontier of the abolition movement. Furthermore, sterner legislation was needed, because the Upper South was not a unit in its social texture. It contained diverse elements, like the Quakers, the Germans of the Shenandoah Valley, settlements of Northern immigrants, and the individualistic

[42] *Acts Passed at the Second Session of the Ninth Legislature of Louisiana* (Donaldsville, La., 1830), p. 96; George M. Stroud points out, in *A Sketch of the Laws Relative to Slavery* (Philadelphia, 1856), p. 251, that the circulation of the Declaration of Independence was proscribed by this law.

[43] *Acts of the General Assembly of the State of South Carolina Passed in December, 1859* (Columbia, S. C., 1860), pp. 768-769.

[44] *Acts Passed at the Eighth Sesssion of the General Assembly of the State of Arkansas* (Little Rock, 1851), p. 23.

mountaineers of the Appalachians, whose loyalty to the slave regime was doubtful.

Much of the Southern legislation on seditious publications depended on the interpretation by the courts as to whether the liberty of speech and of the press was actually abridged. Northern historians have tended to render a verdict of intolerance largely on the basis of laws and of the Southern blockade against "foreign" abolition publications. But the enforcement of law and its modification by public opinion afford a more realistic basis on which to judge the Southern people. The evidence for the Upper South shows that the extreme laws limiting the freedom of discussion were tempered in nearly every case, by giving the law its most constricted and humane interpretation. Indeed, the courts of these states preserved traditions of liberality and fairness that were noteworthy. This maintenance of poise is all the more remarkable when it is contrasted with the narrow and intolerant spirit that dominated the Federal courts in applying the Sedition Act of 1918.

In the summer of 1818 a Methodist minister from Pennsylvania named Jacob Gruber spoke before a camp meeting at Hagerstown on "the national sins." About twenty-six hundred white people were in the audience and over four hundred Negroes were on the outskirts of the crowd. The bold evangelist attacked slavery as being inconsistent with the Declaration of Independence and criticized the slave trade as inhuman and cruel. Consequently, he was indicted by the grand jury for attempting to incite slaves to rebellion. So incensed were the people in the neighborhood of Hagerstown that the counsel for the defense, Roger Brooke Taney, secured the removal of the case to Frederick.

Taney based his defense of the accused man on the ground that his punishment would violate the Maryland laws guaranteeing freedom of speech and of the press. His argument at this time reveals an idealistic side to Taney's nature that in later years, when he guided the Supreme Court in the Dred Scott case, seems to have been obscured. In an impassioned address, Taney upheld the right to criticize the institution of slavery in Maryland, and he won a verdict of "Not Guilty" from the jury.[45]

"Any man has a right to publish his opinions on that subject whenever he pleases," said Taney. "It is a subject of national concern, and may at all times be freely discussed. Mr. Gruber did quote the language of our great act of national independence, and insisted on the principles contained in that venerated instrument. He did rebuke those masters, who, in the exercise of power, are deaf to the calls of humanity; and he warned them of the evils they might bring upon themselves. He did speak with abhorrence of those reptiles, who live by trading in human flesh, and enrich themselves by tearing the husband from the wife—the infant from the bosom of the mother: and this I am instructed was the head and front of his offending. Shall I content myself with saying he had a right to say this? That there is no law to punish him? So far is he from being the object of punishment in any form of proceeding, that we are prepared to maintain the same principles, and to use, if necessary, the same language here in the temple of justice, and in the presence of those who are the ministers of the law. A hard necessity, indeed, compels us to endure the evil of slavery for a time. It was imposed upon us by another nation, while we were yet in a state of colonial vassalage. It cannot be easily, or suddenly removed. Yet while it continues it is a blot on our national character, and every real lover of freedom confidently hopes that it will be effectually, though it must be gradually, wiped away; and earnestly looks for the means, by which this necessary object may be best attained. And until it shall be accomplished: until the time shall come when we can point without a blush, to the language held in the Declaration of Independence, every friend of humanity will seek to lighten the galling chain of slavery, and better, to the utmost of his power, the wretched condition of the slave. Such was Mr. Gruber's object in that

[45] For a good account of this case, see Carl Brent Swisher, *Roger B. Taney* (New York, 1935), pp. 95-98.

part of his sermon, of which I am now speaking. Those who have complained of him, and reproached him will not find it easy to answer him: unless complaints, reproaches and persecution shall be considered an answer."[46]

The first case that occurred in Virginia involving the severe law of 1836 was that of the Commonwealth of Virginia versus Barrett. This case reached the Supreme Court of Virginia in December, 1839. Lysander Barrett was charged with the crime of circulating in Virginia a memorial praying Congress to abolish slavery in the District of Columbia. In the memorial slavery was declared to be "a sin against God, a foul stain upon our national character, and contrary to the spirit of our republican institutions."[47] Barrett was able to obtain the signature of only ten persons in Lewis County (western Virginia). The Court interpreted the Virginia law of 1836 strictly and rendered a unanimous opinion, that in order to sustain a prosecution under the act, the person accused must be a member or agent of an abolition or antislavery society. Accordingly, the Court held that the prosecution of Barrett had failed, and reversed the decision of the lower court.

Decidedly the most important of these cases involving the freedom of speech in Virginia was Commonwealth of Virginia versus Bacon. Jarvis C. Bacon was brought to trial in March, 1849, for maintaining that owners had no right of property in their slaves. Bacon was a minister of the Gospel in Grayson County, located in the southwestern part of the present state of Virginia. On the Sunday before Christmas, 1848, he had preached from the text in the New Testament, "Ye are the light of the world." In the course of the sermon, the defendant, without mentioning the names of slaveholders at any time, said: "If I was to go to my neighbor's crib and steal his corn, you would call me a thief, but that it was worse to take a human being and keep him all his life, and give him noth-

[46] David Martin, *Trial of the Rev. Jacob Gruber, Minister in the Methodist Episcopal Church, at the March Term, 1819, in the Frederick County Court, for a Misdemeanor* (n.p., 1819), pp. 42-44.

[47] B. W. Leigh, *Reports of Cases Argued and Determined in the Court of Appeals and in the General Court of Virginia* (Richmond, 1840), IX, 665.

ing for his labor, except once in a while a whipping or a few stripes."[48]

Bacon was fined in the Circuit Court of Grayson County $49.62½, but he appealed to the General Court of Virginia. This case, although it involved only an ignorant and perhaps misguided preacher in a remote county of Virginia, was significant, for it brought clearly to issue the problem of freedom of speech in Virginia. The defense maintained that the Virginia law of 1848 referred only to the denial of the *legal* right of ownership of slaves and not to the moral right. The legislature of the state could not pass a law preventing a person from discussing the moral right of slavery, because it was prohibited by the "freedom of speech" clause in the Constitution of Virginia and the statute of religious toleration. To show the harmlessness of Bacon's utterances, the defense quoted from the doctrines and discipline of the Methodist Church on the evils of slavery.

Judge Lomax delivered the opinion of the Supreme Court, postulating that "any statute tending to restrain the exercise of the freedom of speech or supposed to have such tendency should be strictly construed by the Courts." Under this ruling the Court decided that Bacon did not clearly deny the legal right of slavery. To convict, it was necessary for an express denial of property right to be shown and for such denial to be maintained by adducing facts and arguments. The Court softened the rigor of the law to a degree that almost nullified it, in order that Bacon might be liberated, and perhaps that the honor of Virginia might be vindicated. Commenting on the law of 1848, Judge Lomax said: "If there be any ambiguity in its meaning, why should a Court, guided by the spirit of the Constitution which favors the freedom of speech and of religious faith, reject in this criminal prosecution, this innocent construction and fasten upon another that makes such speaking a crime?"[49] By this liberal interpretation of the law, Bacon

[48] P. R. Grattan, *Report of Cases Decided in the Supreme Court of Appeals and in the General Court of Virginia* (Richmond, 1852), VII, 604.
[49] *Ibid.*, VII, 612.

was released from the previous fine. This great victory for the cause of freedom of speech went unnoticed in the leading Virginia newspapers.

Another striking example of leniency in enforcing the incendiary law of 1848 occurred in the case of Commonwealth versus Curry. In June, 1850, a young man of prepossessing appearance, named Isaac Curry, recently from Pittsfield, Massachusetts, was tried before the Hustings Court of Alexandria on the charge of "improper interference with slaves and teaching them that their owners had not the right to hold them in bondage." Although the jury was forced to bring in a verdict of guilty on the basis of the evidence, they placed only a light fine of ten dollars on him and recommended him to the mercy of the judge. Even the attorney for the commonwealth made a speech in which he said that, although the young man had been convicted of a high crime endangering the safety of the community and in violation of that Christianity which he professed to have taken as his guide, nevertheless he hoped the Court would take his youth and good character into consideration and remit the punishment. The old judge set the young crusader free with an admonition.[50]

The trial of Samuel Janney of Loudoun County in the summer of 1850 is the most illuminating case that involved the liberty of the press in Virginia. Janney was a poet, historian, schoolteacher of girls, and prominent Quaker. In August, President William A. Smith of Randolph-Macon College delivered a lecture in the courthouse at Leesburg, in which he took the ground that slavery was right in itself and was sanctioned by the Bible. Janney published an elaborate refutation in a Leesburg paper, the *Washingtonian*. The Grand Jury of Loudoun County indicted him, at first, for publishing an article which they said "was calculated to incite persons of color to make insurrection or rebellion." This charge was not technically correct, and the Court would not entertain the case. The Grand Jury, then, indicted him a second time for the

[50] Alexandria *Gazette*, June 17, 1850.

same article, on the ground that it denied that "owners had right of property in their slaves."[51] At the trial, which occurred in June, 1850, Janney made a brilliant defense. In his oral argument, he said: "The longer you keep this subject before the people the more there will be of my way of thinking." In his written argument, he rested his case both on the technicalities of the law and on the great principles of constitutional liberty.

This argument may be summed up as follows: (1) He denied the fact alleged in the presentment, that he had maintained that masters have no right of property in their slaves. On the other hand, he had distinctly recognized that slaves were property *in a legal sense of the term.* (2) The statute under which the presentment was made did not apply to the case, when taken in connection with the constitution of Virginia. The legislature could not have intended to violate the constitution concerning the freedom of the press and of religious belief, and the statute must be construed accordingly. (3) If the court should hold that the statute of 1848 did apply to his case, Janney maintained that the law should be disregarded as being in palpable violation of the constitution of Virginia. He cited the decision of Judge Roane in the case of Peter Kemper versus Mary Hawkins. (4) Finally, Janney reviewed the circumstances under which the article was written. A learned divine had gone through Loudoun County maintaining that slavery was right in itself and he had ridiculed the Declaration of Independence. He put the question to the jury: "And can it be possible that freedom of the press is so completely prostrated in Virginia that a native citizen of the county may not be permitted to answer an address thus publicly delivered in which were maintained doctrines at variance with the sentiments of Washington, Jefferson, Madison, Patrick Henry, and all the great statesmen of Virginia?"[52]

The court which heard the case was composed of the magistrates of the county, most of whom were slaveholders. After

[51] Samuel M. Janney, *Memoirs* (Philadelphia, 1881), pp. 97-98.
[52] *National Era,* July 11, 1850.

listening to Janney's defense, they quashed the proceedings against him, and the presiding justice gave him a lecture on the necessity of great care and caution in meddling with the delicate question of slavery.[53]

A case which attracted considerable attention in the South was the trial of Mrs. Margaret Douglass at Norfolk in 1854 for teaching Negro children to read and write. For nearly a year she and her daughter had conducted a school in Norfolk for Negro children, having an enrollment of twenty-five pupils. In 1853 she was indicted by the Grand Jury for violating the Virginia laws. Being of a bold spirit and very poor, she determined not to hire a lawyer but to plead her own case before the jury. In the antibloomer state of Virginia this procedure created not a little astonishment and wonder. She showed that most of the Negro children attending Sunday schools of the city could read and in some cases had been taught by prominent people in Norfolk. So effective was her argument that the jury recommended a nominal punishment, but the judge imposed a sentence of imprisonment in the city jail for one month. He declared in his decision that to render a formal judgment of imprisonment for a week or a day would be regarded by all true advocates of justice and law as mere mockery. He justified the Virginia law prohibiting Negro education as a necessary measure of self-defense against Northern incendiaries.[54]

In 1857 Prince William County in northern Virginia, which had received a considerable infusion of Yankee immigrants, became the scene of prosecutions of antislavery men. A resident of that county named Crawford was committed to jail by Justice Kankey, charged with declaring himself an abolitionist, who "believed a Negro was as good as he was, if he behaved himself; and maintaining by speaking, that persons have not the right of property in slaves under the law."[55] Also,

[53] Janney, *Memoirs*, chap. x.
[54] Margaret Douglass, *The Personal Narrative of Mrs. Margaret Douglass* (Boston, 1854), pp. 40-50; also Richmond *Enquirer*, Nov. 20, 1853.
[55] *National Era*, Aug. 27, 1857.

John Underwood, one of these Yankee settlers, who had even attained the position of justice of the peace, was presented by the Grand Jury for "uttering and maintaining that owners have no right of property in their slaves." He was later found guilty by the court and fined $312.50. He appealed on the ground that the statute upon which the prosecution was founded was void and unconstitutional.[56] The most intolerant side of Southern character was revealed in dealing with Northern men and Northern publications.

In North Carolina, no prominent cases involving the liberty of speech and of the press appeared until 1850. With the coming of autumn in that year, the Greensborough *Patriot* printed a violent article directed against Jesse McBride and Adam Crooks, two antislavery preachers from beyond the Ohio River. The author of the article had heard McBride preach in Guilford County to an audience containing twenty or thirty negroes, and deemed his discourse highly incendiary. McBride, he said, had protested against the barbarity of the state law prohibiting the teaching of slaves to read and write, and had excoriated the Southern churches and preachers for hypocrisy.[57] The Greensborough *Patriot* commented on the activities of McBride and Crooks as follows: "Public attention is thoroughly aroused to the matter; official vigilance is awakened; and any tampering with slaves, or dissemination of incendiary sentiments dangerous to the community will not escape detection and such punishment as outrages of the kind deserve before the fall circuit of the Superior Courts is over."[58]

McBride and Crooks, in consequence of the agitation, were arrested and in October, 1850, were tried before the Superior Court of Forsyth County (western Piedmont). James T. Morehead, a brother of former Governor Morehead, and George Mendenhall were the counsel for the defense. Every

---

[56] *Liberator*, Aug. 28, Nov. 29, 1857. The case did not reach the Supreme Court; see Grattan's *Reports*, Vols. XIII-XV, covering 1855-60.

[57] Greensborough *Patriot*, Sept. 28, 1850. According to the picturesque language of the writer, McBride had, "in one sentence, sent the *whole Southern Church* to hell—declaring it impossible for them to be saved."

[58] Greensborough *Patriot*, Oct. 5, 1850.

disposition was shown to give the prisoners a fair and impartial trial. They were accused of violating the North Carolina law of 1830 prohibiting the circulation of incendiary publications. It was proved that Jesse McBride had given an incendiary pamphlet to a little girl ten or twelve years old at the home of a Mr. Kenedy, where he had spent the night. The pamphlet in question was described as "a sort of running commentary on the Ten Commandments, couched in the violent and canting language of the abolitionists and intended to show that slaveholders live in the habitual violation of all said commandments."[59] McBride was convicted of having violated the law, but Crooks was liberated. Public sentiment seems fully to have upheld the decision.[60] When McBride was sentenced to prison for one year, to stand in the pillory for one hour, and to be whipped with twenty lashes, the Raleigh *Standard,* leading newspaper of the state, declared: "We wish the law could take hold of their necks instead of their backs."[61] Apparently the press did much to fan the flame of intolerance and to revive a law that was almost a dead letter.

Ten years later the next important case was decided which bears on the freedom of the press in North Carolina. Daniel Worth was indicted for circulating Helper's *The Impending Crisis.* Worth was born in Guilford County, North Carolina, but he had emigrated to Indiana. In this environment he had become a Wesleyan minister and had been elected to the legislature. Later he returned to his native state with something of the ardor of a crusader. In July, 1859, he wrote a letter to the *National Era* at Washington, D. C., describing his work in North Carolina. He said that he had been in North Carolina nearly two years, "yet all is peace and quiet." During that

[59] Raleigh *Register,* Oct. 23, 1850, and the *North State Whig,* Washington, N. C., Nov. 13, 1850.

[60] Years later an echo of the McBride-Crooks affair was reported in Albion Tourgée's *A Fool's Errand* (New York, 1880), p. 80. Squire Hyman, who was a leader in the demonstrations against the two abolition preachers, defended his action in a conversation with Tourgée by declaring: "Such doctrines lead at once and naturally to insurrection among the blacks and threaten us with all the horrors of San Domingo."   [61] Raleigh *Standard,* Oct. 23, 1850.

interval he had distributed "a large number of our standard anti-slavery authors, so that my books are doing a work little inferior to the living preacher."[62] He had denounced slavery with burning zeal, but as yet he had not been molested! His downfall came with the violent excitement that followed the John Brown raid of October, 1859.[63]

Worth was tried at Greensboro in the spring of 1860. Being six feet and four inches in height and having a fine intellectual forehead, he made an impressive appearance as he conducted his own defense before the jury. In the trial several witnesses were called who asserted that Worth sold them Helper's book for one dollar, recommending it as a good book, but warning them to be careful concerning it.[64] It was proved also that he had declared that the laws of North Carolina were made by "a set of drunkards, gamblers, and whoremongers." The prosecution read to the jury some of the most invidious sections of *The Impending Crisis*. The extracts compared the existence of slavery to the introduction of smallpox in a community and threatened to accomplish the destruction of slavery, if it were not done voluntarily, with the aid of the abolitionists of the North and the slaves, who "in nine cases out of ten, would be delighted to cut their masters' throats." The defense maintained that a violation of the incendiary law of 1830 did not apply to distributing antislavery literature to free white persons, but only in the sale or delivery of such a publication to a slave or free Negro.[65] Worth was given the lightest penalty consistent with the law, imprisonment for twelve months. He thereupon appealed to the Supreme Court.

His relative, Jonathan Worth, a very prominent leader in the political life of the state, wrote a letter on the eve of the

[62] Letter from Daniel Worth, New Salem, N. C., July 5, 1859 (printed in *National Era*, Aug. 4, 1859).

[63] John Harriss wrote Governor Ellis that Worth had been circulating seditious books in Randolph County and that a suspicious long box had been sent to his boardinghouse, which was believed to contain muskets (John Harriss to Gov. Ellis, Dec. 30, 1859, Executive Papers of North Carolina, MSS).

[64] *North Carolina Standard*, April 7, 1860.

[65] H. G. Jones, *Reports of Cases at Law Argued and Determined in the Supreme Court of North Carolina* (Salisbury, N. C., 1860), VII, 489.

trial to secure leniency for the accused. He feared that the full rigor of the law would be enforced against his cousin, which meant, besides imprisonment, confinement for a certain space of time in the pillory and public whipping. Worth pointed out that if a gray-haired man of sixty-seven years should be whipped for the offense, abolitionists both at home and in the North would turn the episode to account. He regarded his relative as "an enthusiastic monomaniac," whom all his kinsmen tried to persuade to leave the state. He commented on the state of feeling in North Carolina: "His zeal had the better of his discretion. Nobody here will countenance the circulation of a book denouncing slaveholders as worse than thieves, murderers, etc." Jonathan Worth himself, however, thought that the harsh law of 1830 should be carried out only against those who produced dissatisfaction among the slaves. He urged the mitigation of the punishment of Daniel Worth on the ground that to show some laxity in enforcing the law would be evidence of conscious security on the part of the community.[66]

In the hearing before the Supreme Court, June, 1860, Worth was ably represented by James Morehead, who owned many slaves. The Supreme Court, however, refused to reverse the decision of the lower court. The justices decided that it was not necessary to circulate an incendiary publication among negroes to make the act criminal, for in a mixed population reading matter put into circulation would inevitably reach the blacks. Justice Manly, in announcing the decision of the Court, emphasized the intent of a publication in determining its criminality. "Without going into a detailed consideration of the offensive matter," he ruled, "it is sufficient to say, the expressed object of the book, as disclosed by the extracts, is to render the social condition of the South odious, and to put an end to that which is held up as the odious feature, by force, and arms, if necessary." At the same time he hastened to interpret the law so that no injustice might be done to persons who were not

[66] J. G. deR. Hamilton (ed.), *The Correspondence of Jonathan Worth* (Raleigh, N. C., 1909), I, 110-113.

bona fide abolitionists. He held that to circulate a book like *The Impending Crisis,* not for the purpose of propagating its principles but for the sake of gratifying curiosity and for placing it in the hands of reliable persons, would not involve punishment. The criminality consisted in the intent, which must be gathered from the circumstances.[67]

The courts of the Lower South were also guided by the spirit of liberality in interpreting the laws restricting freedom of speech. The Supreme Court of Alabama in 1837 reviewed the case of a free Negro, apparently, named McDonald, who was accused of trying to instigate an insurrection among the slaves. He had talked with a slave named Moses about plans of raising a slave army of five hundred men who would seize arms and ammunition, march to Mobile or Pensacola, and press a ship to carry the conspirators to Texas, which he called a free land. The court held that since no actual or meditated insurrection took place, the conviction of the defendant was unauthorized.[68]

A case was appealed to the Supreme Court of Louisiana in 1851 involving a yeoman named Read. The latter had been indicted for uttering the following language in public discourse: "The Negroes . . . are as free as the white men. This is a free country, and that the Negroes have no right to call any man master. . . ." The jury found the accused guilty, though recommending him to the mercy of the court, but the trial judge condemned him to hard labor in the penitentiary for five years. The Supreme Court, however, arrested judgment in this case, Chief Justice Eustis declaring: "The indictment contains no charge of any criminal intent, and the word *feloniously* . . . is omitted, . . . nor is it charged that the words were uttered in the presence . . . of slaves or persons of color. . . . When a man's life is put in jeopardy for language made use of, we think the language itself ought to be charged in the indictment . . . with the same particularity as a libel."[69]

---

[67] Jones, *Reports,* VII, 489-494.
[68] Catterall, *Judicial Cases Concerning American Slavery and the Negro,* III, 141-142.   [69] *Ibid.,* III, 613-614.

The surprising fact about Southern laws curtailing freedom of discussion is that they were so rarely invoked. For
considerable periods, especially in Virginia and North Carolina, they were allowed to become dead letter laws, and were
revived only in time of alarm or passion, as during the violent
excitement of 1835-36 or after the John Brown raid. Otherwise, persons of Southern birth might express antislavery opinions almost with legal impunity. The courts, also, when called
into action, tended to moderate the harshness of the written
code, and to throw the mantle of protection around minorities.
There was, of course, always the silent pressure of public disapprobation, and occasionally the violence of the mob.[70]

In one respect the Southern people were highly intolerant
at all times, in their attitude toward "foreign emissaries" and
toward the insulting publications of the North. Rhodes is
probably right when he says: "While the Southern advocates
of the rightfulness of slavery were heard willingly at the North
in joint debate, or from the lyceum platform, the life of a
Garrison or Parker would have been forfeited had they gone
South and attempted to get a hearing."[71] It was precisely
against the activities of this type of person that the Southern
laws were passed and enforced, rather than to suppress the
discussions of moderate Southern men. Whether the Southern
States should have exercised forbearance and permitted the
bold Northern crusader to speak freely in regard to slavery is
a grave question that different ages would answer differently.

[70] Andrew Jackson proposed ostracizing those who sympathized with the abolitionists. He advised Postmaster General Kendall that abolition papers should be
delivered by Southern postmasters only to subscribers who demanded them; "and
in every instance the Postmaster ought to take the names down, and have them
exposed thro the publik journals as subscribers to this wicked plan of exciting
the negroes to insurrection and to massacre . . . few men in society will be
willing to acknowledge that they are encouraging by subscribing for such papers
this horrid and most wicked procedure; and when they are known, every moral
and good citizen will unite to put them in coventry, and avoid their society. This,
if adopted would put their circulation down everywhere, for there are few so
hardened in villainy, as to withstand the frowns of all good men" (letter to Amos
Kendall, Aug. 9, 1835, in John Spencer Bassett, ed., *Correspondence of Andrew
Jackson*, Washington, D. C., 1931, V, 360-361).

[71] J. F. Rhodes, *History of the United States from the Compromise of 1850 to the
End of the Roosevelt Administration* (New York, 1928), I, 375.

Chapter VI

THE CALHOUN INFLUENCE

In the decline of Jeffersonian liberalism, the agitation of sectional politicians was a potent and insidious instrument. This imponderable force might well be called "the Calhoun influence," since Calhoun was the greatest and the most articulate of the Southern politicians who agitated the slavery issue. His figure looms above his contemporaries in the ante-bellum South and raises the question whether his magnetic leadership was responsible for a new orientation of Southern thought. The answer to this riddle involves "the great man theory" of history, the assumption that the personality of some great leader gives character and direction to his period. If any individual in the land of Dixie played the role of "the great man" it was Calhoun. Did he lead the South astray, or was his influence on the destinies of his section negligible as compared with the dominant economic trends and intellectual currents of his day?

Calhoun was the South's most profound political theorist since the time of Jefferson. But his political theory was only a logical statement of the *status quo* in the South Carolina of his day. The mighty authority of the dead Greek philosopher, Aristotle, happened to harmonize with and justify such a political state as he saw before his eyes. Thus Aristotle took a place in his trinity of the Constitution, the Bible, and Aristotle —all agreeing with the infallible mind of Calhoun. Boldly he discarded those elements of Jeffersonian liberalism that did not suit the new trends in Southern life. Vernon Parrington has called him a realist, because he frankly recognized that men are unequal, that liberty is the reward of capacity and not the birthright of all, and that the natural rights philosophy is largely a dream. In place of the contract theory of government, which had exalted the individual, he taught that government was an organic function of society, a doctrine that exploded the old idea of the eighteenth-century aristocrats that government was a necessary evil.[1]

The South, a minority within the nation, needed a political theory of defense. Calhoun fashioned it. No more ingenious devices could have been contrived for that purpose than his doctrine of the concurrent majority and his application of the dogma of indivisible sovereignty to the older Jeffersonian concept of States' rights. Calhoun observed that the numerical majority can be as tyrannical as the most absolute despot. It is the duty of a genuine constitutional government, therefore, to protect the rights of minorities from a selfish and unscrupulous numerical majority. The safeguard which Calhoun offered was the concurrent voice, by which no action affecting the vital interests of the minority should be adopted unless the minority and the majority concurred.[2] His practical proposal was the adoption of the state veto. There was wisdom, in truth, in this advocacy of balance in the national life, of the majority listening to the minority, of recognizing the virtue of compromise in a country of such vast proportions and of such diverse economic interests as the United States.

Furthermore, certain elements in his political theory, especially its emphasis on the protection of the rights of minorities, made a permanent contribution to the preservation of freedom in the nation. For this recognition of the supreme importance of protecting minority rights contained the seed of tolerance. But Calhoun's defiant eyes, beneath their shaggy brows, looked far off beyond the Potomac to curbing the Federal power, and failed to see the imperative need of protecting intellectual minorities, the critics and dissenters within the frontiers of the South. Had he possessed the culture of Jefferson,

[1] Sources for the study of Calhoun's ideas on government are found in his "Disquisition on Government" and "Discourse on the Constitution and Government of the United States," in Richard K. Crallé (ed.), *The Works of John C. Calhoun* (New York, 1888), Vol. I. See also the excellent commentaries by C. E. Merriam, *A History of American Political Theories* (New York, 1920), pp. 228-242, 267-284, and by Parrington, *The Romantic Revolution in America*, pp. 69-82.

[2] See J. T. Carpenter, *The South as a Conscious Minority 1789-1861* (New York, 1930), chap. v.

had he been less provincial, he might have realized the evils of slavery and the wisdom of tolerating the expression of anti-slavery opinions. Instead, he applied his doctrine of the protection of minorities only to the defense of the economic and political interests of the planter class against the Northern majority. His practical influence, moreover, on his own generation was to accentuate the development of an intolerant spirit in the South. From the philosopher's pedestal he stepped down to lead the politicians and fire-eaters who agitated the slavery "issue." Perhaps his greatest influence on his section was exerted in this role of agitator, seeking to arouse and unite the South to a stern resistance against the abolition movement.

The opponents of Calhoun maintained that his towering ambition to be elected President played a dominant part in determining his agitation of the slavery question. A bitter enemy, Thomas Hart Benton, made the charge that the South Carolina leader, after the subsiding of the nullification excitement, sought a new issue with which to inflame the South.[3] Opposition to the tariff did not offer as universal an appeal to Southern prejudices (especially to the sugar interests of Louisiana) as did the slavery question. Therefore this ambitious politician seized upon the latter issue as a steppingstone to the Presidency. James Knox Polk confided to his diary that Calhoun mounted the slavery controversy as a political hobby to keep himself before the public in his designs on the Presidency.[4] In the spring of 1850 Fredrika Bremer saw the funeral procession of Calhoun pass by and observed the idolatry of the dead leader on the part of the South Carolinians, but, conversing with Joel Poinsett at his plantation on the Pee Dee River, she learned that this wise old gentleman thought that Calhoun had been great only in ambition.[5]

Nor have the historians been kinder to his memory. According to a recent student of the antislavery movement, Cal-

[3] Thomas Hart Benton, *Thirty Years' View* (New York, 1854), I, 612.
[4] M. M. Quaife (ed.), *The Diary of James K. Polk, during His Presidency, 1845 to 1849* (Chicago, 1910), II, 458.
[5] Bremer, *The Homes of the New World*, I, 298-299, 304-305.

houn began his violent agitation against the reception of abolition petitions in Congress because he saw splendid political
capital in opposing them.[6] James Ford Rhodes found the
spring of action in Calhoun in his "restless craving for the
presidency."[7] An eminent Southern historian has even suggested that the failure of the country to elect him chief magistrate may have been directly responsible for the Civil War.[8]
The real monument to Calhoun, a New England scholar
has written, was not the marble shaft erected to his memory
in St. Philip's Churchyard, but the graves of young men and
a South ruined by the Civil War.[9]

This traditional view of Calhoun, however, needs correc-
tion. He was more devoted to principle and less subject to
expediency than any of the prominent statesmen of the period.
"His theories and his sense of duty alone dominated him,"
wrote Varina Howell Davis with a woman's shrewd percep-
tion of character.[10] The fat Senator Dixon H. Lewis, who
knew Calhoun intimately, admired the latter's aloofness from
petty politics and electioneering.[11] In a similar vein Rev. William Barnwell declared shortly after the death of Calhoun that
the unbounded influence of the statesman in his native state
was not due to the arts of a demagogue.[12] The editor of
the New Orleans *Picayune* came near to a true estimate of the
Carolina leader in his editorial on the "Death of Calhoun."
He pointed out that Calhoun had "breasted a flood of adverse
public opinion" during his life, and that his support of nullification was an act of "self-immolation." The Carolinian had
unfortunately carried his love for his native South into fanati-

---

[6] Barnes, *The Antislavery Impulse*, p. 110.

[7] Rhodes, *History of the United States*, I, 41-45.

[8] William E. Dodd, *Statesmen of the Old South* (New York, 1926), pp. 110-111.

[9] S. E. Morison, *The Oxford History of the United States, 1783-1917* (London, 1928), II, 104.

[10] Varina Howell Davis, *Memoir*, I, 211.

[11] Dixon H. Lewis to Calhoun, May 6, 1845 (MS in Clemson College Library). The Calhoun papers in the Clemson College Library contain many unpublished letters written to Calhoun.

[12] J. P. Thomas (ed.), *The Carolina Tribute to Calhoun* (Columbia, S. C., 1857), p. 202.

cism.[13] But the greatest tribute to the essential nobility of Calhoun's character was paid by Robert Barnwell Rhett. "Altho' my who[le] public-life," he wrote in 1854, "seems to me to have been a failure and to have ended in vanity, yet I thank God, that so much of it was spent in association with one so worthy of my esteem and admiration. . . . We fought for the South. He fell dead in the cause—I, living. Had he lived we would together have conquered. As it is—neither of us will be able to vindicate ourselves. But time will do it for us—at least for him, for my name will be too feeble to be connected with his great fame."[14]

Calhoun's efforts to alarm and arouse the Southern people over the menace of abolition were based on a clearer view of the future than most of his contemporaries could conceive. This clairvoyance caused him to urge a policy of "forcing the issue" before the North had grown too strong.[15] So convinced was he of the rightness of his vision that he became perhaps the most uncompromising man in the South. He became the statesman of the ultimatum. But he was in no sense a pioneer in agitating the explosive question. Senator William Smith, Governor George McDuffie, Dr. Thomas Cooper, Thomas R. Dew, and others had earlier developed aggressively the proslavery dialectic.[16] The Southern people, indeed, were moving rapidly forward to an intolerant position on the slavery question when the Carolina statesman assumed command of the extreme proslavery faction.

From a quiescent defense of the South's peculiar institution, Calhoun was aroused to a militant mood by the deluge of antislavery petitions that began to inundate Congress in 1835-36. Two practicable ways were open to Southern states-

[13] New Orleans *Picayune*, April 2, 1850. The editor of the *Picayune* had been a severe critic of the ultraism of Calhoun.

[14] Rhett to Richard K. Crallé, Oct. 25, 1854 (*American Historical Review*, XIII, 312, Jan., 1908).

[15] J. F. Jameson (ed.), "Correspondence of John C. Calhoun," *Annual Report of the American Historical Association for the Year 1899* (Washington, D. C., 1900), II, 386, 416.

[16] See Jenkins, *Pro-Slavery Thought in the Old South*, pp. 65-81.

men in dealing with these petitions. One course of action, which was advocated by Senator Bedford Brown of North Carolina, Felix Grundy of Tennessee, Senator King of Georgia, Henry Clay of Kentucky, and Calhoun's own colleague, W. C. Preston of South Carolina, was to ignore the abolitionists as much as possible, to dispose of their petitions with the least agitation. This group feared the consequences of denying virtually the right of petition. They warned the Southern extremists that their course of agitation in the halls of Congress was precisely what the abolitionists wished, and that if the cause of the abolitionists should become identified with "the sacred right of petition," the sentiment of the Northern people, a vast majority of whom abhorred the fanatics, would change.[17]

Deliberately Calhoun rejected this conciliatory course in favor of a policy of meeting the enemy "on the frontier." The true policy of the South, he urged, was to vote against receiving abolition petitions, for their reception would recognize the jurisdiction of Congress over slavery. "If there must be an issue," he said, "now is our time. We never can be more united or better prepared for the struggle, and I, for one, would much rather meet the danger now, than turn it over to those who are to come after us."[18] But his fellow Southerners would not stand beside him at this pass of Thermopylae. They adopted, instead, a compromise presented by a South Carolina Congressman, the famous Pinckney Gag of 1836, which provided for receiving the petitions but immediately laying them upon the table without debate.

Another occasion arose in this same year for Calhoun to alarm and arouse the South over the slavery issue. President Jackson had suggested to Congress the advisability of passing

[17] *Congressional Globe*, II, 79-80 (1835-36); IV, 37 (1837-38). For a résumé, see Crallé, *Works of John C. Calhoun*, III, 140-202.

[18] Crallé, *Works of John C. Calhoun*, II, 486. A few years later he reiterated this advice: "The true policy is to take bold ground and force an issue as soon as possible" (Calhoun to J. R. Mathews, Feb. 24, 1838, Calhoun MSS in Library of Congress).

laws to prevent the circulation of incendiary abolition publications through the mails. Calhoun opposed this method of dealing with the danger.[19] As chairman of a special committee he made an inflammatory report on the subject and introduced a bill which would leave to the states the authority to determine what were incendiary publications. Congress should merely pass a law prohibiting postmasters from receiving or transmitting through the mails publications whose circulation was prohibited by the states. Calhoun's report expressed the extreme States' rights interpretation of the Constitution. The laws of nations were declared to be in force between the sovereign states, except in so far as modified by the compact. One of these laws was that a nation is obligated to suppress subversive propaganda against a neighboring state. The Southern States were justified in demanding that their Northern neighbors suppress the abolition societies and presses.[20]

Calhoun, wrote Benton, alarmed the South by his insidious report on incendiary publications. He made it appear that there was an impending danger of the abolition of slavery in all the slave states.[21] There is no denying that this report portrayed the consequences of the abolitionist propaganda, if unchecked, in the darkest colors—the instigation of servile war, with all its horrors, the degradation of both races in the South, the destruction of property worth nine hundred and fifty millions, and the bursting of the bonds of the Union, engulfing the country in a sea of blood.

Yet the Carolinian looked far ahead of his time, and his fears were thoroughly justified. He declared that he did not fear the circulation of these incendiary publications in the slaveholding states, for the people of those states were protected. But he viewed with consternation the effect of these inflammatory publications upon the population of the non-slaveholding states. The abolition societies were infusing their

[19] See Calhoun's autobiography, attributed to R. M. T. Hunter, entitled *Life of John C. Calhoun, presenting a Condensed History of Political Events from 1811 to 1843* (New York, 1843), p. 58.

[20] Crallé, *Works of John C. Calhoun*, V, 201-202.

[21] Benton, *op. cit.*, I, 584.

poison into the rising generation, teaching one whole section to hate another. Inevitably the result would be the destruction of the Union. He sincerely believed that the way to preserve the Union was to suppress the abolitionists.

At the close of the year 1837 the state of Vermont introduced resolutions in Congress urging the abolition of slavery in the District of Columbia and the prohibition of the internal slave trade. These resolutions by a sovereign state provoked Calhoun to a defense of slavery as it existed in the South. "This agitation," he declared, "has produced one happy effect, at least—it has compelled us of the South to look into the nature and character of this great institution, and to correct many false impressions that even we had entertained in relation to it. Many in the South once believed that it was a moral and political evil. That folly and delusion are gone. We see it now in its true light, and regard it as the most safe and stable basis for free institutions in the world."[22] It was left to James Henry Hammond to state explicitly "the mudsill theory" of slavery.[23] But Calhoun in various speeches in the Senate affirmed that slavery was a positive good, that it was the best solution to the race problem, and that it freed the South from the evils of a conflict between capital and labor.

From 1835 to his death in 1850 Calhoun was an agitator and an alarmist on the slavery issue. "The great point is to rouse the South and to unite it," he wrote to a Charleston follower.[24] His effectiveness as an agitator was weakened, however, by his devotion to abstract ideas. Supremely confident in the infallibility of his reason, he introduced abstract resolutions in Congress, which seemed to him to be indisputably the truth and destined to triumph. Such an addiction to metaphysics and to pushing logic to extreme limits was a decided drawback to him in politics. None the less, he made few of the usual concessions adopted by politicians to win the fickle favor

[22] Crallé, *Works of John C. Calhoun,* III, 179-180.
[23] Jenkins, *Pro-Slavery Thought in the Old South,* pp. 286-287.
[24] Calhoun to H. W. Conner, July 3, 1844 (Henry William Conner Papers, 1843-50, photostats in Library of Congress).

of the people. He devised no popular slogans; he scorned the florid oratory characteristic of his period; he refused to electioneer by speech-making tours. On the other hand, led by an unquenchable ambition to be President, he wrote a campaign biography in 1843, whose authorship was assumed by R. M. T. Hunter at Calhoun's request, and he carried on an extensive correspondence with his political lieutenants in different parts of the country. Too much of a philosopher, he could not qualify as a natural agitator, but was forced into this role by a keen realization of the dangerous minority position of the South.

This underdog psychology of the Southern people was accentuated by the quarrel that flared up between the sections over the Wilmot Proviso. Calhoun took a prominent part in inflaming Southern opinion over this question. "We ought rather than to yield an inch, take any alternative, even if it should be disunion," he wrote.[25] The territory recently conquered from Mexico, he pointed out, had been purchased by the common blood and the common treasure of both sections. Any discrimination against slaveholders carrying their human property into this region would be a denial to the South of equality in the Union. It made little difference to him or other Southern extremists that the territorial question was largely an abstraction, since the vast semiarid regions of the Southwest were not suited to the extension of slavery.[26] Southerners could not submit to such debasement, he declared, without destroying their honor and the spirit of freemen.

In thus appealing to "Southern honor," Calhoun was exploiting a powerful emotional force that warped cool and realistic consideration of Southern problems. Southern honor was really a romantic concept. It was an obligation to assert "the rights" of the South, even when those rights were abstractions or were likely to plunge the country into internecine war. The "rights" which honor required the South to assert were equal-

[25] Jameson, "Correspondence of John C. Calhoun," p. 763.
[26] See Chauncey S. Boucher, "*In Re* That Aggressive Slavocracy," *Mississippi Valley Historical Review*, VIII, 48 (June-Sept., 1921).

ity in the territories (i.e., the claim of the slaveholder to carry his slaves into the territories) and freedom from "the subjugation" of the Black Republican party. The Charleston *Mercury* quoted Alexander H. Stephens, a statesman who had arisen from the yeomanry, as saying that the Southern people should assert their rights, "at any hazard, though there be nothing at stake but their honor."[27] The truculent governor of Virginia, Henry A. Wise, declared that although he loved the Union, he would not hesitate to burst its bonds, if Southern honor were touched by as much as a pin prick.[28] Such statements were considered idle threats in the North, but often they were the expressions of a quixotic romanticism. Calhoun rationalized the romantic concept of "Southern honor" by warning his countrymen that nothing but disaster would result from yielding any of their rights. They could not hope to placate the North by so doing, but would only encourage the Northern antislavery men to further aggression and at the same time weaken Southern morale.

The most striking document to arouse the people that the Carolina strategist drew up was the "Address of the Southern Delegates in Congress to their Constituents," written in 1849. In this appeal to his compatriots Calhoun stated the Southern grievances—the violation of the Fugitive Slave Act by Northern states, the ceaseless agitation of the abolition societies, and the attempt to exclude the Southern slaveholders from the territory recently conquered from Mexico. He depicted the direful consequences of an emancipation of the slaves by a dominant majority in the North. The freedmen would be elevated to a political and social equality with their former owners by giving them the right of voting and of holding office. They would then become the firm political allies of the North and hold the Southern whites in subjection. To prevent this prostration of the white race, what must South-

---

[27] Dwight L. Dumond (ed.), *Southern Editorials on Secession* (New York, 1931), p. 41.

[28] Charleston *Mercury,* Oct. 8, 1856. Speech of Wise delivered in Corinthian Hall, Richmond, Sept. 20, 1856.

erners do? Calhoun's answer was for the South to unite, disregarding party ties and party success, anxiety for which had
formerly paralyzed their efforts for self-defense. The resolute
stand of a united section would cause the North to pause and
calculate the consequences.[29] In his very last remarks in the
Senate, on March 5, 1850, condemning the conciliatory speech
of the Mississippi Senator Foote, Calhoun pointed out that
every portion of the North entertained feelings more or less
hostile to the South. His last days were devoted to feverish and
despairing activity in urging the calling of the Nashville Convention and in preparing the Southern mind for secession.

The influence of Calhoun on his section was not fully revealed until ten years after his death. When South Carolina
left the Union, the citizens of Charleston paid tribute to his
leadership by unfurling a banner bearing a picture of his
statue. The news that South Carolina had seceded caused a
crowd in New Orleans jubilantly to deck the bust of Calhoun
with a cockade.[30] His ceaseless agitation of the necessity of the
South to resist the aggressions of the North and his dogma of
state sovereignty had borne fruit. The leading Secessionists
were devout followers of Calhoun, like Robert Barnwell Rhett,
W. L. Yancey, Albert Gallatin Brown, Senator Louis Wigfall,
Jefferson Davis, and Roger Pryor. Just before his death Calhoun called Robert Toombs to a conference, at which he expressed his despair of the South's obtaining its rights within
the Union. Upon Toombs's shoulders as leader of the younger
group of Southern statesmen he let fall his mantle.[31] This
dynamic Georgian, more than any other individual, was responsible for the secession of his state.

The tragedy of Calhoun was that he loved the Union, and
yet took the very course to destroy it. His love of liberty and
his concern for what he regarded as the interests of his section,
were stronger than his attachment to the national govern-

[29] Crallé, *Works of John C. Calhoun*, VI, 290-313.
[30] Rhodes, *History of the United States*, III, 93.
[31] Phillips, *The Life of Robert Toombs*, p. 79.

ment.[32] Gifted to an uncanny degree with the power of prophecy, he saw only a dark future for the South. The only way that disaster could be averted from his native section, he proclaimed, was by suppressing the antislavery crusade and by giving the South a veto in Congress against hostile legislation. The New Orleans *Picayune* declared after the death of Calhoun that his statement should be accepted "that it was because he loved the Union that he uttered such fearful vaticinations of its fate" if his remedies should not be applied.[33]

What effect did this agitation of Calhoun and the fire-eaters have in arousing an intolerant spirit in the South? "He was the first, I believe, of great statesmen in the country," declared Rhett shortly after Calhoun's death, "who denounced the cant—that slavery is an evil—a curse."[34] More than any other propagandist for the righteousness of slavery, Calhoun could reach the popular ear. For a period of nearly fifteen years he spoke from the rostrum of the Senate urging a policy of no compromise with abolitionists. His speeches were spread broadcast over the South, through the newspapers and through printed pamphlets. To a people alert to the drama of politics they were more potent instruments of changing public opinion than the literary essays of Dew, Harper, and Simms.

His agency in converting many wavering minds to the belief that slavery was a positive good cannot be gauged. Judge Nathan Green testified in 1858: "I have long considered it [slavery] an evil. Until the last twenty-five years I never heard any well-informed Southern gentlemen give expression to any contrary sentiments. About that time Mr. Calhoun first announced the opinion that the institution was a desirable one. Now many Southern men following Mr. Calhoun—and pressed by aggressive attacks from the North—hold the same opinion."[35] Calhoun cleverly harmonized a support of slavery

[32] See Jameson, "Correspondence of John C. Calhoun," p. 716, and Crallé, *Works of John C. Calhoun*, IV, 531.

[33] New Orleans *Picayune*, April 2, 1850.

[34] Thomas, *The Carolina Tribute to Calhoun*, p. 360.

[35] *National Era*, Aug. 19, 1858.

with the deep democratic instinct of his constituents, or in the phrase of Vernon Parrington, he invoked the dream of a Greek democracy. Against the trend of the whole civilized world, he envisaged slavery as a permanent institution in the South, or at least one extending far into the future. He elevated its preservation above the saving of the Union. So closed was his mind to any other point of view that one of his reasons for opposing national nominating conventions was that Southerners would go to these conventions and fraternize with avowed abolitionists.[36]

Important as was his influence in establishing the cult of slavery and in popularizing secession, he was never able to attain a political ascendancy in the South. In his native state alone did he reign supreme. "For many years," wrote B. F. Perry, "Mr. Calhoun was absolute in South Carolina, and all who sought promotion in the State had to follow and swear by him. He thought for the State and crushed out all independence of thought in those below him."[37] But outside of South Carolina he had only a minority of devoted followers. The voluminous correspondence addressed to Calhoun, which is preserved at Clemson College, shows that he had many supporters scattered throughout the South, but it also demonstrates that they were fighting with their backs against the wall.[38] The stain of nullification could never be erased from Calhoun's escutcheon, and, besides, he was regarded as too theoretical and too extreme to be a safe leader. Howell Cobb, spokesman of the Georgia Democracy, wrote in 1849, "Calhoun is our evil genius."[39] Consequently, his frequent efforts to secure the Democratic nomination for the Presidency were always futile. The focal state of Virginia, under the

[36] Calhoun to H. W. Conner, April 4, 1848 (Conner photostats).

[37] Perry, *Reminiscences of Public Men*, p. 49.

[38] Some of the most valuable of these letters have been published by Chauncey S. Boucher and Robert P. Brooks, "Correspondence Addressed to John C. Calhoun, 1837-1849," *Annual Report of the American Historical Association for the Year 1929.*

[39] U. B. Phillips (ed.), "The Correspondence of Robert Toombs, Alexander H. Stephens, and Howell Cobb," *Annual Report of the American Historical Association for the Year 1911*, II, 164.

leadership of Thomas Ritchie, resolutely refused to vote for him, despite the zealous efforts of R. M. T. Hunter, James A. Seddon, and Richard K. Crallé.[40]

The inability of Calhoun to dominate the South politically was shown by his failure to build up a Southern bloc in Congress. His Address of the Southern Delegates in Congress of 1849 was signed by only forty-eight of the eighty-eight members of Congress who attended the Southern caucus. None of the Senators from Kentucky, Maryland, North Carolina, Tennessee, Georgia, or Texas signed it.[41] The Whigs attended the meeting to control and crush it. Robert Toombs bluntly told Calhoun that "the Union of the South was neither possible nor desirable until we were ready to dissolve the Union."[42] Furthermore, President Polk was hostile to the movement, and, according to Calhoun, succeeded in keeping "the party hacks" from signing the address.[43] Howell Cobb, John H. Lumpkin of Georgia, and other prominent Democrats felt that Calhoun's Southern movement was unwise, since it was designed to destroy the national character of the Democratic party in the South, and make it purely sectional.[44]

Calhoun's agency in causing his section to abandon the liberal principles of Jefferson and Madison was only one of many contributory factors. Following the development of cotton as the great Southern staple, the stage was set for a profound social change in the land of Dixie. Calhoun stepped upon the stage, not as a creator of public opinion, but as the articulate voice of certain social trends. When he changed from the pursuit of a nationalist career to a sectional course during the nullification controversy, he did it reluctantly, apparently

[40] See Duff Green to R. K. Crallé, Sept. 5, 11, 1831; Feb. 17, 1832 (Duff Green Letters, 1831-53, MSS in Library of Congress); Thomas C. Reynolds, editor of the Petersburg *Republican,* a Calhoun organ, to Calhoun, July 29, 1844 (Calhoun MSS at Clemson College). See especially various letters in C. H. Ambler (ed.), "Correspondence of R. M. T. Hunter, 1826-1876," *Annual Report of the American Historical Association for the Year 1916,* Vol. II.

[41] Gaillard Hunt, *John C. Calhoun* (Philadelphia, 1907), p. 307.

[42] *Correspondence of Toombs, Stephens, and Cobb,* pp. 139, 141-142.

[43] Calhoun to H. W. Conner, Feb. 2, 1849 (Conner photostats).

[44] *Correspondence of Toombs, Stephens, and Cobb,* p. 164.

forced by the minor political leaders of the state.[45] Some of
his friends outside of South Carolina urged him to step forward and arrest the nullification movement, for fear that it
would ruin his chances to be President. To Virgil Maxcy of
Tulip Hill, Maryland, he wrote that it was a great mistake to
think that he could quiet the excitement in his state over the
tariff. On the contrary, for him "to attempt to stay the present
current would be madness."[46] In truth, if Calhoun wished to
remain in public life, it was necessary for him to represent the
dominant sentiment of his section. His powerlessness to
change the direction in which the Southern States were moving is indicated also by their utter disregard of his warnings
of the folly of the Mexican War.[47]

In the decline of free thought and speech below the Potomac, the significance of Calhoun lies primarily in his role as
an agitator. He was the chief of a group of politicians and
sectional statesmen who exploited the slavery issue and created
stereotypes in the minds of the Southern people that produced
intolerance. The lesser fry were not imitators of the Carolina
leader, but collaborators. These politicians of the ante-bellum
period would not have resorted to such issues as the slavery
question and "Southern honor" if they had not been popular.
They waved the flag of "white supremacy" and of "equality
within the Union" as vigorously and effectively as the politicians during Reconstruction days flaunted "the bloody shirt."
In so doing they stirred the fires of intolerance and contributed
to the suppression of the mild antislavery man within the borders of the South as well as the reckless radical.

Northern politicians and editors were also guilty of gener-
ating sectional hate and intolerance in their struggle for power.
Violent partisans like Slade of Vermont, Joshua K. Giddings,
Ben Wade, and Charles Sumner aroused bitter passions in the

[45] See D. F. Houston, *A Critical Study of Nullification in South Carolina* (Cambridge, Mass., 1896), and C. S. Boucher, *The Nullification Controversy in South
Carolina* (Chicago, 1916).

[46] Calhoun to Virgil Maxcy, Sept. 11, 1830 (Galloway, Maxcy, Markoe Papers).

[47] For a good account, see Meigs, *The Life of John Caldwell Calhoun*, II, 381-
390.

North against Southern people. The splendid opportunity for emotional propaganda arising from the struggle in Kansas between the free state and proslavery factions was utilized to the full by Republican politicians and editors in the North. During "the bleeding Kansas" episode, the Baltimore *Sun* condemned those Northern agitators, who, for the sake of political effect, exaggerated conditions in Kansas and tried to irritate Northern feeling against the Southern people by a campaign of vilification and misrepresentation.[48] The Northern press feasted its readers on horrible stories from Kansas, the editor maintained, to win votes for Frémont.[49] He predicted that Kansas would continue to be "one vast field of blood—in the newspapers" until the Presidential campaign had ended.

Doubtless many of the office seekers appealing to the shirt-sleeve democracy of the South used the issue of white supremacy insincerely. In the early stages of the slavery controversy Thomas Ritchie accused the Virginia Whigs of trying to create a panic over abolitionist activities in order to defeat Van Buren. Vincent Witcher, said the wily editor, carried in his pocket the worst pamphlets of "the fanatics" and the most odious pictures he could obtain from Gerrit Smith, Tappan, and Company. He exhibited them to the inhabitants of Pittsylvania County "by way of frightening his people into Whiggery, as if they were so many children."[50]

Benjamin F. Perry, the editor of the Greenville *Mountaineer,* was disgusted at this exploitation of the slavery issue by the politicians. On August 8, 1835, he wrote in his diary that the Nullifiers had exploited the excitement over the abolition pamphlets found at Charleston. The extreme proslavery newspapers were making extracts from these pamphlets and doing the very thing that the fanatics wished. "The course which the Southern people ought to pursue," he wrote, "is one of profound silence on the subject of slavery."[51] By constantly writing and talking about the abolitionists and printing extracts from their incendiary pamphlets, the Southern people

[48] Baltimore *Sun*, Aug. 30, 1856.   [49] *Ibid.*, Sept. 9, 1856.
[50] Richmond *Enquirer*, April 1, 1836.   [51] Diary, Aug. 8, 1835.

might excite their slaves to an insurrection.[52] Furthermore, the agitation of the slavery question, he thought, was the only thing that would unite the whole South against the North.

Patriots of an older generation, such as Joel Poinsett, William A. Graham and Sam Houston, looked with sadness upon the agitation of the slavery question by politicians. To Edward Coles, Poinsett wrote on March 28, 1851: "Depend upon it the interests of the slaveholder and the slave, the bond and the free throughout these United States will best be promoted by calming as early and as far as possible the dangerous agitation, which originated and has been kept up by political Demagogues for their own sordid purposes."[53] William A. Graham of North Carolina, Vice-Presidential candidate of the Whigs in 1852, pointed out that it was regarded as fine party capital, both in the North and in the South, to go to extremes in denouncing the other section or in supporting or in attacking slavery.[54] Blunt, realistic, old Sam Houston was disgusted with the Southern politicians who agitated the slavery "issue," which could only have the effect of increasing excitement on this subject and of producing an incurable discord between the two sections.[55]

The pernicious work of agitation was carried on after Calhoun's death by orators and politicians like James H. Hammond, Robert Barnwell Rhett, David Yulee, Senator Iverson, W. L. Yancey, Albert Gallatin Brown, and Henry A. Wise. Senator Albert Gallatin Brown was one of the most colorful of these later agitators. He represented the poor whites and small slaveholders of Mississippi, who sustained him at the polls by an unbroken line of victories from 1833 to 1861. Brown was more intolerant, more violent and bombastic in his denunciation of antislavery men and the Northern people

[52] The *United States Telegraph,* Calhoun's organ in Washington, was one of the offenders. On April 16, 1833, for example, Duff Green published choice inflammatory extracts from the *Emancipator.*
[53] Joel R. Poinsett Papers, XVI, 191.
[54] Letter from W. A. Graham, Nov. 17, 1858 (William A. Graham Papers, MSS in archives of North Carolina Historical Commission).
[55] New Orleans *Picayune,* March 17, 1849.

than was Jefferson Davis, who represented the planting interest in the Democratic party.[56] An example of Brown's technique in arousing the intolerance of the poor man toward any
movement for freeing the slaves was his dark prophecy of
what would happen after emancipation. "The rich will flee
the Country," he warned. "Then the non-slaveholder will begin to see what his real fate is. The Negro . . . will insist on
being treated as an equal . . . that his son shall marry the
white man's daughter, and the white man's son his daughter.
. . . Then will commence a war of races such as has marked
the history of San Domingo."[57]

These fire-eaters were the Southern counterpart of the abolitionists. Some of them, like Yancey or Edmund Ruffin, were
as unselfishly devoted to the cause of the South as Garrison or
Weld was to the cause of the slave.[58] Extremes tend to produce extremes. The violent attacks of the abolitionists built
up a war psychosis in the South. It was not rhetoric that
caused Henry A. Wise of Virginia to exclaim when only ten
Senators voted against receiving abolition petitions: "The
South lies low and bleeding. Oh, God! for energy for the
occasion."[59] He felt an overmastering resentment at the unjust attacks of "the fanatics" and a corresponding deep sectional patriotism. In such a war-charged atmosphere tolerance was difficult to maintain. The ceaseless agitation of the
slave question by politicians, by fire-eaters, and by political-
minded editors must be put down as one of the major causes
for the decline of liberal thought and free speech in the Old
South.

[56] Ranck, *Albert Gallatin Brown,* pp. 20, 147-148, 180.
[57] Quoted by Avery Craven in a review of Ranck's *Albert Gallatin Brown,* in
American Historical Review, XLIV, 412 (Jan., 1939).
[58] See Avery Craven, *Edmund Ruffin, Southerner* (New York, 1932), chaps.
iii, v, and vii.
[59] Wise to a person in Gloucester County, Va. (name torn from the letter),
March 12, 1836 (Henry A. Wise MSS in Library of Congress). See also Clement
Eaton, "Henry A. Wise and the Virginia Fire Eaters of 1856," *Mississippi Valley
Historical Review,* XXI, 495-512 (March, 1935).

CHAPTER VII

THE FREEDOM OF THE PRESS IN THE UPPER SOUTH

IN EVERY AGE there are certain subjects of high emotional voltage which it is perilous for editors to discuss. The danger consists, not in the conflict with laws and the police, but in opposing some powerful vested interest or some overwhelming popular prejudice. Obviously an editor must conduct his paper so that it will have adequate financial support. The subject that was most dangerous to discuss in the Old South was the eradication of slavery. Since most Southern editors sincerely agreed with their readers on the slavery question, they did not feel that their freedom of discussion was limited. Furthermore, they felt that no useful purpose was to be served by opening their columns to antislavery communications.

The editor with reforming tendencies, on the other hand, had to face the hostility of slaveowners who feared a loss of property from unrestrained discussion of emancipation. Not only were four billion dollars of property at stake, but conservative men foresaw the disastrous effect of sudden liberation upon the whole economic life of the section.[1] Penetrating critics like Olmsted pointed out that the sentiment for emancipation in the Southern States waxed and waned with the price of cotton and slaves. The intangible influence of the slave power was so great, he declared, that if any man had the audacity to offer himself as a candidate for political office in Virginia on the platform of abolition of slavery, there probably would not be a single newspaper in the state that could afford to support him.[2] Yet the slaveowners seldom spoke of the influence of

[1] The enormous decline of agricultural production in the British West Indies after the adoption of emancipation was frequently cited as proof of the folly of liberating the Southern slaves. See E. N. Elliott, *Cotton Is King and Pro-Slavery Arguments* (Augusta, Ga., 1860), pp. 139-149; for a modern study, see L. J. Ragatz, *The Fall of the Planter Class in the British Caribbean, 1763-1833* (New York, 1928).

[2] Olmsted, *Seaboard Slave States*, pp. 248, 301.

their vested interests in determining the policy of silence which they sought to impose. Almost invariably the appeal was made to the need of safeguarding the community from the danger of servile insurrection. This argument for controlling the press appealed to the deepest instinct in human nature and was efficacious with the great mass of nonslaveholders.

Over the head of the outspoken editor frequently hung the sword of Damocles—the imminence of the *code duello*. Cartoonists exaggerated this unpleasant aspect of the journalistic profession in the South by portraying the Southern editor with a dueling pistol in one hand and a pen in the other. The feeling prevailed in many Southern communities, perhaps a hangover from frontier days, that it was cowardly and unmanly to resort to the courts to sue a man for slander or insult. Hence there was an astonishing mortality among Southern editors. A splendid example of how the practice of dueling constituted a threat to the freedom of the press in the Old South was the case of Benjamin F. Perry, whose attacks on the Nullifiers of South Carolina nearly cost him his life. They imported a rival editor to goad him to a duel and kill him. But the plot miscarried, for Perry killed his opponent on the dueling grounds on an island in the Tugalo River. Before this fatal encounter he wrote in his diary, "I commit myself to Almighty God for protection," and after his bloody victory he prayed fervently.[3] At the close of the ante-bellum period, Jennings Wise, editor of the Richmond *Enquirer*, a young man who prayed every night before retiring, fought eight duels in less than two years, in one of which he seriously wounded Sherrard Clemens, a Congressman from western Virginia.[4]

In the period 1800-30, before laws were adopted which limited the press in discussing slavery, the silent pressure of public opinion operated powerfully to control the press. The career of Joseph Gales, editor of the Raleigh *Register*, shows the limitations which a journalist was forced to recognize in a slave

[3] Benjamin F. Perry Diary, Aug. 5, 11, 23, 1832 (MS in Library of the University of North Carolina).

[4] John S. Wise, *The End of an Era* (Boston, 1902), pp. 95-96.

community.[5] In 1816 he was requested by some Quakers to publish an antislavery address which had been delivered before their Manumission Society. He replied in a frank letter: "I am not willing to insert it in the *Register*. It is on a subject which the people of the state will not hear discussed with temper at present, it might also produce consequences of a direful kind by getting into the hands of slaves, for many of them can read. I wish with you that an end could be put to slavery, but it will be of no use to attack the people's prejudices directly in the face, it must be brought about by slow but gradual means. If you wish the copy returned, say so, Yours Respectfully, Jo. Gales."[6]

The Quakers of North Carolina produced an editor who had the fiery spirit of a crusader in William Swain of the Greensborough *Patriot*. Swain belonged to that rare class of men who believe in toleration as a principle. Accepting enthusiastically Jefferson's sentiments on tolerance and the protection of minorities, he asserted the right of the people to hear a free discussion of all public subjects—since this is a government of opinion.[7] Immediately he received a letter from a canny old Tar Heel protesting against such a libertarian policy in respect to slavery, since "the people are so sensitive upon even the most delicate allusion to the subject that it might and probably would check the circulation of your paper and thus operate against its usefulness to meddle with it at all."[8]

Swain, however, never wavered from his original policy of conducting his newspaper as a fearless and independent critic of men and measures. One factor that made his journal so vital and interesting was that he opened its columns to letters from all types of people. In 1830 he revived a pamphlet written on the evils of slavery by a North Carolinian thirty years

[5] For a short sketch of Joseph Gales, see W. E. Dodd, *Nathaniel Macon* (Raleigh, N. C., 1903), p. 158.

[6] *Historical Papers of the Trinity College Historical Society*, IX-XII, 46. This letter is all the more valuable, since it comes from a man of such marked independence and courage. Gales had been editor of the Sheffield *Register* in England, whence he was driven on account of his liberalism.

[7] Greensborough *Patriot*, May 23, 1829.

[8] *Ibid.*, May 30, 1829.

before. Swain explained in a preface that he did not agree with everything in it, but published it as a remarkable product emanating from a slaveholding state. The old writer regarded slavery as a subject of "awful delicacy" about which there must be no rash expression of opinions. Nevertheless, he dared to maintain that the slave system was radically evil, that it was founded on injustice and cruelty, and that it was a fruitful source of pride, idleness, and tyranny.[9]

· When North Carolina passed her harsh laws on incendiary publications, Swain hurled back a defiance in two notable editorials. He declared that it had become an indictable offense to write or speak, or even to dream, on a subject so exceedingly "delicate" as slavery. Still, the evils of the institution ought to be discussed by the people, notwithstanding the prohibition of the civil authority. He served notice on all prosecuting officers who should try to enforce the gag laws that if they wanted business they must subscribe to his paper.[10] On November 19, 1834, he made an eloquent statement of his devotion to the liberty of the press and to the inviolable right of private opinion. "Before we will relinquish our right to think, speak, print, and publish our own deliberate opinions in relation to *public* men and *public* measures," he affirmed, "we will renounce existence itself. Take away our rights as a free man and life has no charms for us! We shall deal plainly with the people, not caring who may be affected by our course. We would rather bask for one hour in the approving smiles of an intelligent and undeceived people, than to spend a whole eternity amidst the damning grins of a motley crew of office-hunters, despots, demagogues, tyrants, fools and hypocrites."[11] His challenge was not accepted, for he was unmolested by the courts until his death.

Swain lived true to his faith despite the storms of opposition and condemnation which his course aroused. His tumultuous career as editor has been described by Levi Coffin, the North

[9] *Address to the People of North Carolina on the Evils of Slavery* (Greensborough, N. C., 1830).
[10] Greensborough *Patriot*, March 20, 1833.
[11] *Ibid.*, Nov. 19, 1834.

Carolina Quaker reputed to have been president of the underground railway: "He advocated the manumission of slaves,
and though he met with a storm of opposition and was assaulted by other papers, he continued his course boldly and
independently. He received letters from various parts of the
state full of threats and warnings. These he published in his
paper and replied to them in editorials. Many public speakers
and writers engaged in discussion with him, but they could
not cope with him and generally retired from the combat
much worsted."[12] He was fortunate, however, in the location
of his newspaper in Guilford County, which was the center
of Southern Quakerdom. After his death in 1834, the *Patriot*
lost its old fire and independence and became an intolerant
organ of the proslavery interests. Swain's example of fearless
discussion of slavery was not followed by any other newspaper
of the state.

In Tennessee the freedom of the press in respect to slavery
was championed only by two obscure editors in the eastern
part of the state, one of whom was Elihu Embree, a Quaker,
engaged in iron manufacturing near Jonesborough. Although
Embree remained a slaveholder until his death, he belonged
to the Manumission Society of Tennessee. In 1819 he began
to publish a weekly newspaper, the *Manumission Intelligencer,*
the title of which was later changed to the *Emancipator.* This
publication was the first periodical in the United States devoted
exclusively to the abolition of slavery. The organ of the Tennessee Manumission Society, it pursued a mild policy, pointing
out the moral sin of slavery, and urging its gradual eradication. Embree sent his paper to the governors of every state in
the Union. The governors of Georgia, North Carolina, Alabama, and Mississippi returned their copies. The chief executive of North Carolina wrapped his copy in such a fashion as to
cost Embree one dollar postage, while Governor Poindexter
of Mississippi subjected the Quaker editor to a charge of
twenty-five cents to inform him that he did not "wish to receive it on any terms." Poindexter declared that the publishing

[12] *Reminiscences of Levi Coffin* (Cincinnati, 1879), p. 74.

of the *Emancipator* was a mischievous effort to disturb the public tranquility and to interfere with the work of Providence in bringing an end to slavery.[13] Before Embree died in December, 1820, his courageous paper had attained a circulation of two thousand subscribers. After his death the torch of antislavery agitation was borne by Benjamin Lundy, who from 1821 to the summer of 1824 published the *Genius of Universal Emancipation* at Greeneville, Tennessee.[14]

The Virginia press, in the period 1800-30, did not dare to tread on the dangerous ground of discussing the evils of slavery. During the debate on emancipation in the Virginia legislature in 1832, Thomas Ritchie, editor of the Richmond *Enquirer,* observed: "The seals are broken which have been put for fifty years upon the most delicate and difficult subject of state concernment. We publish speeches in the House of Delegates to-day, which at no other period would have been delivered but behind closed doors. In the same spirit the press fearlessly speaks its own sentiments—unawed by the tocsin of denunciation or the menaces of proscription."[15] Another prominent Richmond editor, John Hampden Pleasants, described with rich imagery the bondage of the press. "In a free land, with a free Press," he wrote, "one subject was prohibited and guarded from free discussion with Turkish jealousy. Nat Turner, and the blood of his innocent victims have conquered the silence of fifty years. Exposed to the danger of having the throats of their wives and children cut any night in the year, men have broken the chains which a morbid sensibility imposed upon their tongues and hands. Imprisoned for years by this unreasonable jealousy, the thoughts of men have burst forth with warmth and vivacity proportioned to the long previous confinement."[16] These statements are confirmed by an examination of the files of the leading Virginia papers during that period. One striking exception to the general silence of the

[13] Murphy, *The Emancipator*, pp. 91, 111-112.
[14] Harvard University Library's file extends only from May, 1831, to Aug., 1832; the file of the Library of Congress covers only the years 1832-33.
[15] Richmond *Enquirer*, Jan. 19, 1832.   [16] Richmond *Whig*, Jan. 12, 1832.

Virginia press on the slavery question was a series of essays indirectly attacking slavery published by Samuel Janney in the Alexandria *Gazette* during 1827.

Unquestionably the press of the Upper South enjoyed its greatest freedom in the brief period immediately following the Nat Turner rebellion. At this crisis in the life of the state, Thomas Ritchie performed the most idealistic and courageous act in his tortuous career as a leader of opinion.[17] He demanded that the legislature, which was deliberating on the question of emancipation, should not disappoint the people by reporting a bill only to remove the free blacks. He described slavery as a great evil which had seriously crippled the progress of Virginia as revealed by contrast with the free states of the North. "We are not fanatics," he protested, "nor friends of the *Amis des Noirs*. But something ought to be done—means sure, but gradual, systematic, but discreet, ought to be adopted for reducing the mass of evil which is pressing upon the south, and will still more press upon her, the longer it is put off."[18] Nevertheless, he made the pessimistic prediction that nothing adequate would be done by the General Assembly to meet the crisis.

A few days afterwards, Ritchie received a letter from Senator Nathaniel Alexander of Mecklenburg County, one of the large slave counties of the state, cancelling his subscription.[19] Alexander followed this curt note by a public letter in the Richmond *Whig* attacking Ritchie. In this communication he said that all sensible men recognized the utter impracticability of any safe scheme of emancipation. Therefore, it was folly to stimulate fresh agitation of the subject, which could only result in stirring the blacks to further acts of violence. In order to crush the *Enquirer,* he proposed that meetings should be called "to take into consideration the propriety of discontinuing the use of that paper, as the only effectual means of making them feel your disapprobation of their untimely interfer-

[17] For the career of Ritchie, see C. H. Ambler, *Thomas Ritchie* (Richmond, 1913).   [18] Richmond *Enquirer,* Jan. 7, 1832.
[19] Printed by Ritchie in the *Enquirer,* Jan. 12, 1832.

ence with a question which so vitally concerns the peace and happiness of Eastern Virginia."[20] This protest was not the isolated voice of an individual, for soon thereafter a large proportion of the citizens of Mecklenburg County met in the courthouse at Boydton and issued a memorial in appreciation of the position of Senator Alexander and declaring that they would support no newspaper that advocated emancipation.[21]

The *Enquirer* replied to this attack by appealing to the sacred right of a free press, by quoting the venerable authority of Jefferson on emancipation, and by pointing out the moderate tone of its expressions. Ritchie was not daunted by such a storm of opposition, but continued to print the antislavery speeches made in the Virginia Assembly and to open his columns both to proslavery and antislavery advocates.[22] This celebrated debate on emancipation in the Virginia legislature was tremendously significant, for it was the last great effort of the Virginia liberals to deal with the slave problem.[23] As a result of the open debate in the Virginia legislature and the unwonted freedom of the press, many letters were printed in the columns of the *Enquirer* and the *Whig* discussing the absorbing topic of the hour. Some of them urged the adoption of a plan of gradual emancipation, but most of them, like that of "Old Planter," admonished the young bloods of the legislature not to meddle with property rights for the sake of gathering flowers of eloquence.[24]

The brilliant editor of the Richmond *Whig,* John Hampden Pleasants, took a prominent part in criticizing the slave regime. On January 17, 1832, he wrote an editorial promising to publish in full the debates on slave emancipation in the Virginia legislation. At the time that William Lloyd Garrison was waging his crusade against the slave master, Pleasants was making the bold prediction that slavery was doomed. He declared: "The moment statesmen were permitted to ex-

[20] Reprinted by Ritchie in the *Enquirer,* Jan. 12, 1832.
[21] Richmond *Whig,* Jan. 22, 1832.   [22] Richmond *Enquirer,* Jan. 12, 1832.
[23] For a discussion of the debate in the legislature, see T. M. Whitfield, *Slavery Agitation in Virginia, 1828-1832* (Baltimore, 1930), chap. iv.
[24] Richmond *Enquirer,* Jan. 31, 1832.

amine the moral foundation and the pernicious effect of slavery, and the press was unshackled to proclaim their sentiments and to combat in the cause of reason, justice, and the common good, that moment the decree of abolition was registered in the book of fate. It must be so, and it cannot be otherwise. This year may not see the vast work commenced, nor the next, nor the next; a half century may not see it completed. But commenced it *will be*—completed—completed it will be."[25] A few days later Pleasants wrote another earnest editorial, in which he prophesied that the slave master would be abandoned by the other classes—the mechanic, the small slaveholder, and the professional man—to fight alone for the maintenance of slavery.[26] The tone of the *Whig* editorials was more vehement and outspoken than that of its Democratic rival.

The most formidable attack on the freedom of the press at this time was made by a writer under the pseudonym, "Appomattox."[27] After the latter had shown the impossibility of a servile insurrection attaining success but the necessity for restrictive legislation, he took up the problem of how much freedom could be allowed the press in a slave state like Virginia. "Let us pay no regard to the claim which may be asserted for the independence of the press," "Appomattox" wrote; "if in the exercise of their independence, they choose to print, we in the exercise of our independence may choose to suppress, to the uttermost of our power, what we deem inflammatory, dangerous, mischievous. Every man has a perfect right to withdraw his subscription from any newspaper, and to discourage the circulation of it; and if he thinks the opinions it maintains likely to produce evil, he is bound in duty to his country, to exercise that right."[28] Therefore, he stoutly maintained, the newspapers that advocated emancipation in Virginia should

[25] Richmond *Whig*, Jan. 17, 1832.   [26] *Ibid.*, Jan. 20, 1832.
[27] Pleasants attributed this pamphlet to Benjamin Watkins Leigh, a prominent Whig (*ibid.*, Feb. 7, 1832).
[28] Published in Richmond *Enquirer*, Feb. 4, 1832.

be suppressed. He issued an earnest appeal to his fellow citizens to "discourage, every man by his own example, and by advice to his neighbors, the circulation among them of the Virginia abolition presses, upon the like reasons of common prudence, that would not tolerate the dissemination of writings wilfully incendiary."[29] The letter of "Appomattox" was unquestionably an able presentation of the point of view of the conservative classes.

This intolerant brochure aroused the liberal forces in the state and the champions of a free press. The editor of the Richmond *Whig* responded with a defiant editorial, branding the letter of "Appomattox" as an attempt to prevent the press of Virginia from discussing slavery by holding over them *in terrorem* the club of proscription. Comparing this effort to muzzle the press to the infamous Sedition Law of 1798, John Hampden Pleasants expressed his scorn of the perpetrators and declared that the people of Virginia would arise to the support of a press so threatened.[30] Ritchie also paid his respects to the author in the same issue in which he published the notable letter. "The author of *Appomattox,*" Ritchie wrote, "wishes us to exercise a sort of practical bull. He uses the liberty of the press for the purpose of extinguishing that liberty."[31] The editors of the *Enquirer,* he maintained, had kept a cool head, they had pursued a middle path between two extreme parties and had thus aroused the unfriendliness of both.

During these hectic days of 1832, meetings were held in eastern Virginia to condemn the discussion of emancipation by the legislature and by the press. The citizens of Northampton County drew up an address condemning the discussion of emancipation in the House of Delegates, a subject which the wisdom of past times considered fit only for secret

---

[29] *The Letter of Appomattox to the People of Virginia,* reprinted in pamphlet form (Richmond, 1832) by T. W. White, later proprietor and editor of the *Southern Literary Messenger.* See p. 29 of the pamphlet.

[30] *Constitutional Whig,* Feb. 6, 1832.   [31] Richmond *Enquirer,* Feb. 4, 1832.

deliberation, and of far too delicate and dangerous character to be openly debated. The memorial then directed attention to the widespread influence of the Richmond *Enquirer* and the *Whig*: "It behooves them, therefore, to be extremely cautious, how they admit into their columns articles of questionable tendency, or such as may mislead public opinion abroad in regard to the sentiments and intentions of Virginia upon this delicate subject."[32] The assembly demanded that the leading journals of the state should set an example of great circumspection and of reserve in referring to the emancipation of the slaves. Another meeting in Essex County, presided over by the aristocratic Dr. Austin Brockenborough, tried to organize public opinion to crush the freedom of the press in Virginia. It adopted resolutions threatening to discontinue all subscriptions of the members to newspapers that advocated the doctrine and projects of "the abolitionists in the last legislature." The meeting also demanded that the circulation of the abolition speeches made in the legislature should be suppressed, because they were capable of doing as much harm as the incendiary literature of the North.[33]

This assault on the press gave Ritchie an occasion to assert the independence of his newspaper. "In laying the proceedings of our fellow-citizens of Essex before our Readers," he wrote, "we give the strongest evidence we can furnish of the Liberty of the Press. That Press must be free, when those whose course is calculated to shackle its liberty, are free to use it as the organ of their sentiments."[34] John Hampden Pleasants also replied to the Essex assembly with his usual verve. He expressed a vehement contempt for such an effort to bind the press by appealing to the baser motives of the fears and interests of the editors. "Were all at the meeting in Essex and

---

[32] Richmond *Enquirer*, March 1, 1832. The influence of these newspapers in an era of personal journalism was much greater than their circulation would indicate. The Richmond *Whig*, for example, reputed to have the largest number of subscribers in Virginia, could muster only three thousand subscribers (Fincastle *Democrat*, Sept. 8, 1845).

[33] Richmond *Enquirer*, May 4, 1832.   [34] *Ibid.*, May 4, 1832.

all who concurred in it," he declared, "to withdraw their support from us, we have little question that, even in that county, independent spirits enough would be found to stand up for the Liberty of the Press, and indemnify any insignificant injury we might sustain."[35]

Certain newspapers of Tennessee expressed sympathy with the debate on emancipation in Virginia. The Nashville *Republican and State Gazette* declared that the whole South and West were silently watching its progress, feeling that they had much at stake in the result.[36] The Knoxville *Register* was outspoken in its approval of the Virginia emancipationists. In an appeal addressed to the legislature of Tennessee, the editor declared: "The citizens of Virginia are more alive to the subject than any other state, and various plans have been suggested for finally ridding the country of the calamity. We most cordially wish them all the success the greatness of the undertaking and the benevolence of the design merits. But while others are so sensitive on the subject, shall Tennessee continue with folded arms and do nothing? Cannot our present Legislature do something to check the growing evil, at least so far as to prevent emigration from other states."[37]

A leading newspaper of Georgia, the Milledgeville *Southern Recorder,* on the other hand, expressed the conservative point of view toward the Virginia debates. "Although we have been hitherto entirely silent upon this part of the proceedings of the Legislature of Virginia," the editor wrote, "it must not be supposed that this has proceeded from indifference on our part to a matter so momentous. But we have believed, and still believe, that the *less* that is said upon this subject (at least in our own State) the better: and acting upon this belief, we shall abstain from any future notice of this matter, until the final action of Virginia upon it, when we will lay the result before our readers."[38] Likewise, the Charleston

---

[35] Richmond *Whig,* May 1, 1832.
[36] Nashville *Republican and State Gazette,* Dec. 3, 1831.
[37] Knoxville *Register,* Nov. 30, 1831.   [38] *Southern Recorder,* Feb. 2, 1832.

City Gazette viewed with alarm the Virginia debate, fearful that a policy might be adopted that would assail the interests of South Carolina.[39]

The few years following the Nat Turner insurrection marked the greatest period of freedom in the ante-bellum history of the Southern press. It was, indeed, the impact of personal danger that shook men out of the rut of routine thinking. The violent irruption of the blacks in Southampton County gave the antislavery men an opportunity to raise their heads and boldly speak their sentiments. Although the chief advocates of emancipation came from the western part of Virginia, where slavery had a weak foothold, it is significant that the two leading editors of Richmond, Ritchie and Pleasants, were outspoken advocates of gradual emancipation. The press discussion and the debates in the Virginia legislature during 1832 influenced other states of the Upper South to relax their censorship of the tabooed subject. But this unshackling of the press was largely an emotional reaction. The period of free discussion came to an end almost as quickly as it had arisen.

From 1835 to 1861 the South pursued a policy of silence in regard to the removal of slavery. The Southern mind seemed to have lost the power of imagination necessary to envisage a free society consisting of blacks and whites. The institution of slavery had been inherited from many generations of Southerners and rested upon the land with an almost hopeless inertia. It required a critical mind above the average to condemn a way of life, a system of race relationships, that had been sanctioned by so many honorable men and women. A demonstration of the unfitness of Negroes for freedom in a white civilization was presented by the daily spectacle of the shiftless and disorderly lives of the free Negroes in Southern communities. More important than any economic influence arising from the invention of the cotton gin was the feeling that slavery was needed to control the blacks, to make them work, to prevent crime, and to keep the South "a white man's country." The

---

[39] *City Gazette and Commercial Daily Advertiser*, Jan. 25, 1832.

Negroes were regarded as children who needed discipline and supervision. To this sentiment responded the humblest cracker as well as the master of a thousand slaves. This social philosophy, containing so much common sense and truth in it, was balanced against the need to preserve a free press.

The fate of James G. Birney was a solemn warning to those in the South who thought of urging radical measures in abolishing slavery. Birney belonged to the aristocratic planter-class of Kentucky. After receiving an education at Princeton, he settled in Huntsville, Alabama, where he practiced law and operated a cotton plantation with slave labor. While acting as an agent of the American Colonization Society in 1832, he was converted from an innocuous liberalism on the slavery question to radical antislavery views by the abolitionist, Theodore D. Weld, who was then on a visit in the South. Thereupon, he returned to Danville, Kentucky, emancipated his own slaves, and organized in March, 1835, the Kentucky Anti-Slavery Society, an auxiliary of the American Anti-Slavery Society.[40] It was this active co-operation with the Northern abolitionists that made it impossible for him to enjoy freedom of speech and of the press in Kentucky.

The experience of Birney gives a good insight into the power of the vested interests in controlling the press. In late August, 1834, he sent a letter on emancipation to the editor of the *Western Luminary,* but the latter returned it, saying that "it was too strong for the times and rather too high a wrought picture of the sin of slavery in the Presb Church—fearing too it would injure the cause—that I wished to advance."[41] Birney at this time planned to establish an antislavery paper in Kentucky "tho' some of the bulls of Bashan are roaring." Two weeks later, he breakfasted with Henry Clay in Lexington and conversed with him on the possibility of an antislavery movement in Kentucky. This brilliant and popular leader

[40] For facts about his life see William Birney, *James G. Birney and His Times* (New York, 1890).

[41] Birney to Theodore Weld, Sept. 2, 1834 (James G. Birney Papers, MSS in Library of Congress).

maintained that slavery existed in so mitigated a form in Kentucky as not to be looked upon as a great evil. He pointed out "that men's interests in *property* had been found an insurmountable barrier to gradual emancipation then (in 1799)—that *now* they were more formidable—the case was hopeless by any direct effort, and was to be left to the influence of liberal principles as they should pervade our land. He spoke of Mr. Robert Breckinridge having put himself down in popular estimation by his having advocated emancipation and that he and Mr. John Green, two gentlemen of great worth, had disqualified themselves for political usefulness by the part they had taken in reference to slavery."[42]

Undeterred by this chilling advice, Birney continued to lay plans for founding an antislavery paper in Kentucky. When he announced in 1835 his intention of publishing at Danville an abolition paper to be known as the *Philanthropist,* a mass meeting of the citizens of Danville appointed a committee to inform him that he would not be permitted to publish an abolition paper in Kentucky. In a solemn letter, the committee warned him "to beware how you make an experiment here, which no *American Slaveholding community* has found itself able to bear," and it reprobated his abominable doctrines that would poison the minds of contented and happy slaves.[43] Upon Birney's refusal to give up his plans, the committee bought out the printer, and the postmaster of Danville announced that he would exclude the obnoxious newspaper from the mails. Birney then tried to secure a printer for his paper in Lexington, Frankfort, and Louisville, but failed completely.[44] Finally, he crossed the Ohio River and began publishing the *Philanthropist* near Cincinnati, but a mob destroyed his press, while the mayor looked on.[45]

In passing judgment on the South for its hostility toward

[42] James G. Birney Diary, Sept. 16, 1834 (MS in Library of Congress).

[43] Dwight L. Dumond (ed.), *Letters of James Gillespie Birney 1831-1857* (New York, 1938), I, 197-200; Birney's reply, I, 204-210.

[44] McDougle, *op. cit.,* pp. 106-108.

[45] G. H. Barnes and D. L. Dumond (eds.), *Letters of Theodore Dwight Weld, Angelina Grimké Weld, and Sarah Grimké, 1822-1844* (New York, 1934), I, 324.

antislavery editors, Northern mobs, such as the Ohio one that wrecked Birney's press, should not be omitted from the picture. No crime against the press was ever committed in the land of Dixie comparable to the murder of Elijah Lovejoy by an Illinois mob.[46] When Lucian Minor, a Virginian, traveled through New England in 1834, he discovered that the overwhelming majority of the people were intolerant toward the abolitionists. The fellow passengers of his stagecoach expressed general approval of the action of the Tappan mob in New York (July 4, 1834) against abolitionists, "sarved 'em right." In Boston he was told by the editor of the *Columbian Centinel,* by the rich merchant, Henry Lee, and by Professor Simon Greenleaf of Harvard that the enlightened and respectable people of New England regarded Garrison as "a miserable fanatic" and the abolitionists as contemptible.[47] The mobbing of the editor of the *Liberator* in Boston in 1834 revealed that the persecuting spirit of the Puritans had not died out. In 1835, Rev. Samuel J. May, an abolitionist, was mobbed five times in Vermont.

Despite the unfortunate experience of Birney, Kentucky remained the most liberal state in the South during the decade of the 1830's. At Louisville, the *Western Messenger,* a literary and religious magazine edited by James Freeman Clarke, took a sane antislavery stand.[48] Clarke published extracts in his magazine from the writings of William Ellery Channing showing the moral turpitude of slavery. He himself declared slavery to be a monstrous evil, and maintained that he would devote his life to the great cause of emancipation, if by so doing he could hasten that event one year. Nevertheless, he did not believe that slaveholders should be condemned as sinners for continuing to hold slaves under the conditions that existed in

[46] See *Memoir of Rev. Elijah P. Lovejoy, Who Was Murdered in Defense of the Liberty of the Press at Alton, Ill., November 7, 1837, by Joseph C. and Owen Lovejoy* (New York, 1838).

[47] James Russell Lowell (ed.), "A Virginian in New England Thirty-Five Years Ago," *Atlantic Monthly,* XXVII, 674-676 (June, 1871). These letters were earlier published in the *Southern Literary Messenger* for 1834-35.

[48] Mott, *A History of American Magazines, 1741-1850,* pp. 658-663.

the South. In the August, 1836, issue of the *Western Messenger,* he asserted that liberty of speech in regard to slavery prevailed in Kentucky and that "we are not afraid of discussing this or any other subject here."[49] In later days he affirmed that the people in Kentucky, while he was a resident from 1833 to 1840, did not think that there was anything improper or dangerous in discussing the subject of slavery fully. The Kentuckians at that time were in the habit of declaring that their state would be the first to emancipate.[50]

A few years after Birney left his native state, a limited discussion of slavery occurred in the Kentucky press as a result of an agitation for the calling of a constitutional convention. The advocates of this measure were chiefly those who desired a modification of the Constitution to permit gradual emancipation. The Lexington *Observer,* pointing out that some of the most enlightened men of the state believed slavery to be a great moral and political curse, demanded a full, free, and manly discussion of emancipation in order to allay the restlessness in the public mind.[51] The Flemingsburg *Kentuckian* and the Paris *Citizen* published a letter from a Bourbon County slaveholder, urging that the proposed constitutional convention should follow the example of New York and Pennsylvania and adopt a system of gradual emancipation, followed by the colonization of the freed Negroes.[52] The editor of the Flemingsburg *Kentuckian* wrote editorials in favor of gradual emancipation and admitted both antislavery and proslavery articles to his columns, for he wished "to see the subject fully and fairly discussed and presented to our readers in as impartial a light as possible."[53] He believed that if Kentucky emancipated her slaves, she would set an example that other Southern states would follow. Nevertheless, he violently resented any innuendo that he was an abolitionist.[54] The move

[49] *Western Messenger,* IV, 58 (Aug., 1836).
[50] James Freeman Clarke, *Anti-Slavery Days* (New York, 1883), pp. 22-27.
[51] *Genius of Universal Emancipation,* Jan., 1838.
[52] Flemingsburg *Kentuckian,* July 6, 1838.
[53] *Ibid.,* Aug. 3, 1838.   [54] *Ibid.,* Aug. 10, 1838.   .

to summon a constitutional convention was finally voted down by the people, who were urged to this course by Henry Clay.

It was an easy and effective way to discredit an enemy by accusing him of being an abolitionist. Early in 1846 an article appeared in the Richmond *Enquirer* accusing John Hampden Pleasants of a design to establish an abolition paper in the capital of Virginia. The veteran Whig editor replied to the charge in a caustic letter, in which he assailed the editors of the *Enquirer* for endorsing the article and maligning him when they knew his opposition to abolitionists. He proceeded then to define his position on the slavery question as that of a pragmatist. In 1832 he had taken precisely the same view that Thomas Ritchie, Senior, and most of the prominent men of Virginia, had held, that slavery was an evil and should be gotten rid of, and he had not changed his opinion. "Such is my opinion still," he wrote, "and if they constitute me an abolitionist, I can only say that I would go farther to see some of the abolition leaders hanged than any man in Virginia. In respect to slavery I take no pious, fanatical view. I am not opposed to it because I think it morally wrong, for I know the multitude of slaves to be better off than the whites. I am against it for *the sake of the whites,* my own race. I see young and powerful commonwealths around us, with whom, while we carry the burthen of slavery, we can never contend in power, and yet with whom we must prepare to contend with equal arms or consent to be their serfs and vassals—we or our children."[55]

Pleasants and Thomas Ritchie, Junior, who had succeeded his father as editor of the *Enquirer,* carried on their correspondence of vituperation, until the latter called the old veteran a coward. Pleasants, always a man of fiery spirit, challenged his young rival to a duel, in which the challenger was mortally wounded. Young Ritchie had silenced the voice of the most courageous antislavery man in Virginia. The jury

[55] *Full Report of the Commonwealth of Virginia vs. Thomas Ritchie, Jr.* (Richmond, 1846), p. 4. A pamphlet.

summoned to adjudge the case awarded a verdict of "Not Guilty" to Ritchie.

Western Virginia, the section of the state where slavery was weakest, and where many Northern settlers lived, was also the area where several free presses arose in the decade of the fifties. Most of these newspapers were localized in the Panhandle of Virginia, a long narrow strip sandwiched between Pennsylvania and Ohio. In 1860 the Panhandle section of Virginia had only one hundred and forty-nine slaves out of a total population of forty-five thousand.[56] Furthermore, the Panhandle was the home of a large foreign-born element. Ohio County alone had approximately five thousand, five hundred persons of foreign birth, constituting one seventh of the foreign-born population of the state. Wayne County, the seat of Eli Thayer's colony and of his antislavery paper, the Ceredo *Crescent,* had only one hundred and eighty-nine slaves out of a population of over four thousand. In such areas slavery could be discussed by the press with practically no danger to the community and without attacking the property rights of any considerable class.

One of the liberal leaders of this western section of Virginia was Enos W. Newton, editor of the *Kanawha Republican.* His newspaper throws light on his progressive policies, although only the files from December 4, 1841, to December 25, 1844, are preserved.[57] In his journal he was constantly advocating the development of free common schools, the adoption of a vigorous program of internal improvements, and the encouragement of the temperance reform. He was also an ardent champion of a protective tariff when the South was bitterly opposed to it. However, he dodged any discussion about slavery.

His enemy, the editor of the *Kanawha Valley Star,* unremittingly taunted him about his Northern birth and his coolness on the slavery question. In 1856 he was charged with being tinctured with Free Soilism because he had opposed the Democratic policy in Kansas.[58] By 1860 "Father Newton" had

---

[56] J. C. McGregor, *The Disruption of Virginia* (New York, 1922), p. 12.

[57] In the West Virginia State Library, Charleston, W. Va.

[58] *Kanawha Valley Star,* Jan. 23 and Feb. 13, 1856 (file in the State Library, Charleston, W. Va.).

weathered many a storm during his long career as editor of the *Kanawha Republican*. At this time he was superintendent of the Kanawha Free Schools, as well as superintendent of a Northern Methodist Sunday school in Charleston. Nevertheless, the editor of the *Kanawha Valley Star* launched an attack on him, calling him an "Onion River Yankee" because he was born on the banks of the Onion River in Vermont. He accused him of circulating "incendiary publications" under the guise of religious papers while he was occupying the position of Sunday school superintendent. To this attack Newton replied that it was folly to charge him with not being sound on slavery. He had entered the South in 1817 as a young man, had married a Southern woman, and his children were born on Virginia soil. "Upon the subject of slavery," he said, "we never entertained any opinions not in accordance with those entertained by the intelligent slave-holders themselves."[59]

In 1857 Eli Thayer founded a newspaper, the Ceredo *Crescent,* for his settlement of New Englanders at Ceredo, Wayne County, in western Virginia. The *Crescent* was a remarkably sane and well-balanced paper, with a clear realization of the conditions of success in a Southern community. The editor announced at the outset: "We will not place ourselves in opposition and hostility to the people among whom we intend to make our home and burial place, but will win their sympathy and support by proving a valuable friend and independent advocate, by daring to speak our sentiments upon their constitutional and legitimate rights without hope of emolument or fear of loss."[60] Although the *Crescent* deprecated the use of mob violence, it was, considering its New England antecedents, singularly free from antislavery articles.[61]

Perhaps the most daring of the abolition newspapers of Virginia was the *Clarke Journal* published by Alexander Parkins at Berryville, in the lower Shenandoah Valley. Parkins had the bravery to advocate moderation in dealing with John

[59] *Ibid.,* Jan. 16, 1860.
[60] Ceredo *Crescent,* Oct. 24, 1857 (in the Library of the American Antiquarian Society, Worcester, Mass.).   [61] *Ibid.,* July 3, 1858.

Brown and his followers. He favored the exercise of mercy on the ground of expediency. "Will it do more good to go on shedding blood," asked Parkins, "or to stop now and confine the rest for life? Our judgment is, and we are bound to give it, (if every subscriber stops his paper, as we have been threatened to some extent) in favor of the latter. More good can be done as a pure question of policy, by staying the effusion of blood. Now if this be treason, make the most of it. We will be as ready to die for a conviction as John Brown."[62] The Richmond *Enquirer* attacked Parkins as "a hired traitor in our midst" because he published the prospectus of the New York *Tribune* as an advertisement. The *Enquirer* professed to believe that Parkins was a paid agent of the execrable Greeley, and that the prosecuting attorney of Clarke County should take cognizance of his incendiary efforts. Furthermore, the editor of the Richmond paper recommended that the people of Clarke and the surrounding counties should suppress "this incendiary sheet" as a measure of safety.[63]

Wheeling, which was a semi-Northern city, was the focus of the antislavery newspapers of the Upper South. One of the important free lance presses of this city was the *Times and Gazette,* edited by a Mr. Wharton. In an early issue of his paper, he courageously stated his attitude toward slavery: "We are in favor of taking the earliest possible means for getting rid of slavery in the state of Virginia, with justice to the master, safety to the state, and comfort and convenience to the laboring population now in it."[64] The antislavery articles in this independent paper incited the champions of the opposition to call a meeting to suppress such publications. At the appointed time about two thousand citizens crowded in the courthouse. A proslavery speaker arose and offered some resolutions to suppress an incendiary press, but his proposals were greeted with hisses. Instead of condemning Wharton, the meeting voted that the citizens of Wheeling "would have and sustain one newspaper which did not fear to boldly speak the

[62] Richmond *Enquirer,* Nov. 15, 1859.
[63] *Ibid.*   [64] *National Era,* April 19, 1854.

truth."[65] The Richmond *Whig,* in commenting on the heterodox views of the Wheeling editor, said that they would meet
with little or no countenance in Virginia, for there was no
material diversity of opinion among Virginians on the slavery
question.[66]

The Wheeling *Intelligencer,* under the editorship of A. W.
Campbell, became the most outspoken of the influential dailies
of the South. Campbell was born in Ohio and as a young
man had attended the law school of Hamilton College, New
York. In 1856 he bought the Wheeling *Intelligencer* and made
of it a remarkably courageous and public-spirited paper. He
allied himself with the Republican party and was sent as a
delegate from Virginia to the Republican National Convention which nominated Lincoln. When the secession question
was being debated, he stood for the Union, and was one of
the leaders in the creation of the new state of West Virginia.
After the war he showed his devotion to liberal principles by
swaying the West Virginia delegation to oppose the nomination of Grant for a third term.[67]

He announced his intention of publishing an independent
and liberal newspaper, "one toward which all phases of public
opinion can look for a fair representation of their views."[68]
Bold to express his views on political matters, he bitterly sati-
rized the champions of the "dimmycratic party," and declared
that Virginia was retrograding like Spain because her politicians pretended a devotion to democracy but cared nothing for
the people, and because Virginia had clung to "the cankering
embrace of a trade in serf-flesh."[69] When Alfred Caldwell,
senator from the Wheeling district, made a speech in the legislature in favor of the interests of free labor as against the
slavery regime, Campbell commended him for his courage in
exercising freedom of speech.[70] In reply to the demand of the
Wheeling *Times* and the Wheeling *Argus* that Senator Cald-

[65] *Ibid.,* April 19, 1854.   [66] Richmond *Whig,* April 18, 1854.
[67] Judge G. L. Cranmer, *History of the Upper Ohio Valley* (Madison, Wis.,
1890), pp. 241-245.   [68] Wheeling *Intelligencer,* Oct. 9, 1856.
[69] *Ibid.,* Feb. 5, 1859.   [70] *Ibid.,* Feb. 7, 1859.

well should resign "while opportunity is left him," Campbell
wrote two columns of lament over the loss of freedom of
speech in the South. He said that it was a disgrace for
two journals of Wheeling to propose delivering up another
victim to the Moloch of the slave power.[71] On February 18,
1859, he wrote an editorial in which he declared that Wheeling ought to belong to Pennsylvania and that it would be
much better for the Panhandle to be cut off from Virginia.
Wheeling as a free community would be far ahead of the
present slave-tainted city.[72] In this year Campbell was also
active in trying to secure for Wheeling the honor of being selected as the meeting place of the National Republican Convention of 1860.

In Baltimore, the *Sun* upheld high standards of independent and courageous journalism. This newspaper, founded in
1837, was the first penny paper below Mason and Dixon's line.
Consequently, it was read by the mechanics and poorer people
of the city who could not afford to purchase "the respectable
sixpenny papers" of the time. The publisher was A. S. Abell
and Company who had previously established the Philadelphia
Public Ledger.[73] In its early issues, the *Sun* announced that it
would pursue a policy of neutrality in politics. Accordingly,
when Slade of Vermont created an uproar in the House of
Representatives by discussing the evils of slavery, thereby causing Southern extremists to threaten secession, the *Sun* cried
shame on anyone who would urge a dissolution of the Union.
"We do not take side with either section, North or South,"
the editor declared. "We are unwilling to say with the South,
petitions shall *not* be received, for we hold the right of freemen to petition among the most valuable of a freeman's privileges. We are equally unwilling to say with the North, dis-
possess the South of their property because they do not agree
with us on the subject of Negro servitude."[74] Standing between

---

[71] *Ibid.*, Sept. 28, 1859.   [72] *Ibid.*, Dec. 3, 1859.

[73] W. G. Bleyer, *Main Currents in the History of American Journalism* (Boston,
1927), p. 179. See also Gerald Johnson, Frank R. Kent, H. L. Mencken, and Hamilton Owens, *The Sunpapers of Baltimore* (New York, 1937).

[74] Baltimore *Sun*, Dec. 23, 1837.

the extremes was a difficult but wise policy for a newspaper to maintain in a state like Maryland, which was partly Southern and partly Northern.

Twenty years later the *Sun* was still trying to preserve a detached position amidst the violent passions of partisan politics. It expressed strong disapproval of Preston Brooks for his brutal assault on Sumner.[75] It also spoke with sadness of a mob that broke up a Republican meeting in Baltimore in 1856. The leaders of this Frémont rally had been subjected to great indignities, their tall silk hats had been smashed in, their long coattails had been cut off and distributed in pieces to a jeering mob of two thousand people. The editor commented: "We can only characterize such proceedings as disreputable, and unworthy of a people who profess to honor the freedom of speech."[76] Opposing the principles of the Republican party, the *Sun,* nevertheless, declared that such assaults upon a peaceful meeting would do more harm than Republicanism could ever do in Maryland.

The difficulty of maintaining a free press in slave territory was exemplified in the hardships and final suppression of the *True American* at Lexington, Kentucky, in 1845. This paper had been launched by Cassius M. Clay after he had been denied access to the columns of the press of Kentucky.[77] Clay was well fitted by nature and training to be the leader of a forlorn cause. He was born into an aristocratic slaveholding family and was given an excellent education at Transylvania University and at Yale.[78] At the latter college he heard William Lloyd Garrison speak, and his innate dislike for slavery ripened into a positive opposition to the institution. Upon his return to Kentucky, he entered a career of politics as an enthusiastic Whig, but this was soon terminated in 1841 when he was defeated for re-election to the legislature on account of his pronounced antislavery views. After his defeat, he

---

[75] *Ibid.,* Aug. 27, 1856, editorial, "Congressional Heroics."

[76] *Ibid.,* Sept. 12, 1856.

[77] *The Life of Cassius Marcellus Clay, Memoirs, Writings, and Speeches* (Cincinnati, 1886), I, 106.

[78] For an account of Clay's life, see *ibid.* and E. Merton Coulter's "Cassius M. Clay," *Dictionary of American Biography,* IV, 169-170.

toured the Northern States, making many speeches, and returned to Kentucky a more violent and determined opponent of slavery than ever before.

It was then that he established the *True American* at Lexington, though his truculent temperament was bound to lead to conflict with his fellow townsmen. Yet the prospectus of the publication was a temperate document. It announced a policy of appealing to the interests and reason of the people of Kentucky, and not to their passions, "a paper devoted to gradual and constitutional emancipation."[79] Another object, not avowed at this time, was the organization of the non-slaveholders as a class against the wealthy slaveholders. In this attempt, Clay was a forerunner of Hinton R. Helper, the author of *The Impending Crisis*. Although most of the articles and editorials in the *True American* were temperate and well balanced, Clay would occasionally be goaded into violent outbursts and would challenge his critics to duels.[80] He also provoked hostility by fortifying his printing office, by placing two brass cannon on a table breast high so as to command the door, and by building a trap door in the roof in order that in the last extremity the defenders might escape. The final touch to these ingenious arrangements was the location of a keg of powder, with a fuse attached, in a position where it could blow up the office and its invaders if the need arose.[81]

For over two months the *True American* was published without disturbance. It attained a circulation of seven hundred subscribers in Kentucky and twenty-seven hundred, including Daniel Webster, in other states. On August 12 an editorial and a leading article appeared which bitterly aroused the pro-slavery faction of Lexington. The pronouncement that excited feeling was a paragraph in Clay's editorial: "But remember, you who dwell in marble palaces—that there are strong arms and fiery hearts, and iron pikes in the streets, and panes

---

[79] Horace Greeley (ed.), *The Writings of Cassius Marcellus Clay* (New York, 1848), contains a prospectus of the *True American*, pp. 211-212.
[80] See *True American*, June 3, July 8, 1845 (partial file in Library of American Antiquarian Society).   [81] Clay, *Memoirs*, I, 107.

of glass only between them and the silver plate on the board and smooth skin woman on the ottoman—when you have mocked at virtue and denied the agency of God in the affairs of men and made rapine your honied faith; tremble for the day of retribution is at hand—and *the masses will be avenged.*"[82] Such a passionate protest against the slaveholding oligarchy gave the enemies of Clay just the opportunity for which they had been waiting.

On August 18 a tremendous public meeting was held in Lexington to decide the fate of the *True American.* After listening to a fiery speech by Thomas F. Marshall, the assembly resolved that no abolition organ ought to be tolerated in Kentucky and appointed a committee of sixty to dismantle the presses of the obnoxious paper. When the committee reached the office of the *True American,* they were met at the door by the mayor, who gave notice that they were acting against the law but that the city authorities could offer no forcible resistance. The keys were surrendered to the city marshal, and the presses were boxed up and sent to Cincinnati, expenses being paid by the committee. Several of the high-handed group were later prosecuted in Lexington, but the defendants pleaded not guilty to the charge of riot, alleging that they were engaged in abating a public nuisance and had used just enough force to accomplish that end. The jury, having listened to the arguments of both sides, did not hesitate to acquit the accused.[83]

The speech of Thomas F. Marshall before the public meeting at Lexington contained the most cogent argument produced by the ante-bellum South for the suppression of the freedom of the press. He based the right of suppressing antislavery newspapers on the principle *salus populi suprema lex.* An abolition newspaper in a slave state he regarded as a nuisance of the most formidable character, since by its agency the

[82] *History and Record of the Proceedings of the People of Lexington and Its Vicinity in the Suppression of the True American* (Lexington, Aug. 25, 1845), p. 8.

[83] Lewis Collins, *History of Kentucky* (Covington, Ky., 1874), I, 51. When Clay returned from the Mexican War, restored once more to popular favor, he sued James B. Clay, the son of Henry Clay, and the members of the committee of sixty, and received a verdict for damages of $2,500 (Clay, *Memoirs,* I, 108).

slaves might be stirred to insurrection. He asked the pertinent question: "Who shall say that the safety of a single individual is more important in the eye of the law than that of a whole people? Who shall say that when the case of danger—real danger of a great and irreparable injury to the whole community—really occurs, that it is not armed legally with the rights of self-preservation?"[84] He declared that it would be impossible to abate the nuisance of publishing the *True American* save by direct action of the people. No law existed which prevented the establishment of an antislavery paper. Even if the *True American* could be enjoined, it would be published under another name. The people therefore must act outside the law to safeguard the public interest.

The newspaper editors of the Upper South watched the proceedings in Lexington with decided approval. The Richmond *Whig* gave an account of the suppression of the *True American* and commented coldly: "We feel no sympathy for Mr. Clay, a member of that family of fanatics, who, pernicious ever to society and its peace, are more especially pernicious to the cause which they undertook to promote."[85] The Alexandria *Gazette,* discussing the suppression of the *True American,* said: "The incendiary article wantonly published (and in the case referred to nothing could be grosser) in the midst of a community, situated as the people are in Kentucky, could not with safety to themselves be tolerated. They abated the nuisance as peaceably as they could."[86] The Richmond *Enquirer* succinctly stated the judgment of most Southerners: "We feel that our existence could not be free from danger whilst a fiery fanatic like Cassius M. Clay was allowed to continue an abolition paper, and hurl his incendiary missiles into every corner of the South. Filled with this conviction, the people of Lexington met in solemn council, and resolved to expel from the state the madman, whose wanton attacks perilled the lives of themselves and their families."[87] The press of the South heart-

[84] W. L. Barre, *Speeches and Writings of T. F. Marshall* (Cincinnati, 1858), p. 208.   [85] Richmond *Whig,* Aug. 26, 1845.
[86] Alexandria *Gazette,* Aug. 27, 1845.   [87] Richmond *Enquirer,* Sept. 2, 1845.

ily supported the suppression by a mob of an independent paper that was expressing unpopular opinions.[88] The editors of the Southern papers did not feel that their freedom of speech was denied, because they had no desire to publish anti-slavery articles. An idealist like Cassius Clay was regarded as a "fanatic" allied with Northern abolitionists; therefore, they could have no fellowship with him nor any sympathy for his fight to maintain a free press.

The suppression of the *True American* revealed the great power of the proslavery faction in agitating a Southern community into acts of intolerance. In the final act the driving out of the obnoxious paper was accomplished with the approval of the great body of citizens. Yet this unanimity of feeling was carefully worked up by a clique of interested persons, bitter political and personal enemies of Cassius Clay.[89] Prentice, the editor of the Louisville *Journal*, believed that after Clay had promised to exercise caution in discussing slavery, the people of Lexington would not have molested him or his premises had not a small faction been actively engaged in inciting the mob to violence.[90] Clay himself did not believe his opponents were sincere in maintaining that his paper would incite the slaves to revolt. "I regard the idea of insurrection in Kentucky, where there are about six whites to one black," he said, "as ridiculous and only used by the slaveholders as a bugaboo, to maintain the ascendancy of their power in the state."[91]

After the destruction of his paper, Clay volunteered to fight in the Mexican War, hoping to restore his prestige so that he could work more effectively for the great reform. Upon his return, he became a candidate for governor on a

[88] When a mob at Parkville, Mo., destroyed a free soil press, the *Industrial Luminary*, in 1855, the act was condoned by a leading Missouri newspaper on the ground that it sometimes becomes necessary to act without regard to law to secure peace to a community (W. E. Smith, *The Francis Preston Blair Family in Politics*, New York, 1933, I, 303; *Liberator*, May 4, 1855).

[89] C. M. Clay, *Appeal of Cassius M. Clay to Kentucky and the World* (Boston, 1845); also Greeley, *The Writings of Cassius Marcellus Clay*, Introduction.

[90] *National Intelligencer*, Aug. 26, 1845.

[91] *History and Record of Proceedings at Lexington*, p. 10.

platform of gradual emancipation and received five thousand votes. He was supported in his candidacy by an antislavery newspaper published at Lexington and Louisville, entitled the *Progress of the Age*.[92] His ardent efforts for the antislavery cause brought him such popularity in the North that he received over a hundred votes for Vice-President in the Republican convention of 1860.[93]

Despite the suppression of the *True American*, Kentucky continued to be an arena of Southern antislavery newspapers. In 1847, the *Examiner* was established at Louisville by John C. Vaughan, a South Carolinian, and F. Crosley, a Kentuckian, for the purpose of advocating the cause of emancipation. Although the editors worked valiantly for the election of antislavery delegates to the constitutional convention of 1849, their editorial policy was dominated by common sense and the spirit of moderation. They warned the advocates of emancipation during the campaign to be "extremely careful to keep aloof from angry and embittered controversy, which always confirms the prejudices of the opponent. Be gentle, discreet, and yet firm. Do not hazard any wild propositions. Keep attention fixed on those evils which result from slavery and are sufficiently manifest in every section of the state. Let slavery in the abstract, as it is called, alone, and talk of slavery as it exists around us."[94] But the efforts of the *Examiner* to bring about emancipation were fruitless, for, although ten thousand votes were cast for the election of antislavery delegates, not a single candidate was elected.[95] James Freeman Clarke explained this failure by observing that the Democratic and Whig parties in Kentucky at that time were nearly equal in strength and were engaged in a bitter rivalry. Both parties

[92] *Progress of the Age*, April 19, 1851.

[93] Lincoln recognized the services of Clay by appointing him Minister to Russia. He lived to be over ninety years of age, but his latter years were spent in bitter disillusionment (Horace Greeley, *The American Conflict*, Hartford, Conn., 1865, I, 321).

[94] Martin, *The Anti-Slavery Movement in Kentucky*, pp. 122-123.

[95] *Ibid.*, p. 134.

were afraid to touch the dangerous issue of emancipation.[96] Shortly after the convention met, the idealistic *Examiner* perished for want of financial support.

In 1858 a Northern mechanic, named William Bailey, printed a quixotic paper, the *Free South,* at Newport, Kentucky. In its editorial columns he urged the nonslaveholding whites of Kentucky to use their votes to exterminate slavery. On December 31, 1858, he issued a stirring call to battle: "Working men of Kentucky, think of yourselves! See you not that the system of slavery enslaves all who labor for an honest living. You, white men, are the best slave property of the South, and it is your own votes that make you so."[97] Bailey would have starved had he not received support from the abolitionists of the North.[98] He had resolved, however, to remain at his post in "the enemy's own territory," but after the John Brown raid a mob broke into his printing establishment and wrecked his presses.[99]

By far the most influential ante-bellum newspaper of Kentucky was the Louisville *Journal.* George D. Prentice, the editor, came to Kentucky in 1830 to write a campaign biography of Henry Clay. After he had completed his task he was persuaded to stay and edit a Whig newspaper.[100] So well did he adapt himself to his Southern environment and with so much verve did he write that the *Journal* became the most extensively read paper in Kentucky and attained a large circulation in the free states of Illinois and Indiana. The popularity of this journal was partly due to the delightful flavor of wit which Prentice gave to his editorials and news squibs.[101] He was a staunch partisan, championing the chief Whig measures, and lashing his opponents with vitriolic wit. As a consequence, he had to fight several duels, despite his aversion to "the code of

[96] Clarke, *Anti-Slavery Days,* pp. 26-27.
[97] *Free South,* Dec. 31, 1858.   [98] *Ibid.,* March 9, 1859.
[99] Tarboro (N. C.) *Southerner,* Nov. 19, 1859.
[100] William H. Perrin, *The Pioneer Press of Kentucky* (Louisville, Ky., 1888), pp. 76-81.
[101] In 1860 Prentice collected some of his most telling witticisms in *Prenticeana: or Wit and Humor in Paragraphs* (New York, 1860).

honor." When the Lower South seceded, Prentice wrote virile editorials in favor of Kentucky's remaining in the Union.[102]

No editor in the ante-bellum South showed greater skill in maintaining the delicate balance between discussing such a dangerous subject as emancipation in a slave state and preserving at the same time the influence of his paper unimpaired. After Prentice had rebuked the people of Lexington for suppressing the *True American* he announced that he would discuss the question of emancipation when he judged the time ripe for it, and when such discussion should serve the public interest.[103] On October 8 he wrote an extended editorial in which he undertook to show the inexpediency of discussing slavery at that particular time. He pointed out that the effect of the suppression of the *True American* was to close men's minds in Kentucky against the free discussion of slavery for a long time to come. Intelligent observers sympathetic to emancipation had expressed the view that the Lexington affair would tend to prevent the free discussion of slavery for five years. So aroused were the people that Prentice believed the public mind was not in the proper state to discriminate between abolition and the policy of substituting free for slave labor in Kentucky.

In meditating upon the situation Prentice arrived at a very striking theory of the freedom of the press in a slave state. He announced that he would not engage in the discussion of emancipation until the people themselves called for it. This policy was not dictated by fear or pecuniary motives, but by the need of preserving the unity of the Whig party. His mission, he wrote, was to uphold Whig principles, to cement and strengthen as far as possible the ranks of the Whig party. Con-

---

[102] Two of his sons joined the Confederate army, but he remained loyal to the Federal government throughout the war. When he died in 1870, the great journalist, Henry Watterson, said in a memorial address before the legislature: "From 1830 to 1861, the influence of Prentice was perhaps greater than the influence of any political writer who ever lived." Shortly before Prentice's death his paper was sold and its name changed to the *Courier-Journal* (Henry Watterson, *George Dennison Prentice: A Memorial Address*, Cincinnati, 1870, p. 16).

[103] Louisville *Weekly Journal*, Sept. 3, 1846.

sequently, the Louisville *Journal* was silent on the slavery question from 1845 to 1849.

In this latter year an agitation in favor of emancipation occurred prior to the assembly of the constitutional convention of 1849. At first Prentice refused to permit the discussion of the problem in the columns of his paper, but later he lifted his ban. He explained that there could be no harm in discussing emancipation as a simple social question. Fanaticism arose when slavery was discussed as a moral evil or when the argument rested on the postulate that "all men are created equal."[104] Prentice affirmed again and again that slavery would disappear gradually by "the slow process of public opinion and the gentle influence of moral causes." The instruments of this silent revolution were to be: (1) public opinion, (2) the press, (3) the religious teachers, and (4) the fact that slave labor was more expensive than free.[105] Believing that time would cure the evil, he opposed the agitation of a question which would fill the state with strife and discord. This note of resignation expressed the orthodox point of view of that "truly conservative party," whose chief Southern leaders were Henry Clay, John Bell of Tennessee, and Willie P. Mangum, and George Badger of North Carolina.[106]

The failure of Cassius Clay and George Prentice to persuade the people of Kentucky to tolerate a free press revealed, first, the irresistible power of wealth and the vested interests in the Old South, and secondly, the unreasonable fear of servile insurrection. The approach of the two men to the problem of reform was in vivid contrast—Clay was the bold and outspoken radical, ready to take desperate chances, while Prentice was the thoroughly realistic conservative who felt that no real good could be accomplished by tilting against the strongly intrenched dragon of slavery. Slavery benefited only the small

[104] *Ibid.,* Feb. 21, 1849. See also an article by Clement Eaton, "The Freedom of the Press in the Upper South," *Mississippi Valley Historical Review,* XVIII, 479-499 (March, 1932).

[105] *Ibid.,* editorials of Feb. 28 and March 7, 1849.

[106] See Henry Clay MSS, John Bell MSS, and Willie P. Mangum MSS in Library of Congress; also A. C. Cole, *The Whig Party in the South,* pp. 104 ff.

upper class, while five sixths of the people were injured by it. The majority of Kentuckians looked upon slavery as a real evil, yet an active and able minority dictated public sentiment in the state. They made it dangerous for a man to express independent views on slavery in a public speech or newspaper. Their resolute and implacable hostility to antislavery reformers caused an editor who hoped to have any influence, or aspired to be a party leader, to pause before incurring the charge of being unsound in regard to the inviolable institution.

This group was immensely aided by the fact that the South suffered from a pathological fear of servile insurrection. The common people could be easily thrown into a panic by the term "abolitionist."[107] The stereotype of the abolitionist hurling firebrands into a magazine was used time and again to rally the common people against the critics of slavery.[108] Thus, on the ground of insuring the public safety, freedom of the press was denied to the mild opponent of slavery, who was often purposely confused with the dangerous fanatic.

Yet there were other factors that confirmed the Southerners in their policy of repressing hostile discussion of their peculiar institution. Intolerance was undoubtedly generated by the rise of the Northern abolitionists who were unrelentingly scourging the South for her sins. The need to silence slavery agitation in order to hold a political party together sealed the tongues of some editors. Moreover, Southerners consented to the silencing of the press because slavery was so inextricably intertwined with the fabric of society that radicalism became to an extraordinary degree dangerous and repellent to them. Robert E. Lee expressed this feeling in a letter of 1856, in which he wrote that the holding of slaves was an evil, but he added that their emancipation would result sooner from the mild and melting influence of time than from the storms and contests of fiery controversy.[109] This attitude on the part

---

[107] See Phillips, "The Central Theme of Southern History," p. 32.

[108] Walter Lippmann has pointed out the extreme importance of stereotypes in producing intolerance (*Public Opinion*, New York, 1922, pp. 79-156).

[109] Freeman, *R. E. Lee: A Biography*, I, 372.

of idealistic opponents of slavery blunted the militant edge of the crusade against the great evil. The Upper South contained a surprising number of nonconformists, recruited chiefly from the professional classes, but they were isolated individuals who could not compel a hearing in the columns of the press or on the hustings.[110] Consequently, the freedom of the press in respect to the question of emancipation was enjoyed only for brief interims in the border states of the Upper South.

[110] See chap. x, "Free Lances of the Upper South."

Chapter VIII

CENSORSHIP OF THE MAILS

THE LIBERAL tradition of America emphasizes the necessity of reducing the dangerous power of censorship to the minimum consistent with national safety. A valuable case history in the use of censorship to restrict social criticism, extending far beyond the requirements of public safety, is afforded by the experience of the ante-bellum South in imposing a rigid censorship on incoming mail from the Northern states. The Southern record demonstrates the difficulty of suppressing pernicious and dangerous propaganda without at the same time destroying the literature of reform, of protest, and of sanative criticism. The recognition of such a distinction is the very heart and core of the problem of censorship.

The freedom of the mails is inextricably connected with the broader freedom of the press. Calhoun pointed out this fact in a report to the Senate on February 4, 1836, opposing a federal censorship of the mails. "The object of publishing is circulation," said this great defender of minority rights; "and [for the federal government] to prohibit circulation is, in effect, to prohibit publication."[1] If the federal government should act as a censor of the mails, it would place a formidable power in the hands of the majority party that happened temporarily to be in control of the administration. Those who fight for the precious rights of the freedom of the press and of the mails are usually minority groups who wish to propagate ideas that are repugnant to the ruling class. Seldom are these advocates of toleration for themselves, however, imbued with the spirit of tolerance, nor do they have any genuine interest in the preservation of the freedom of the press and of the mails as a democratic principle. Rather, these agitators and reformers tend to become intolerant extremists, ill-balanced and wrongheaded, whom the majority

[1] Gales and Seaton, eds., *Register of Debates in Congress,* 24 Cong., 1 sess., XII (Washington, 1836), Part 4, Appendix, 73.

of people heartily dislike. The Northern abolitionists of the decade 1830-40, for example, were a minority group disliked both in the North and the South. They believed that slavery was the number one moral and political problem of the nation, and not a purely Southern problem. Consequently they demanded the right to use the United States mails to protest against this crying evil. But this right of using the mails for transmitting their propaganda was opposed by another minority group within the nation, the Southerners, who contended that their safety was involved in the issue of the freedom of the mails. The fact that a virtual censorship of the mails crossing the Mason and Dixon line was established after 1835 indicates the ascendancy of the Southern group in federal politics during the ante-bellum period. Such a censorship could not be maintained without the acquiescence of the federal government.

In the summer of 1835 the Southern people became keenly aware of a new danger that threatened the tranquillity of their social system. A powerful, concerted effort of propaganda had been launched against the Southern way of life by the abolition societies of the North.[2] Both the American and the New England antislavery societies had resolved upon an aggressive campaign to distribute their publications in the South. It was not the object of these societies, so they declared, to distribute such abolitionist literature among slaves or free Negroes in the South. They hoped, rather, to revolutionize public opinion below the Mason and Dixon line by scattering their radical publications "unsparingly" throughout the land of Dixie.[3] Accordingly, tons of antislavery pamphlets, magazines, and

[2] Propaganda is used in this paper, according to its original definition, as the literature of propagating certain beliefs or doctrines. It is used in a neutral sense, without the modern connotation of a deliberate distortion of the truth to attain an end, or the sinister concealment of authorship. There was a great variety in the abolitionists' publications, which ranged from rational discussion to lurid emotionalism, but a common denominator in most of this propaganda was a complete failure to understand the complexities of the problem of removing Southern slavery, especially the race problem involved, and the vast social and economic dislocations that would result from a sudden abolition of slavery.

[3] *Fourth Annual Report of the Massachusetts Anti-Slavery Society* (Boston, Jan. 20, 1836), pp. 17-18; *Second Annual Report of the American Anti-Slavery Society* (New York, May, 1835), pp. 48-53.

newspapers were sent through the mails to prominent Southerners—justices of the peace, ministers, editors, members of Congress, state officials—in other words, the leaders of public
opinion.[4]

The impact of this deluge of fervid publications on the
Southern mind produced a wave of excitement and of anger.
In the summer of 1835 a mob of citizens, led by ex-Governor
Robert Y. Hayne, entered the post office at Charleston, South
Carolina, and destroyed several sacks of mail containing antislavery pamphlets.[5] The federal government made no effort
to arrest or prosecute those who thus violated the property and
the laws of the United States. The postmaster at Richmond,
Virginia, announced that a number of the newspapers and
pamphlets of the abolitionists had been mailed to his office and
that he had been requested by several gentlemen of respectability
to stop their circulation.[6] Postmaster Thomas Scott, of Raleigh,
received at his office some of "the Northern fanatical publications" addressed to the most respectable citizens of the capital
city. He sternly withheld them from circulation.[7] The postmaster at Orange Court House, Virginia, reported that many
incendiary papers had been sent to people who did not subscribe
to them and who returned them with appropriate notes on
them.[8] At Greensborough, in the rich black belt of Alabama,
the circulation of copies of the *Emancipator* caused passionate
mobs to arise.[9] The grand jury of Tuscaloosa County, Alabama,
returned a true bill of indictment against Robert G. Williams,

[4] The magnitude of this propaganda drive is shown by the fact that in a single year,
May, 1836, to May, 1837, the American Anti-Slavery Society alone published 9,000
copies of *The Anti-Slavery Magazine*, 130,150 copies of *The Slave's Friend*, 103,000
copies of *The Anti-Slavery Record*, 189,400 copies of *Human Rights*, 217,000 copies
of the *Emancipator*, as well as numerous bound volumes, tracts, pamphlets, and prints.
Not all of this material crossed the Mason and Dixon line. *Fourth Annual Report of the
American Anti-Slavery Society*, reprinted in *The Quarterly Anti-Slavery Magazine*
(New York, July, 1837), p. 348.

[5] Theodore D. Jervey, *Robert Y. Hayne and His Times* (New York, 1909), pp.
379-81.

[6] Richmond *Enquirer*, Aug. 25, 1835.

[7] Raleigh *Standard*, Aug. 6, 1835.

[8] Salem (N. C.), *The Farmer's Reporter and Rural Repository*, Aug. 15, 1835.

[9] Henry Watson, jr., to Julius Reed, Aug. 23, 1835. Henry Watson, jr., MSS. (in
Duke University Library).

editor of the *Emancipator,* published at New York, for circulating within the state "pamphlets and papers of a seditious and incendiary character, and tending to gross misrepresentation, and illicit appeals to the passions of the slaves to excite them to insurrection and murder."[10] Throughout the Southern states arose a movement to establish a *cordon sanitaire* against the invasion of inflammatory propaganda. Indeed, Southerners regarded the activities of the abolition societies and the antislavery press of the North somewhat in the same light as Austria prior to World War I viewed the propaganda of the Serbian societies in Bosnia-Herzegovina.[11]

One of the most effective measures of safeguarding Southern society from subversive propaganda was the exercise of a censorship over the incoming mails. In 1836 the Virginia legislature passed a law requiring postmasters to notify justices of the peace whenever they received incendiary publications or publications "denying the right of masters to property in their slaves and inculcating the duty of resistance to such right." The justice of the peace should then inquire into the circumstances of the case, and if he were convinced that such writings were dangerous, he should have such books, pamphlets, and other publications burned in his presence· and should arrest the addressee, if the latter subscribed for the said book or pamphlet with intent to aid the purposes of the abolitionists or antislavery societies.[12] This law gave a single justice of the peace inquisitorial power over the mails and, by extension, a dictatorship over the kind of mental food his neighbors were permitted to enjoy. A Maryland act of 1841 commanded the grand juries to summon before them at every term of court all the postmasters in their respective counties and ex-

[10] Tuscaloosa (Ala.) *Flag of the Union,* Aug. 22, 1835.
[11] For evidence see Resolutions of the General Assembly on Incendiary Publications, *Acts of the General Assembly of the State of North Carolina, 1835-1836* (Raleigh, 1836), p. 120.
[12] *Acts of the General Assembly of the Commonwealth of Virginia, 1835-36* (Richmond, 1836), chap. 66, sec. 3. In South Carolina a somewhat similar law was passed in 1859, making it the duty of a postmaster to notify the magistrate of any person receiving abolition literature in the mail. H. M. Henry, *The Police Control of the Slave in South Carolina* (Emory, 1914), p. 162.

amine them as to whether they had received publications of an inflammatory character, "having a tendency to create discontent among and stir up to insurrection, the people of color of this State."[13] These laws, which certainly interfered with the free transmission of the mails, never came before the Supreme Court to test their constitutionality and afford a striking example of the nonassertion of federal power.

Postmaster General Amos Kendall, who entered the cabinet of President Jackson from the slave state of Kentucky, was complaisant to Southern demands that abolition publications be excluded from the Southern mails.[14] Although he admitted that he had no legal authority of censorship in this matter, he encouraged an unofficial exclusion of abolition literature from the Southern mails by individual postmasters. He adopted the Southern contention that the abolition publications were calculated to fill every family with black assassins and to repeat the horrors of Santo Domingo. He commended the postmaster of New York City for his efforts to persuade the abolition societies voluntarily to renounce sending their publications through the mails to Southern addresses and, upon their refusal of this request, his decision not to be an accomplice of "fanatics" in forwarding dangerous missiles to the South.[15] In his report of December 1, 1835, Kendall declared that the state laws against the circulation of incendiary publications should be obeyed by the officers of the general government. He also reported his action in regard to the Charleston mob, and he observed that his policy had prevented the circulation of "obnoxious" publications in the South.[16]

[13] *Session Laws of Maryland, 1841-42* (Annapolis, 1842), chap. 272, sec. 3. This law was modified the following year, so that grand juries were required to summon postmasters only when they deemed it necessary.

[14] Kendall was born at Dunstable, Massachusetts, and was a graduate of Dartmouth College, but he had emigrated to Kentucky as a young man.

[15] Amos Kendall to J. D. Townes of Petersburg, Va., Aug. 20, 1835, and to Samuel Gouverneur of New York City, Aug. 22, 1835. *Niles' Weekly Register*, XLIX, 7-9 (Sept. 5, 1835).

[16] Report of the Postmaster General, Dec. 1, 1835, to the President of the United States. Blair and Rives, eds., *The Congressional Globe*, 24 Cong., sess., II-III (Washington, 1836), Appendix, 8-9. In checking references the author discovers that apparently different libraries either bind or number early volumes of the *Congressional*

President Jackson approved thoroughly of the policy of his Postmaster General in regard to abolition publications. He wrote to Kendall: "we can do nothing more than direct that those inflamatory [sic] papers be delivered to none but who will demand them as subscribers; and in every instance the Postmaster ought to take the names down, and have them exposed thro the publik [sic] journals as subscribers to this wicked plan of exciting the negroes to insurrection and to massacre." He declared that when such subscribers "are known, every moral and good citizen will unite to put them in coventry, and avoid their society. This, if adopted, would put their circulation down everywhere, for there are few so hardened in villainy, as to withstand the frowns of all good men."[17]

Jackson was a man of action, however, not content to let the matter rest with public opinion. In his message to Congress, December 7, 1835, he recommended that Congress pass a law to prohibit the circulation through the mails in the Southern states of "incendiary publications intended to instigate the slaves to insurrection."[18] He pointed out that the invasion of these publications in the slave states had produced a great excitement, and that the federal post office, which had been established to promote friendly feelings between the states, was being used for an opposite purpose. This recommendation normally would have been referred by the Senate to the Post Office Committee, which was composed of a majority of members from the free states. But Calhoun managed to have a special committee chosen to consider the President's recommendation. Calhoun himself was appointed chairman of this select committee, in which slaveholders predominated.

The great Nullifier objected to Jackson's proposal of a

Globe differently. The citations in this article are to the set in the library of Lafayette College. See *Checklist of United States Public Documents, 1789-1901*, I (Washington, 1911), 1466, for comment which applies presumably to the set in the Library of Congress.

[17] Jackson to Amos Kendall, Aug. 9, 1835. John Spencer Bassett, ed., *Correspondence of Andrew Jackson*, V (Washington, 1931), 360-61.

[18] James D. Richardson, *A Compilation of the Messages and Papers of the Presidents, 1789-1897* (Washington, 1896), III, 175-76.

federal law prohibiting the circulation through the mails of incendiary publications in the slave states. Instead he reported a bill making it illegal for any deputy postmaster knowingly to receive and put in the mail any pamphlet, newspaper, handbill, or other printed paper, or pictorial representation, touching the subject of slavery, directed to any person or post office in those states where the laws prohibited their circulation.[19]

In urging the adoption of this bill Calhoun drew a dark and alarming picture of the consequences of abolition agitation, and he predicted that this agitation would not only endanger the safety of the South but would also cause both sections to hate each other and thus bring about a destruction of the Union. It is clear that Calhoun was primarily concerned in stopping the antislavery agitation of the North, not because he had any great dread of servile insurrection, but because he feared it would eventually convert the North to the antislavery cause and might disturb the loyalty of Southern non-slave-holders.[20] His report on the circulation of incendiary publications through the mails contained the grave warning to the rich and governing classes in the North that they had an important stake in preserving the *status quo* of capitalistic society, both above and below the Mason and Dixon line, from the corroding effect of subversive propaganda. "Let those who are interested remember," he said, "that labor is the only source of wealth, and how small a portion of it in all old and civilized countries, even the best governed, is left to those by whose labor wealth is created."[21] Calhoun was a realist in bluntly stating that in all civilized communities one portion of the people lived on the labor of another, and his argument unmistakably suggested that the industrial capitalists of New England in their exploitation of white labor were not more righteous than "the cotton capitalists" in their exploitation of black slave labor.

The method which he advocated to stop the subversive

---

[19] *Cong. Globe*, 24 Cong., 1 sess., II-III, 165 (Feb. 4, 1836).

[20] Gales and Seaton, *Register of Debates in Congress*, 24 Cong., 1 sess., XII, Part 4, Appendix, 76.

[21] *Ibid.*

agitation of the abolitionists was by state action. The Northern states, he demanded, should suppress their abolition presses. These fanatics were engaged in a moral and religious war against the South, the most violent and bitter of all wars. The law of nations, which prohibited campaigns of hostile propaganda against a peaceful and unoffending nation, applied to the relations between the sovereign states of the Union. Furthermore, the federal government should cooperate with the Southern states to help them enforce their own laws against the invasion of incendiary publications.[22] He pointed to the recognition by the federal government of its obligation to observe state quarantine laws as an example of such co-operative procedure. In an able speech before the Senate, April 12, 1836, discussing the great constitutional issue involved in Jackson's proposal of a federal law controlling the transmission of incendiary publications through the mails, he pronounced it a step toward centralization that would invade the rights of the states. Such a law "would place in the hands of the General Government an instrument more potent to control the freedom of the press than the Sedition Law itself," for it would give to the federal government the right to decide what publications were incendiary and what were not and of enforcing the transmission of those deemed not incendiary.[23] Calhoun was opposed to federal censorship of the mails partly because he foresaw the consequences that might befall Southern institutions once the antislavery forces obtained control of the national government.

Much of this excitement over the issue of incendiary publications was due to political motives. Calhoun had a deep-seated grudge against Jackson, the enemy who had thwarted his presidential ambitions and who had taken a resolute stand against nullification. Since Jackson's choice for President in 1836 was Martin Van Buren, Calhoun was eager to discredit this New Yorker in the South by attaching to him the stigma

[22] If Calhoun had lived to witness the prohibition era, he would have noted with grim satisfaction that the federal government accepted his principle and aided the dry states to enforce their prohibition laws.

[23] Richard K. Crallé, *Works of John C. Calhoun* (New York, 1888), II, 512-14.

of being allied with the Northern abolitionists.[24] The Carolina leader saw an opportunity to unite the South by magnifying the importance of the abolitionists. Accordingly, his report on the bill to exclude abolition literature from the mails was definitely an alarmist document.[25] In private letters Calhoun revealed his desire to unite the South by agitating the slave question. To Armistead Burt he wrote:. "We stand stronger than we ever did on the Slave question. The South is more united, and the nature of the question is better understood both north and South than it has ever been. But we must not relax. The abolitionists are numerous, zealous, and active."[26] Calhoun ignored the fact that the vast majority of Northern people at this period, even John Quincy Adams, did not approve of the abolitionists.[27]

Loyal Southerners and pro-Jackson men like Senators King of Alabama, Cuthbert of Georgia, and Felix Grundy of Tennessee protested against Calhoun's making a party question out of the exclusion of incendiary publications from the mails.[28] Benton records a story showing Calhoun's partisan zeal against Van Buren. Calhoun and the anti-Jackson men brought about a tie vote on the engrossment of the bill concerning incendiary publications. Van Buren, the presiding officer of the Senate, happened to be absent from his chair temporarily when the vote was taken. But Calhoun called eagerly and loudly for his rival to cast the deciding vote.[29] The oily Albany politician, however, disappointed him by voting with the Southern senators. Subsequently, the bill was defeated by a vote of twenty-five to nine-

[24] Claude G. Bowers, *The Party Battles of the Jacksonian Period* (Boston, 1922), pp. 443-49.

[25] Francis Blair, friend of Jackson, and editor of the Washington *Globe,* pointed out the political nature of Calhoun's agitation of the slave question. W. E. Smith, *The Francis Preston Blair Family in Politics* (New York, 1933), I, 120.

[26] Calhoun to Armistead Burt, June 28, 1836. *Annual Report of the American Historical Association for the Year 1899* (Washington, 1900), II, 361.

[27] Professor Avery Craven maintains that Adams concealed the fact that he was a "thorough-going abolitionist" to further his designs of agitation. *The Coming of the Civil War* (New York, 1942), pp. 176-77. Later the abolitionists such as Weld and Birney converted great numbers of people in the Middle West to their cause.

[28] *Cong. Globe,* 24 Cong., 1 sess., II-III, 37, 353 (Dec. 21, 1835; Apr. 18, 1836).

[29] Thomas Hart Benton, *Thirty Years' View* (New York, 1854-56), I, 587.

teen, in which seven Southern senators, including Henry Clay and Thomas Hart Benton, cast negative votes.[30]

The political press of the South undoubtedly inflamed the Southern people on this issue of excluding abolition publications from the slave states. The powerful Richmond *Whig,* for example, accused Thomas Ritchie, editor of the Richmond *Enquirer,* of "keeping the peddle soft" when writing about the Northern "fanatics" because this politician-editor feared to injure the prospects of Van Buren by a bold stand against the abolitionists.[31] The *Enquirer* later retorted by asserting that the Whigs were trying to create an abolition panic in order to defeat Van Buren. Mr. Vincent Witcher, said the wily Democratic editor, carried in his pocket the worst pamphlets of "the fanatics" and the most odious pictures that he could obtain from Gerrit Smith, Tappan, and Co. He exhibited them to the inhabitants of Pittsylvania County "by way of frightening his people into Whiggery, as if they were so many children."[32]

In July, 1836, Congress passed a drastic law reorganizing the Post Office Department, which had recently been criticized by the enemies of Jackson for corruption and mismanagement.[33] One of its provisions prohibited any postmaster, under severe penalty, from unlawfully detaining in his office any letter, package, pamphlet, or newspaper and refusing to deliver the same to the person to whom it was addressed.[34] Such legislation should have restored to the abolitionists the right to use the mails to send their literature into the slave states. But this law remained a dead letter so far as the Southern mails were concerned and was ignored with impunity during the ante-bellum period.

The Northern public did not arise to defend the freedom of

[30] *Cong. Globe,* 24 Cong., I sess., II-III, 539 (June 8, 1836).

[31] Richmond *Whig,* July 24, 1835.

[32] Richmond *Enquirer,* Apr. 1, 1836; see C. H. Ambler, *Thomas Ritchie: A Study in Virginia Politics* (Richmond, 1913), p. 166.

[33] See William Stickney, ed., *Autobiography of Amos Kendall* (Boston, 1872), chaps. XII-XIII.

[34] Laws of the United States of a Public Nature, No. 64, Sec. 32, Gales and Seaton, *Register of Debates in Congress,* XII, Part 4, Appendix XXXII.

the mails. No spectacular and prominent figure appeared to fight for the removal of the censorship of the mails until 1859, when Horace Greeley unsheathed his sword to attack "Post-Office Despotism."[35] One important reason for this neglect was that the attention of the Northern people was focused on the dramatic battle that William Slade and John Quincy Adams were making in Congress to secure the freedom of petition in regard to antislavery petitions. The abolitionists themselves realized that "the petition strategy" had far more popular appeal to American democratic instincts than the insistence on the right to use the Southern mails for their propaganda. They concentrated, therefore, on the fight against the Gag Rule in Congress until it was abandoned in 1844. Furthermore, the vast majority of Northern people at this period were indifferent to the violation of the freedom of the mails, because they lacked sympathy for the abolitionists, whose civil rights were being denied.[36]

An exception to the general apathy of the North was shown by William Leggett, acting editor of the New York *Evening Post,* who vigorously condemned the indirect bureaucratic censorship of the mails by the postal department. He declared that neither the federal post office nor the general government itself possessed any power to prohibit the transportation by mail of abolition tracts, but that it was the duty of the government to protect abolitionists in their constitutional right of free discussion. Although he was opposed to the doctrines and practices of the abolitionists, he proclaimed that he was still more opposed to any infringement of their political or civil rights. "If the government once begins to discriminate as to what is orthodox and what heterodox in opinion, what is safe and what unsafe in tendency," he warned, "farewell, a long

[35] New York *Tribune,* Dec. 28, 1859.

[36] The editor of the Philadelphia *National Gazette,* for example, condemned both the Charleston mob for rifling the mails and also the abolitionists for attempting to circulate their publications in the slave states. He printed a long article declaring that the Postmaster General ought not to hesitate to take the responsibility of excluding the incendiary publications of the abolitionists from the mails. The *National Gazette,* Aug. 8, 22, 1836.

farewell to our freedom."[37] For this courageous criticism of Kendall's ruling on the transmission of the mails, the *Evening Post* was deprived of its government patronage. The advertisment for uncalled-for letters in the New York post office was transferred to a rival newspaper.[38]

The ablest protest in the North against the violation of the freedom of the mails was a pamphlet published at Worcester, Massachusetts, in 1836 by "Cincinnatus." "Cincinnatus" was the pen name of William Plumer, a former governor and United States senator from New Hampshire. In this document, entitled "Freedom's Defence: or a Candid Examination of Mr. Calhoun's Report on the Freedom of the Press," Plumer sought to arouse the yeomanry and the laboring men of the North to defend the freedoms of the press and of the mails, which were threatened by Southern slaveholders. Calhoun's bill and his insidious report on the circulation of incendiary publications through the mails were represented by Plumer to be a menace to the democratic spirit of America. He pointed out that Calhoun would deny the freedom of the press and the use of the mails for laboring men to protest against the exploitation of labor. At great length he refuted Calhoun's analysis of a community of interest between the capitalists of both sections, as well as a close analogy between the slaves of the South and "the operatives" of the North. Calhoun justified "grinding the faces of the laboring classes."[39] His proposed bill on the circulation of abolition publications was a dangerous attack on the liberty of the press and on free institutions, violating the bill of rights in the constitutions even of the Southern states and preventing the free play of truth to vanquish error.

After the excitement of the 1830's, the fear of a flood of abolition publications inundating the South subsided, not to

[37] Allan Nevins, *The Evening Post: A Century of Journalism* (New York, 1922), p. 148.

[38] J. M. Lee, *History of American Journalism* (Boston, 1917), p. 223.

[39] *Freedom's Defence: or a Candid Examination of Mr. Calhoun's Report on the Freedom of the Press, Made to the Senate of the United States, Feb. 4, 1836*, by Cincinnatus (Worcester, 1836), p. 14. A pamphlet loaned to the writer by the courtesy of Dwight L. Dumond.

be revived to any great extent until 1856, when a bitter political campaign agitated the Southern people. One reason for this decline of alarm over incendiary publications was the fact that the Northern abolition societies abandoned their campaign of sending propaganda to leading Southerners.[40] Furthermore, this emotional propaganda was prevented from circulating in the slave states by the action of mobs as well as the censorship of the Southern mails by postmasters. Occasionally some of the abolition publications managed to pass the blockade and reach their destination in the South. The editor of the Flemingsburg *Kentuckian,* for example, noted that about a dozen copies of the *Emancipator* had been sent to the citizens of his village, and that he had received a copy marked "Read, calmly reflect, and be convinced!"[41] The editor of the *Hiwassee Patriot* at Madisonville, Tennessee, declared that he had seen copies of *Human Rights* circulating in his county, an abolitionist publication that should be committed to the flames, since it had "no other tendency than to corrupt and disaffect our slaves."[42] In 1849 some abolition publications were sent to the post office at Pendleton, South Carolina, but a mob seized the mails and destroyed the offending abolition matter, a procedure which George Prentice, the influential editor of the Louisville *Journal,* strongly condemned.[43]

Although the danger from obvious abolition publications thus decreased, Southerners detected a more subtle method of smuggling antislavery sentiments across the Potomac and Ohio rivers in religious magazines, in literary periodicals, and in the metropolitan newspapers of the North. Consequently a movement arose in the latter part of the ante-bellum period to boycott Northern magazines, such as *Harper's Magazine, Putnam's,* the *Saturday Evening Post,* and the *Atlantic Monthly,* that were unfavorable to Southern slavery.[44] In 1846 a motion was passed

[40] G. H. Barnes, *The Antislavery Impulse, 1830-1844* (New York, 1933), pp. 100-104.

[41] Flemingsburg *Kentuckian,* Mar. 30, 1838.

[42] *Hiwassee Patriot,* Feb. 26, 1839.

[43] Louisville *Daily Journal,* Oct. 4 and Oct. 11, 1849.

[44] Raleigh *Register,* Aug. 22, 25, 29, 1855; *Southern Literary Messenger,* XXV (Dec., 1857), 472; *De Bow's Review,* XXII (Jan., 1857), 100.

in the Virginia house of delegates ordering the Attorney General to investigate the question whether the Baltimore *Saturday Visitor* was an incendiary publication circulating in Virginia contrary to the law of 1836. It had printed a speech of Cassius Marcellus Clay of Kentucky, a gradual emancipationist.[45] Near the close of the ante-bellum period a mass meeting was held in Taylor County, Virginia, which passed the following resolution: "Resolved, That the five *Christian Advocates* published in the cities of New York, Pittsburgh, Cincinnati, St. Louis, and Chicago, having become abolition sheets of the rankest character, we ask our Commonwealth's attorneys and postmasters to examine them and if found to be of an unlawful character to deal with them and their agents as the laws of the State direct."[46] The New York *Tribune,* under the editorship of Horace Greeley, won a premier place as an incendiary publication to be banned from circulation in a Southern state. After the John Brown Raid, Postmaster R. H. Glass of Lynchburg, Virginia, informed the editor of the *Tribune* that he would not in the future deliver copies of this paper that came to his office. This decision was based on the following reason: "I believe them to be of that incendiary character which are forbidden circulation alike by the laws of the land and a proper regard for the safety of society."[47]

The general policy of the federal Post Office Department toward the circulation of incendiary publications through the mails remained unchanged from the time of Amos Kendall to the outbreak of the Civil War.[48] One of the most important statements concerning this policy was issued by the Attorney General of Franklin Pierce, Caleb Cushing, a proslavery native of Massachusetts. In 1857 the postmaster of Yazoo City, Mis-

[45] Lexington (Ky.) *True American,* Feb. 18, 1846.
[46] Norfolk (Va.) *Southern Argus,* Mar. 19, 1858.
[47] Wheeling (Va.) *Intelligencer,* Dec. 13, 1859; *The Liberator,* Dec. 30, 1859; see also the New York *Tribune,* Nov. 17 and Dec. 17, 1859, for other instances.
[48] See Lindsay Rogers, *The Postal Power of Congress: A Study in Constitutional Expansion,* Johns Hopkins Studies in Historical and Political Science, Ser. XXXIV, No. 2 (Baltimore, 1916), pp. 140-43. The records of the Post Office for this period ("outgoing correspondence") which are preserved in the Historical Library of the Post Office Department are fragmentary and not available to the public for examination. No "incoming" correspondence of that period has been retained in the department.

sissippi, refused to deliver a copy of the Cincinnati *Gazette* to a Mr. Patterson, alleging that it was an incendiary publication. When the Cincinnati *Gazette* protested this arbitrary interference with the free transmission of the mails, the Postmaster General requested that Cushing give a legal opinion on the issue. The latter ruled that a federal postmaster was not required to deliver mail which was designed or had the tendency to promote insurrection in a slave state. He admitted, however, that the postal authorities could not take final action in determining whether the subscriber had a right to receive the newspaper in question, or whether it violated the Mississippi law prohibiting any white person from circulating publications containing sentiments, doctrines, advice, or innuendoes, "calculated to produce a disorderly, dangerous, or rebellious disaffection among the colored population." The only lawful way ultimately to decide these questions, the Attorney General declared, was recourse to the courts of the state or of the federal district.[49]

Two years later a similar policy of the virtual censorship of the Southern mails was sustained by Postmaster General Holt. This Southern cabinet officer held the typical point of view of his section, that the circulation of abolition publications in the slave states was like throwing firebrands into a powder magazine. In a letter to the postmaster at Falls Church, Virginia, who had written to ask whether he should obey the Virginia law relating to postmasters and incendiary mail, Holt made the following rule:

> You must under the responsibilities resting upon you as an officer and as a citizen determine whether the books, pamphlets, newspapers, etc., received by you for distribution are of the incendiary character described in the statute, and if you believe they are, then you are not only not obliged to deliver them to those to whom they are addressed, but you are empowered and required by your duty to the State of which you are a citizen to dispose of them in strict conformity to the provisions of the law referred to.

[49] United States Department of Justice, *Official Opinions of the Attorneys General of the United States Advising the President and Heads of Departments in Relation to Their Official Duties,* comp. by Caleb Cushing (Washington, 1858), VIII, Yazoo City Post Office Case, 489-502.

The people of Virginia may not only forbid the introduction and dissemination of such documents within their borders, but if brought there in the mails, they may by appropriate legal proceeding have them destroyed.[50]

The Assistant Postmaster General, however, took a more liberal position in regard to the censorship of the mails. The postmaster of a little Virginia village, Luney's Creek, wrote to the editor of the *Religious Telescope* of Dayton, Ohio, after the John Brown Raid, that he was no longer permitted to deliver the latter publication and would burn any copies that came into his custody. The Assistant Postmaster General repudiated this arbitrary ruling. He declared: "Because a single copy of any particular newspaper contains matter decided by the state authorities to be incendiary in character, it does not, therefore, follow that any subsequent numbers of the same paper are to be condemned for that cause. Each and every number of the paper must be acted upon and disposed of separately."[51] Thus he stated one of the most important principles in American censorship.

After the abnormal excitement of the John Brown Raid, postmasters wrote from remote Virginia towns to Governor Wise to ascertain what action they must take in regard to delivering the New York *Tribune* and other papers of that character. The governor referred the matter to his Attorney General, John Randolph Tucker. The latter, in reply to the postmaster of a little town in Doddridge County, quoted the Virginia law requiring postmasters to notify a justice of the peace when they thought that incendiary publications came to their offices. The justice of the peace should determine whether the paper in question was incendiary, and if it were such, he should burn it and arrest the consignee if the latter was cognizant of the incendiary character of the publication. The Attorney General declared that this state law was entirely constitutional and did not, properly considered, conflict with

[50] *Congressional Record,* 53 Cong., 2 sess., Vol. XXVI, Part IX, Appendix, Part 1 (Washington, 1894), p. 4.
[51] New York *Tribune,* Feb 8, 1860.

the federal authority in the establishment of post offices and post roads. "This Federal power to transmit and carry mail matter, does not carry with it the power to publish and circulate," he ruled. "With the transmission of the mail matter to the point of its reception the Federal power ceases."[52]

The Southern censorship of the mails during the last three decades before the Civil War could be justified only on the ground that the safety of the people is the supreme law. Undoubtedly a nation, and probably a regional society, has the right to protect itself against subversive propaganda. Southerners feared that, if abolition publications were allowed free circulation in the South, eventually these inflammatory writings would fall into the hands of some brooding Nat Turner or Denmark Vesey.[53] Many slaves in the South could read. Although the majority of Southern states had laws prohibiting the teaching of slaves to read and write, in Kentucky, Maryland, and Tennessee there were no legal impediments to slaves' acquiring this knowledge. Even in those states which prohibited the teaching of the mystery of letters to the slaves, a considerable number of house servants were instructed by indulgent masters.[54] An examination of over 350 advertisements for fugitive Kentucky slaves by McDougle reveals the surprising fact that in seventy-one cases the masters mentioned the fact that the absconding Negro could read, which would seem to indicate that one fifth of the runaway slaves in the Upper South could read.[55]

The fear of servile insurrection was only one element in the complex of motives that led to the Southern censorship of the mails. It is likely that "the cotton capitalists" viewed with uneasiness the circulation of abolition propaganda, comparable to

[52] Letter of J. R. Tucker, Richmond, Nov. 26, 1859, *Cong. Rec.,* as cited in n. 50 above. Also quoted in *The Liberator,* Dec. 23, 1859.

[53] Clement Eaton, *A History of the Old South* (New York, 1949), Chapters 11 and 16.

[54] Carter Woodson, *The Education of the Negro Prior to 1861* (New York, 1915), p. 228; also Woodson's *The Mind of the Negro as Reflected in Letters* (Washington, 1926) and *Life and Times of Frederick Douglass Written by Himself* (New York, 1941), chaps. x-xi.

[55] I. E. McDougle, *Slavery in Kentucky, 1792-1865* (Lancaster, 1915), p. 79.

the modern communist propaganda, that might disturb the minds of the white non-slaveholders and yeomen who were injured economically by the institution of slavery. The supression of the circulation of Hinton Rowan Helper's *Impending Crisis,* which was addressed solely to the white non-slaveholders and not to the Negroes, whom he hated, indicated a fear among the ruling class of the South that a realistic discussion of slavery might set non-slaveholders against slaveholders. So strong, however, was the desire among the yeomanry and poor whites to keep the South a white man's country that there was little immediate danger of the development of a class struggle initiated by the dialectic of a free labor society.[56] Furthermore, the nature of the abolitionists' indictment, frequently out of line with reality and filled with the most violent vituperation of the whole of Southern civilization, was provocative of intolerance among all classes of society in the land of Dixie.[57] Southern public opinion became so inflamed over the abolitionist publications that even the most rational discussion of slavery was branded as "incendiary" and not permitted to circulate in the Southern states.[58] Thomas Ritchie, an influential leader in forming public opinion in the Upper South, who had been an avowed antislavery man at the time of the Virginia debate on emancipation in 1832, declared eight years later; "Certainly the fanatics at the North have taken the most effective means not to leave a single friend of emancipation in the Southern states."[59]

[56] Roger W. Shugg, *Origins of Class Struggle in Louisiana: A Social History of White Farmers and Laborers during Slavery and After, 1840-1875* (University, La., 1939), chaps. IV-V.

[57] This theme has been stated by F. L. Owsley in an essay, "The Irrepressible Conflict," in *I'll Take My Stand: The South and the Agrarian Tradition, by Twelve Southerners* (New York, 1930; Harper Torchbook edition, 1962), and by Avery Craven in *The Repressible Conflict, 1830-1861* (University, La., 1939). For an objective point of view see H. H. Simms, "A Critical Analysis of Abolition Literature, 1830-1840," *Journal of Southern History,* VI (1940), 368-82.

[58] See Dwight L. Dumond's discussion of this subject in *Antislavery Origins of the Civil War in the United States* (Ann Arbor, 1939), chaps. II-IV. Professor Dumond shows also how bitterly persecuted the abolitionists were in the North during the decade 1830-40.

[59] Richmond *Enquirer,* Feb. 18, 1840.

The effectiveness of the Southern censorship depended partly on a remarkable unity of public sentiment within the South in regard to the abolition publications. But the co-operation of the federal postal authorities was also necessary in imposing a censorship of the mails. This co-operation was given by the administrations of Southern presidents and of Northern presidents with Southern sympathies. It indicated among the responsible leaders of the federal government that the Southerners had a good case in demanding the exclusion of antislavery propaganda from the Southern mails. Since it was difficult to draw the line between incendiary publications and lawful literature of reform and criticism, the postal authorities took the path of least resistance and made no attempt to discriminate between the two types of propaganda. Consequently the radicals of the North found that they were denied the use of the federal mails in forwarding their publications across the frontier of the land of Dixie. When the election of Lincoln transferred the executive branch of the federal government from Southern to Northern control, Southerners feared that a hostile Postmaster General would be appointed who would try to enforce a free transmission of abolition publications through the mails and thus destroy the "dike of silence."[60]

The continuity of censorship by the postal department was illustrated by the suppression of socialist and communist propaganda during World War I and during "the big red scare" of 1920's. In this relatively modern case intolerance was a defense mechanism against a danger, the Bolshevist menace, which was greatly exaggerated in the popular mind. Censorship in wartime belongs to a different category from censorship in peacetime, but the habit of regulating expression of opinion during a national emergency is likely to carry over into normal times. In President Wilson's cabinet the Attorney General and the Postmaster General were responsive to the intolerant atmosphere of the period. Postmaster General Burleson exercised a despotic and unjustifiable censorship, practically denying the use of the

[60] Carl Russell Fish, *The American Civil War* (London, 1937), pp. 44-45.

PLATE I

Gunston Hall on the Potomac By courtesy of Louis Hertle
George Mason Portrait [after Hesselius] owned by Virginia Historical Society Library

PLATE II

Berry Hill, near Halifax, Virginia

PLATE III

"A Cotton Plantation on the Mississippi"
From a Currier and Ives pint

Cooleemee, on the Yadkin River, North Carolina
Sketch by Margaret Eaton Smithdeal

PLATE IV a

Grand Stairway at Cooleemee
Sketch by Margaret Eaton Smithdeal

PLATE IV b

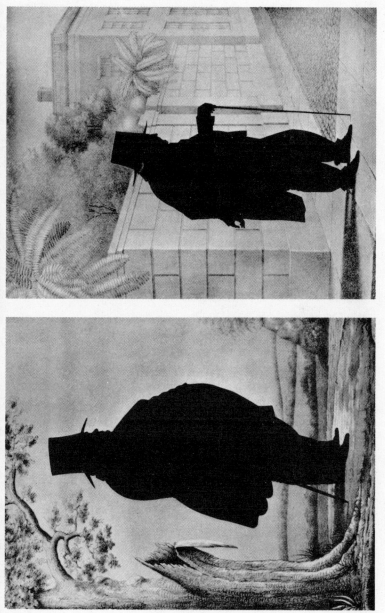

PLATE V a   Senator Dixon H. Lewis of Alabama
Silhouette by William H. Brown

PLATE V b   Doctor Thomas Cooper
Silhouette by William H. Brown

James Louis Petigru
Engraving in the Library of Congress
PLATE VI a

Henry A. Wise
Photograph from J. P. Cook
PLATE VI b

Cassius Marcellus Clay
Photograph in the New York Public Library
PLATE VII b

John Hampden Pleasants
Engraving owned by the Virginia Historical Society
PLATE VII a

PLATE VIII

Fort Hill, Calhoun's home, near Pendleton, South Carolina

mails to certain radical publications. In the Milwaukee *Leader* Case, March 7, 1921, the Supreme Court upheld this arbitrary and unenlightened use of the power of censorship by the postal department.[61] Although sixty years had intervened since the censorship of the Buchanan administration, no marked progress was discernible in the *practice* of tolerance in the United States of the 1920's. Individuals such as Judge Learned Hand, Justice Oliver Wendell Holmes, and Professor Zechariah Chafee had made notable contributions to the *theory* of toleration, but they were dissenting voices in the postwar world. Ordinary human nature seemed to be incapable of practicing tolerance, save in unessential or indifferent matters.

[61] Zechariah Chafee, jr., *Free Speech in the United States* (Cambridge, 1941), pp. 42-51, 98-99, 298-305; J. R. Mock, *Censorship, 1917* (Princeton, 1941), pp. 148-52, 230-31; F. L. Mott, *American Journalism* (New York, 1941), pp. 605, 623-25.

CHAPTER IX

ACADEMIC FREEDOM BELOW THE POTOMAC

IN BRIGHT CONTRAST to the apathy of the Old South toward the education of the masses was her record in collegiate education. Realizing the need for training leaders, the Southern States were the first to establish state universities. As the economic prosperity of the land of Dixie increased and as the religious denominations entered into an aggressive rivalry, new colleges were founded and the older ones increased their enrollment. This notable expansion occurred despite the fact that many sons of wealthy planters were attracted to Northern institutions. According to the census of 1860, Virginia had twenty-three colleges with an enrollment of 2,824 students, Georgia, thirty-two colleges with 3,302 students, while New York had only seventeen colleges with an enrollment of 2,970 students, and Massachusetts eight institutions of higher learning with 1,733 students.[1] Undoubtedly some of the institutions designated as colleges in the South were not much more than academies, or "log-cabin colleges." It should be noted, however, that aristocratic Virginia annually spent fifty thousand dollars more than Massachusetts on colleges, indicating that she realized the need of trained leaders. In 1857 there was one college man to every six hundred and sixty-six white inhabitants in Virginia as compared with one to every nine hundred and forty-four white inhabitants in Massachusetts.[2] The enrollment at Harvard in 1856 was three hundred and sixty-one students, while the University of Virginia had five hundred and fifty-eight students.[3]

[1] *The Eighth Census of the United States; Mortality and Miscellaneous Statistics*, p. 505.
[2] *Southern Literary Messenger*, XXIV, 165-166 (March, 1857).
[3] *Catalogue of the Students of Harvard University for the Academical Year 1855-56* (Cambridge, Mass., 1856), p. 23, and *Catalogue of University of Virginia, Session of 1855-'56* (Richmond, 1856), p. 16.

Not all Southern colleges, however, were prospering in these last decades of the Old South. The University of Georgia lost many of its best professors during this period, and by 1856 had declined in enrollment to seventy-nine pupils.[4] William and Mary College was in such a languishing condition in 1848 that George Frederick Holmes in disgust resigned his professorship that paid him the princely salary of one thousand dollars. He declared that he saw no hope for a revival of the college, torn as it was by dissensions in the faculty and unsupported by the people of the state.[5] South Carolina College, which attained an enrollment of two hundred and thirty-seven men in 1849 while the brilliant orator, W. C. Preston, was president, had only one hundred and seventy students in 1860. Transylvania University, after a burst of splendor under President Horace Holley in the 1820's, went into a long decline.

Following the example of Northern institutions of higher learning, the Southern colleges routinized their intellectual life around the classics. There was little in the collegiate education of the Old South to direct the minds of students to the grave economic and social evils that surrounded them. The freshman and sophomore years in most Southern colleges were devoted almost exclusively to the classics and mathematics. The most striking omission in the curriculum of the ante-bellum college was the absence of courses in modern history, both European and American. If the teaching of the classics often degenerated into a well-worn treadmill, occasionally a brilliant man, like Basil Gildersleeve at the University of Virginia, would make his courses a contribution to genuine culture. A few realists, like Thomas S. Grimké of Charleston, Matthew Fontaine Maury, and Philip Lindsley, President of the University of Nashville, protested against the dominance of the classics. Grimké roundly declared that young men wasted some of the most valuable years of their lives in studying dead lan-

[4] Coulter, *College Life in the Old South,* pp. 250-256.
[5] Holmes to Col. McCandlish, Rector of the Board of Visitors, Jan. 22, 1848 (G. F. Holmes Papers, MSS in Library of Congress).

guages which were useless in practical life.[6] Maury protested: "When our young men leave college most of them (some exceptions) are prepared as little for entering upon the world as they were when they entered college. The reason of this is that every young man is taught to believe Latin and Greek, of the first importance; consequently everything that is solid and practical, such as mathematics, chemistry and the like is made to occupy a subordinate place and only a smattering of them is obtained. West Point is considered to be the only tolerable institution in the United States; and why it is so is owing to the circumstance that the humbuggery of the Learned Languages is not tolerated there. . . . Does it not appear strangely inconsistent that in our colleges we should always have Professors of Hebrew, Greek and Latin, and not of the English language, when there are so few persons who can write or speak a half dozen sentences without committing some blunder."[7] Lindsley, a native of New Jersey and a graduate of Princeton, attempted to push the classics into the background, and to educate Southern youth for the manifold activities of life, including government, commerce, manufacturing, fencing, swimming, and gymnastics.[8]

Although the classics reigned supreme on rural campuses of the South, scientific studies were also taught. At the University of Virginia, which had an enrollment of five hundred and fifty-eight students in 1856, one hundred and ninety-one students were taking courses in chemistry and one hundred and forty-three, courses in natural philosophy.[9] Able professors of science were established in the leading colleges and universities of the South. At Transylvania University in Kentucky, the eccentric professor, Constantine Samuel Rafinesque, taught botany; at the University of Nashville, Gerard Troost taught science in the midst of a confusion of stuffed

[6] Perry, *Reminiscences of Public Men*, p. 276.

[7] Maury to Anne Maury, Aug. 28, 1836 (M. F. Maury Papers, I, MSS in Library of Congress).

[8] George P. Schmidt, "Intellectual Crosscurrents in American Colleges, 1825-1855," *American Historical Review*, XLII, 57-58 (Oct., 1936).

[9] T. C. Johnson, *Scientific Interests in the Old South* (New York, 1936), p. 14.

birds, turtles, fossils, minerals, chemical apparatus, and books.[10] William Barton Rogers, later the founder of Massachusetts Institute of Technology, lectured at the University of Virginia. In Chapel Hill, President Joseph Caldwell built an astronomical observatory, where the first systematic observations of the stars and planets in the United States were begun; here also the distinguished geologist, Elisha Mitchell, taught until his tragic death on Mount Mitchell. Oglethorpe University had on its faculty James Woodrow, who became a champion of the evolution theory in the South. At the University of Georgia and at South Carolina College, the LeConte brothers were brilliant teachers of science, while at the youthful University of Alabama, Frederick A. P. Barnard, Michael Tuomey, and John W. Mallet added lustre to Southern scholarship by their scientific studies. But in the city of Charleston, where the College of Charleston and the Medical College of South Carolina were located, a distinguished center of scientific interests flourished. Here John Bachman, author of *The Quadrupeds of North America,* Lewis R. Gibbes, a versatile scientist, Francis S. Holmes, the eminent authority on fossils, and John Edward Holbrook, author of a learned work on the reptiles of North America, taught in the college, while the Ravenels, Joel Poinsett, Stephen Elliott, Joseph Mellichamp, and others, did significant work as amateurs or patrons. Louis Agassiz gave two courses on science in Charleston in 1847-48, a city which several years later established the most valuable museum of natural history in the South.[11]

The emphasis on the classics at the expense of the exact sciences in the colleges of the Old South was not so great an abuse as the suppression of academic freedom. Academic freedom in the Old South included the rights of professors to select their own textbooks, to speak their thoughts on slavery and politics, and to hold unorthodox views on religion. In a

---

[10] See Philip Lindsley, "Discourse on the Life and Character of Professor Gerard Troost, M.D.," in L. J. Halsey (ed.), *The Works of Philip Lindsley, D.D.* (Philadelphia, 1866), I, 591-640.

[11] Easterby, *A History of the College of Charleston,* pp. 108-113.

rough and tumble world academic freedom cannot possibly exist without certain limitations. Even in the most liberal university of the South, the University of Virginia, Jefferson, the founder, was unwilling that the law faculty should choose their own textbooks, lest young Southerners should imbibe false doctrines at variance with republican government.[12] All kinds of practical considerations limited the freedom of the Southern professors. State legislatures and boards of trustees, who were composed of the most respectable men of the state, squires, judges, colonels, generals, and honorables, were heavily interested in "cotton capitalism" and Negro slaves. The criticism of slavery became therefore a tabooed subject in the classic halls and beneath the towering oaks of Southern campuses.

In the early phases of the development of the proslavery philosophy, the colleges produced a few antislavery critics. The Catholic jurist, Judge William Gaston, who was invited to deliver the commencement address at the University of North Carolina in 1832, used the occasion to warn the young men of that institution of the dangers that lay in the continuance of slavery. Less than a year had elapsed since the Nat Turner insurrection, and he recognized the fact that " a morbid sensitiveness" prevailed in respect to the discussion of slavery. Nevertheless, he courageously declared that slavery more than any other cause had kept the South back in the career of improvements. He pointed out that slavery was not only injurious from an economic point of view, but that it "poisons morals at the fountain head."[13] Although he openly advocated the abolition of such an unwise system of labor, he was enthusiastically cheered by his audience. So popular was this speech among the students that five editions of it were published, the last in 1858. Not long after this memorable address, he was elevated to the Supreme Court of North Carolina by the legislature.

[12] H. A. Washington (ed.), *The Writings of Thomas Jefferson* (Washington, D. C., 1854), VII, 397.

[13] William Gaston, *Address Delivered before the Dialectic and Philanthropic Societies at Chapel Hill, N. C., June 20, 1832* (4th ed.; Raleigh, N. C., 1849).

The students and faculty of Centre College, Kentucky, took an attitude toward the discussion of slavery more liberal than that of any other college in the South. President J. C. Young wrote a pamphlet advocating the gradual emancipation of the slaves.[14] On September 30, 1834, James G. Birney recorded in his diary the report that fourteen of the students were firm abolitionists.[15] It is a significant fact that the Kentucky State Anti-Slavery Society, organized the following March, elected Professor Buchanan of Centre College as its first president and Professor Luke Munsell corresponding secretary.

The trustees of the college, however, frowned upon anti-slavery zeal. This conservatism was revealed when Birney sought a permanent appointment on the faculty. In 1834 he had taught two hours daily during the absence of Professor Breckinridge, while the latter was attending the legislature. He felt that he had succeeded as a teacher, but the trustees rejected him, he was informed by President Young, on account of his abolition views.[16] A year later Professor Buchanan resigned his professorship because of the prejudices aroused by his prominence in the abolition movement.[17]

In 1837 Professor George Tucker of the University of Virginia published an economic attack on the peculiar institution, entitled *The Laws of Wages, Profits, and Rents,* in which he garnered the cream of his lectures to his students.[18] He maintained that slave labor was less productive than free, and that it had an injurious economic effect on the white population, in leading to idleness, drunkenness, and dissipations. Such a system of labor, he declared, could not exist in the more advanced stages of society because of the need of industry and economy. He predicted, accordingly, that slavery must expire when the Lower South had used up its best lands, an eventuality which would probably not take place for forty or fifty

[14] William Birney, *James G. Birney and His Times,* pp. 154-155.
[15] James G. Birney Diary, 1834 (MS in Library of Congress).
[16] Birney to Theodore D. Weld, July 17, 1834 (James G. Birney Papers).
[17] Dumond, *Letters of James Gillespie Birney,* I, 277-280.
[18] For a recent study of Tucker, see Leonard C. Helderman, "A Social Scientist of the Old South," *Journal of Southern History,* II, 158-174 (May, 1936).

years.[19] He thought that the Northern abolitionists had done much to create an intolerant spirit, so that the advocates of emancipation in the slave states found it prudent to conceal their opinions. But when Tucker published his *History of the United States* in 1858, he had joined his compatriots of the Old Dominion and had become an apologist for the institution. He then maintained that slavery led to social ease and grace, to self-discipline and moderation among the planters, that the slave regime had produced extraordinary and noble characters, and he also asserted that the condition of the Southern slave was equal to that of the laboring class in any other country.[20]

During the latter part of the ante-bellum period college presidents or professors could not express any sympathy with the antislavery movement without serious danger of losing their jobs. In 1849 the president of Georgetown College in Kentucky, Dr. Howard Malcolm, a Northern man by birth, stirred up violent excitement by voting for an emancipation candidate to the constitutional convention. As a result of the resentment produced by this act, he felt compelled to hand in his immediate resignation to the board of trustees. The trustees by a unanimous vote expressed the belief that the continuance of Dr. Malcolm in the presidency would seriously injure the college.[21]

Without a doubt the most striking example of interference with academic freedom that occurred in the Old South was the dismissal of Professor Benjamin Sherwood Hedrick from the University of North Carolina. Hedrick was born near Salisbury, North Carolina, in the Piedmont area of the state. He lived on one of the main highways between Virginia and South Carolina, and here he could see coffles of slaves passing on their way to the Lower South. He was also impressed

---

[19] George Tucker, *The Laws of Wages, Profits, and Rents* (Philadelphia, 1837), chap. iii; also, *The Progress of Population in the United States* (New York, 1855), p. 17.

[20] George Tucker, *History of the United States* (Philadelphia, 1856-58), I, 98; III, 263.

[21] Louisville *Examiner*, Aug. 18, Sept. 1, 1849; see also L. W. Meyer, *Georgetown College: Its Background and a Chapter in Its Early History* (Louisville, Ky., 1929), p. 73.

by the fact that nearly one half of his neighbors, friends, and kindred abandoned the state to seek homes in the free West.[22] His antislavery views were strengthened while he was a student at Harvard University. He was not an abolitionist, however, but a free-soiler.[23] In 1854 he was appointed professor of chemistry at the University of North Carolina, where he devoted himself to his work and refrained from expressing his views on the explosive subject of slavery.

During the campaign of 1856, Hedrick was asked if he would vote for Frémont. He replied that he would if a Republican electoral ticket should appear in the state. When W. W. Holden heard the rumors of Hedrick's free-soil principles, he began a venomous attack on him in the Raleigh *Standard*. On September 17 he wrote an editorial entitled "Frémont in the South," which closed with these ominous words: "If there be Frémont men among us, let them be silenced or required to leave. The expression of Black Republican opinions in our midst is incompatible with our honor and safety as a people. If at all necessary we shall refer to this again. Let our schools and seminaries of learning be scrutinized, and if Black Republicans be found in them, let them be driven out. That man is neither a fit nor a safe instructor of our young men, who even inclines to Frémont and Black Republicanism."[24]

Shortly after this tirade, the *Standard* published a letter from a law student at the University charging one of the professors with being a Frémont supporter and expressing the opinion that he should be required to leave. Hedrick replied in an able letter of defense, calling to witness Jefferson and the great statesmen of the South who had condemned slavery. The Executive Committee held a meeting and resolved unanimously to persuade Hedrick to resign through the agency of President Swain and Charles Manly, former governor and at that time secretary and treasurer of the University. Manly

[22] Bassett, "Anti-Slavery Leaders of North Carolina," p. 291.

[23] Some of the Hedrick letters giving his views are preserved in the vault of the University of North Carolina.

[24] J. G. deR. Hamilton, "Benjamin Sherwood Hedrick," *James Sprunt Historical Publications*, X, 8.

wrote to Swain "to put on his Diplomatic Cap and manage this thing right."[25] The great danger to the University, he pointed out, was that Hedrick might wish to be dismissed "that he may fly to Yankeedom as the *Great Proscribed;* and find refuge in the bosom of Black Republicans with the blood of martyrdom streaming from his skirts, then he will not resign but will want to be kicked out." Hedrick was burnt in effigy by the students on the college campus; and the faculty, with the exception of Harrisse, passed resolutions censuring his course and exculpating themselves from any sympathy with his political views. The Executive Committee of the University also passed resolutions declaring that Hedrick had greatly impaired, if not entirely destroyed, his usefulness as a professor in the University. Notwithstanding, he persisted in holding his place. The University authorities did not wish to push the matter until after the election, but outside pressure throughout the state led to his dismissal.[26]

Professor Harrisse, who supported Hedrick, had a brilliant and bold mind that did not harmonize with the drowsy environment of Chapel Hill. In his later career he became world-famous for his work as a bibliographer and investigator of early American voyages. Harrisse was teaching French and studying law at the University when the Hedrick affair occurred. He had previously written for the university magazine an article of keen sarcasm entitled "Popular Delusions." In this he ridiculed the popular taste for seeing "the greatest wonder in the world" or hearing "the greatest fiddler in the world," or "the sweetest voice in the world," while real artists were neglected because they were unwilling "to be puffed up

[25] Charles Manly to David Swain, Oct. 4, 1856 (David L. Swain Papers in archives of North Carolina Historical Commission).

[26] Some representative newspapers which attacked Hedrick were: The Wilmington *Journal,* Oct. 10, 1856. Of Hedrick the editor wrote: "We would not contribute to give this vain yet designing youth the notoriety and profitable martyrship after which he evidently aspires. Of course, he can no longer retain a position in the university of a state, to whose institutions he is a traitor, nor enjoy even common respect among her citizens."

The *Carolina Watchman* of Salisbury, Oct. 28, 1856, said that Hedrick deserved to be dismissed: "The professorships should be sifted and weeded of those who may covertly circulate opinions not in sympathy with our social institutions."

in newspapers of all sizes, and handbills of all colors, by the side of Mustang Liniment or *Jew David's Hebrew Plaster*."[27] When Hedrick was assailed for his opinions, President Swain wrote to Charles Manly that he feared Harrisse would write "something foolish or worse," for he was a great admirer of Hedrick. He did write a most interesting article on the Hedrick affair for a French newspaper published at St. Louis, *La Revue de L'Ouest*. In an article on "Les Universités et L'Élection," he praised Hedrick for his brave loyalty to his convictions. "What was our joy," he exclaimed, "on reading a sincere republican profession of faith, open, bold, yet modest, joined to a perfectly plausible eulogy of Mr. Frémont. What happiness to compare this act of courage with the cowardly denunciation which had occasioned it."[28]

He closed with a scathing denunciation of Southern intolerance: "You may eliminate all the suspicious men from your institutions of learning, you may establish any number of new colleges which will relieve you of sending your sons to free institutions. But as long as people study, and read, and think among you, the absurdity of your system will be discovered and there will always be found some courageous intelligence to protest against your hateful tyranny. Close your schools, suppress learning and thought, you have nothing else to do in order to be faithful to your principles, and it is the only means which remains to you of continuing the struggle with some chances of success."[29] Harrisse became very unpopular at the University, got into trouble over discipline, and had to leave.[30]

In this same year a professor at the University of Virginia, A. T. Bledsoe, published an *Essay on Liberty and Slavery,*

[27] *University of North Carolina Magazine* (Second Series), II, 368-370 (Oct., 1853).

[28] *La Revue de L'Ouest*, St. Louis, Mo., Oct. 25, 1856. Translated by Professor W. M. Dey of the University of North Carolina.

[29] I am indebted to the late Professor E. V. Howell of the University of North Carolina for access to some of the source materials on Harrisse that he had collected.

[30] For a short biography, see Henry Vignaud, *Henry Harrisse* (Paris, 1912); also Adolf Growell, *Henry Harrisse, Biographical and Bibliographical Sketch* (New York, 1899).

which was an apology for slavery. One of his colleagues, Professor Charles B. Shaw, wrote an anonymous reply, in which he maintained that slavery had greatly injured the whites in Virginia, although it had elevated the Negroes. Shaw opposed immediate abolition, for he believed that both the slaves and their masters needed preparation for the accomplishment of emancipation. Nevertheless, he held that, admitting the danger of teaching the slaves to read and write, danger should be encountered for humanity's sake. He regretted the denial of free speech at the South, due partly to the growth of the fanatical abolition movement in the North. "Gradually a funeral pall has been drawn over any rational discussion of the slavery question," he wrote, "and if there be any now here who hold the sentiments once openly expressed, they are only whispered in confidence; even the moderate, the candid, and the humane, deem it impolitic to strengthen the hands of outside meddlers by any concessions to their views. No person can safely reside in the South who is suspected of liberal views on the subject of slavery."[31] Shaw's discussion of slavery was so reasonable and well tempered that it could not have been regarded as incendiary by any moderate person, but he did not dare to publish it under his signature.

It is surprising that Francis Lieber, with his antislavery views, was able to maintain his position as professor in South Carolina College for twenty years. His correspondence is filled with expressions of loathing for slavery; "I was not born for niggery."[32] That he lived in an atmosphere of repression is indicated by a letter to one of his Northern friends, "Don't let anything I have written slip into the papers."[33] Although he was very prudent in concealing his antislavery convictions from the scrutiny of his Southern neighbors, nevertheless, he sought to influence public opinion to accept the Wilmot Proviso. In a series of public letters addressed to Calhoun, he

[31] [Charles B. Shaw,] *A Reply to Professor Bledsoe* (Boston, 1857), p. 7.

[32] Lieber to Ruggles, Dec. 30, 1855 (Lieber MSS); notwithstanding, he owned slaves, whom he sold when he left Columbia (E. L. Green, *A History of the University of South Carolina*, p. 61).

[33] Lieber to Ruggles, July 14, 1842 (Lieber MSS).

made a noble plea for freedom of discussion in respect to
ridding the South of slavery. He declared that the rest of the
world recognized the value of the liberty of the press, but in
South Carolina, the freedom of the press was suspended on
all subjects relating to the inviolable institution. Addressing
the Carolina statesman directly, he wrote: "I know you, sir,
too well to fear from you the answer that no law prohibits
such discussion. You know as well as I do that it cannot
be done. . . . But if you fear discussion, if you maintain that
the South cannot afford it, that every man who differs from
your community, or who sees deficiencies in the institution
must be hushed, then you admit at the same time that the
whole institution is to be kept up by violence only and is
against the spirit of the times and unameliorable."[34]

In 1858 the Montgomery *Advertizer and Gazette* demanded the removal of Professor Nathan Green from the faculty of Cumberland University at Lebanon, Tennessee. The
editor asserted that Professor Green had talked with students
about his dangerous antislavery views. This liberal professor
was an eminent man in Tennessee, having resigned as Chief
Justice of the Supreme Court to head the law department of
Cumberland University.[35] He felt the need, nevertheless, to
reply to this accusation. Admitting frankly that he had long
considered slavery an evil, morally, socially, and politically,
he defended himself by declaring that he was born and reared
in Virginia and had owned slaves for fifty years. He considered the evil of slavery to be suffered chiefly by the master
and not by the slave.[36] His distinguished character commanded respect so that he was not displaced from his position
in the university. In the revolution of public opinion that
changed the Southern viewpoint to look upon slavery as a
positive good, he had remained unconvinced, a belated Jeffersonian.

The universities of the Old South had reason to fear ex-

[34] Perry, *Life and Letters of Francis Lieber,* pp. 235-236.
[35] W. P. Bone, *A History of Cumberland University, 1842-1935* (Lebanon,
Tenn., 1935), pp. 80-83.   [36] *National Era,* Aug. 19, 1858.

pression of antislavery sentiments by both faculty and students, for they were at the mercy of a powerful public sentiment that controlled the purse strings. In pursuance of a cautious policy, President Swain of the University of North Carolina stated to the faculty during the excited campaign year of 1856: "The sermons delivered on the Sabbath in the college chapel, have been confined to an exhibition of the leading doctrines of Christianity, with respect to which no difference of opinion exists among us; and no student during the last twenty years has been permitted to discuss upon the public stage any question of party politics."[37]

Augustus Baldwin Longstreet was a fair representative of the official attitude of Southern colleges toward religion and politics. He could speak with authority, for he had served as president, successively, of Emory University, Centenary College of Louisiana, the University of Mississippi, and at last, of the University of South Carolina. He regarded the encroachment of scientific discoveries upon the sacred mysteries of religion with profound intolerance; and college education, in his Methodist eyes, was always subordinate to religious orthodoxy. As to slavery and secession, he stood in the front rank of the fire-eaters. During the fierce struggle over slavery within the Methodist Church that led to the schism of 1844, Longstreet declared that "Abolition among Churchmen is a mania, a fanatical monster, an insatiable polyphemus, which will tear to pieces and devour everything sacred and all political and religious institutions."[38] Longstreet also openly encouraged secession sentiments among the students at the University of South Carolina, in defiance of Petigru's warning that the trustees would condemn a president who engaged in politics.

In the decade of the 1850's a powerful movement developed to sterilize the Southern colleges from antislavery ideas. Not only were attempts made to expurgate dangerous ideas from

[37] Hamilton, "Benjamin Sherwood Hedrick," p. 17.
[38] John Donald Wade, *Augustus Baldwin Longstreet: A Study of the Development of Culture in the South* (New York, 1924), p. 280.

the textbooks used both in colleges and schools, not only was an extensive campaign launched to dissuade wealthy Southerners from sending their sons to Northern colleges, but also a definite effort was made to establish colleges that would be free from the radical teachings of the North. In advocating the establishment of a university in Mississippi (1844) Governor Albert Gallatin Brown declared that the practice of sending Southern youths to be educated in other sections ought to be discouraged. They should be kept at home and shielded from the inculcation of false doctrines and prejudices against home institutions.[39] All of these efforts were attacks on the freedom of academic life; if they had matured they would have converted the Southern colleges and schools into institutions of propaganda.

The migration northward of many young Southerners to study in schools and colleges had long been gall and wormwood to the fire-eaters. Yet the pull of Northern colleges was too strong to be resisted. Even the ardent pro-Southern Governor Wise had been educated at Washington College, Pennsylvania. Calhoun had received his scholastic training at Yale and Litchfield, to be followed by lesser lights, such as Augustus Baldwin Longstreet, Cassius Marcellus Clay, Judah Benjamin, Governor James H. Adams of South Carolina, the ardent champion of reopening the African slave trade; Robert Toombs had studied at Union College; William Lowndes Yancey had matriculated at Williams College; while West Point trained a host of Southerners, including Jefferson Davis and Robert E. Lee. The famous law school at Litchfield, Connecticut, turned out nearly two hundred graduates from the Southern States, representing one fifth of the total number of its graduates.[40] At the University of Pennsylvania, of the four hundred and thirty-two students attending in 1846, two hundred and sixty-five were from the South, mostly medical students.[41] Yet these Northern colleges, as Professor Arthur

[39] Ranck, *Albert Gallatin Brown*, p. 33.
[40] Wade, *Augustus Baldwin Longstreet*, p. 40.
[41] Edward Ingle, *Southern Side-lights* (New York, 1896), p. 144.

Cole has pointed out, had slight success in nationalizing the Southern students who attended them.[42] Such an alarming patronage of Northern institutions by the gifted youth of the South seemed to be a confession of weakness in the idyllic slave regime, as though the repression of free thought in the South had dwarfed her institutions of learning.

After the John Brown invasion there began a hegira of Southern students from the North. On December 22, 1859, an extra train arrived at Richmond bringing over two hundred medical students from Philadelphia. The faculty and students of the Richmond Medical College, the town council, and the Southern Rights Association exultantly welcomed them. All formed in procession and marched to the governor's mansion past the beautiful capitol designed by Jefferson. The armory band preceded them, playing martial and stirring airs. Here they listened to Governor Henry A. Wise, standing on his porch and indulging in a tirade of incandescent Southern oratory. One of the students gracefully responded. Then they retired to the Columbian Hotel, where the hospitality of the Old South had prepared "a beautiful collation" for them.[43]

Governor Wise, fond of magniloquent phrases, exclaimed, "Let Virginia call home her children!" He assured them that they had acted wisely in leaving a hostile community to build up Southern schools and rebuke the North for its fanaticism. Thus the reproach so often made against the South, that negro slavery paralyzed learning and science, would be proved untrue. In his typical perfervid way, he exhorted: "Let us employ our own teachers, (applause), especially that they may teach our own doctrines. Let us dress in the wool raised on our own pastures. Let us eat the flour from our own mills, and if we can't get that, why let us go back to our old accustomed corn bread. (Loud applause.)"[44]

A similar point of view was expressed by Powhatan Ellis, a politician of the Deep South. "I have never known a young

[42] Arthur C. Cole, The Irrepressible Conflict, 1850-1865 (New York, 1934), p. 52.
[43] Richmond Semi-Weekly Enquirer, Dec. 23, 1859.
[44] Richmond Daily Dispatch, Dec. 23, 1859.

man educated at Yale or Cambridge," he wrote, "but what he returned to us a complete Yankee, and would lecture his parents in regard to the sin of holding human beings in Slavery. I think all these things ought to be considered in sending young men to college. They ought to be prepared by education, to make useful citizens in the society where their property is, and where they are destined to live."[45]

The campaign to persuade Southern youths to withdraw from Northern colleges and enter home institutions was condemned by some national-minded Southerners, such as John A. Gilmer of North Carolina, later to be considered for a Cabinet position by Lincoln. In a speech at Philadelphia (1859) Gilmer spoke of those Southerners who withdrew their children from Northern schools on account of sectional prejudices as "silly men."[46] A compromise position on this question was presented by the Southern historian, Francis Lister Hawks. His proposals were: (1) let the South educate her sons at home, but let her make educational opportunities as good as those of the North; (2) let her use no violence against incendiaries and abolitionist emissaries detected within her borders, except in accordance with the law; (3) let Southerners discriminate between friends and enemies at the North; (4) let the South develop her own manufactures and establish direct trade with Europe.[47]

The enrollment of Southern students in Northern colleges was not affected by this agitation of orators, newspapers, and Southern commercial conventions as much as one might expect. The number of students at Harvard from the Southern States increased from sixteen in 1830 to sixty-five in 1850 and declined by only two students in 1860. At Yale the enrollment in 1830 was sixty-nine students from the South, seventy-two in 1850, followed by a decline to thirty-three in 1860. At Prince-

---

[45] Powhatan Ellis to Powhatan, Jr., May 2, 1859 (Munford-Ellis Papers in Library of the University of North Carolina).

[46] *North Carolina Standard* (Raleigh, N. C.), Jan. 7, 1860.

[47] Francis Lister Hawks to David Swain, President of the University of North Carolina, Jan. 3, 1860 (Swain Papers, MSS in archives of North Carolina Historical Commission).

ton, however, the increased enrollment from the South was striking: seventeen in 1830, one hundred and fifteen in 1850, and a slight decline to one hundred and thirteen in 1860.[48] This patronage of Northern colleges continued through the ante-bellum period despite the notable expansion of Southern institutions of higher learning.

Some of the most ardent Southern partisans demanded the exclusion of Northern textbooks from the South. President William A. Smith of Randolph-Macon College was a zealous propagandist for expurgating from the textbooks abolition sentiments or innuendoes. "The poison which our texts now contain," he declared, "must be distilled from them by the learned of the land."[49] The *Southern Argus,* published at Norfolk, declared that the Northern schoolbooks used in the South were permeated with sectional bias. "The primers have slurs and innuendoes at slavery; the geographies are more particular in stating the resources of the Northern States; the histories almost ignore the South; the arithmetics contain in their examples reflections upon the Southern States; the classical works have marginal notes denouncing the institution, and the moral philosophies teem with free-soil doctrines."[50] The editor proposed establishing four large publishing houses in the South to provide the right kind of textbooks. Such Northern schoolbooks as Peter Parley's histories, Appleton's *Complete Guide of the World,* and Wayland's *Moral Science* (a college textbook) were described as too dangerous for young Southern minds.[51] *De Bow's Review* and the Southern commercial conventions were continually calling on the South to boycott Northern colleges and Northern textbooks.[52]

[48] See tables compiled by C. F. Thwing, *A History of Higher Education in America* (New York, 1906), pp. 254-255.

[49] William A. Smith, *Lectures on the Philosophy and Practice of Slavery* (Nashville, Tenn., 1856), p. 29.

[50] *Southern Argus,* March 23, 1858.

[51] Bessie Louise Pierce, *Public Opinion and the Teaching of History in the United States* (New York, 1926), pp. 135-146.

[52] *De Bow's Review,* XX, 67-77 (Jan., 1856); XXVIII, 434-440 (April, 1860); *Official Report of the Debates and Proceedings of the Southern Commercial Convention Assembled at Knoxville, Tennessee, Aug. 10, 1857* (Knoxville, Tenn., 1857), p. 50.

Northern men holding positions in Southern universities were not entirely protected from popular prejudice by the acquisition of slaves. President Barnard of the University of Mississippi, although a slaveholder and an educator quite sound on the slavery question, found his Yankee birth to be the wedge for a vicious attack on his administration in 1859-60. A student assaulted a Negro servant of Barnard, and was brought to trial before the faculty. The majority of the faculty refused to convict on Negro testimony (following the practice of Southern courts), but Barnard and two other Northern men voted for the expulsion of the student. This act of justice caused charges to be made that Barnard was unsound on slavery. The accusations were investigated by the board of trustees, but he was triumphantly sustained by resolutions of that body.[53] Barnard felt, however, that his position was insecure in the South, that the best interests of the University were always at the mercy of an unintelligent legislature that would threaten to withdraw appropriations and even to attack its charter.

President David L. Swain was bitterly assailed in 1858 for appointing a Northern man to a professorship in the University of North Carolina. He defended himself by pointing out that when the University of Virginia was founded every professor was a foreigner.[54] The powerful editor of the Fayetteville *Observer* contemptuously brushed aside this defense. "In both those Institutions [the universities of Virginia and of South Carolina]," he wrote, "filled with foreigners and Northern men, there have been most deplorable outbreaks, and riots, and rows, and breaking up of Faculty organizations. Both have been noted for the prevalence and propagation of infidel notions in religion. And both in our opinion, are far below our own University in all that a thoughtful man can regard indispensable in education."[55]

The movement to convert the schools and colleges of the

[53] John Fulton (ed.), *Memoirs of Frederick A. P. Barnard* (New York, 1896), pp. 246-253.
[54] Swain to E. J. Hale, Feb. 3, 1858 (David L. Swain Papers, MSS in archives of North Carolina Historical Commission).
[55] E. J. Hale & Son to David L. Swain, Feb. 5, 1858 (*ibid.*).

South into propaganda institutions reached its culmination
in the founding of the University of the South at Sewanee,
Tennessee. Bishop Leonidas Polk of the Episcopal Church
proposed as early as 1856 the establishment of a university at
which sound doctrines on slavery should be taught.[56] Thus
a native ministry for the Episcopal Church would be educated,
and Southern youths would be protected from the radicalism
rife in the North.[57] A writer in *De Bow's Review* gave his
blessing to this enterprise as an instrument for unifying the
South and welding the Southern States into a nation. Here
at Sewanee the sons of Southern planters could drink "pure
and invigorating draughts from unpolluted fountains" and no
longer be corrupted by Northern colleges. The University of
Virginia could not qualify as the educational center of the
South, for it was not central enough nor "sufficiently cot-
tonized."[58] In October, 1860, the cornerstone of the first building of the university was laid by Bishop Polk. He secured
nearly ten thousand acres of land and a half million dollars
as an endowment for the university, but the Civil War prevented the realization of his dreams of a university the equivalent of Oxford or Göttingen in the wilderness of Tennessee.

While Leonidas Polk was seeking to found an institution
at Sewanee that would satisfy the most conservative planter of
the Cotton Kingdom, within the interior of Kentucky John
G. Fee was struggling to establish a radical college, modeled
after the notorious Oberlin College. Fee, the son of a Kentucky slaveholder and a Quaker mother, was converted to
abolitionist views during his student days at Lane Theological
Seminary. Since the very name *abolitionist* was anathema to
Southern people, he joined the cause only after he had wrestled
with the Lord in a vacant lot. His father disinherited him
as a result of this decision. Fee resolved to carry on his work

[56] W. M. Polk, *Leonidas Polk, Bishop and General* (New York, 1894), I,
209-215.
[57] George R. Fairbanks, *History of the University of the South at Sewanee,
Tennessee* (Jacksonville, Fla., 1905), pp. 12-18.
[58] "A Central Southern University: Political and Educational Necessity for Its
Establishment," *De Bow's Review*, XXIII, 490-503 (Nov., 1857).

as a preacher and as a propagandist in his native state, despite
the great dangers he was bound to encounter. He was mobbed
twenty-two times, but continued to preach his antislavery
views until his final expulsion in 1859.[59] He carried no weapons, and would pray for the mobs or start preaching to them
as they persecuted him. Although he prosecuted the leaders
of mobs in the criminal courts of Kentucky, he had little success in securing convictions. With grim satisfaction, he noted
in his autobiography, however, the violent deaths that, one by
one, overtook the leaders of these mobs.[60] He established an
academy and a church at Berea in Madison County on a plot
of land given him by Cassius Clay. Here a little community
developed, devoted to the principles of race equality, co-
education of Negroes and whites, and opposition to sectarianism. Several Oberlin students came to Berea to teach in the
only school in the South where black and white children
studied side by side. But even Cassius Clay frowned upon
such recognition of race equality and the acceptance of the
higher law doctrine.

In 1858 Berea College was started as a biracial institution
supported by funds from the North. While Fee was on a
money-raising tour in the Northern States, John Brown's raid
occurred. He was invited to preach in Henry Ward Beecher's
church in Brooklyn, where he declared, "We want more John
Browns, not in manner of action, but in consecration; not to
go with carnal weapons but with spiritual. . . ." The Louisville *Journal,* edited by George D. Prentice, garbled the remarks of Fee as reported in the New York *Tribune,* by asserting that "John G. Fee is in Beecher's Church calling for more
John Browns."[61] These misrepresentations were published in
the Lexington *Observer* and the *Mountain Democrat* of Richmond, Kentucky, together with the allegation that a box of
Sharp's rifles had been sent to Fee. It was not surprising,

[59] Edwin Rogers Embree, "A Kentucky Crusader," *American Mercury,* XXIV,
102 (Sept., 1931).

[60] *Autobiography of John G. Fee, Berea, Kentucky* (Chicago, 1891), p. 124.

[61] *Ibid.,* pp. 146-147.

therefore, that the people of Kentucky arose in wrath against the settlement at Berea. Seven hundred and fify men met at Richmond and pledged themselves to remove Fee, J. A. R. Rogers, and their co-laborers. The citizens of Berea appealed to the governor of Kentucky for protection, but he refused to intervene, and, as a result, the reformers were forced to cross the Ohio River into a free state.[62] When Fee returned from the North to Bracken County, another large public meeting held at Brookville passed resolutions that Fee and his associate, John G. Hanson, be ordered to leave the country. Realizing that resistance would be futile, they abandoned their native state, and settled in Cincinnati until the outbreak of the Civil War.

The conservative atmosphere of Southern colleges was maintained and accentuated by the thoroughly conservative character of the student body. The University of Virginia was looked upon as an institution patronized almost wholly by aristocrats and "cotton snobs." Consequently, young men living in counties beyond the Blue Ridge preferred to attend colleges in Ohio and Pennsylvania, in preference to the snobbish university, "V. M. I.," or William and Mary. In 1857 only thirteen students from western Virginia were enrolled in the university, while the enrollment from the rest of the state was three hundred and twenty.[63] The aristocratic tone of the College of Charleston was resented by some of the poor students, for example, Francis Asbury Mood. He recollected that during his college course the entire corps of professors and trustees never spoke twenty words to him outside of the recitation room, although they cultivated the friendship of students from aristocratic families.[64] Tharin, another poor boy, was offended by the arrogance of his fellow students who judged each other by "their Ethiopian attachments," and were fond

[62] See John A. R. Rogers, *Birth of Berea College* (Philadelphia, 1903).

[63] C. H. Ambler, *Sectionalism in Virginia from 1776 to 1861* (Chicago, 1910), p. 282.

[64] C. C. Cody, *The Life and Labor of Francis Asbury Mood, Founder and First Regent of South-Western University* (Chicago, 1886), p. 82.

of comparing "nigger-rolls."[65] Furthermore, the homogeneity of Southern colleges was not broken by any stimulating clashes with Northern students. Indeed, a Northerner enrolled in a Southern college was "a rare bird." During the period, 1800-61, only eleven Northern students, chiefly sons of politicians in Washington, attended William and Mary College.[66] The conservative cast of student opinion in the South was displayed at Chapel Hill when the students burnt an effigy of Professor Hedrick. Young Willie P. Mangum, the son of Senator Mangum, wrote concerning Hedrick's brave independence in supporting Frémont: "It is another evidence of the one-sided views and idea of self-importance which characterize the learned only in books."[67] With student opinion so hostile to independent thought, and with trustees and newspapers solidly lined up against freedom of expression, it is no wonder that academic freedom was a frail reed in the Old South. Yet it would be an error to conclude that only in the South academic freedom was suppressed. During the abolition crusade three professors were dismissed from Western Reserve College at Hudson, Ohio, because they agreed with the Southern attitude toward slavery. Years later John Fiske was not reappointed instructor at Harvard on account of his evolution views; President Andrews of Brown University felt constrained to resign because he believed in bimetallism; and Professor Schafer of the University of Minnesota was dismissed in 1917 because he refused to succumb to war hysteria.[68]

[65] R. S. Tharin, *Arbitrary Arrests in the South; or Scenes from the Experience of an Alabama Unionist* (New York, 1863), pp. 173-174.

[66] Herbert B. Adams, *The College of William and Mary* (Washington, D. C., 1887), pp. 49-50. "While southern students went in considerable numbers to Yale, Harvard, and Princeton, northern students were almost unknown in the annals of southern colleges."

[67] W. P. Mangum, Jr., to his sister, Chapel Hill, 1857 (Willie P. Mangum Papers in Library of Congress).

[68] Edward P. Cheyney (ed.), "Freedom of Inquiry and Expression," *Annals of the American Academy of Political and Social Science* (Philadelphia), CC, 103, 104, 116 (Nov., 1938).

CHAPTER X

ALIENS IN A SLAVE COUNTRY

A BASIS OF dissent from the prevailing views of the section was provided by the alien elements within the population of the South. Not only did the foreign stocks, such as the Germans, the Irish, the Creoles, and the Jews, come within this category, but also the Northerners who settled below Mason and Dixon's line and the Quakers with their clannish and unworldly religion, all of these represented extraneous elements in Southern society. It is a fascinating problem in the study of human nature to determine to what extent these various elements succumbed to the Southern environment. Did they, possessing different backgrounds, produce rebels and critics? Did they rather accept the dominant views and beliefs of the communities in which they lived?

The foreign element congregated in the cities, along the river chain of the Mississippi and in the seaports. There was a surprisingly large foreign-born population in these cities, which, despite their cosmopolitan constituents, retained a provincial point of view. In 1860 New Orleans led the Southern cities with a foreign-born population of 44.5 per cent of the white inhabitants, while Savannah, Mobile, Louisville, and Memphis had alien elements of over one third their white populations. Montgomery, Richmond, and Charleston were more homogeneous, with only thirteen per cent, twenty-two per cent, and twenty-seven per cent foreign residents. St. Louis, a semi-Southern and semi-Western city, had a foreign-born population of nearly sixty per cent of its entire population. By comparison, Northern cities, like Chicago, New York, and Milwaukee had an alien element of approximately one half of the population.[1]

During the eighteenth century a large band of Germans

[1] *The Census of 1860: Population*, pp. xxxi, xxxii. Percentages derived by the author. The ratio of foreign-born in the South was greater in 1860 than in 1900.

had settled in the Great Valley of Virginia and had pushed
through a wild country into the Piedmont area of the South.
The centers of German colonization were the valley counties
of Shenandoah, Page, and Rockingham in Virginia, Rowan
County, and the little Moravian settlement of Wachovia in
North Carolina. Professor Wayland has estimated that by
1840 the population of the above-named counties in Virginia
was about three-fourths German, and that the proportion of
Germans in the neighboring counties was about one half.[2]
They emigrated almost entirely from Pennsylvania, where
they had been unaccustomed to slavery, bringing with them
the free-state atmosphere as well as the system of cultivating
small farms. The census of 1850 revealed that the three German counties of Page, Rockingham, and Shenandoah, occupying the fertile limestone valley of Virginia, contained a very
small proportion of slaves, twelve, ten, and six per cent respectively. Some of the adjoining counties, predominantly
English, had a slave population of over fifty per cent. In
North Carolina, Rowan, the central German county, had only
twenty per cent slaves, and Forsyth, the Moravian county,
had only twelve per cent.

The Germans of Virginia were, on the whole, antagonistic
to slavery, but they were not aggressive in their opposition.
In 1818 Rev. Johannes Braun, pastor of certain German
churches in the Shenandoah Valley, wrote a treatise entitled
*Circular-Schreiben an die Deutschen Einwohner von Rocking-
ham und Augusta und den benachbarten Counties,* discussing
slavery at length. He held that slavery was opposed to the
spirit of Christianity, and showed that he was much influenced
by St. George Tucker and Thomas Jefferson in advocating a
plan of gradual abolition. One of the Moravian bishops, Gloss-
brenner, is reported to have expelled his own father-in-law
from the church in Augusta County for slaveholding.[3] Au-

[2] J. W. Wayland, *The German Element of the Shenandoah Valley of Virginia*
(Charlottesville, Va., 1907), chap. vii, based on county records. See also T. K.
Cartmell, *Shenandoah Valley Pioneers and Their Descendants* (Winchester, Va.,
1909), and Samuel Kercheval, *A History of the Valley of Virginia* (Winchester, Va.,
1833), chaps. iii and v.   [3] Wayland, *op. cit.,* pp. 181, 182, 239.

gusta County with its large German population was prominent in memorializing the Virginia legislature in 1831 to adopt
a plan of emancipation. The representative of this county,
John McCue, presented a striking petition from two hundred
and fifteen women of Augusta praying for the abolition of
slavery, and made a vigorous speech in support of it. His
stand was approved by his constituents, for in the following
election he was returned to the legislature.[4] Other petitions,
signed by many people, were circulated in Augusta County,
asking for the abolition of slavery.

In 1847 Dr. Henry Ruffner, of German stock, presented his
antislavery views and a scheme of gradual emancipation in
a public speech at Lexington. So great an impression did it
make that he was requested in a formal letter signed by twelve
of the leading citizens to publish his views in pamphlet form.
Accordingly, he published *An Address to the People of West
Virginia, Shewing That Slavery Is Injurious to the Public Welfare,* one of the ablest attacks ever made on the peculiar institution by a Southern man.[5] He carefully dissociated himself
from the abolitionists of the North, whom he regarded with
aversion. In fact, he attributed to them the intolerance of the
Southern people toward any unfavorable criticism of their
institutions. His objections to Southern slavery were based on
economic and social grounds. He showed, for example, that
it was a wasteful and unsound system of labor. The free
farmer of the Middle States, he pointed out, produced agricultural products to the value of about two hundred and sixty-
five dollars to the hand, while the planter of old Virginia
produced only about one hundred and thirty dollars value to
the hand. He called attention to the fact that Virginia had
lost her prosperity and a large number of her sons had emigrated to avoid the depressing effects of slavery. Ruffner was
an ardent advocate of a free school system, of giving the West
a fair share in the control of the government, and of appro-

[4] J. A. Waddell, *Annals of Augusta County, Virginia* (Richmond, 1886), p. 244.
An excellent county history.
[5] Henry Ruffner, *An Address to the People of West Virginia, Shewing that
Slavery Is Injurious to the Public Welfare* (Lexington, Va., 1847).

priating money for internal improvements. With these objects close at heart, he struck some formidable blows at the
conservative slave system, which blocked their attainment.

Hermann Schuricht, a journalist of Richmond, has given
some valuable information as to the German-Virginian attitude toward slavery. He came to Virginia in 1859 from Germany and founded a German newspaper at Richmond, *Die
Virginische Zeitung*. In January, 1860, he accepted an offer
to merge his paper with the influential and well-established
Richmond *Enquirer* and to edit the German section of that
paper, stipulating in his contract that he should not be obliged
to write articles in favor of slavery. Schuricht observed that the
German population of Virginia opposed slavery but feared
that agitation about it would lead to a split of the Union.
They favored the removal of slavery in a lawful and peaceful
manner and opposed any rash action that would endanger
the Union.[6]

The Germans in the older South were staunch and loyal
Democrats, so much so that the three valley counties of Virginia were called "The Tenth Legion."[7] They were enthusiastic supporters of Governor Henry A. Wise partly because
he had fought so valiantly against the nativistic Know-Nothings. The warm friend and adviser of Jefferson Davis was
the German, Karl Minnegerode, pastor of the aristocratic
Church of St. Paul at Richmond.[8] Those Germans who had a
burning hatred for slavery, the political refugees of 1848, with
few exceptions avoided the older South.[9] Furthermore, the
German Jews who came to the land of Dixie had no aversion
to slavery; some of the most flourishing slave traders were
Jews.[10] When war broke out in 1861, the Germans living in
the South loyally followed their section in fighting in the cause

[6] Hermann Schuricht, *History of the German Element in Virginia* (Baltimore,
1898-1900), II, 61, 63.

[7] For an explanation of this attachment to the Democratic party, see A. B.
Faust, *The German Element in the United States* (Boston, 1909), II, 126-127.

[8] Gustav Körner, *Das Deutsche Element in den Vereinigten Staaten von Nord-
amerika* (Cincinnati, 1880), p. 410.

[9] See Ernest Bruncken, *German Political Refugees in the United States, 1815-
1860* (Chicago, 1904).   [10] Schuricht, *op. cit.*, II, 93.

that would save slavery. The famous German Friendly Society of Charleston, South Carolina, showed its devotion to the Southern cause by giving the lead weights in the window frames of its assembly room to the Confederate government.[11] Reichard, the Prussian consul at New Orleans, raised a regiment of Germans for the Confederate service and later became a Confederate general.[12]

Among the yeomanry of German descent in western North Carolina arose the most noted antislavery man that the old South produced, Hinton Rowan Helper. Helper's family (the name was originally spelled Helfer) came from the vicinity of Heidelberg. His father was a small farmer of the uplands, who owned a single family of slaves.[13] With considerable justice he may be called the Karl Marx of the nonslaveholding whites. What made Helper a radical critic of slavery was not sympathy for the slave, but the outside impulse of travel. In 1855 he wrote a book about his travels in California, entitled *The Land of Gold, or Romance Unveiled,* in which he early displayed a temperament that delighted in iconoclasm and a taste for statistics. He took occasion to observe that free labor was superior to slave labor, and that slaves should be segregated in the country and not allowed in the city. This animadversion on the institution of slavery was noticed only after the work had been accepted for publication and was in the course of being printed. The editor, who was a Virginian, refused to finish printing the book unless the passages offensive to slaveholders should be expunged. Helper was forced to accede to this demand, but such censorship aroused all the exaggerated combativeness of his nature. Accordingly, he advanced from advocating the banishment of slavery from cities to complete hostility to slavery.

[11] G. J. Gongaware, *The History of German Friendly Society of Charleston. South Carolina, 1766-1916* (Richmond, 1935).
[12] M. L. Bonham, *The British Consuls in the Confederacy* (New York, 1911), p. 15.
[13] Helper gives invaluable biographical details in his *Noonday Exigencies in America* (New York, 1871), and *Nojoque; A Question for a Continent* (New York, 1867); see also Bassett, "Anti-Slavery Leaders of North Carolina," *Johns Hopkins Studies in History and Political Science,* XVI (1898).

Helper later attributed his vehement assault on slavery to this interference with his freedom of publication. He had come to the conclusion "that there was not in any part of the South at that time any medium of the press through which thought could be disseminated, save only where the thinking, honest or dishonest, had been done with a view to the more positive security and aggrandizement of slavery. Deeply impressed with this conviction, I solemnly vowed that I would if possible, have a hearing on the subject upon which I had thus been unjustly silenced."[14] His antislavery sentiments were fired also by reading the census of 1850. In 1857 he published in New York City, the first edition of his scathing denunciation of the South called *The Impending Crisis,* in which he tried to show that the North was far superior to the South, in economic productivity, education, and general civilization.[15] He used statistics with telling effect. He stated, for example, that the Northern hay crop alone was worth more than all the cotton, tobacco, rice, hay, and hemp produced in the fifteen slave states.[16] He also developed the view that the slaveholding oligarchy had conspired to keep the poor whites in an abject, illiterate state.

Helper proclaimed himself an *immediate* abolitionist, opposed to granting remuneration to the holders of slave property. At the same time he regarded the colonization of the liberated Negroes as imperative. So violent was his hatred of the Negro race that in later years he refused to patronize a restaurant which employed Negro waiters. He wrote one of the most passionate books of racial hatred that has ever been penned, *The Negroes in Negroland.* The source of this ungenerous hostility was his sympathy for the poor whites, whose opportunities in life were decreased by the competition of the Negroes.

[14] Helper, *Noonday Exigencies in America*, p. 161.

[15] W. H. Gehrke, in an article entitled "Negro Slavery Among the Germans in North Carolina," maintained that Helper wrote this book in Baltimore or New York City (*North Carolina Historical Review*, XIV, 321, Oct., 1937).

[16] H. R. Helper, *The Impending Crisis of the South: How to Meet It* (New York, 1859), p. 45.

Helper's book had all the elements necessary to prevent its circulation or consideration by the Southern people. In the first place, he hurt Southern pride by making an invidious comparison of the two sections. In the second place, he launched violent tirades against the morality and intelligence of Southerners who supported the institution of slavery. Finally, the book was actually incendiary. He proposed an organization of nonslaveholders against the aristocratic classes. In case of conflict, the nonslaveholders, he declared, could count on the reinforcement of "the Negroes, who, in nine cases out of ten, would be delighted with the opportunity to cut their masters' throat."[17]

The Impending Crisis did not at first create a sensation. In 1858 Horace Greeley, "the arch priest of abolition," undertook to publish it as a campaign document for the Republican party. With this purpose in view he secured the endorsement of over fifty members of the Republican party. Only then did *The Impending Crisis* arouse a storm of indignation and intolerance in the South.[18] In 1859, when the House of Representatives was engaged in choosing a Speaker, a Southern member introduced a resolution that no one who had endorsed the Helper book should be considered fit to be Speaker. This provoked a bitter debate, in which one Southern Congressman after another denounced Helper or anyone who had given him countenance. Senator Asa Biggs of North Carolina branded him as a man of low character, who had stolen three hundred dollars from his employer in Salisbury, North Carolina.[19] The Republican candidate for Speaker, John Sherman, had been one of the endorsers of *The Impending Crisis,* a fact which prevented his election.

It became a crime to circulate this book in the South, as the conviction of Daniel Worth at Greensboro proved; even to own a copy was dangerous. The newspapers of the Southern States did not try to refute its arguments but engaged in

[17] *Ibid.,* p. 149.
[18] H. M. Wagstaff, *States Rights in North Carolina* (Baltimore, 1906), p. 106.
[19] *Congressional Globe,* April 5, 1858.

violent invectives against its author. William E. Stevenson, afterwards governor of West Virginia, was indicted for circulating *The Impending Crisis* in Wood County, but he was not brought to trial.[20] Some Southern men, out of curiosity to taste of forbidden fruit, smuggled an occasional copy within the borders, but when caught possessing a copy, they protested their strong disapproval of its doctrines.

The later years of Helper were tragic. An outcast from his native state, he became alienated from the Republican party because its reconstruction measures neglected the poor white and elevated the negro. He grew fanatically interested in a gorgeous scheme for building a railroad from Bering Sea to the Straits of Magellan, and in prosecuting this dream he spent seventy thousand dollars of his fortune. In 1909, an old man of eighty years, he committed suicide in a room on Pennsylvania Avenue, declaring despondently, "There is no justice in this world," and affirming that "he was tired of living anyway."[21] Thus died ingloriously one of the most independent spirits that the ante-bellum South produced. He was never able to make that adjustment with his environment which leads to happiness.

The placid Moravian villages of North Carolina did not produce any outstanding critic of slavery, like Helper or Ruffner. Their German inhabitants adapted themselves to the environment about them, contributing to it, however, a tone of kindliness and fraternal feeling. Miss Adelaide Fries, the official historian of Wachovia, has written an admirable statement of their attitude toward slavery: "The records show that when they came they made a careful study of North Carolina law, and their obedience to it often annoyed their neighbors who had a less high ideal of citizenship. I have never seen any entry to show that they considered slavery wicked; they seem to have accepted it as part of the custom of the land, just as they accepted other customs. They were too industrious to feel the need of many slaves, but did hire or buy occasionally

[20] G. D. Hall, *The Rending of Virginia* (Chicago, 1902), p. 72.
[21] Charlotte (N. C.) *Observer*, March 10, 1909.

when they felt it right and necessary. There was no church rule about it, so far as I know."[22] Miss Fries's grandfather, a prominent leader in Wachovia, owned about forty slaves at the time of the Civil War. The Moravians were solicitous for the souls of the slaves, for whom they built special churches and organized missions.[23] Occasionally also, some unusual individual among these thrifty people would liberate his slaves; for example, Dr. Schuman in 1836 set free seventeen of his slaves who wished to go to Liberia.[24]

The Moravians did not countenance abolitionists. The Salem Diary, October 11, 1850, records the fact that the minds of the brethren had been excited by the trial of two abolitionists, McBride and Crooks, who had given a girl a tract discussing slavery in relation to the Ten Commandments. The latter had been called to account by several of the brethren.[25] In 1847 the Virginia Conference of Moravians resolved by a vote of eighteen to four "that this Conference, from the fact that the *Religious Telescope,* our church paper, is calculated to hinder, rather than promote, the church within the bounds of our Conference, in consequence of its containing abolition matter from time to time, take into consideration the propriety of publishing within its own borders, a religious paper for its own benefit."[26]

The large German element in western Texas was also strongly affected by the Southern environment. The Germans in Texas were estimated in 1857 at about thirty-five thousand persons. Olmsted reported: "Few of them concern themselves with the theoretical right or wrong of the institution and while

[22] Miss Adelaide Fries, Archivist of the Moravian Church in America, Southern Province, in a letter to the writer, Feb. 2, 1927.

[23] For the work of the Moravians among the negroes, see L. T. Reichel, *The Moravians in North Carolina* (Salem, N. C., 1857), p. 139; also, J. T. Hamilton, *History of the Moravian Church* (Baltimore, 1900), p. 404.

[24] Extract from "The History of St. Philip's Church (Colored)," by Miss Adelaide Fries (MS in Winston-Salem, N. C.).

[25] Salem Diary, Oct. 11, 1850 (MS, written by Rev. George Bahnson). Translated from the German for the writer by the courtesy of Miss Adelaide Fries. See also J. H. Clewell, *History of Wachovia in North Carolina* (New York, 1902), p. 211.

[26] A. P. Funkhouser and O. F. Morton, *History of the Church of the United Brethren in Christ, Virginia Conference* (Dayton, Va., 1921), p. 101.

it does not interfere with their own liberty or progress, are careless of its existence."[27] In 1854 Dr. Adolph Douai, editor of the San Antonio *Zeitung,* published some radical antislavery views, thereby exciting a storm of opposition among the newspapers of the state, and causing the American merchants to withdraw their advertisements from the columns of the paper. The Germans who were implicated by the rash action of Dr. Douai hastened to disavow him. In Comal County the German residents drew up resolutions disclaiming any responsibility for Dr. Douai's sentiments. The Germans of Lockhart, after demanding that Douai should be removed from the editorship, passed the following resolution: "We recommend to our German countrymen to discountenance and suppress attempts to disturb the institution of slavery, upon which is founded the prosperity and happiness of our Southern country."[28] Dr. Douai was forced to abandon his paper and become an exile in the North.[29] The Germans in Texas, it should be noted, employed *free labor* almost entirely.

The Germans in St. Louis, constituting nearly a third of the population, were strongly antislavery and almost solidly Republican in their political affiliations. In August, 1860, they invited Carl Schurz of Wisconsin to deliver an address. His subject was "The Doom of Slavery," in which he showed that the institution of slavery throttled free discussion, prevented the education of the slaves, and was incompatible with free labor. The Germans organized themselves into Wide Awake Clubs, and paraded in torchlight processions for the election of Lincoln. In 1861 they furnished three fourths of the volunteers for the militia companies to preserve the Union. Their aid, organized by Francis P. Blair and the redheaded Captain Nathaniel Lyons, was responsible for preventing Missouri from seceding.[30]

[27] F. L. Olmsted, *A Journey through Texas* (New York, 1860), p. 432.

[28] G. G. Benjamin, *The Germans in Texas* (Philadelphia, 1909), p. 101. See also Moritz Tiling, *The German Element in Texas* (Houston, Texas, 1913).

[29] Dr. Douai later published a book on the civilization of the United States, entitled *Land und Leute in der Union* (Berlin, 1864).

[30] Galusha Anderson, *The Story of a Border City during the Civil War* (Boston, 1908), pp. 16-19, 85.

Among the Germans of Baltimore were two radical jour-
nalists who edited a German language newspaper, *Der Wecker,*
from 1851 to the outbreak of the Civil War. The founder of
this liberal antislavery paper was Carl Heinrich Schnauffer,
a student of Heidelberg, a poet, and a revolutionist of 1848.
In 1851 he emigrated to Baltimore and established *Der Wecker,*
which he edited until his death in 1854. After his death, his
wife carried on its publication with the same liberal principles.
In 1857 Wilhelm Rapp, an exile of '48 and president of the
Turnerbund, became editor. He supported the policies of the
Republican party in this German language newspaper, the
only newspaper in Baltimore to do so. He declared that he
wished to wage war on slavery, not from afar, but in the territory of the slavocracy. In April, 1861, a mob drove him from
the city. The presses of *Der Wecker* were saved from being
demolished only by the heroism of Mrs. Schnauffer, who with
a young child in her arms stood on the threshold of the printing
establishment and defied the mob.

The Catholic Irish who emigrated to the Southern States
quickly adopted the native point of view in regard to slavery. T. C. Grattan, who traveled extensively in America
during the 1850's, reported that the Southern Irish approved
of slavery. They wished to have some class lower than themselves over whom they could domineer: ". . . they would, if
possible, place the Negro lower than he is that they might on his
degradation rise above the level assigned to themselves."[31]
This feeling is understandable when it is realized that the Irish
day laborers were the chief economic competitors of the slaves.
In fact, Irishmen were used in the South to perform dangerous labor, dig ditches, handle the bounding cotton bales in
loading ships.[32] The loss of a fifteen-hundred-dollar Negro was
a serious misfortune, but the loss of an Irishman was lightly
regarded.

[31] T. C. Grattan, *Civilized America* (London, 1859), II, 41-42. It is to be
noted that the Irish fought valiantly for the Confederate cause, one of their great
leaders being Major General Patrick Ronayne Cleburne, who in January, 1864, advocated recruiting negro slaves in the Confederate army.
[32] Olmsted, *Seaboard Slave States,* p. 551.

The hundred thousand Irishmen, approximately, in the South were seldom planters or slaveholders.[33] The more energetic and prosperous were businessmen in the cities, but the large majority occupied the slum areas of Southern cities, like "Pinch" in Memphis.[34] The profound attachment of the Irish to the Catholic Church was a factor in drawing them to the cities.[35] When the sons of Erin acquired farms in the South they usually cultivated them by their own labor and that of their large families. In 1850 about fifty families from Tipperary settled in Taliaferro County, Georgia, where they raised cotton and corn. None of them owned slaves. By industry and sobriety, however, they built up a prosperous community.[36]

The Irish bishop at Charleston, John England, in a series of letters published in 1840, made it clear that his countrymen and the Catholic Church had never held slavery in itself as sinful. After clearing himself from any charge of abolitionism, he maintained that the rights of slaves, especially the validity of marriage ties, should be respected by the masters. "I have been asked by many a question which I may as well answer at once," he wrote, "viz., whether I am friendly to the existence or continuation of slavery? *I am not.* But I also see the impossibility of now abolishing it here. When it can and ought to be abolished is a question for the legislature, and not for me."[37] Bishop McGill of Richmond also condemned the Southern people for their failure to protect the slaves in their marriage relations. The only notable agitator against slavery that the Southern Irish produced was James G. Birney, a son of Irish expatriates.

The Creoles were like the Irish in their acceptance of slavery. The Creole planters usually treated their slaves kindly but did not feed them as well as did the Anglo-Saxon mas-

---

[33] This number is derived from *The Seventh Census of the United States,* Table XV, p. xxxvi.

[34] Capers, *The Biography of a River Town,* pp. 60, 108.

[35] John F. Maguire, *The Irish in America* (London, 1869), p. 255.

[36] *Ibid.,* p. 259.

[37] Ignatius A. Reynolds, *The Works of the Right Rev. John England, First Bishop of Charleston* (Baltimore 1849), III, 190.

ters.[38] The laws of Louisiana in regard to slavery were the most humane in the Southern States. The Creoles were too indolent and lacking in ambition, however, to become reformers and rebels against convention. Their lives revolved around passionate pleasures, gambling, dancing, and making love. There were a number of cultured and aristocratic families among them, but the majority neglected the education of their children.[39] The French Acadians of Louisiana, indeed, were comparable to the poor whites in their illiteracy, poverty, and lack of ambition. The most important leader of the Creoles was Governor A. B. Roman, a fine gentleman, who was a moderate in regard to abolitionists and an opponent of secession. The two leading Creole newspapers, *L'Abeille de la Nouvelle-Orleans* and *Le Courrier des Opelousas,* were strong supporters of slavery and advocates of the suppression of incendiary publications.[40] In 1860 *L'Abeille* opposed the movement for disunion and urged the election of John Bell, while *Le Courrier* was a Breckinridge paper.

The Jewish element, confined to a few cities and small towns, were loyal Southerners. At the beginning of the nineteenth century the Jewish community of Charleston, wrote Elzas, was "the largest, the most cultured, and the wealthiest Jewish community in America."[41] One of the most prominent of the Charleston Jews was J. N. Cardozo, editor of the *Southern Patriot* and later of the *Evening News.* Cardozo valiantly opposed the nullification party in South Carolina, a fact which caused him a serious loss of patronage.[42] Another outstanding Hebrew of Charleston was Isaac Harby, who in 1825 was elected one of the teachers in the free schools of the city. In Columbia the Hebrew physician, M. H. DeLeon, attended

[38] Olmsted, *Seaboard Slave States,* p. 650; Tasistro, *op. cit.,* II, 113.

[39] Eliza Ripley, *Social Life in New Orleans* (New York, 1912), chaps. xxiv-xxv, gives an intimate picture of refined Creole families.

[40] *Le Courrier des Opelousas,* Aug. 25, 1860. A file of this rare paper is preserved in the library of Louisiana State University.

[41] B. A. Elzas, *The Jews of South Carolina from the Earliest Times to the Present Day* (Philadelphia, 1905), p. 147.

[42] Cardozo to Poinsett, Nov. 8, 1832 (Joel Poinsett MSS).

Dr. Thomas Cooper, after whom he named one of his sons.[43] To the Confederate armies the Jews of South Carolina contributed A. C. Myers, Quarter-Master General, and David C. DeLeon, Surgeon General.

In the Lower South the leading Hebrews fitted harmoniously into the conservative proslavery society. Philip Phillips was a member of the South Carolina nullification convention before he moved to Alabama, where he was elected to Congress.[44] The fire-eating Senator David Levy Yulee of Florida was one-fourth Jewish in blood.[45] Solomon Cohen, postmaster of Savannah, was a conservative leader of the Democratic party of Georgia.[46] Judah P. Benjamin was perhaps the most brilliant lawyer of the Old South, a Senator from Louisiana, and Confederate Secretary of State. He had an intimate contact with slavery through the operation of his large sugar plantation of Bellechasse, below New Orleans.[47] More than any of these politicians, however, the philanthropist, Judah Touro, won the affection of the Southern people. Touro, the son of a Rabbi of Newport, Rhode Island, emigrated in 1802 to New Orleans, where he began to sell soap, candles, and codfish, and eventually became a millionaire. Touro had many eccentricities; during his long domicile in the South, he never left the city of New Orleans except to fight under Jackson; he had a horror of riding in carriages; and he was painfully modest. His fame was based on his philanthropies, and when he died the whole city mourned his death.[48]

One of the most versatile Jewish families of the Upper South was the Mordecai family of North Carolina and Virginia. Gratz Mordecai founded a female academy at Warren-

---

[43] Dictionary of American Biography, V, 224.

[44] The South in the Building of the Nation, X, 561.

[45] Dictionary of American Biography, XX, 638.

[46] I. W. Avery, The History of the State of Georgia from 1850 to 1881 (New York, 1881), pp. 115, 206.

[47] Pierce Butler, Judah P. Benjamin (Philadelphia, 1906), pp. 51-63.

[48] For accounts of Touro's life, see D. C. Adelman, Life and Times of Judah Touro (published by the Touro Fraternal Association, n.p., 1936), and Freeman Hunt, Lives of the American Merchants (New York, 1858), II, 441-467.

ton, North Carolina, in 1809, which was highly successful.[49] His son, Samuel, became a merchant in Richmond and the author of a volume entitled *Richmond in By-Gone Days.*[50] Another son, Alfred, was graduated from West Point and became a major in the United States Army. A third son, George Washington, was a prominent lawyer of Raleigh, a leader in the Episcopal Church, the president of a bank, and the owner of a plantation. In regard to his slaves he wrote: "I would much sooner trust myself alone on my plantation surrounded by my slaves, than in one of your large manufacturing towns when your labourers are discharged from employment and crying aloud for bread for themselves and their little ones."[51] Both Sam and George Washington were opposed to the agitation of the slavery question, and were staunch for the Union until the South seceded.[52]

There were exceptional individuals among the Southern Jews, nevertheless, who were antislavery men.[53] Judah Touro emancipated the single slave that he possessed and aided other slaves to obtain their freedom. Solomon Heydenfeldt, a lawyer and judge of Tallapoosa County, Alabama, was known to be an antislavery man. In 1849 he published *A Communication on the Subject of Slave Immigration, addressed to the Hon. Reuben Chapman, Governor of Alabama,* in which he proposed an amendment to the state constitution to prohibit the further immigration of slaves into Alabama. This dissent from the prevailing opinion of his neighbors seems to have hampered his career to such an extent that he moved to California in 1850. Here he became a judge of the supreme court of the state.[54] Lewis N. Dembitz, a Jewish lawyer of Louis-

[49] *Gratz Mordecai, Founder and Proprietor from 1809 to 1818 of the Warrenton (N. C.) Female Seminary.* A pamphlet.

[50] Samuel Mordecai, *Richmond in By-Gone Days* (Richmond, 1856).

[51] G. W. Mordecai to a Northern Republican, Dec. 28, 1860 (Mordecai Papers).

[52] Samuel Mordecai to George, Dec. 17, 1860 *(ibid.).*

[53] See M. J. Kohler, "The Jews and the American Antislavery Movement," *Publications of the American Jewish Historical Society* (Washington, 1897), No. V, pp. 137-155; (Baltimore, 1901), No. IX, pp. 45-56.

[54] *The Jewish Encyclopedia* (New York, 1904), VI, 378; A. M. Friedenberg, "Solomon Heydenfeldt, a Jewish Jurist of Alabama and California," *Publications of the American Jewish Historical Society* (Baltimore, 1902), No. X, pp. 129-140.

ville, Kentucky, was a delegate to the Republican National Convention of 1860 that nominated Lincoln for President. Rabbi David Einhorn of Baltimore attacked Southern slavery in a monthly that he edited, *Sinai,* and in the pulpit.[55]

The Southern Jews do not seem to have aroused any pronounced anti-Semitic sentiment until during the Civil War. John Hampden Pleasants published in 1828 an eloquent defense of the Hebrew race by a young Jew of Richmond named Isaac Leeser. Pleasants commended the article to the readers of the *Whig* and condemned anti-Semitic prejudice.[56] Mary Boykin Chesnut, a social leader in South Carolina and Washington, was on intimate terms of friendship with a beautiful Charleston Jewess, "Mem" Cohen.[57] But during the Civil War prejudice was aroused against the Jewish merchants by their illicit trade with the enemy and the extortionate prices for goods that they demanded.[58] The unpopularity of Abraham C. Myers, the Quarter-Master General of the Confederacy, and of Judah P. Benjamin, Secretary of War and the favorite of Jefferson Davis, contributed to the growth of anti-Semitism in the Confederacy.[59]

The Quakers of the Upper South were another alien element, not because of race, but because of a singular religion, which set them apart from their neighbors. They represented the backbone of antislavery sentiment in their section. Most of them had emigrated from Pennsylvania and the island of Nantucket. The centers of Quaker colonization were Loudoun, Fairfax, and Frederick counties in northern Virginia and Guilford County (Piedmont), North Carolina. Among the notable Quaker families who produced antislavery leaders were the Janney and Pleasants families in Virginia and, in North Carolina, a group of families that came from the island

[55] *The Jewish Encyclopedia,* I, 650.

[56] Herbert T. Ezekiel and Gaston Lichtenstein, *The History of the Jews of Richmond, 1769-1917* (Richmond, 1917), p. 54.

[57] Chesnut, *op. cit.,* p. 166.

[58] Howard Swiggett (ed.), *A Rebel War Clerk's Diary at the Confederate States Capital by J. B. Jones* (New York, 1935), I, 128, 133, 221, 289.

[59] See William E. Dodd, *Jefferson Davis* (Philadelphia, 1907), p. 343, and Gamaliel Bradford, *Confederate Portraits* (New York, 1914), chap. v.

of Nantucket, the Coffins, the Swains, and the Worths. About 1800 the Quaker churches of Virginia disowned any member who persisted in buying or holding slaves.[60] Such opposition to slavery was based almost entirely upon moral grounds and upon aversion to the use of force in human relations. The Quakers exerted themselves to remove the guilt of slavery by forming manumission societies, by memorializing the legislature, by using the press, by teaching negroes to read and write, and even by supporting the Underground Railway.

Their efforts to further the antislavery cause through the press have not been properly appreciated. Charles Osborn, a North Carolina Quaker, after establishing antislavery societies in his native state and Tennessee, removed in 1816 to Mt. Pleasant, Ohio, where he edited the *Philanthropist,* the first newspaper in America to come out for immediate and unconditional emancipation.[61] The significance of Elihu Embree, the founder of the *Emancipator* of Jonesborough, Tennessee, has been discussed in a previous chapter. Benjamin Lundy acquired his antislavery zeal at Wheeling, Virginia, as he worked at the saddler's trade. In 1821 he began to print his *Genius of Universal Emancipation* in Ohio, then at Greeneville, Tennessee, and finally at Baltimore. William Swain, a North Carolina convert of Lundy and for six months his assistant editor in Baltimore, returned to North Carolina and edited the Greensborough *Patriot* in Guilford County.[62] Benjamin Lundy gave support to his young disciple in North Carolina, and from time to time reprinted in the columns of his paper extracts from the Greensborough *Patriot*. William Lloyd Garrison also assisted Lundy in publishing his antislavery paper and was profoundly influenced by this Quaker enthusiast.

The most prominent Quaker in Virginia who utilized the press to champion the cause of the slave was Samuel Janney

[60] J. P. Bell, *Our Quaker Friends of Ye Olden Time* (Lynchburg, Va., 1905), pp. 149-150.

[61] George W. Julian, *The Rank of Charles Osborn as an Anti-Slavery Pioneer* (Indianapolis, 1819), p. 6.

[62] Thomas Earle, *Life, Travels, and Opinions of Benjamin Lundy* (Philadelphia, 1847), p. 27.

of Loudoun County—a real abolitionist who successfully kept his footing in Virginia during the storm and stress period. He was a literary man, a poet, and a capable historian. But his attempt to operate a cotton mill in Virginia was a failure, and he had to descend to conducting a boarding school for girls. A universal reformer like Garrison, but with a better balanced mind, in 1826 he organized among the Quakers and a few Methodists of Alexandria a benevolent society, whose purpose was to create an antislavery sentiment in Virginia. In January of the following year he began to write for the Alexandria *Gazette* a series of articles against slavery in which he maintained that the discussion of slavery was necessary in order to remove the evil. Predicting that it would take many years of persevering effort and agitation to accomplish this end, he tried to show that slavery would lead to the economic decay of states in which it formed the basis of labor. Finally, he advocated the education of the slaves and the adoption of the *post-nati* system of gradual emancipation.[63]

Janney set out with the aim of becoming a propagandist in the interest of emancipation, seeking financial aid for this purpose among rich Quakers in the North. From such sources he hoped to raise one hundred dollars to enable him to write articles against slavery in Southern newspapers. He argued that he could do more effective work for the antislavery cause since he was a native Virginian and understood the temper and prejudices of Southern people. "One of the best methods at present," he wrote, "is to insert anti-slavery pieces in the southern papers and purchase a good many extra numbers of the paper for circulation. They pass better through the post-office than tracts."[64] In accordance with this plan, Janney actually published in the Richmond *Whig* a series of articles indirectly hostile to slavery entitled "The Yankees in Fairfax County." He insinuated the doctrines of abolitionism by describing a model free-labor colony in northern Virginia and by showing how

[63] Alexandria *Phenix Gazette,* April 30, July 18, 1827.
[64] Janney, *op. cit.,* p. 87.

much more prosperous its members were than their slaveholding neighbors. After his courageous stand for the freedom of speech and of the press in 1850, Janney devoted himself to the pursuits of author and of traveling Quaker preacher. He is a striking example of how much freedom a native Virginian with tact and estimable character could actually enjoy in expressing his opinions on slavery.

Quaker environment and Quaker inheritance furnished the background of other notable antislavery leaders in the South. Among them there stands out prominently George O. Mendenhall, a lawyer of Guilford County, North Carolina. He was a descendant of the influential Quaker family that had emigrated from New Garden, Pennsylvania, to Guilford County in the eighteenth century. He was the lawyer who defended McBride and Crooks when they were tried in 1850 for circulating incendiary publications. That he was willing to sacrifice much for his opinions is shown by the fact that he gradually liberated his eighty slaves and transported them to the Northwest, involving a property loss of seventy thousand dollars. He brought his last group of slaves to Ohio in 1857, locating them on farms.[65] Rev. Daniel Worth, who created so much disturbance by his circulation of *The Impending Crisis,* also came from a Quaker community in North Carolina and was of Quaker stock. Jesse Burton Harrison, who wrote the noble refutation of Dew's proslavery argument, was reared in a home of Quaker traditions.[66] John G. Fee, the abolitionist founder of Berea College, was the son of a Quaker mother. John Hampden Pleasants, the independent editor of the Richmond *Whig,* was the son of Governor James Pleasants of Goochland County, who was a member of a noted antislavery Quaker family.[67] Pleasants as a young man had been editor of a small newspaper in Lynchburg, which was dominated by Quakers.

[65] *African Repository,* Aug., 1857; also *National Era,* Washington, D. C., Aug. 13, 1857.
[66] Mrs. J. M. Cabell, *Sketches and Recollections of Lynchburg* (Richmond, 1858), p. 97.
[67] R. A. Brock, *Virginia and Virginians* (Richmond, 1888), I, 138-140.

Because of the activity of the Quakers, by 1827 North Carolina had fifty antislavery societies with a membership of three thousand, Tennessee had twenty-five societies with a thousand members, and Virginia had eight societies with two hundred and fifty.[68] Another indication of the strength of the antislavery sentiment in the state was the fact that the *Genius of Universal Emancipation* had more subscribers in North Carolina, although a slaveholding area, than in any other state of the Union.[69] The North Carolina Quakers were active supporters of the Colonization Society. They had sent about a thousand slaves to free governments by 1834, and spent nearly twenty thousand dollars in transporting them, assisted by the Friends of the London Yearly Meeting. Of this number, one hundred and nineteen slaves were sent to Haiti, and several hundred to Liberia.[70] Levi Coffin, a Quaker of Guilford County, transported slaves by the Underground Railway, of which he later became president. He was credited with having aided over three thousand fugitives to escape to free territory, or about a hundred a year. Most of this rescue work was accomplished after he moved to Indiana in 1826.[71]

By 1830 the Quakers realized the hopelessness of changing Southern sentiment on the slavery issue. The minutes of the Manumission Society, March 14, 1830, reveal the lethargic spirit prevailing in so many "sleeping branches." The reason for this falling away from the cause was stated: "the work to be accomplished is one too great to be accomplished by our puny efforts."[72] In 1834 the last meeting of the North Carolina Manumission Society was held at Marlborough with only three

[68] According to a statement in the *Genius of Universal Emancipation*, Oct. 13, 1827; Earle, *op. cit.*, p. 218. See also P. M. Sherrill, "The Quakers and the North Carolina Manumission Society," *Historical Papers of the Trinity College Historical Society*, IX-XII (1914).   [69] Earle, *op. cit.*, p. 199.

[70] Letter from Jeremiah Hubbard of Deep River, Guilford County (*African Repository*, Sept., 1834, p. 215).

[71] R. M. Jones, *Later Periods of Quakerism* (London, 1921), II, 582.

[72] Minutes of the General Association of the Manumission Society of North Carolina, 1816-36 (MS in the Library of Guilford College). The minutes have been published in recent years by H. M. Wagstaff in *James Sprunt Historical Series*, XXII, but the correspondence, memorials, and other papers of the Quaker antislavery leaders in the Guilford College library remain unpublished.

branches represented. The cause of this decline was principally the migration of the antislavery Quakers to the West. The great exodus of Quakers from the South occurred between the years 1800 and 1830. Along the Kanawha trail or through the Cumberland Gap, they went to found homes in Ohio and Indiana where free labor was honored. By 1860 the Quakers in North Carolina had dwindled to only fifteen hundred and thirteen members.[73] Along with the Quakers went a large element of nonslaveholding whites, led by land hunger and a desire to escape slavery.[74] The conservatives were left behind. The passing of the antislavery Quakers from the South removed a vigorous element of dissent, and thus weakened the cause of free speech and a free press.

The influence of Northerners in the ante-bellum South toward the preservation of free speech and a free press has never been adequately investigated. During the latter half of this period Northern men moved into Virginia to purchase and cultivate some of the abandoned tobacco fields, an infiltration which John M. Daniel's Richmond *Examiner* called "The Vandal Invasion of Virginia." Shortly after 1841 some Yankees from New Hampshire and Connecticut entered Fairfax County and bought farms at five dollars an acre, introducing rotation of crops, and tilling their lands with free white labor. As a consequence of exemplary thrift and industry they became prosperous and their lands greatly increased in value.[75] Samuel Janney advertised their success in his articles on "The Yankees in Fairfax County," published in the Richmond *Whig* and the Alexandria *Gazette*. The Northern colonists were welcomed at first. The Richmond *Enquirer,* in commenting on the agitation started by the Agricultural Society of Petersburg to get Northern farmers to come to Virginia, observed: "An infusion

[73] For the best account of the westward movement of the Quakers, see S. B. Weeks, *Southern Quakers and Slavery* (Baltimore, 1896).

[74] Many of the immigrants of Southern upland stock were favorably disposed to slavery, even striving to secure its adoption in Illinois and Indiana. See T. C. Pease, *The Frontier State, 1818-1848* (Springfield, Ill., 1918), chaps. iv and xx, and J. P. Dunn, *Indiana, a Redemption from Slavery* (Boston, 1896), chap. xii.

[75] For a description, see Sir Charles Lyell, *A Second Visit to the United States* (New York, 1849), I, 207.

of a little Yankee industry and capital into the arteries of Virginia will produce a beneficial effect. We have seen it done successfully in the County of Fairfax."[76] The *Enquirer* attributed the success of Northern farmers where Southerners had failed to the social nature of the latter, which led them to gather around the courthouse and country stores to smoke, chew, talk politics, and, in general, to waste time.

In 1857 a new period of Yankee migration into Virginia took place. Eli Thayer conceived of the plan of purchasing large tracts of Virginia land and transporting Northern settlers in organized social groups. He founded a little town called Ceredo in western Virginia near the Ohio River. Here manufacturing enterprises were started, a free public school was erected, and a printing press established, which issued the Ceredo *Crescent*. Thayer conceived of his adventure as a missionary enterprise. "Let Ceredo speak to her neighbors," he said, "not through pamphlets but through her steam engines and her prosperity."[77] Furthermore, he believed that the colonization scheme would be instrumental in cementing the Union more strongly than ever "by uniting on the same soil, the social, political, and pecuniary interests of remote and sometimes hostile sections." At the close of 1858 Ceredo was a thriving little town with a population of over five hundred persons.[78]

Thayer's flamboyant scheme of colonization raised an outcry of protest from the Virginia newspapers. The Richmond *Whig*, doubtless recalling his connection with Kansas, regarded the movement as an outrage against the Old Dominion: "We have sadly mistaken the character of the Virginia people if they will ever permit the colonizing among them of the vile and viperous set of abolitionists who impudently and defiantly announce their intention beforehand of revolutionizing our social organization and establishing upon its ruins the corrupt, dangerous, anarchy producing system of free so-

[76] Richmond *Enquirer*, June 26, 1845.
[77] Ceredo *Crescent*, Oct. 24, 1857. A fragmentary file is in the Library of the American Antiquarian Society, Worcester, Mass.
[78] *People's Press* (Salem, N. C.), Dec. 3, 1858.

ciety which prevails in the Northern States."[79] The editor of
the Richmond *Examiner* declared that it was "the duty of an
indignant public opinion summarily to expurgate and purge
the commonwealth of every solitary apologist of the enter-
prize." He thought that the South could not stand the shock
of "fragrant hordes of adventurers fresh from the onion
patches of Connecticut and the codfisheries of the Bay State"
who would convert "lower Virginia into a paradise of onions,
squashes, string-beans and 'liberty.' "[80] Other representative
Virginia papers took a calmer view of the menace. The *Southern Argus,* Norfolk, asserted that many Virginians were too
sensitive on the subject of Southern institutions, and that it
was ridiculous to fear Eli Thayer's colonists.[81] The Richmond
Enquirer extended a welcome to honest lawabiding settlers
from the North who would stand by Southern institutions and
obey the laws of Virginia.[82]

Enlightened men, even in the Deep South, like Eli J. Capell
of Pleasant Hill, Amite County, Mississippi, wished Northern
farmers to settle in Dixie and teach the natives better methods
of agriculture and the virtues of thrift and sobriety. Capell
wrote to the editor of the *American Agriculturist,* July 1, 1845:
"I wish that more of your northern farmers and mechanics
could be induced to settle among us. We are about one hundred years behind you in improvement. This could be made
a splendid country, if there were more of the northern enterprise here. . . . If they were opposed to slavery, they need not
have any here unless they wish it."[83]

The intensely chauvinistic city of Charleston was a prominent center of Northern men in the South. In 1819 the New
England Society of Charleston was founded with forty-nine
original members. One of the most distinguished of its mem-

[79] Richmond *Whig,* extract in New York *Tribune,* March 18, 1857.

[80] Richmond *Examiner,* May 22, 1857.   [81] *Southern Argus,* April 22, 1857.

[82] Ceredo *Crescent,* Oct. 24, 1857. Extract from the *Enquirer.*

[83] W. H. Stephenson, "A Quarter-Century of a Mississippi Plantation: Eli J.
Capell of 'Pleasant Hill,' " *Mississippi Valley Historical Review,* XXIII, 363 (Dec.,
1936).

bers was Samuel Gilman, pastor of the Unitarian Church, who composed the college song, "Fair Harvard" (1836). A large proportion of the members of the New England Society were substantial merchants. Benjamin Faneuil Dunkin, a graduate of Harvard, was the Chief Justice of South Carolina and a signer of the Ordinance of Secession. James B. Campbell, a native of Massachusetts, came to South Carolina as a schoolteacher, married the daughter of a former governor of the state, and became a prominent Union leader. In fact, the New Englanders in Charleston were, with few exceptions, conservative Union men. If they disapproved of slavery, they prudently left no records of their dissent.[84]

Individuals from the North settled in the Southern States as teachers, businessmen, and editors. In North Carolina a considerable proportion of the editors were Northern men. Wheeler names six editors from beyond Mason and Dixon's line in his survey of the newspapers of the state in 1851: (1) Dennis Heartt of Connecticut, editor of the Hillsboro Recorder; (2) William Mayhew of Massachusetts, editor of the Newbernian; (3) D. Dimmick, a native of Maine, editor of the North State Whig; (4) Talcott Burr, a native of Rhode Island, editor of the Wilmington Herald; (5) W. B. Gulick of New Jersey, editor of the Goldsboro Patriot and Republican; (6) Thomas Loring of Massachusetts, editor of the Wilmington Commercial.[85] The Raleigh Standard, the leading Democratic organ of the state, was founded in 1834 by Philo White, a New Yorker.[86]

An astonishing number of prominent Southern editors were originally from the North. The commanding figure in the newspaper world of Kentucky was the Connecticut Yankee, George Prentice, editor of the Louisville Daily Journal.

[84] See William Way, History of the New England Society of Charleston, South Carolina, for One Hundred Years, 1819-1919 (Charleston, S. C., 1920).

[85] J. H. Wheeler, Historical Sketches of North Carolina from 1584 to 1851 (Philadelphia, 1851), Vol. I, chap. vii.

[86] W. W. Holden, Address on the History of Journalism in North Carolina, delivered at Winston, N. C., June 21, 1881.

Connecticut Yankees, Thaddeus Sanford and George Jeremiah Harris, also edited the Mobile *Register* and the Nashville *Union*. The Charleston *Courier* for many years prior to the Civil War was edited by Aaron Willington of Massachusetts. The Kanawha *Republican* and the Wheeling *Intelligencer* were edited respectively by Enos W. Newton, a Vermont schoolteacher, and A. W. Campbell of Ohio. In Georgia at this period three of the most influential newspapers of the state were edited by Northern men: the Savannah *Republican,* the Augusta *Chronicle,* and the Macon *Journal.*[87] The New Orleans *Picayune* was founded by George W. Kendall, a Yankee who had worked with Horace Greeley on the New York *Tribune.*

Another branch of intellectual leadership in the South, the profession of teaching, received many recruits from the North. At the University of Virginia Professor William H. McGuffey, famed for his *Eclectic Readers,* taught many years. The University of North Carolina had a Northern president, Joseph Caldwell, and several excellent Northern professors, James Phillips and Elisha Mitchell (whose name the highest mountain in the Alleghany range bears). The University of Georgia (then called Franklin College) had among its faculty three New Englanders, President Josiah Meigs and Professors Stephen Olin and Nahum Hiram Wood.[88] Perhaps the most distinguished of the Northern educators in the South was Frederick A. P. Barnard, professor at the University of Alabama from 1837 to 1854, and later president of the University of Mississippi. During the Civil War he returned North and became president of Columbia University.[89] Dr. George Junkin, President of Washington College, Lexington, Virginia, opposed aggressive abolitionism, but at the same time he taught his classes a strongly national interpretation of the Constitution. When some of his students raised the Palmetto flag over

[87] R. H. Shryock, *Georgia and the Union in 1850* (Durham, N. C., 1926), p. 84.
[88] Coulter, *College Life in the Old South,* pp. 15, 86, 87.
[89] "Autobiographical Sketch of Dr. F. A. P. Barnard," *Mississippi Historical Society Publications* (University, Miss., 1912), XII, 107-121.

one of the college buildings, he had it burned, and when secession took place, he departed for the North."[90]

Sergeant Prentiss and John A. Quitman are examples of
young Northern men who went South to make their fortunes
and grow up with the country. They settled in Natchez and
became thoroughly converted to the Southern viewpoint.
Prentiss wrote a remarkably well-balanced letter to his brother
in Maine explaining his views on slavery. "That slavery is a
great evil, there can be no doubt," he wrote," and it is an unfortunate circumstance that it was ever introduced into this,
or any other country. At present, however, it is a necessary
evil, and I do not think admits of a remedy."[91] He observed
that the slaves were well clothed, well fed, and kindly treated,
and he believed they were fully as happy as their masters. To
free them and let them remain in the South would not be ren-
dering a service to them. So thoroughly assimilated to his
Southern environment did Prentiss become, that he fought
many duels, including a celebrated one with Henry S. Foote.
Quitman was so enthusiastic for Southern institutions that he
might be regarded a fire-eater.[92] They both lived in beautiful,
aristocratic homes outside of Natchez.

Less notable than Prentiss and Quitman were two Massachusetts men, Horace Maynard and Franklin Plummer, who
became successful politicians in the South. Horace Maynard
was valedictorian of his class at Amherst College. After gradu-
ation, he came to Knoxville, Tennessee, where for a number
of years he was a professor in the East Tennessee University.
From 1857 to 1861 he represented the Knoxville district in
Congress. His Yankee birth was a drawback to him in his
political career, making him extremely cautious in his public
speech. One of his party associates described this characteristic as follows: "He seemed sensibly to realize that the Southern

[90] D. X. Junkin, *The Reverend George Junkin, D.D., LL.D., A Historical Biography* (Philadelphia, 1871), pp. 491, 519-520.

[91] Prentiss to his youngest brother, July 25, 1831 (*A Memoir of S. S. Prentiss
Edited by His Brother*, I, 107).

[92] Claiborne, *Life and Correspondence of John A. Quitman*, I, 138-139.

people would not tolerate in a native of Massachusetts the boldness of speech that they accepted in a native of the South."[93] Consequently, he steered clear of attacking slavery, but in 1861 he became one of the most important Union leaders of his state. Franklin Plummer was a plausible Yankee who settled in Pearlington, Mississippi, where, with his New England common school education, he was regarded as "a walking encyclopedia."[94] From teaching school in a log cabin, he arose to the position of one of the most astute politicians the Southwest ever had.

The career of Henry Watson, who came from Connecticut to Alabama as a tutor but finally settled as a lawyer, is typical of that of many Yankees in the ante-bellum South. Fresh from New England, he wrote to his father, August 23, 1835: "I abominate slavery but I consider the abolitionists of the North a dangerous set of men, and so far as they attempt to circulate such papers as the 'Liberator' and 'Emancipator' among the slaves as guilty of murder."[95] After he had lived years among the Southern people, he assimilated their point of view in regard to slavery. Especially he deprecated the agitation of the slavery question by aspiring politicians and raving fanatics. "In the state of things as they exist," he wrote, "emancipation is impossible—with immediate emancipation the two races could not exist in the same country."[96] During the secession crisis he strove valiantly to save the Union, but remained loyal to the state of his adoption.

In addition to the bona fide Northerners in the South there were a number of Southern men born of Northern parents. Senator James H. Hammond of South Carolina, an ardent proslavery man, was the son of a Yankee schoolteacher who was graduated from Dartmouth in the same class with Daniel Webster and came south to teach school. Benjamin F. Perry,

[93] Oliver P. Temple, *Notable Men of Tennessee from 1833 to 1875: Their Times and Their Contemporaries* (New York, 1912), pp. 137-138.

[94] J. F. H. Claiborne, *Mississippi as a Province, Territory, and State* (Jackson, Miss, 1880), I, 423-425.

[95] Henry Watson Papers in Duke University Library.

[96] Letter of June 22, 1858 (Watson MSS).

a leader of the Union party in South Carolina, was the son of a native of Massachusetts. President David L. Swain of the University of North Carolina was the son of a Massachusetts doctor who had settled at Asheville. The father of the great classicist and professor at the University of Virginia, Basil Gildersleeve, was a Connecticut Yankee. One of the most striking of Northern men with Southern relationships was Thomas G. Clemson, who married Anna Calhoun, and aided his father-in-law in managing the Fort Hill plantation and in working Calhoun's gold mine at Dahlonega.[97] All of these men were strongly attached to Southern institutions and accepted slavery tranquilly.

There were a few Northern men living in the South, however, who retained their antislavery views and dared to express them. An outstanding example of a Northern colonist who did not surrender his convictions was John C. Underwood, a native of New York and a graduate of Hamilton College. He came to Clarke County, Virginia, as a schoolteacher, but soon he was able to buy a farm of eight hundred acres, which he tilled with free labor. In 1856 Underwood was a delegate from Virginia at the Republican convention which nominated Frémont as candidate for the Presidency. Shortly afterwards, a meeting of citizens of Clarke County adopted a set of resolutions condemning Underwood as guilty of moral treason against the commonwealth and threatening him with violence if he ever returned to the state.[98] During the Reconstruction period he was one of the radical leaders and was appointed a Federal judge.

According to the census of 1850, there were 29,537 Northerners residing in Virginia (of whom 11,447 came from New Jersey and 6,323 from Pennsylvania), 4,250 in Georgia, and 14,566 in Louisiana.[99] The migration of Southerners to the

[97] See A. G. Holmes and G. R. Sherrill, *Thomas Green Clemson: His Life and Work* (Richmond, 1937).

[98] New York *Daily Tribune*, Sept. 12, 1856; *Liberator*, Aug. 15, 1856; *Dictionary of American Biography*, XIX, 113-114. For another example of the suppression of a Northern antislavery man, see John H. Aughey, *The Iron Furnace of Slavery and Secession* (Philadelphia, 1863).

[99] Compiled from *The Seventh Census of the United States*, Table XV, p. xxxvi.

North was much greater than the movement of Northerners into the South. In 1850 there were 608,626 people of Southern birth living in free states, but only 199,672 Northerners residing in the South.[100] Here one might have expected an important element of dissent, but very few of them raised their voices in opposition to the prevailing sentiment of the communities in which they lived. Some Northerners undoubtedly refrained from expressing their convictions about slavery from considerations of prudence. But many others, having observed the institution at close quarters, felt as did their Southern-born neighbors, that abolition was a dangerous and unwise measure. T. O. Larkin, a Massachusetts man who kept a store at Wilmington, North Carolina, before he became famous as the Consul of Monterey, believed that if the Northern abolitionists could live in the South a few years they would change their ideas about Southern slavery.[101] Those émigrés who did rebel against their Southern environment were usually men who had recently come from the North. Although certain racial groups in the South, like the Germans, started with antislavery prejudices, they quickly assimilated the Southern point of view. The removal of the antislavery Quakers from the South, leaving the conservatives behind, also weakened the forces that might have fought for freedom of expression on the slavery issue.

[100] R. R. Russel, "The General Effects of Slavery upon Southern Economic Progress," *Journal of Southern History*, IV, 40 (Feb., 1938).

[101] Robert J. Parker, "A Yankee in North Carolina; Observations of Thomas Oliver Larkin, 1821-1826," *North Carolina Historical Review*, XIV, 340-341 (Oct., 1937).

CHAPTER XI

FREE LANCES OF THE UPPER SOUTH

THE COTTON STATES, an eminent historian has asserted, presented in respect to slavery "the most perfect agreement ever known in Anglo-Saxon history."[1] Ministers of the Gospel, professors, poor whites, and gentlewomen agreed with the planters that it was best to keep the Negro subjected to the discipline of a master. This uniformity of thought, however, was not so rigid in the Upper South, where a surprising number of individuals refused to accept the dogmas of the pro-slavery apologists. These nonconformists deserve to be termed "the free lances of the Old South."

The imperialism that an idea can wield over a section was cogently illustrated in the widespread acceptance of the pro-slavery ideology in the South. Beginning in the decade of the 1820's, even before the violent attack of the abolitionists had provoked a defense, the South was subjected to thorough propaganda on the rightfulness of the institution, which overwhelmed many vacillating minds.[2] The Upper South contributed more than its share of brilliant champions to this evangelism. Thomas R. Dew, professor at William and Mary College, wrote a pioneer work defending slavery in 1832, which was followed ten years later by a volume from the pen of Rev. Thornton Stringfellow of Culpepper County, Virginia, showing that slavery was sanctioned by the Bible. In 1856 Professor A. T. Bledsoe of the University of Virginia composed a philosophical *Essay on Liberty and Slavery,* and President William A. Smith of Randolph-Macon College published his lectures to his senior class on the morality of slavery.[3] Dur-

---

[1] Dodd, *The Cotton Kingdom,* p. 70.

[2] The most recent study of the development of the proslavery philosophy is Jenkins's *Pro-Slavery Thought in the Old South.*

[3] W. A. Smith, *Lectures on the Philosophy and Practice of Slavery* (Nashville. Tenn., 1856).

ing these years Edmund Ruffin was maintaining by lectures and spirited essays in Southern periodicals that slavery was both just and well adapted to Southern economy. George Fitzhugh, a Virginian, published in 1854 his *Sociology for the South,* in which he claimed the superiority of the slave system over the free, competitive system of the North. From Kentucky came an able apology for the peculiar institution, *Methodism and Slavery,* by Rev. H. B. Bascom, President of Transylvania University. At Sewanee, Tennessee, Bishop Leonidas Polk established the University of the South to serve as a bulwark for proslavery interests. In North Carolina, Calvin H. Wiley, an outstanding educational reformer, published his defense of slavery entitled *A Sober View of the Slavery Question,* while Professor Elisha Mitchell of the University of North Carolina presented a similar point of view in a curious pamphlet, *The Other Leaf of the Book of Nature and the Word of God.*[4]

When one surveys this overwhelming propaganda by the most distinguished men of the South, when one takes into consideration that the Old Testament and Saint Paul sanctioned slavery, and when one realizes the formidable police problem of regulating semibarbaric Negroes and the great property loss arising from emancipation, the surprise comes, not at the uniformity of opinion in the South, but at the number of men who did think independently on the slavery question.

The strata of Southern society from which one might expect outspoken critics of slavery to arise were the poor whites, the yeomen, and the mechanics. It is a mistake, nonetheless, to think that the poor whites and the yeoman classes of the South would countenance any free criticism of slavery. Kenneth Rayner, prominent in North Carolina politics during the ante-bellum period, declared: "The masses of the non-slaveholding population of the South were more violent in their op-

---

[4] In the Lower South, two significant works defending slavery were published: *The Pro-Slavery Argument* (Charleston, S. C., 1850) and E. N. Elliott's *Cotton Is King and Pro-Slavery Arguments* (Augusta, Ga., 1860).

position to 'abolition' and 'abolitionists' than were the slave-owners themselves. They had in their minds a fixed and definite meaning attached to the word 'abolitionist.' They regarded it as meaning one who was in favor of setting free all the Negroes in the country, to remain there among themselves, and to have all the rights and privileges of, and be on an equality with, the poor white man. Thus it was a question of caste, of social position, of personal pride, in regard to which, above all other things in the world, human nature is most sensitive."[5] D. R. Hundley, who wrote a pioneer book on Southern sociology, observed that the poor whites were proslavery in sentiment almost to a man.[6] Even W. R. Gilmore, who was paid to travel in the South and write an antislavery book, admitted that the poor whites had a bitter hatred for the Negro and also for the abolitionist.[7] Olmsted, however, during his journey on horseback through the back country of Virginia, North Carolina, and Tennessee in 1854 talked with a number of mountain whites who were hostile to slavery.[8] The poor whites supported the Democratic party with its platform of slavery extension.

J. D. B. De Bow wrote a masterly pamphlet on *The Interest in Slavery of the Southern Non-Slaveholder*. Two powerful motives, he asserted, operated to attach the nonslaveholder to the slavery regime: (1) most nonslaveholders hoped to acquire slave property; (2) they feared the consequences of emancipation. De Bow maintained that there was no competition between the yeoman farmers and the slaves, for the labor of the latter was exhausted in cane, cotton, rice, and tobacco culture, while the labor of the former was devoted chiefly to cultivating corn, wheat, and potatoes, and raising hogs. He pointed to a striking phenomenon of Southern society: "The sons of the non-slaveholders are and always have been the leading and ruling spirits of the South, in industry as well as in politics. . . .

---

[5] [Kenneth Rayner,] *Life of Andrew Johnson by a National Man* (New York, 1866), p. 244.

[6] Hundley, *Social Relations in Our Southern States*, p. 273.

[7] Gilmore, *Among the Pines*, p. 69.

[8] Olmsted, *A Journey in the Back Country*, pp. 250-266, 270.

In this class are the McDuffies, Langdon Cheves, Andrew Jacksons, Henry Clays, and Rusks of the past; the Hammonds, Yanceys, Orrs, Memmingers, Benjamins, Stephens, Soules, Browns of Mississippi, Simms, Porters, McGraths, Aikens, Maunsel Whites, and an innumerable host of the present; and what is to be noted, these men have not been made demagogues, but are among the most conservative among us."[9] Basing his conclusion on a wide and accurate investigation of Southern conditions, he declared that there did not exist at the South a class conscientiously objecting to the ownership of slave property.[10]

The hope of acquiring slaves on the part of the yeoman class was a strong deterrent to any radical criticism of the institution. The acquisition of slaves by a poor man marked a step upward in the social ladder, an advance in the esteem of his neighbors—the imprimatur of success. The ownership of such property was the highest ambition of the enterprising nonslaveholder, according to D. R. Hundley. He relates an anecdote of a yeoman who had recently purchased his first slave. With an air of pride the farmer called, "Jeff! you, Jeff! Come here you big black nigger, you!" When Jeff responded, "Bres God, Mas'r, what's de marter?" his master said, "O, Nuthin, *I only wanted to see how 'twould sound jist—that's all!*"[11] Frequently overseers, sprung from lowly origins, like Ephraim Beanland, who managed James Knox Polk's plantation in Mississippi, aspired to become planters or slaveowners —and succeeded.[12]

The leaders of the nonslaveholding whites used more vio-

[9] J. D. B. De Bow, *The Interest in Slavery of the Southern Non-Slaveholder* (New York, 1860), p. 10.

[10] In an article in the *American Historical Review*, previously cited, entitled "The Central Theme of Southern History," U. B. Phillips shows how determined were the nonslaveholding whites to keep the Negro in slavery. He quotes a striking prayer of an overseer on a Louisiana sugar plantation written in the plantation journal, June 13, 1861: "My honest convicksion is that every man, wome, and chile, that has gave aide to the abolishionist are fit subjects for Hell" (p. 32).

[11] Frederic Bancroft, *Slave-Trading in the Old South* (Baltimore, 1931), p. 345.

[12] Bassett, *The Southern Plantation Overseer as Revealed in His Letters*, pp. 91-93.

lent and more picturesque language in condemning antislavery men than did the aristocratic planters. "Parson" W. G. Brownlow of Tennessee, editor of the Knoxville *Whig* and later leader of the Unionists of East Tennessee, for example, was a vigorous upholder of slavery. He challenged any Northern man to a public debate on the question of slavery, first specifying that he must not be a Negro. In 1858 an abolitionist by the name of Prynne accepted his challenge and a notable debate took place in Philadelphia. Brownlow characteristically based his main defense of slavery on a very literal interpretation of the Bible.[13] Andrew Johnson, who likewise represented the prejudices of the Tennessee yeoman, was another staunch defender of slavery. When he grew sufficiently wealthy, he purchased and kept eight slaves. Not only did he oppose the reception of abolition petitions in Congress, but when Senator Bell voted against the Kansas-Nebraska Bill, Johnson supported the movement in Tennessee to force him to resign. Johnson's attitude toward slavery was forcibly expressed in the question: "If you liberate the Negro, what will be the next step? . . . What will we do with two million Negroes in our midst? . . . Blood, rape and rapine will be our portion. You can't get rid of the Negro except by holding him in slavery."[14] Another leader of the nonslaveholders, W. W. Holden, who had begun life as a printer's devil, was chiefly responsible for driving Benjamin Sherwood Hedrick from his professorship at the University of North Carolina because of the latter's support of Frémont, the Republican Presidential candidate.[15] In the Lower South Joseph E. Brown, Alexander Stephens, and Albert Gallatin Brown, sprung from the small farmer class, were ardent supporters of the peculiar institution.

The yeomanry of North Carolina, however, did produce two outstanding critics of the slavery regime in Hinton Rowan

[13] W. G. Brownlow, *Ought American Slavery to be Perpetuated? A Debate Between Brownlow and Prynne* (Philadelphia, 1858).

[14] Robert W. Winston, *Andrew Johnson, Plebeian and Patriot* (New York, 1928), pp. 118-119.

[15] See W. K. Boyd (ed.), *Memoirs of W. W. Holden* (Durham, N. C., 1911).

Helper and Daniel Reaves Goodloe.[16] The latter suffered the cruel blows of Fortune that are often reserved for the man who refuses to be a timeserver. In his youth he was apprenticed to a printer in Oxford, North Carolina, a circumstance which affiliated him with the mechanics class. His antislavery views made North Carolina an uncongenial place for him, and he went to Washington. There he secured a clerkship under President Taylor's administration, which he quickly lost when he wrote a letter favorable to *Uncle Tom's Cabin* that was published in the *Key to Uncle Tom's Cabin*. Goodloe was for a while editor of the *National Era,* the moderate antislavery paper published at Washington. After the Civil War he was appointed marshal in North Carolina by President Johnson, but was turned out in 1869 "for the grave offense of exposing the knaveries of the carpet-baggers."[17]

Goodloe explained his conversion to antislavery views by asserting that the Virginia debates of 1831-32 "fixed me as an Emancipationist from which I never swerved back. I am a home-bred anti-slavery man—not northern."[18] In 1842 some of his friends tried to persuade him to run for a political office, promising to nominate him, but he refused. He declared later: "I had a profound conviction of the evils of slavery, moral and economic. The agitation had not then reached the fever heat, but it was rising, and it began to be seen that the interest of slavery underlay and touched every other question. I should have been called upon to define my views on the subject which I could not have done without injury to the Whig cause, to my friends, and to myself."[19]

In the previous year (1841) he had written an antislavery pamphlet entitled *Inquiry into the Causes Which Have Retarded the Accumulation of Wealth and Increase of Population*

---

[16] For valuable studies of Goodloe and other antislavery men in the South, see S. B. Weeks, "Anti-Slavery Sentiment in the South," *Publications of the Southern History Association* (1898), II, 87-130.

[17] D. R. Goodloe Papers, Biographical Notes (MSS in Library of the University of North Carolina). [18] *Ibid.*

[19] Bassett, "Anti-Slavery Leaders of North Carolina," p. 49; see also the biographical sketch of Goodloe in *Dictionary of American Biography,* VII, 390-391.

in the Southern States.[20] Goodloe was a forerunner of Helper in attacking slavery from an economic point of view. Unlike Helper, he did not vitiate his writings with bitterness or brand slaveholders as criminals, but sought rather to convince them that slavery was injurious to their best interests, especially by reference to the census reports of 1840. He followed his first attack by another antislavery pamphlet, *The Southern Platform,*[21] in which he gathered the statements of the great leaders of the South who had opposed slavery in an earlier age, that he might awaken a generous sympathy for emancipation. One of the most valuable portions of this pamphlet consisted of extracts from the Virginia debates of 1831-32. There is no evidence that Goodloe's pamphlets circulated in the Southern States to any extent.

Across the Great Smoky Mountains in Tennessee where dwelt a hardy yeomanry, a number of independent persons opposed slavery openly in the decade of the 1830's. When the constitutional convention of Tennessee met in the summer of 1834, memorials for the adoption of a scheme of gradual emancipation were signed by eighteen hundred and four persons, chiefly from Greene and Washington counties.[22] The convention, however, resolutely refused to be drawn into a controversy over emancipation. A committee was appointed to draw up a report stating the reasons of the convention for refusing to consider the question. This report, presented by John A. M'Kinney and adopted by a vote of forty-four to ten, admitted that slavery was an evil: "To prove it to be a great evil is an easy task, but to tell how that evil can be removed is a question that the wisest heads and the most benevolent hearts have not been able to answer in a satisfactory manner."[23] The committee declared that any steps toward emancipation in Tennessee

[20] D. R. Goodloe, *Inquiry into the Causes Which Have Retarded the Accumulation of Wealth and Increase of Population in the Southern States* (Washington, D. C., 1846), first printed in 1844.

[21] D. R. Goodloe, *The Southern Platform* (Boston, 1858).

[22] *Journal of the Convention of the State of Tennessee Convened for the Purpose of Revising and Amending the Constitution thereof* (Nashville, Tenn., 1834), p. 125.   [23] *Ibid.*, p. 88.

would merely lead to the removal of the slaves to the Lower South, where their lot would be rendered worse. Furthermore, the emancipation of the slaves might result in the bloody scenes of San Domingo. A small minority of the convention, on the other hand, protested against the report as apologizing for slavery and as contrary to the Declaration of Independence and the Bible.[24] Joseph Kincaid's written protest was a noble assertion of liberal principles in regard to the South's gravest problem. Even the warm advocates of a scheme of emancipation did not urge its adoption without provision for the removal of the freedmen from Tennessee.

A fascinating figure in the early history of Memphis, Major Marcus Winchester, displayed an audacious liberalism in regard to race relations. An officer in the War of 1812, he settled in Memphis as the leading merchant, built an imposing house on the Bluff, and was elected the first mayor. His handsome face, excellent education, and courtly manners won the favor of such sharp-tongued ladies as Frances Trollope and Mrs. Anne Royall. Nevertheless, he braved public opinion by marrying a French quadroon, the cast-off mistress of Thomas Hart Benton, and reared a family of mulatto children. Such flagrant disregard of the color line led to his ostracism for a while, but later he was elected to the legislature. Winchester sought to aid his slaves to emancipate themselves by an intelligent plan of self-help. He opened up an account for each of his slaves, crediting them with their services and deducting outlays and expenses. "Always ready to catch at passing isms," he was a sympathizer and adviser of Frances Wright, who attempted to carry out a scheme of emancipation, somewhat similar to his, at Nashoba.[25]

The letters of Ezekiel Birdseye of Newport, Tennessee, to Gerrit Smith present a wealth of information on some of the rather obscure antislavery men in the Upper South. Birdseye was a Connecticut Yankee who had come to Tennessee to

[24] *Ibid.,* pp. 102-104.
[25] J. D. Davis, *History of Memphis and the Old Time Papers* (Memphis, 1873), pp. 70-83. See also Capers, *The Biography of a River Town,* pp. 52-53.

develop some coal mines. His letters to Gerrit Smith during the year 1841 have been preserved in the Gerrit Smith Papers at Syracuse University. Birdseye carried on a correspondence with the Northern philanthropist, giving him the names of the antislavery Southerners to whom abolition documents and papers could be sent. He mentioned a number of men in East Tennessee who were opposed to slavery and who would receive antislavery literature, like Rev. Josiah Rhoton of Claiborne County, Professor Craig of Maryville College, Dr. J. M. Recca of Mossy Creek, Mr. Kirkpatrick, postmaster of Bent's Creek, Judge William B. Reace (Reese) of the Supreme Court, J. W. Lucky, an attorney of Jonesborough, the venerable Samuel Johnstone of Monroe County, and a Mr. Patterson, president of the Manumission Society of Jefferson County.[26] Birdseye wrote that this manumission society had over six hundred members, but owing to the oppressive laws of the state, it did not dare to hold meetings. Indeed, Patterson had sold his farm and purchased land in Indiana, unwilling to remain longer in a slave state. Birdseye was a vigorous advocate of the separation of East Tennessee from the parent state as a means of advancing the antislavery cause. He found, however, that it was "prudent" to say but little on the subject of the extermination of slavery until the act of separation had been accomplished.

By 1860 few of these antislavery men of East Tennessee remained, or they had become inarticulate. It is a striking fact that of the numerous Union leaders in East Tennessee described by a contemporary, Oliver Temple, in his *Notable Men of Tennessee,* not one was a declared opponent of slavery. He describes the vague fears of the abolitionists that dominated the people of his section: "No one dared any longer to suggest its removal or its amelioration. All, whether slaveholders or non-slaveholders, felt the crushing power and the ómnipotence of this despotism of public opinion. The least suspicion of disloyalty to slavery, the least hint of anti-slavery sentiments

[26] W. F. Galpin, "Letters of an East Tennessee Abolitionist," *East Tennessee Historical Society Publications* (Jan., 1931), No. III, pp. 134-149.

on the part of anyone, brought upon such person infamy and the curse of social outlawry."[27]

It would be natural to suppose that the most brilliant, the most original, and the most tolerant minds of the Old South should be found among the planters and the political leaders. They were the top rank of the aristocracy. Yet Southerners liked to compare themselves to the Romans, a practical race, impatient of theory, with a genius for law, politics, and government, while the Yankees were likened unto the Greeks, theoretical, literary, mercantile. The planters and political men were conservative. The Bible and the Constitution were their palladium and the final arbiter of all disputes. As practical men they believed that slavery was the best solution of the race problem. As owners of slave property they could not permit a devastating criticism that might deprive them of their vested interests.

A few strong personalities, nevertheless, arose above the prejudices and point of view of the ruling class into which they were born. Edward Coles was one of these men. He possessed the advantage of having been reared in a mellow, aristocratic environment. His father's home had received as guests the great men of Virginia—Patrick Henry, Jefferson, Madison, Monroe, Wirt, the Randolphs. The youthful heir had been sent to college at Hampden-Sydney and William and Mary. As a climax to his education, he was appointed the private secretary of President Madison, in which position for six years he moved in the refined society of Washington.

At college he formed decided antislavery opinions and eagerly read everything he could find on the subject. While he was secretary to Madison, he wrote a letter to Jefferson (July 31, 1814) beseeching the old statesman as the philosopher of the rights of man, to lead an emancipation movement in Virginia. He expressed his opposition to slavery in terms of moral principle and strong aversion to holding slaves. He said that he had resolved to emigrate to a state where slavery did not exist.

[27] Temple, *Notable Men of Tennessee*, pp. 34-35.

In reply, Jefferson with delicate irony turned the tables on the young reformer. After referring to his services in the cause of emancipation, he reminded the youth that he was an old man, and that Coles was bidding Priam buckle on the armor of Hector. Jefferson then rebuked the young idealist for his decision to abandon his native state. Let him come forward, *the young and valiant champion,* with the years before him, and as a missionary insinuate abolition doctrines into the minds of his fellow citizens.[28]

Coles, stung apparently by the gentle rebuke of the great man, wrote a second letter in which he said that he would remain in Virginia if he thought that he could be instrumental in liberating the slaves or in ameliorating their lot. But he was convinced that he would be unable to accomplish either purpose. He maintained that, not the young who are with little influence and unripened powers, but the experienced and illustrious statesmen, must take the lead. To break the apathy of society required a strong impulse, but around the standard of Jefferson a great party would rally.

In 1819 he started from his plantation in Virginia with his negroes on the long journey to the free soil of Illinois. When he arrived at this mecca of freedom, he liberated them, giving one hundred and sixty acres of land to each head of a family. In 1824, as governor of Illinois, he valiantly defeated the attempt to amend the state constitution so as to permit slavery. It is an indictment of Virginia plantation society that it could drive out such an idealist and forceful leader as Edward Coles.[29]

James Coles Bruce of Halifax, Virginia, was another prominent planter who opposed slavery, but not on moral grounds. In 1847 he made a notable address before the agricultural clubs of Mecklenburg and Granville counties. He prefaced his remarks by saying that he proposed to speak plainly and candidly on the system of labor employed by the South. To ward off op-

[28] Ford (ed.), *The Writings of Thomas Jefferson,* IX, 477.
[29] See E. B. Washburne, *A Sketch of Edward Coles* (Chicago, 1882); and Henry Wilson, *The Rise and Fall of the Slave Power in America* (Boston, 1873), I, 163-164.

position, he declared that he had no sympathy with the abolitionists; the African was not yet fit for freedom. Slave labor, he
observed, was suited only to a virgin soil, and for that reason
it was not adapted to Virginia and North Carolina. The average planter, consequently, had made no profit on agriculture
in Virginia for the last four years. He advised his hearers to
sell their slaves while the demand from the Lower South held
up their price. He clinched his economic argument against
slavery by the following appeal to the dictates of common
sense: "Certainly, if the labor be unproductive, it is folly to
keep it. The slave adds nothing to the moral and physical
strength of the country, and if his labor be profitless, of course
he is a nuisance, and the sooner we rid ourselves of him the
better. His place will be supplied with a better population, and
in the meantime the poorer lands will be thrown out of cultivation."[30] This speech was to be quoted by Southern critics
of slavery who were under fire for their views.

General John Cocke, of Bremo, was likewise a Virginia
planter who possessed unusual independence of mind. He had
played a noble role in the founding of the University of Virginia. A puritan cavalier, he became a temperance advocate,
an opponent of dueling, and a supporter of the colonization
movement. Believing that the excessive cultivation of tobacco
and slavery were the twin evils of Virginia, he "dared to sport
a new idea" and to discourage the cultivation of tobacco as
the staple crop. In 1855 not a tobacco plant was grown on any
of his plantations. Slavery appeared to him as a cancer eating
into the vitals of Southern society, and in 1846 he had predicted that Virginia would witness profound changes touching the peculiar institution. He carried out his convictions by
emancipating some of his slaves. Strikingly free from intolerance, he received *Uncle Tom's Cabin* with sympathy, as a
work destined to hasten the fall of slavery.[31]

The American Colonization Society Papers reveal some

---

[30] Richmond *Enquirer*, Aug. 24, 1847.
[31] P. A. Bruce, *History of the University of Virginia* (New York, 1922), I,
161-163; *Dictionary of American Biography*, IV, 253-254.

planters who were willing to sacrifice their pecuniary interests to liberate their slaves. The will of General Sam Blackburn, who had lived near Staunton, Virginia, emancipated his forty-six slaves, and provided that their passage to Liberia be paid by his estate.[32] James Green left twenty-five thousand dollars to the American Colonization Society to be devoted to the emancipation and colonization in Liberia of slaves from Mississippi.[33] William Thompson of Harrodsburg, Kentucky, a student at Yale College, wrote to the society proposing to give up his thirty-three slaves for the purpose of sending them to Liberia.[34] Captain Ross, owner of Prospect Hill, near Port Gipson, willed his estate, including one hundred and seventy slaves, to the Colonization Society. The agent of the society, who had to defend the will against the heirs, wrote that Captain Ross treated his negroes more like children than slaves: "To render them happy appears to have been the great object of their master. Captain Ross was an excellent planter, yet for many years, instead of endeavoring to increase his estate, its great resources were developed and applied to increase the comforts of his people."[35]

Dr. William J. Holcombe of Lynchburg, Virginia, also followed an idealistic course in regard to slavery. After liberating his slaves, he aided some of them to pay their passage to Liberia. His magnanimity was shown by his refusal to accept a large inheritance because part of it consisted of slaves. In 1843 he moved his family to Indiana, that he might bring up his younger children in a free state. But his older son, Professor James P. Holcombe of the University of Virginia, became an advocate of the institution of slavery, and one of the most ardent secessionists in the Virginia Convention of 1861.[36]

Some of the vigorous young men who spoke so eloquently

[32] John H. Peyton to James Laurie, Aug. 8, 1835 (African Colonization Society Papers in Library of Congress).
[33] R. R. Gurley to P. R. Fendall, June 3, 1836 (ibid.).
[34] William Thompson, Jan. 14, 1857 (ibid.).
[35] R. R. Gurley to Philip R. Fendall, July 12, 1836 (ibid.).
[36] Bruce, History of the University of Virginia, III, 72; Dictionary of American Biography, IX, 134.

against slavery in the Virginia Assembly of 1832 recanted their political heresies in later life.[37]   Robert Eden Scott, on the other hand, preferred to sacrifice his political ambitions and preserve his independence of spirit.   In 1849 he made a brave speech in the Virginia House of Delegates, opposing resolutions that condemned the Wilmot Proviso.   Declaring slavery to be "an institution reprobated by the world, acknowledged to be a social and political evil," he condemned any policy of forcing it on the people of a territory against their consent.   Scott could not be regarded, however, as an immediatist on the question of liberating the slaves.   Rather, he expressed the point of view of liberal and moderate Southerners who frankly acknowledged the disadvantages of slavery, but believed that it would be unwise to emancipate the slaves without some plan of removing the unfortunate race from the South.   "The extinction of slavery," he declared in a public speech, "must be the work of time and proceed from the voluntary exercise of our own free will."[38]   This speech was printed in the Virginia papers at the time and was later appealed to by Southern antislavery men.   Letcher quoted extracts from it when he was attacked in 1859 for his early antislavery sentiments.[39]   Samuel Janney heard Scott speak when he was a young man and was impressed by the nobility of his character.   As a consequence of his bold expressions on slavery, he was defeated for re-election to the legislature, and retired from political life.[40]

Another Virginian who was punished for his antislavery opinions by political retirement was McDowell Moore. He had been one of the signers of the Ruffner pamphlet. In 1860 his name was placed on the Whig ticket as a Presidential elector. On account of his relation to the notorious document, he felt obliged to withdraw his name in order to prevent discord. He did not try to atone for his act in endorsing the antislavery sentiments of Dr. Ruffner as did John Letcher. Instead, he

[37] For example, James McDowell; see *John P. Branch Historical Papers*, IV, 30; and Charles Faulkner, *Speech on the Basis Question* (Richmond, 1851), p. 9; McDowell's Papers, preserved in the Duke University Library, are silent as to the reasons for this *volte-face*.   [38] Alexandria *Gazette*, Feb. 15, 1849.
[39] Richmond *Enquirer*, May 17, 1859.   [40] Conway, *Autobiography*, I, 76.

preferred to keep the esteem of "that able, patriotic, and good old man, Henry Ruffner, which was worth more than the inconvenience of incurring the ill-will of those who condemned him."[41]

An astounding figure of Virginia politics during the ante-bellum period was Charles Fenton Mercer, a freethinker and iconoclast. He was the scion of an illustrious Virginia family, who had received a liberal education at Princeton and in Europe. He entered politics and was so successful in retaining the respect of his constituents that he was kept in Congress continuously from 1817 to 1840.[42] In 1845 he wrote *An Exposition of the Weakness and Inefficiency of the Government of the United States of America,* in which he made a vigorous attack on slavery. The book was anonymous and privately printed.[43]

The opposition of General Mercer to slavery had its source not so much in economic considerations, or sympathy for the slave, but in the feelings of a patriot, the belief that slavery tainted politics and corrupted Southern society. He predicted that a quarrel would arise over this institution that would result in disunion. He compared the abolitionists to the Crusaders of old fighting in a holy cause. With vivid clearness he delineated the effect that slavery had on the morals of slaveholders. It developed in them, he said, domineering manners, disregard for the law, resulting in lynch law and duels, licentiousness, drinking, and gambling.[44] He described how it dominated politics, so that everything had to be decided, not on its own merits, but how it affected the slave interests. In order to protect the peculiar institution, the Southern States had denied the sacred right of petition, had established an intolerable censorship over the mails, and had violated the right of trial by jury.

The other evils which weakened the government of the

---

[41] *Southern Argus,* March 20, 1860.

[42] J. M. Garnett, *Life of Charles Fenton Mercer* (Richmond, 1911).

[43] Harvard University has a copy of this edition presented by the author. During the Civil War a second edition was published by a "member of the Middle Temple, London."

[44] [C. F. Mercer,] *Exposition,* pp. 168-172. See footnote 92.

United States were also painted in bold colors by Mercer. The master evil, he thought, was the States' rights doctrine which tended to make the national government "a nominal thing." Another fault was the lack of education of the voting masses, which unhappily the Federal government was powerless to remedy. He believed that public lectures should be given and lyceums founded to educate the older generation. With complete disregard of prevailing trends of Southern society, he sketched his ideal government—a republic in which the executive should be chosen for a ten-year term, the judges appointed for life, and electors should have a real estate qualification, education should be a national concern, all religions tolerated, manufacturing protected, the three-fifths ratio abolished, and Congress should consist of only one chamber.

A more aggressive figure in Virginia politics who opposed the proslavery group was John Minor Botts of Richmond. Botts resembled a bulldog, always barking, valiant, ruggedly honest, and plain-spoken. No man in Virginia was so persistently ridiculed as he "the unspeakable Botts," "the terrible Botts," whose very name was the signal for merriment. Sergeant Prentiss maliciously called him "the Great Groom of Gohanna."[45] Something of the temper of the man can be seen in his opposition to the nomination of General Taylor for President. He was a loyal Whig, who realized the availability of the hero of Buena Vista, but he believed that candidates should be chosen on the basis of their principles.[46] His devotion to free speech was shown in his courageous support as Congressman of John Quincy Adams in the latter's efforts to repeal the Gag Resolutions. Botts supported this hated enemy of the South because he believed in the sacred right of petition.[47] In 1850 he was a staunch advocate of the Great Compromise. His attitude toward slavery at this time was

[45] Wheeling *Intelligencer*, May 14, 1859.

[46] J. M. Botts, "To the Whigs of Virginia," an address in a volume of collected speeches of J. M. Botts (Harvard University Library).

[47] C. C. Webster, "John Minor Botts, Anti-Secessionist," *Richmond College Historical Papers*, I, 14 (June, 1915). See also A. C. Cole, *The Whig Party in the South*.

expressed in a public speech at Powhatan Courthouse, June 15, 1850, in which he deplored the bondage of the black man as an evil and said that the South would welcome as a great benefactor the man who found some satisfactory and practical way to get rid of the incubus, yet he feared that it was perfectly utopian to attempt it.[48]

On August 8, 1856, he delivered a memorable address in the African Church at Richmond. He began with the remark that he spoke as a private citizen, having become utterly disgusted with politics and politicians. He had become a branded man, because he had dared to vote against the Kansas-Nebraska Bill, foreseeing that it would precipitate a violent sectional conflict. He had increased his unpopularity by voting in Congress with the abolitionists to censure the conduct of Preston Brooks. On the present occasion he arose to address Virginians with a repressed feeling of bitterness for the treatment he had received. His guiding principle, he avowed, was nationalism: "I know no North, no South, no East, no West." Then he reaffirmed his antislavery views and his devotion to the cause of free speech. "My position on the question of slavery is this," he said, "and so far from wishing to conceal it, I desire it should be known to all. Muzzles were made for dogs, and not for men, and no press and no party can put a muzzle on my mouth so long as I value my freedom. I make bold to proclaim that I am no slavery propagandist."[49] Botts declared that he was a slaveholder and the man who called him an abolitionist was a fool or a knave—yet he was unwilling to force slavery on a reluctant people. He was a strange combination of radicalism and conservatism, of violent and pugnacious speech, and of moderate and conservative measures.

Lacking the devotion to principle, characteristic of Botts, "Honest John" Letcher sought to lead the democracy of his state without alienating the aristocrats. Serious handicaps blocked his path: his humble birth, the idealism of his early

[48] J. M. Botts, *Speech at Powhatan Court House, June 15, 1850*, a pamphlet. For further material on Botts, see *Dictionary of American Biography*, II, 472-473.

[49] J. M. Botts, *Speech at the African Church, Richmond, June 15, 1856*, p. 12. A pamphlet.

career, and the fact that he was a Western man. He was, more-over, the son of a Methodist butcher.[50] He himself began his career inauspiciously as a tailor in Lexington, Virginia, but his restless and ambitious nature led him to seize all the opportunities for self-culture within his reach. He joined a debating society at Lexington, named after the illustrious prototype of the American self-made man, Benjamin Franklin. Here young Letcher inclined strongly to radicalism, speaking in the society to advocate a dismemberment of the state and the removal of slavery from the western half.

He was one of the twelve endorsers of the Ruffner pamphlet. In later life he recanted the idealistic vagaries of his young manhood, for political ambitions made him a conservative. His opinion of the pamphlet was changed as early as 1850, when he was a candidate for office. "At the time of the publication of that address [the Ruffner pamphlet]," he pleaded in extenuation of his offense, "I state frankly that I did regard slavery as a social and political evil. I did not regard it then, nor since, as a moral evil, for I was at that time, have been ever since, and am now, the owner of slave property, by purchase and not by inheritance."[51] During his successful gubernatorial campaign of 1860, his connection with the Ruffner pamphlet again rose to plague him, and he made a complete recantation. He explained his apostasy by the statement that later study had convinced him that slavery was a beneficial institution. In attaining his object, he lost the support of the radicals who reproached him for abandoning his principles "to placate a one-idea oligarchy."[52] Yet on the eve of the Civil War he was the chief executive of the Old Dominion.

The Whig party of the Upper South contained many men who prided themselves on their devotion to principle and their moderation of views. They resisted the agitation of the slavery

    [50] For biographical details, see E. B. Prettyman, "John Letcher," *John P. Branch Historical Papers*, III, 314-349; Brock, *Virginia and Virginians*, I, 231; and *Dictionary of American Biography*, XI, 192.
    [51] *John P. Branch Historical Papers*, III, 332. Also Richmond *Enquirer*, Nov. 30, 1858, and May 17, 1859.
    [52] Wheeling *Intelligencer*, Feb. 5, 1859.

question both by the fire-eaters and the abolitionists—a course motivated primarily by a strong national feeling. There is little evidence that the Whig leaders valued freedom of speech as a vital necessity of democratic government. Indeed, their efforts were directed toward suppressing the discussion of the slavery question on the grounds of expediency. Their large property interests in slaves made them apprehensive of controversy over the slavery issue. Although the Whigs were less intolerant toward antislavery men than were the more radical Democrats, many of them were violent partisans, bitterly prejudiced against the Democratic party.[53] Especially in Kentucky, East Tennessee, and in North Carolina were they influential.

After Henry Clay had given up all Presidential ambitions, which had caused him to keep his antislavery opinions in the background, he came forward during the campaign preceding the constitutional convention of 1849 and boldly advocated the adoption of a plan of gradual emancipation for Kentucky. In the famous letter to Richard Pindell at this time, he proposed a plan of emancipation by which slaves born after 1855 or 1860 should become free upon attaining the age of twenty-five years, but they should be hired out by the state for a period of three years to pay their expenses to Liberia.[54] Clay believed that emancipation would not work in the South unless it were accompanied by a plan of colonization. It is significant that shortly after writing the Pindell letter he was returned to the Senate by a large vote, despite his emancipation sentiments.

The agitation for the revision of the Kentucky Constitution during the years 1847-49 brought to the surface many prominent Kentuckians who championed the gradual abolition of slavery. Louisville, where there were a larger industrial popu-

[53] See letter of Thos. R. R. Nelson to John Bell, Jan. 10, 1851, proposing to "unmask the *sinuosities* of Democracy for the last twenty years" (John Bell Papers, MSS in Library of Congress).

[54] Carl Schurz, *Life of Henry Clay* (Boston, 1898), II, 316-317, 333. On May 22, 1849, J. V. Harrison of Fayette County wrote to Joseph Holt that Clay was "looked to as the head of this [the Emancipation] party—though too old to take an active part in the campaign" (Joseph Holt Papers, Vol. XIII, MSS in the Library of Congress).

lation and a better school system (managed by New England men) than in any other community in the state, was the center of the antislavery sentiment. William L. Breckinridge, editor of the Louisville *Presbyterian Herald,* 1838-45, was one of the most influential of these humanitarians. In 1848 some of the most eminent leaders in Kentucky signed an "Address to the People of Kentucky" which urged the adoption of a plan of emancipation similar to the one which had worked so successfully in ridding Pennsylvania, New York, and New Jersey of slavery. The address recognized that the most serious impediment to emancipation was the problem of the free Negro and that any plan of freeing the slaves should be accompanied by colonization.[55] One of the signers was James Speed (afterwards in Lincoln's Cabinet). Speed contributed a series of antislavery letters to the Louisville *Courier* at this time, and ran for election to the constitutional convention on an emancipation platform, but was defeated.[56] The Emancipation Convention of Frankfort, held April 25, 1849, also brought together one hundred and fifty delegates from twenty-four counties who were opposed to slavery. Among the distinguished delegates were both of Kentucky's Senators, Henry Clay and Joseph R. Underwood, as well as Robert J. Breckinridge, and Cassius M. Clay. Indeed, many of the Kentucky advocates of emancipation were slaveholders.

One of the Whigs from the Upper South who attracted attention by his independence of mind was T. L. Clingman, Congressman from the extreme western district of North Carolina. In 1844 he voted for the repeal of the famous "Gag Rule" that prevented the reception of abolitionist petitions in Congress. In an able speech he held that this rule was an infringement of the right of petition. Taking a pragmatic view of the situation, he maintained that repression would only strengthen the hands of the abolitionists in the North by allying their

[55] Martin, *Anti-Slavery Movement in Kentucky,* p. 123. Another circular by a group of Louisville men, Jan., 1849, was sent to prominent leaders in the Upper South appealing for funds to publish tracts and newspapers showing the moral economic, and social evils of slavery (Zebulon Vance Papers, I, MS, Raleigh, N. C.).

[56] *Dictionary of American Biography,* XVII, 440-441.

cause with that of freedom of speech. Furthermore, he said that any attempt to head off the discussion of slavery in Congress could only be regarded as an admission of weakness on the part of the South. At the same time Clingman was an ardent defender of slavery and the rights of the South.[57]

Willie P. Mangum, Whig Senator from North Carolina, held liberal views on slavery. He had been taught as a boy by John Chavis, a free Negro who had studied at Princeton College. Chavis carried on a correspondence with the Carolina Senator, discussing politics, giving advice, and lecturing him on occasion.[58] According to Daniel Reaves Goodloe, who knew him at Washington, Mangum became affiliated with Senator Benton and adopted the mild type of free-soilism and emancipation which Benton advocated in his late years, but he never made them public.[59] His papers preserved in the Library of Congress give no indication of antislavery views.[60]

Kenneth Rayner was another liberal North Carolina Whig who gave offense to the ultraists on the slavery issue. Hinton Rowan Helper placed Rayner in the group of Southern men "who entertain sentiments of the Immortal Fathers of the Republic that slavery is a great moral, social, civil, and political evil to be got rid of at the earliest practical period."[61] In a speech on the floor on Congress, Rayner declared that slavery was not a blessing but a misfortune to any people among whom it existed. "But if it were ten times greater an evil than it is," he warned, "we will never suffer those who are uninterested in the matter to interfere with us.—And I can assure Northern gentlemen that the course of the abolitionists has riveted the chains of slavery with double and triple bolts of steel. It has thrown back the cause of non-slavery in the South, at least a

[57] T. L. Clingman, *Speeches and Writings* (Raleigh, N. C., 1877), pp. 197, 259.

[58] A number of these letters are preserved in the Mangum Papers in the Library of Congress, copies of which are in the archives of the North Carolina Historical Commission.

[59] D. R. Goodloe MSS in the Library of the University of North Carolina; notes on political leaders at Washington, p. 38.

[60] Although this collection of letters is very voluminous, most of the letters are written to Mangum.

[61] Helper, *The Impending Crisis*, pp. 167-168.

century."[62] Rayner belonged to the group of "politiques" in the South who discouraged the agitation of the slavery question lest it lead to disunion. He accused the Democratic party of keeping the country in an eternal turmoil and confusion about "niggers, niggers." He was pursued with tigerlike ferocity by the Democratic press because he had urged the Union-loving men of the South to unite and oppose the ceaseless agitation of slavery and to vote for Fillmore. Rayner was the owner of a hundred slaves, but he was accused of sympathizing with the abolitionists and of advocating a coalition with Frémont. These accusations so enraged him that he attempted to give a caning to Editor Holden of the Raleigh *Standard* who had made them.

Francis H. Pierpont was also a Southern politician who looked at slavery from the viewpoint of its political effect. His boyhood was spent near Fairmont in western Virginia. After graduating from Allegheny College at Meadville, Pennsylvania, he taught school in Mississippi and later married a Northern wife who had abolitionist views. The Ruffner pamphlet (a copy of which was found among his papers) influenced him. Pierpont opposed slavery as a political power that exploited the western part of the state and denied to that section opportunities of growth. Also, he realized the evil effects of slavery on the social life of the people, which Jefferson had earlier pointed out. Nevertheless, he was conservative about expressing public opposition to slavery.[63]

The literary men of the Old South, with few exceptions, followed the example of William Gilmore Simms, Beverley Tucker, and John Pendleton Kennedy, in romanticizing slavery. Only Jesse Burton Harrison, William Alexander Caruthers, George Tucker, and the historian, Howison, escaped the romantic blight in dealing with the evils of the sacred institution. In 1832 John Pendleton Kennedy wrote *Swallow*

---

[62] Kenneth Rayner, *Speech on Receiving Abolition Petitions in Congress, June 15, 1841*, p. 12. A pamphlet. See Rayner Papers (MSS in Library of the University of North Carolina), and a letter to Edward Crudup, Feb. 20, 1856, in the Mangum Papers. Also see Raleigh *Register*, Dec. 10 and 24, 1856.

[63] Charles H. Ambler, *Francis H. Pierpont* (Chapel Hill, 1937), chap. iv.

Barn, in which he portrayed the Southern slaves as happy creatures, always whistling and singing, and condemned any intermeddling with the institution of slavery by outsiders.[64] William Gilmore Simms became an ardent defender of Southern slavery as a beneficent system of labor, contributing an essay on "The Morals of Slavery" for *The Pro-Slavery Argument* (Charleston, S. C., 1852). Finally, William J. Grayson wrote sixteen hundred lines of poetry, *The Hireling and the Slave,* glorifying slavery and attacking the abolitionists.

An attractive type of the Southern amateur in literature was Jesse Burton Harrison of Lynchburg, Virginia. After receiving an admirable classical education at Harvard, he traveled and studied in Europe. In 1832, when the great debate on emancipation was resounding through Virginia, Harrison wrote "A Review of the Slave Question," first published in the *American Quarterly Review,* and later issued as a pamphlet. John Hampden Pleasants, in a preface to the pamphlet, praised it for its "calm and philosophical spirit of enquiry" and pronounced it as more worthy of circulation than Thomas R. Dew's essay on the same subject. Harrison made an eloquent appeal for freedom of discussion and for a gradual liberation of his native state from the incubus of slavery. "We exhort the sons of Virginia," he wrote, "to toil for the diminution of this evil, with all the prudence, delicacy, and gravity requisite in the application of a great public remedy to a wide-spread disease. And in the worst event let them rest assured that history has few places more enviable than would be the lot of the last advocate, who, left without allies, should come, in the grand language of Milton's prose 'through chance of good and of evil report, to be the sole advocate of a discountenanced truth.' "[65]

The first editor of the *Southern Literary Messenger,* James E. Heath, expressed a similar Jeffersonian point of view. In the early issues of the *Messenger,* he published some law lectures of Judge Beverley Tucker, in which Southern slavery was

---

[64] J. P. Kennedy, *Swallow Barn or a Sojourn in the Old Dominion* (New York, 1854), chap. xlvi.

[65] Jesse Burton Harrison, *Review of the Slave Question* (Richmond, 1833), p. 6.

defended. Although he concurred with the learned judge in
viewing Southern slavery as a problem exclusively for Southerners to settle, he vigorously dissented from the doctrine that
it was a moral or political benefit. "We regard it, on the contrary," he wrote, "as a great evil, which society sooner or later
will find it not only to its interest to remove or mitigate, but
will seek its gradual abolition, or amelioration, under the influence of those high obligations imposed by an enlightened
Christian morality."[66]

Among the literary men of the Old South who displayed
independence of mind was the genial and cultivated Virginian,
William Alexander Caruthers. After receiving an education
at Washington College, Lexington, Virginia, he removed to
Savannah and practiced medicine. In his leisure hours he wrote
several novels that contributed much to building up the romantic tradition in the South. He preserved sufficient detachment, however, to realize the evils of slavery and the desirability
of emancipation. He pointed out that slavery destroyed the
yeoman class of the South and debased the poor white. The
free-labor settlement of Salem, North Carolina, long inhabited
by the Moravians, he held up as a healthy spot in a land of
slavery. Southerners should seek out the sources of the prosperity of these thrifty people and imitate them.[67]

Writing a history of Virginia in 1848, R. R. Howison, a
Virginian who oscillated between preaching and practicing
law, was bold enough to declare that slavery was one of the
causes for the decline of his native state.[68] He analyzed public
opinion in Virginia in regard to slavery as follows: "First, we
hold that this institution as it exists among us is lawful, and
that we only have the right to control it.—Secondly, we apprehend that, in general, the people of Virginia hold slavery to
be an enormous evil bearing with fatal power upon their pros-

[66] *Southern Literary Messenger*, I, 254 (Jan., 1835), quoted by Mott, *A History
of American Magazines, 1741-1850*, p. 632.
[67] Parrington, *The Romantic Revolution in America*, p. 43; see also article by
Carl Holliday in *Library of Southern Literature*, II, 753-757.
[68] For a short biography of Howison, see *The South in the Building of the
Nation*, XI, 522-523.

perity."[69] He referred to the Ruffner antislavery pamphlet and to a recent address by James Bruce on the economic evils of slavery. Pointing out the decrease in growth of the negro population due to the slave trade with the Lower South and to the immigration of Northern farmers into Virginia, he wrote that he looked forward to the time when Virginia should become a free state. Howison also took great interest in the movement for free schools in the South.

The ante-bellum preachers of the section did not, as a class, exhibit any independence of mind in regard to the institution of slavery. The frontier sects, Methodist, Baptist, and Presbyterian, which had earlier denounced slavery when their members were poor, wholeheartedly favored the institution as their economic interests became involved.[70] Indeed, most of the prominent leaders of all denominations in the South, Dr. Thornwell, Bishop Elliott, Bishop Bascom, Rev. Thornton Stringfellow, Rev. Augustus Baldwin Longstreet, Bishop Leonidas Polk, Rev. B. M. Palmer, Rev. W. A. Smith, and Bishop Andrew, held that slavery was sanctioned by the Bible. The more extreme clerics connected abolitionism with French infidelity or atheism.[71] Despite this august array of authority, from the Southern ministry came a larger proportion of outspoken critics of slavery than from any other professional group. Such a group of insurgents, isolated though they were, indicate that perhaps the strongest force in producing free lances was moral conviction.

One of the leaders of the Presbyterian Church in the South, who did not follow the crowd, was Dr. John Holt Rice, pastor of a Richmond church and editor of the *Evangelical and Literary Magazine*. Part of his life had been spent in doing religious work among the Negroes and teaching them to read the Scriptures. He traveled frequently in the Northern States and kept up an intercourse with professors at Andover and New

[69] R. R. Howison, *A History of Virginia* (Richmond, 1848), II, 517-520.

[70] W. B. Hesseltine, *A History of the South, 1607-1936* (New York, 1936), p. 340.

[71] Jenkins, *Pro-Slavery Thought in the Old South*, chap. v; also see James G. Birney, *American Churches, the Bulwark of American Slavery* (London, 1840).

Haven, thus liberalizing his views.[72] In a letter to a friend at Norfolk (1827) he declared that a minister could not advocate the eradication of slavery without arousing the strongest opposition. He would be condemned for "touching what are called the rights of property."[73] Dr. Rice believed, at the same time, that the problem could be solved only by the Southerners themselves, and they would, if undisturbed by *foreign influences,* throw off the system entirely in the course of years. He persuaded his wife to liberate her slaves and send them to Liberia.

In the autumn of 1834 James G. Birney made a tour of Kentucky to discover the antislavery men in the state. It is significant that most of the people whom he found sympathetic to his cause were ministers or young men fresh from college. The Rev. Mr. Taylor of Clear Creek Church told Birney that he had preached on the sin of slavery, thereby causing some disturbance among the congregation, but it soon "blew over." With Rev. Robert Holman of Talladega County, Alabama, he had a long conversation on the evils of slavery, prayed with him, and shed tears of joy when the latter agreed to liberate his four slaves.[74] Birney also talked with a young Kentuckian who had recently manumitted two slaves upon whose hire he had been educating himself at Lane Seminary. At Georgetown, Birney found two antislavery men, Rev. Simeon Salisbury and John Johnson, postmaster and Campbellite preacher. Another young antislavery man recently from college (Oberlin and Lane Seminary) was James A. Thome of Augusta, Kentucky. Later he became an agent of the American Anti-Slavery Society and a professor at Oberlin.[75] When Birney completed his tour of exploration in Kentucky, he listed a small handful of preachers whom he knew to be favorable to immediate emancipation. "And this is the whole number of us," he lamented, "most of us very obscure, many

[72] Howe, *Historical Collections of Virginia,* pp. 434-435.
[73] W. H. Foote, *Sketches of Virginia, Historical and Biographical* (Philadelphia, 1845), p. 447.   [74] Birney Diary, Sept. 10 and 14, 1834.
[75] *Weld-Grimké Letters,* I, 149, 501-504.

very young and without influence to do this mighty work in which we have to meet the strongest prejudices as well as the strongest interests and talents."[76] He was encouraged, however, by the action of the Presbyterian Synod which met at Danville in October, 1834. Resolutions were adopted acknowledging the sinfulness of slavery and advising church members to manumit such of their slaves as they thought were prepared for freedom.[77]

Perhaps the boldest thinker that the Southern church produced in ante-bellum days was Moncure Daniel Conway of Falmouth, Virginia. At the age of nineteen he became a Methodist circuit-rider. Thrown into contact with some Hicksite Quakers, whose neat farms contrasted with those of their neighbors, he inquired the reason for their prosperity and was told that it was occasioned by their reluctance to employ slaves. He observed also that slavery was hostile to the widespread education of the people, a cause in which he was ardently interested. After a short period spent as a Methodist preacher, he decided to enter the Harvard Divinity School and prepare himself for the Unitarian ministry. When he returned to the South, he became pastor of a Unitarian church in Washington, where he preached several antislavery sermons. In September, 1854, he wrote his father that he intended to visit him at Falmouth. The elder Conway replied: "It is my sincere advice not to come here until there is reason to believe your opinions have undergone material changes on the subject of slavery. If you are willing to expose your own person recklessly, I am not willing to subject myself and family to the hazards of such a visit.—Those opinions give me more uneasiness just now than your horrible views on the subject of religion, bad as these last are."[78] His father accused him of want of common sense in his attitude toward slavery and said that he merited the intolerance of his old neighbors.

During the next year he disregarded this parental advice

[76] Birney Diary, Sept. 30, 1834.   [77] Ibid., Oct. 8-10, 1834.
[78] Conway, Autobiography, II, 188.

and paid a visit to his home. As he walked along the streets
of the little town, he was accosted by a group of young men,
some of them his former schoolmates, and was ordered to
leave the community. They accused him of being an abolitionist, and said, "There is danger in having that kind of man
among our servants, and you must leave." He left quietly next
morning without explaining the cause of his sudden departure. As the steamboat carried him up the Potomac, an exile
from home, he wept bitterly.[79]

Bishop William Meade of the Episcopal Church of Virginia was also a liberal on the Negro question. During a speech
at Winchester in 1825 he branded slavery as "one of the most
tremendous evils that ever overhung a guilty nation upon
earth."[80] He was an ardent worker for the American Colonization Society and as late as 1856 he aroused opposition by his
aspersions on slavery in an article in the *Southern Churchman*.
He said that slavery had advanced the Negro by giving him
Christianity, but he could never be brought to believe that it
had advanced either the religious, political, or agricultural interests of Virginia. On the contrary, he thought that slavery
had been injurious to the best interests of his section.[81] The
Bishop was attacked by the Richmond *Enquirer* for giving too
much encouragement to slaves in his addresses before them.
In defending himself from such charges, he declared that he
had exhorted slaves to be faithful servants. He could ascribe
the unjust attacks made on him only "to a most sensitive and
morbid state of some minds on the question of slavery."[82] To
Bishop Leonidas Polk, he wrote remonstrating with him for
considering the African slave trade a question of expediency.
Bishop Meade admitted that slavery was sanctioned by the

[79] Conway was a man of considerable literary ability, the author of an excellent
biography of Thomas Paine. He was a moderate reformer, interested in woman's
rights and free schools as well as the abolition of slavery. With Samuel Janney,
he framed a petition to the Virginia legislature to repeal the law which prohibited
the teaching of slaves to read and write, and to restrict the arbitrary separation
of slave families.

[80] *African Repository*, July, 1825, p. 148.

[81] *Ibid.*, June, 1856, p. 222.

[82] *Ibid.*, Sept., 1856, p. 271.

Bible but believed that the African slave trade was a sin, attended by cruelty.[83]

Can a man be more useful to society by opposing its prejudices, or by keeping a tactful silence on a controversial subject? The Rev. Eli Washington Caruthers of Greensboro, North Carolina, apparently thought that he could do more good by pursuing the latter course, until one Sunday morning in July, 1861, he made a confession of faith to his congregation when he prayed that the young men who were in the army "might be blessed of the Lord and return in safety though engaged in a bad cause." For this sentiment he was dismissed. He was known as an antislavery man, but he had not previously aroused opposition by openly expressing his views. His antislavery views had been formed while he was a student at Princeton. At various intervals in his life he composed a treatise entitled *American Slavery and the Immediate Duty of Slaveholders,* but it is significant that it was never published. In his preface, he explained: "The following work would have been published years ago, but for the last fifteen years its publication or circulation would not have been tolerated in any of the Southern States."[84] Caruthers's main reason for opposition to slavery was that it hindered negroes from developing their powers and from becoming Christians. Consequently, he condemned especially the laws which prohibited the teaching of Negroes to read and write and those which permitted the breaking up of families through the domestic slave trade. Pointing out that "their Revolutionary fathers would have spurned ground taken in recent years," Caruthers frankly wrote that the economic motive was responsible for preventing the growth of a liberal attitude toward slavery.[85]

In contrast with the temporizing policy of Caruthers, the most outstanding leader of the Presbyterian Church in Kentucky, Robert J. Breckinridge, pursued a fearless course in

[83] William Meade to Polk, Millwood, Dec. 10, 1856 (Bishop William Meade Papers, MSS in Library of Congress).

[84] Bassett, "Anti-Slavery Leaders of North Carolina," p. 57.

[85] MS in Duke University Library, p. 361.

proclaiming his antislavery sentiments. But he had the advantage of being the scion of an illustrious Kentucky family. After a splendid education in Northern colleges, including Jefferson, Yale, and Union, he began the practice of law at Lexington. For several terms he served in the state legislature, but in 1831 he ran for re-election on a platform of opposition to slavery and Sunday mails, issues which defeated him. He then turned to the Presbyterian ministry, serving as pastor at Baltimore and at Lexington. He became a fierce controversialist, waging war against Catholics, Universalists, the New School party of the Presbyterian Church, as well as whiskey drinking and slavery. In 1849 he led the movement to revise the constitution of Kentucky to permit gradual emancipation, but he was badly defeated. Nevertheless, his high character and powerful family connections made it possible for him to continue to occupy a prominent position in the state. From 1847 to 1853 he was Superintendent of Education in Kentucky, and during the Civil War he was one of the most violent and influential supporters of the Union cause.[86]

The career of Rev. Robert L. Dabney of Union Seminary in Virginia illustrates how youthful radicals on the slavery question were conquered by the prevailing level of thought. In 1840, while he was a student at Hampden-Sydney College, he wrote that it would destroy his happiness to become a slaveholder. Although he repelled the idea that he was an abolitionist, he attacked the weak points in the institution of slavery, for example, the fact that the female slave was not mistress of her own chastity.[87] In later life, nevertheless, after he had attained the dignity of a professor, he became a staunch defender of slavery, urging the leaders of his section to rest their defense on Biblical sanction, with the text, "Thus saith the Lord." He became profoundly incensed at the crusade of the abolitionists, whom he regarded as infidels, and to whom

---

[86] Collins, *History of Kentucky*, I, 477-479; and *Dictionary of American Biography*, III, 10-11.

[87] T. C. Johnson, *Life and Letters of Robert Louis Dabney* (Richmond, 1903), p. 68.

he attributed in large measure Southern intolerance. Against their aspersions on his native state, he wrote an emotional *Defense of Virginia*.[88]

Western Virginia produced several churchmen who not only held antislavery views but boldly published them. The Rev. J. D. Paxton had to abandon his charge at Cumberland, because he contributed an antislavery article to a religious paper. After his expulsion he published a slender volume of *Letters on Slavery*.[89] Making a frontal attack, he declared it to be a moral evil and the duty of Christians to remove it. He criticized the policy of silence which the Southern community imposed on the slavery issue. Full and free discussion, he maintained, would have a tendency to remove the evil and avert the danger. The motive of his attack on slavery was moral, because he believed that it was inconsistent with the spirit of the Gospel and corrupted the character of the masters.

Another outspoken minister in western Virginia was Rev. Wesley Smith. In 1855 he delivered lectures at various places in his section, in which he defended the Methodist Episcopal church from the charge of being an abolitionist and incendiary organization. Boldly declaring that slavery was an evil and the Fugitive Slave Law unjust, he maintained that ministers of the Gospel should not connect themselves with slavery, and that the action of the church in the case of Bishop Andrew was right. Finally, he made a plea for the principle of freedom of speech. The position of his church he defined as not abolitionist but antislavery. When he spoke at Buckhannon, a mob attempted to silence him, and shortly after this episode he published his antislavery lecture as a pamphlet to be distributed.[90]

The stronghold of the antislavery free lances lay in the Upper South, where the negroes were decidedly less concen-

[88] R. L. Dabney, *A Defense of Virginia (and through her of the South) in the recent and pending contests against the sectional party* (New York, 1867).

[89] J. D. Paxton, *Letters on Slavery Addressed to the Cumberland Congregation, Virginia* (Lexington, Ky., 1833).

[90] Rev. Wesley Smith, *A Defense of the Methodist Episcopal Church Against the Charges of Rev. S. Kelley and Others* (Fairmont, Va., 1855). A pamphlet in the State Library at Charleston, W. Va.

trated than in the Black Belt of the Lower South. Consequently, the serious problems that might result from the emancipation of the slaves seemed less insuperable in this region
than appeared to be the case in the Cotton Kingdom. The
experiment of using free labor had also been made in the Upper South by Northern settlers and proved successful. Traces
of Jeffersonian idealism and of Quaker aversion to force had
not been completely obliterated from this border country. Finally, there was an older culture in the Upper South than in
the Gulf States which gave some Southerners an objective
point of view in criticizing the social order. Charleston, Mobile, and New Orleans were likewise centers of culture dating
back to early colonial times, and these cities produced men who
detested slavery, like the merchant John McDonogh of New
Orleans, the brilliant Trescott at Charleston, and Dr. Josiah
C. Nott at Mobile, but these men saw the futility of opposition
to the *status quo* and the reverse side of emancipation with its
appalling difficulties.[91]

The free lances of the Old South sprang chiefly from the
professional classes, the preachers, the college professors, the
lawyers, and the writers. Some of them had been led to disagree with the prevailing ideas of their section by the impulse
of travel; others were men of unusual sensitivity, with tender
consciences; a few were gifted with exceptionally realistic
minds; while still others were temperamentally iconoclasts or
radicals. In most cases they scorned the name of abolitionist,
which had been brought into disrepute by Northern fanatics,
but approached the problem of removing slavery from an economic point of view or that of the evil effects of slavery on
the whites. To them the extinction of slavery was exclusively
a Southern problem to be settled by Southerners. The records
left by the Southern radicals are permeated with a feeling of

[91] McDonogh bought many slaves for the purpose of setting them free and
sending them to Liberia. He sent two Negroes to Lafayette College in Pennsylvania, but he grew discouraged when one of them, refusing to go to Liberia, became a hack driver in New York City. See W. T. Childs, *John McDonogh: His
Life and Works* (Baltimore, Md., 1939), chaps. vii-ix.

hopelessness as they contemplated the tremendous task of solving the race problem outside of the institution of slavery.[92] The suppression of these men furnishes one of the most impressive monuments in history of the ultimate folly of intolerance.

[92] The position of conservative and enlightened Southerners that the removal of slavery should be accomplished by slow and gradual means was undoubtedly sound. A typical expression of this point of view was made by Nathaniel A. Ware, author of *Notes on Political Economy as Applicable to the United States. By a Southern Planter* (New York, 1844). He believed that slavery in the South would become extinct only when it was no longer profitable, a condition that would arise from the growth of density of population. A recent student of Ware's theories maintains that this rather obscure planter and banker wrote the treatise, *An Exposition of the Weakness and Inefficiency of the Government of the United States,* attributed to Charles Fenton Mercer. See William Diamond, "Nathaniel A. Ware, National Economist," *Journal of Southern History,* V, 508-509 (Nov., 1939), and for the orthodox view that Mercer was the author, *Dictionary of American Biography,* XII, 539.

Chapter XII

THE DECLINE OF SKEPTICISM

Skepticism, by which is meant an attitude of doubt toward revealed religion, is an achievement of the intellectual aristocracy. The masses may temporarily be irreligious, as in the South following the Revolution, but they could not properly be called skeptical. Eventually they gravitate to a religion that satisfies their emotions. The skepticism of the Southern aristocracy in the post-Revolutionary period was a transitory stage, rootless, an echo of the age of reason in Europe. Consequently, the erasure of deism and skepticism from the South could be accomplished in a single generation. By 1830 it was practically complete. The epitaph of an era of religious liberals and skeptics was recorded by Benjamin F. Perry, editor of the Greenville *Mountaineer,* who wrote in his diary in 1832 that the man who boasted of his infidelity was either a fool or a scoundrel. "No one," he wrote, "should repose confidence in the honor or integrity of him who boldly proclaims his irreligious notions. It is true we cannot control our opinions, but we may always suppress them when they are prejudicial to our country or society."[1] This sweeping indictment of skepticism represented the voice of the common man in the villages of the South.

Thomas R. Dew, President of William and Mary College, expressed the aristocratic view of skepticism in an article for the *Southern Literary Messenger.* "Avowed infidelity," he reported, "is now considered by the enlightened portion of the world as a reflection both on the head and heart. The Humes and Voltaires have been vanquished from the field, and the Bacons, Lockes, and Newtons have given in their adhesion. . . . The argument is now closed forever, and he who now obtrudes on the social circle his infidel notions, manifests the arrogance

[1] Benjamin F. Perry Diary (1832), p. 36.

of a literary coxcomb, or that want of refinement which distinguishes the polished gentleman."[2]   Caruthers, surveying the religious conditions of his day (1842), noted that the skeptical books of Voltaire, Hobbes, and Paine, which had a vogue in the early part of the century had been burned or concealed so that hardly one of them could be found in North Carolina.[3] The older liberalism of the South, whose departure was thus announced, was the delicate fruit of a colonial aristocracy, different from the cotton capitalism of a later epoch.

This revolution in public opinion was accomplished by several forces. The conversion of the South by waves of evangelism was one of the most efficacious agents. While the aristocratic classes and college men were toying with skepticism, earnest evangelists were traveling through the back country of the South preaching the coming of the Judgment Day. Francis Asbury, Lorenzo Dow—"Crazy Dow," as he was called—Joseph Pilmoor, and John McGehee were the heroes of the great revival movement that swept over the South at the turn of the century. Francis Asbury, one of the bright lights of Methodism, kept a homely journal of his crusade through the Southern States. Taking off his coat and neckcloth, he would preach to great throngs of people out in the open, or in barns, arousing them to repentance by "the awful peals of his voice," provoking often "a copious flow of tears." He found that the people of western Virginia and Carolina were ignorant and indifferent to religion.[4] The ministers who preached to these rural congregations were frequently almost as primitive as their auditors. John Wesley felt the necessity of restraining the zeal of John King, a North Carolina preacher, by the following admonition: "Scream no more at the peril of Your Soul. Speak as earnestly as you can but do not scream. Speak with all your heart but with a moderate voice."[5]   The intense

[2] *Southern Literary Messenger,* II, 768 (Nov., 1836).

[3] E. W. Caruthers, *Life of David Caldwell* (Greensboro, N. C., 1842), p. 263.

[4] Francis Asbury, *Journal* (3 vols.; New York, 1821), *passim.*

[5] W. L. Grissom, *History of Methodism in North Carolina* (Nashville, Tenn., 1905), I, 59.

excitement of preaching and the hard lives of these men tended to shatter their nerves and even to produce insanity.

Joseph Pilmoor traveled on horseback through the ungospelled wilds of the South and found the people touchingly ignorant and imbued with a rough frontier irreligion. He would exhort large congregations of "weeping sinners," using as a text: "He shall baptize you with the Holy Ghost and with fire." His Methodist asceticism made him intolerant of card playing and dancing. He had no mercy on those who delighted in horse racing, condemning "the absurdity of such sport and showing how ridiculous it is for gentlemen of sense to ride many miles to see two or three horses run about a field with negroes on their backs."[6] The dramatic moment in the careers of these itinerant preachers was the conversion of atheists or deists—like the sudden striking down of the prominent atheist, General Bryan, on the New River. The Methodist camp meetings introduced a strong flavor of intolerance into the lives of the plain people of the South.

The revival flame was contagious, sparing no sect save the aristocratic Episcopalians. In Virginia the redoubtable Jesse Lee converted hundreds of "profane sinners, downright skeptics, and God-defying wretches" and herded them into the Methodist fold. Skeptics and hardened sinners would enter the church with sarcastic grins on their faces, and incontinently would be struck down with "the jerks," the "barking exercises," or "the laughing exercises." In 1801 Elder Burkitt returned from Kentucky and reported to the Great Swamp Baptist Association (North Carolina) the vast religious movement in progress in the Western country. This news set the Baptists "on fire," meetings were held throughout the state, and crowds were brought low, weeping copiously, and crying, "What shall we do to be saved?" The Kehukee Association alone baptized fifteen hundred persons in 1802-1803.[7] The Presbyterian

---

[6] *Ibid.* See also Lorenzo Dow, *Journal or History of Cosmopolite* (New York, 1814).

[7] Burkitt and Read, *History of the Kehukee Baptist Association* (Halifax, N. C., 1803), p. 143; see also W. W. Sweet, *Religion on the American Frontier; the*

Church also was revitalized by the evangelistic movement of 1801, and this new zeal expressed itself in sternly repressing dissenters.[8] The revival movement unfortunately elevated harmless pleasures such as card playing and dancing into sins, thus importing a censorious element into the free and easy social life of the Tidewater.

The Episcopal Church, which ministered to the upper classes, was the least touched by the fanatical zeal of the revival movement. Wrote Bishop Ravenscroft of North Carolina, despondent over the slight success of his church in the western part of the state: "If we can keep the Flax smoking until another generation arises, as it will have more information and of course fewer prejudices, our success may be greater. At present the ignorance of the people is too great and too general, either to estimate aright the claims and character of the church, or to see thro the artifices of the Secretaries, who certainly speculate largely on this ground."[9] A clergyman of Petersburg, Virginia, sent a plea for Bishop Meade to come to his parish and tranquilize the people who had been excited by a series of protracted meetings. The distressed preacher felt that his congregation was being drawn off by the exciting machinery of "the anxious bench" and the electioneering devices of the evangelists.[10] Undoubtedly camp meetings and religious excitement were like circuses to the dwellers in monotonous villages and isolated farms of the Old South.

Regardless of the effects of the Great Revival, deism was dying a natural death in the South in the first quarter of the nineteenth century. It was not suited to the romantic spirit that conquered the South. Deism was too cold, too philosophic and reasonable to satisfy the emotional needs of the people. When the colonial-bred aristocracy died out, deism

---

Baptists, 1783-1830 (New York, 1931), for a description of the revival in Kentucky.

[8] Caruthers, *Life of David Caldwell*, pp. 233 and 263.

[9] John S. Ravenscroft to Robert J. Miller, Jan. 22, 1827 (Robert J. Miller Letters, MSS in archives of North Carolina Historical Commission).

[10] N. W. Cobb to Bishop Meade, Dec. 9, 1841 (William Meade Papers, MSS in Library of Congress).

faded imperceptibly from Southern society. Furthermore, the excesses of the French Revolution did much to discredit irreligion and skepticism as a vogue among the well-to-do classes.

Even as late as 1828, nevertheless, Elisha Mitchell, a Yankee professor at the University of North Carolina, found deists and freethinkers who were prominent in their communities. He noted in his diary that he spent the night at the home of Christopher Dudley, a deist who despite his freethinking, was elected seven times senator from Onslow County.[11] Again he supped at the home of a Unitarian, Dr. Satterwhite, an alumnus of the University, and on another occasion he stayed with Colonel Meredith Ballou, of French extraction, who was not a professor of religion, but who liked to collect scandal about the religionists.[12] When Frederick Porcher attended Yale in the 1820's, one of his fellow students was Volney Metcalfe from Mississippi, who had been educated in infidel principles, but who avoided making any display of his views.[13] Buckingham, during his travels in the slave states, attended the public funeral of a recently converted deist at Athens, Georgia. This gentleman, Judge Clayton, was a graduate of the University of Georgia and its most zealous patron. Until the year before his death he had openly avowed himself a deist without affecting his honorable standing in society.[14] But such men were relics of a bygone century.

Jefferson was made to feel the strength of the growing intolerance of his section as early as 1820, when he selected some unconventional professors for the University of Virginia. He was extremely desirous to secure the services and brilliant talents of Dr. Thomas Cooper, who was a freethinker in religion. To the latter was offered a position in the new university with a munificent salary, which was accepted. When the forces of obscurantism began to offer opposition, William H. Cabell

[11] Elisha Mitchell, "Diary of a Geological Tour," *James Sprunt Historical Monographs*, No. 6, p. 9.   [12] *Ibid.*, No. 6, pp. 28-29 and 46.
[13] Reminiscences of Professor Frederick A. Porcher, p. 247 (MS in Library of College of Charleston).
[14] Buckingham, *Slave States of America*, II, 60-61.

wrote to his brother Joseph, Jefferson's right-hand man in establishing the University: "I fear that Cooper's appointment will do the university infinite injury. His religious views are damnable as exhibited in a book published by him shortly after the death of Priestley. You will have every religious man in Virginia against you."[15] On account of the storm of opposition Cooper was forced to look elsewhere for a teaching position. Nevertheless, Jefferson was successful in keeping the University of Virginia free from religious control and sectarian influences.

While the fight against Dr. Cooper's appointment was waging, Jefferson penned a scathing indictment of the Presbyterian clergy. "The Presbyterian clergy," he wrote in a private letter, "are the most intolerant of all sects, the most tyrannical and ambitious, ready at the word of the law-giver, if such a word could now be obtained, to put the torch to the pile, and to rekindle in this virgin hemisphere, the flames in which their oracle Calvin consumed the poor Servetus, because he could not find in his Euclid the proposition which has demonstrated that three are one, and one is three, nor subscribe to that of Calvin, that magistrates have a right to exterminate all heretics to the Calvinistic creed. They pant to re-establish *by law,* that holy inquisition, which they can now only infuse into public opinion."[16] The bitter attacks of the clergy against him in his official career made him prefer the Quakers, who had no priesthood.

Dr. Thomas Cooper found a congenial position at Columbia, South Carolina, as president of the state university. Under his administration, "Infidelity and irreligion took possession of the seat and center of knowledge."[17] At his house prominent South Carolinians gathered, and in the free play of in-

---

[15] Bruce, *History of the University of Virginia,* I, 204. For the fight against Cooper in Virginia see also Herbert B. Adams, *Thomas Jefferson and the University of Virginia* (Washington, D. C., 1888).

[16] Jefferson to William Short, April 13, 1820 (Randolph, *The Writings of Thomas Jefferson,* IV, 322).

[17] Hooper, *Fifty Years Since,* p. 38.

tellect, often startlingly radical views were expressed in regard to religion and politics.[18] In 1822-23 Cooper's attacks on a hired clergy, and especially on the Presbyterian clergy, led to presentments against him by grand juries in the upland counties of Chester and York. A legislative committee investigated the charges, but he was exonerated.[19] Cooper's intransigence was exhibited later in an anonymous pamphlet opposing certain legislation that had been introduced in Congress to stop the carrying of the mails on Sunday. In this pamphlet he declared that avaricious and ambitious priests had ordained the Sabbath, that Christ had prohibited public prayer, and that payment of a clergy was a pernicious practice.[20]

This pamphlet gave a handle to his enemies for launching a second movement to dislodge him from the presidency of South Carolina College. The charges made against him in the legislature by a Mr. Pressly of Abbeville bore a curious resemblance to the accusation of Socrates; Cooper was indicted for promulgating certain religious opinions, "dangerous to the youth and abhorrent to the feelings of the great mass of the community."[21] He was also accused of ridiculing ordinary petitions of prayer and of insulting the clergy. The crowning iniquity of the learned doctor was that he taught that man was no better than an opossum. Among those who raised their voices against Cooper was the Unionist, James Louis Petigru, who used the pragmatic argument for his removal that the enrollment of the student body had declined under his administration.[22] Yet the editor of the *Telescope* thought the excitement raised against Cooper was a master move of the members of the Unionist party, who were antagonistic to the venerable educator for his prominence as a champion of nullification.[23]

[18] G. W. Featherstonhaugh, *Excursion Through the Slave States* (London, 1844), II, 340.

[19] Malone, *Thomas Cooper*, pp. 259-267.

[20] *To Any Member of Congress, By a Layman* (2d ed.; Columbia, S. C., 1831), pp. 10-14.   [21] Columbia *Telescope*, Dec. 20, 1831.

[22] *Ibid.*, Dec. 9, 1831.   [23] *Ibid.*, Dec. 6, 1831.

In an amazing pamphlet defending himself, Dr. Cooper freely admitted his heterodox opinions. He declared that the book of Genesis was not composed to teach astronomy or geology. Furthermore, the New Testament did not countenance a hired clergy, who cost the people of the United States thirteen million dollars annually. He described the classes who were back of the movement to depose him as being the opponents of nullification and the Calvinistic clergy, who wished to dominate the university. At the same time he cleverly referred to his claim to be the first person to suggest the unconstitutionality of the tariff. His chief argument for his defense was legal, based on a strict interpretation of the state constitution and its bill of rights.[24]

Cooper was acquitted a second time by the legislature. During the controversy he wrote to Mahlon Dickerson: "I am not yet conquered, and expect yet to bivouac on the field of Battle."[25] He held the presidency of South Carolina College until the close of 1834, when his position had become untenable. The enrollment of the college continued seriously to decline. After he resigned, a professorship of Christian Evidences was founded, and soon the staunch Presbyterian minister, J. H. Thornwell, was installed as president of the college.

Cooper had, like Tom Paine, a fear that religious fanatics would upon his death "trump up a story about my repentance and conversion from infidelity." In order to forestall such a fraud, he gave to his Jewish physician, M. H. DeLeon, a letter specifically denying that he had recanted. This letter, which has never been published, was the last defiance of Dr. Cooper. In it he stated that he had read all the important authorities on Christianity from the ancient writers of the first four centuries to his own day. The results of his researches were summarized in the following words: "Of the frauds, the forgeries of the Christian writers, I have met with abundant evi-

[24] *The Case of Thomas Cooper, M.D., President of the South Carolina College; Submitted to the Legislature and the People of South Carolina, December, 1831* (Columbia, S. C., 1831), pp. 2, 5, 28, 34, 40.

[25] Cooper to Mahlon Dickerson, Feb. 22, 1832 (*American Historical Review*, VI, 735, July, 1901).

dence; but of satisfactory proof in favor of their supernatural and miraculous pretentions, *none*."[26] He did not wonder that so many wise and good men of his state embraced Christianity, since the evidence on that side of the question, and on that alone, had been pressed upon them from earliest infancy.

Other Southern universities were exposed to the clamor of the masses that only orthodox professors should teach. On account of his religious liberalism Dr. Horace Holley, President of Transylvania University, was bitterly attacked by sectarians in the press, in private conversation, and in pamphlets. A system of espionage was established by his pious enemies, who came to his social entertainments, like serpents into the Garden of Eden, to gather evidence against him in unguarded moments. The fact that nude female statues were exhibited in his home excited horror. Finally, the governor of Kentucky in his message to the legislature attacked him. He was practically forced to resign in 1827, a martyr to the growing intolerance of the churches.[27]

At Charlottesville, Jefferson's policy of the separation of religion from the university was abandoned. Faculty and students by common consent called a chaplain to perform services regularly, chosen in rotation from the different sects. The University of North Carolina at the same time was presided over by the stern Presbyterian, Dr. Caldwell, who was seeking to establish a religious despotism. Students were strictly required to attend religious services. Any freedom of opinion on religion was crushed by an act of the General Assembly which declared: "If any student shall deny the being of a God, or the divine authority of the Holy Scriptures, or shall assert, and endeavor to propagate among the students any principle subversive of the Christian religion, he shall be dismissed."[28] A

---

[26] Thomas Cooper to Dr. M. H. DeLeon, Dec. 15, 1838 (MS in the possession of Mrs. Julian Hennig of Columbia, S. C.).

[27] Charles Caldwell, M.D., *Discourse on the Genius and Character of the Rev. Horace Holley LL.D., Late President of Transylvania University* (Boston, 1828), pp. 218-220.

[28] *Acts of the General Assembly and Ordinances of the Trustees for the Organization and Government of the University of North Carolina* (Raleigh, N. C., 1852), chap. vi, sec. 1. A pamphlet.

jealousy was manifested lest too many of the professors should be chosen from any one sect, such as the Presbyterians or Episcopalians.

A great battle over religious toleration was fought by liberals in the North Carolina Constitutional Convention of 1835. The old constitution prescribed as a qualification for office a belief in the Protestant religion, the existence of a God, and the divine revelation of both the Old and the New Testaments—thus excluding Jews, Catholics, atheists, and deists. These harsh provisions had not been strictly enforced, however, for in 1808 Jacob Henry, a Jew, had represented Carteret County in the legislature, and Judge Gaston, although a Catholic, had held office.[29] A determined effort was now made to remove these religious tests from the constitution.

The advocates of repeal came principally from the Tidewater region of the state. A Mr. Edwards, representing Warren County, made an eloquent speech early in the discussion advocating religious tolerance. Striking his keynote by a quotation from Jefferson that error may be tolerated while truth is free to combat it, he pointed out that the old law fostered a spirit of persecution and encouraged hypocrisy. He thought that it was unjust to exclude from the rewards of government those who share its burdens. He denied the right of any earthly power to impose shackles on the conscience of men, and supported his position by reading a passage from Vattel on religious toleration.[30] The venerable Nathaniel Macon, the friend of Jefferson, raised his voice to speak in behalf of toleration. He said that if a Hindoo were to come to North Carolina and aspire to an office to which his merit entitled him, his religious opinions should not be a bar. He was devoted to toleration because he had an abiding faith in democracy. Judge Gaston supplemented this speech by showing that the Catholic religion was not hostile to free government, nor did it impair

[29] *Niles' Weekly Register*, XXX, 40 (March 18, 1826). Also Wheeler, *Historical Sketches of North Carolina*, II, 75; Hühner, op. cit., pp. 49-51.

[30] *Proceedings and Debates of the Convention of North Carolina Called to Amend the Constitution of the State, Which Assembled at Raleigh, June 4, 1835* (Raleigh, N. C., 1836), pp. 214, 219.

the validity of an oath. He held that reason was the proper umpire of opinion and that the state had no right to interfere with the opinions of its citizens, only with acts and practices.[31]

When a proposal was made by an eastern member that religious opinions of every description should be free from all restraint, even the moderate men arose in violent protest. Many were willing to admit Catholics to toleration, but the overwhelming majority were opposed to showing any leniency to atheists or deists. The latter were regarded as dangerous to the state, particularly because they could not be bound by oath. Wilson of Perquimans County in discussing the repeal of the old law said: "It is very certain if there be any atheists in this state they are few in number and almost unheard of."[32] The constitutional convention, rejecting the plea of its most enlightened members for complete toleration, extended that boon only to Catholics and shut the gates to Jews, skeptics, and atheists.[33]

In Georgia, a few years later (1841), Judge Garnett Andrews of the Superior Circuit Court rendered a decision on the taking of oaths that aroused the opposition of religious liberals. He ruled that the testimony of certain Universalists, who refused to take an oath that they believed in a future state of rewards and punishments, was invalid. This decision was based on the ground that no testimony was entitled to credit unless the witness believed that the violation of an oath would expose him to punishment in the life beyond the grave. This intolerant ruling caused a storm of protest, which contributed to the establishment of a Supreme Court in Georgia, capable of reversing such unpopular decisions.[34]

The sectarianism which was rampant throughout the land

[31] *Ibid.*, pp. 284-285.   [32] *Ibid.*, p. 283.

[33] *Ibid.*, Appendix, sec. 2, p. 416. The revised article declared: "No person who shall deny the being of God, or the truth of the Christian religion, or the divine authority of the Old or New Testament, or who shall hold religious principles incompatible with the freedom or safety of the state, shall be capable of holding any office or place of trust or profit in the civil department within this state."

[34] Green, *Constitutional Development in the South Atlantic States*, pp. 258-259.

of Dixie should have produced a crop of skeptics. Indeed, the turbulent "Parson" Brownlow, who was himself a militant sectarian of the Methodist profession, recognized such a danger when he asserted that the divisions and contentions of the Christian Church were calculated to advance infidelity.[35] In 1834 he contributed to the warfare among the sects by writing an amusingly intolerant book against Presbyterianism.[36] He continued to badger the Presbyterians in a periodical, which he had established expressly to combat the *Calvinistic Magazine* of Abingdon. Brownlow's heaviest artillery, however, was reserved for the Baptist champion, J. R. Graves, who had recently written *The Great Iron Wheel*.[37] Against this polemic he composed a devastating reply entitled *The Great Iron Wheel Examined; or Its False Spokes Extracted*. With this bludgeon in his hands, he whacked the heads of the Baptists for their beliefs in closed communion and baptismal immersion. The Methodists and other denominations, he pointed out, baptized their converts face foremost, but "Our Baptist brethren are almost alone in their vulgarity in *backing into the church of God*."[38] He reminded the Baptists, furthermore, that the waters of the River Jordan were so shallow that it was impossible to baptize in it by immersion.

The celebrated debate between Alexander Campbell and Nathan Rice at Lexington, Kentucky, in 1843, indicated a profound suspicion on the part of some of the Southern clergy that skepticism and collegiate education went hand in hand. Campbell, the leader of the Christian Church in the South, was an experienced debater, having won fame some years before by his debate at Cincinnati with Robert Owen, who had maintained that all religions were bad and contrary to human nature.[39] Rice was a Presbyterian preacher of Paris, Kentucky.

[35] *Jonesborough Monthly Review*, I, 9 (Dec., 1847-April, 1849), in Lawson-McGhee Library, Knoxville, Tenn.

[36] W. G. Brownlow, *Helps to the Study of Presbyterianism or an Unsophisticated Exposition of Calvinism* (Knoxville, Tenn., 1834).

[37] J. R. Graves, *The Great Iron Wheel* (Nashville, Tenn., 1856).

[38] W. G. Brownlow, *The Great Iron Wheel Examined; or Its False Spokes Extracted* (Nashville, Tenn., 1856), p. 203.

[39] *Dictionary of American Biography*, III, 446-448.

The debate was attended by an audience of two thousand people, and lasted for eighteen days, requiring a massive tome of nine hundred and twelve pages to report the published arguments. Campbell maintained that immersion was the only true form of baptism, while his Presbyterian opponent argued for sprinkling. Both based their arguments on the literal word of the Bible. But Campbell in his argument against ecclesiastical creeds made a plea for the abandonment of sectarianism because it led to infidelity. He warned his hearers: "Your schools, your colleges, are full of skepticism. The great majority of your educated men are infidels; some open and acknowledged—many only show it by keeping out of your churches. The reason is, the gospel is blasphemed by the discords, the variance, the hatred, and the strife engendered by your partyism. Abandon your sectarianism, meet on the holy Scripture, and bear with one another's infirmities, . . . and the Lord will pour out his Spirit upon you, and his blessing upon your offspring."[40]

The growing need of defending the institution of slavery, on the other hand, tended to produce religious uniformity in the South. Only by a narrow and literal interpretation of the Scriptures could slavery be given the high moral sanction of the church. Thomas R. Dew in his celebrated polemic in defense of slavery showed what a tower of strength the literal Bible offered to the Southern apologist for slavery. Professor Robert Lewis Dabney, a Presbyterian divine at Hampden-Sydney College, pointed out that the defense of slavery which would reach the common man was not philosophic argument, but the actual words of the Bible. The resting of the Southern case upon the literal interpretation of the Bible, he maintained, would drive the abolitionists to admit their infidelity.[41] By pointing to the undeniable words of the Holy Scriptures, religious leaders like Rev. Thornton Stringfellow, Rev. W. A.

[40] *A Debate Between Rev. A. Campbell and Rev. N. L. Rice on the Action, Subject, Design and Administrator of Christian Baptism* (Lexington, Ky., 1844), p. 905.

[41] Johnson, *Life and Letters of Robert Lewis Dabney*, p. 129. Dabney wrote a series of letters in 1851 for the Richmond *Enquirer* advocating this policy.

Smith of Randolph-Macon, Rev. Bascom of Transylvania University, Professor Thornwell of South Carolina, and Bishop Leonidas Polk presented a plausible defense of slavery and fostered a reactionary movement in the Southern church.

The Northern abolitionists, on the other hand, since the letter of the Bible was against them, appealed to "the spirit of Christianity." Prominent abolitionists like Garrison, Wendell Phillips, and Theodore Parker proclaimed radical ideas in regard to religious dogma, denying miracles, attacking such revered beliefs as the holiness of the Sabbath and the literal inspiration of the Bible.[42] James G. Birney, after he was driven to the North, became a religious skeptic. He wrote in his diary, "Many of the facts & doctrines mentioned in the Old Testament were never inspired by a pure, holy & paternal God—but are solely the doings of man." Birney doubted the miraculous birth of Christ, and after reading the *Vestiges of Creation* accepted the iconoclastic implications of the new geology.[43] Thus the abolitionists tended to discredit religious liberalism in the eyes of Southern people.

The few liberals and skeptics that survived in the South found it prudent to keep their ideas to themselves. The liberal Charles Fenton Mercer observed that although the constitutions of the Federal and state governments guaranteed freedom of opinion and liberty of conscience in respect to religion, few individuals dared to express views that at all departed from the accepted orthodoxy of the leading sects. Men holding heretical views would find that their business and their standing in society would suffer. In this supposedly free country, an individual had to bury his religious opinions in his own bosom from policy. Mercer asserted the impossibility for any free spirit to avow his religious opinions and to be elected to office. No matter how the virtues might adorn him or how intelligent he might be, he would be pursued by the hue and cry of deist, Unitarian, freethinker, or some other epithet that

[42] *Liberator,* Jan. 7, 1848, and W. P. and F. J. Garrison, *William Lloyd Garrison* (Boston, 1889), III, 386.
[43] Birney Diary, 1840-50, May 23, 24, 30, 1850 (MS in Library of Congress).

would make him odious to the crowd. He had listened to the smothered intolerance of the Presbyterians and other sects and had seen how readily they combined against liberty of thought, and he had noted this down as one of the grave weaknesses of the government.[44]

Moncure Daniel Conway had also found his section hostile to divergent views from orthodox Christianity. In his young manhood he had come under the influence of the Hicksite Quakers of Maryland, especially the rationalist leader, Roger Brooke. He was told that Samuel Janney had preached in their neighborhood that "the blood of Jesus could no more save man than the blood of a bullock."[45] He had been strongly impressed furthermore by reading the works of Emerson. Unsettled by such influences, he abandoned his connections with the Methodist Church and became a Unitarian minister. His father refused to give him any aid in this heterodox adventure. Rather, he wrote to his son expressing his pain at such "horrible views on the subject of religion."[46] From his pastorate in a Unitarian church in Washington, D. C., Conway made an excursion into Virginia in 1855, preaching Unitarian sermons at Richmond and Charlottesville.

Another religious radical in the ante-bellum South was John M. Daniel, editor of the Richmond *Examiner*. The independence of his mind was reflected in the advice he gave his cousin, Moncure Daniel Conway: "Whatever you do, don't be a preacher. It is a wretched profession. Its dependence is on absurd dogmas. The Trinity is a theological invention, and hell-fire simply ridiculous."[47] Although he was a fire-eater, he was an extravagant admirer of Emerson, whose works he discussed in his editorial columns. About 1850 this outwardly cynical man, noted for the many duels he had fought, tried to establish a liberal church in Richmond. Toward that end he preached a sermon in "the long-closed Universalist Church

[44] [C. F. Mercer,] *Exposition*, pp. 160-163 (paraphrased).
[45] Conway, *Autobiography*, I, 104.   [46] *Ibid.*, I, 188.
[47] *Ibid.*, I, 79; see also G. W. Bagby, "John M. Daniel's Latch-Key," *Selections from the Miscellaneous Writings of Dr. George W. Bagby* (Richmond, 1884), I. 101-103.

there." Daniel's marked cynicism may have arisen, as his cousin suggested, from his spiritual loneliness.

John C. Calhoun's great intellect elevated him above the uncritical attitude toward religion of his neighbors. Wrote Mrs. Chesnut, "Mr. Calhoun's piety was of the most philosophical type, from all accounts."[48] But she relates an anecdote of the Carolina statesman that indicates he could be sternly intolerant. When one of his guests refused to attend family prayers, Calhoun ordered his servant to saddle his horse and send him away. Benjamin F. Perry was told by Governor Orr that Calhoun was a Unitarian in religion.[49] Nevertheless, he was very reticent about expressing any heretical views, and in the South he attended the Episcopal Church.

Edmund Ruffin found it necessary to conceal his heterodox religious views from public knowledge in his native state. He jotted down in his diary his observation that whoever should dare to use his own judgment and disagree with the interpretation of the Bible by the preachers, would be immediately suspected and charged with opposing the doctrines of the Bible and of the Christian religion. Ruffin's own children thought that his rejection of the commonly accepted interpretation of the Bible was a grave delinquency. He was effectually silenced from discussing religion at all by the intolerant atmosphere of Virginia, and he recorded his surrender to the forces of intolerance by resolving to try to be silent on the subject.[50]

Doubtless there were other isolated individuals in the Southern States who were skeptical of orthodox religion but who were too prudent to proclaim their dissent. Some of these skeptics gave the only indication of their contumacy by staying away from church. The most notable figure of Fredericksburg, John Minor, had the reputation of being an "infidel." When a Presbyterian preacher tried to shame him into going

[48] Chesnut, op. cit., p. 17.
[49] Perry, Reminiscences of Public Men, p. 49; see also Josephine Seaton, William Seaton of the "National Intelligencer" (Boston, 1871), p. 158.
[50] Edmund Ruffin's Diary, June 1 and Dec. 16, 1859.

to church by pointing out that his example of absenting himself from divine services had a bad influence on the community, he turned away the pious man with a witty retort.[51] James Freeman Clarke met a fine old Kentucky gentleman, Judge Speed, who was called an infidel because he refused to accept the prevailing view that every word between the lids of the Bible was the word of God.[52] Lucian Minor, a law professor of William and Mary College, was another unbeliever according to orthodox standards. He was a highly cultivated man, a contributor to the *Southern Literary Messenger*, an advocate of free common schools and of the temperance movement. His skepticism was due to "his faith having been early sapped by the insidious sophistries of Gibbon and Hume."[53] But at his death in 1858 he had retreated from his skepticism.

The profound orthodoxy of the South in 1860 was revealed by the virtual absence of liberal sects below the Potomac. According to the Federal census of that year, only one of the fifty-eight Swedenborgian churches in the United States was located in the South. This section did not contain a single one of the seventeen Spiritualist churches, and only twenty of the six hundred and sixty-four Universalist churches in the country.[54] The moribund condition of the Unitarian Church in the South was indicated by the fact that only three societies were alive at the beginning of the year 1860.[55] The attitude of most Southern people toward the Unitarian faith was expressed by James Henly Thornwell in a letter describing his fellow students at Harvard. "I room in Divinity Hall among the Unitarian students of Theology," he wrote, "for there are no

[51] Conway, *Autobiography*, I, 43, 126.

[52] Clarke, *Autobiography*, p. 77.

[53] James Russell Lowell (ed.), "A Virginian in New England Thirty-Five Years Ago," *Atlantic Monthly*, XXVI, 162 (Aug., 1870).

[54] *The Eighth Census of the United States, 1860: Mortality and Miscellaneous Statistics* (Washington, D. C., 1866), pp. 500-501.

[55] *The Monthly Journal of the American Unitarian Association, January, 1860* (Boston, 1860), pp. 37-41. The total number of societies listed was two hundred and fifty-seven. The three Southern societies were those of Louisville, New Orleans, Charleston (without a pastor). There were societies at Washington, D. C., and at Baltimore also.

others here. I shall expect to meet and give blows in defence of my own peculiar doctrines [Presbyterian]; and God forbid that I should falter in maintaining the faith once delivered to the saints. I look upon the tenets of modern Unitarianism as little better than downright infidelity."[56] Thornwell later occupied the seat of Dr. Cooper as president of South Carolina College, and he was perhaps the most intellectual divine of the Old South.

The decline of Unitarianism in the South was a significant, though practically unnoticed, phenomenon in the history of Southern liberalism.[57] When the Unitarian church in Washington was built (1822), John C. Calhoun gave a large subscription, and was reported to have said, "It will be the religion of the country in fifty years."[58] But this liberal church, instead of fulfilling his prophecy, slowly perished in the South. In 1817 the first Unitarian churches below Mason and Dixon's line were organized at Charleston and Baltimore. The pastor of the Baltimore church was a former Harvard tutor, Jared Sparks. He founded the *Unitarian Miscellany and Christian Monitor* to propagate his faith, and made such a brilliant success of his ministry that he was chosen Chaplain of the House of Representatives in 1821. In addition to the Baltimore and Charleston churches, Unitarian societies were established at Augusta, Savannah, Mobile, New Orleans, Louisville, Wheeling, and Richmond. The dominant element in these churches was the Northern residents in Southern cities, and the ministers were usually trained at Harvard or the Unitarian Seminary at Meadville, Pennsylvania. These Unitarian ministers found it decidedly uphill work to prove that Unitarians were Christians, and not atheists or agnostics, and to free their converts from thralldom to the literal word of the Bible.[59]

[56] B. M. Palmer, *The Life and Letters of James Henly Thornwell* (Richmond, 1875), pp. 117-118.

[57] In this study of Unitarianism in the South I was greatly aided by an essay written by Professor Clarence Gohdes, entitled "Some Notes on the Unitarian Church in the Ante-Bellum South: A Contribution to the History of Southern Liberalism," to be published in a forthcoming volume, *Southern Studies in Honor of William Kenneth Boyd.*

[58] Conway, *Autobiography*, I, 199.   [59] Clarke, *Autobiography*, pp. 74-77.

The radiating centers of religious liberalism in the Old South, indeed, were these isolated Unitarian churches, especially those at Charleston, Louisville, and New Orleans. The Charleston church had been founded by Rev. Anthony Forster, a native of North Carolina. This clergyman was married to a daughter of Joseph Gales, whose wife was a daughter of Joseph Priestley. In trying to convert his father-in-law, Forster read Priestley's works and became a Unitarian. Consequently, the Charleston church was an indigenous outgrowth, not an offshoot of New England Unitarianism.[60] The second minister, however, was Samuel Gilman, a graduate of Harvard, who served as pastor from 1819 to 1859. His wife, Caroline Gilman, the poetess, wrote to a Northern friend: "Mr. Gilman's congregation ranks about where Mr. Lowell's does in Boston, highly respectable, but engrossing little of the fashions and aristocracy of the place."[61] In 1820 Gilman was instructing nearly one hundred children of his church in the catechism.[62] Although the church record book was destroyed during the Civil War, Mrs. Gilman wrote down from memory in 1869 the names of the members of the church. She listed one hundred and thirty-five communicants, including six colored persons.[63]

The church in Louisville, Kentucky, was particularly fortunate in having as its minister, James Freeman Clarke. This young graduate of the Harvard Divinity School had come to Kentucky in 1833 inspired by missionary zeal. At Louisville he edited the *Western Messenger,* making it an organ for the propagation of the Unitarian religion in the South and West. In its pages he printed the sermons of New England divines and the contributions of transcendentalists, like Emerson and Margaret Fuller. But its circulation probably never reached a thousand copies.[64] Clarke won the confidence of the people of

[60] E. C. L. Brown, "Historical Sketch of the Unitarian Church," *Charleston Year Book* (Charleston, S. C., 1882), p. 416.

[61] Caroline Gilman to Mrs. Harriet Fay, March 4, 1821 (Caroline Gilman Letters, MSS in Library of South Carolina Historical Society).

[62] Caroline Gilman to Mrs. A. M. White, March 27, 1820 *(ibid.).*

[63] "List of Communicants made by Mrs. Caroline Gilman, 1869" (MS in Record Book of the Unitarian Church at Charleston, S. C.)

[64] Mott, *A History of American Magazines, 1741-1850,* pp. 658-663.

Louisville, so that in 1839 he was appointed superintendent of the public schools. He commented on this appointment: "It was a proof of the liberality of the place that my religious opinions were no barrier."[65] Nevertheless, the Unitarian church in Louisville made such slow progress that Clarke had a distinct feeling of ineffectuality, which led him in 1840 to remove to Boston.[66]

The most independent minister of the Old South, perhaps, was the Unitarian Dr. Theodore Clapp of New Orleans, who despite his liberalism justified slavery.[67] He was a native of Massachusetts, a graduate of Yale and of Andover Theological Seminary. In 1834 Dr. Clapp abandoned the Presbyterian Church after he had been bitterly attacked for his unorthodox beliefs and set up an independent church, which became exceedingly popular and was attended by many fashionable people.[68] With religious views quite similar to the Unitarian doctrines, he became an advocate of tolerance toward all classes of people, Catholics, atheists, and skeptics. "He never burned brimstone under the noses of his auditory, nor frenzied their imaginations with impassioned appeals to supernatural agencies."[69] Rather, he preached a rational and enlightened religion. New Orleans, with its large floating population, was in the opinion of this kindly man, the most tolerant place in Christendom.[70] His liberalism, however, was strongly contrasted with the intolerant doctrines of Dr. B. M. Palmer, pastor of the First Presbyterian Church of New Orleans.[71]

The Unitarian faith was not suited to thrive in the South in competition with sects like those of the Methodists, the Baptists, and the Presbyterians. The fact that the Unitarian clergy

[65] Clarke, *Autobiography*, p. 131.   [66] *Ibid.*, pp. 101, 128-129.
[67] Theodore Clapp, *Autobiographical Sketches and Recollections* (Boston, 1857), pp. 403-404.
[68] Ripley, *Social Life in Old New Orleans*, chap. xii, "Dr. Clapp's Church."
[69] W. H. Sparks, *The Memories of Fifty Years* (Philadelphia, 1882), p. 542. At frequent intervals in 1849 and 1850 the New Orleans *Picayune* published his sermons on the front page. One of the best of these sermons was devoted to discouraging revivals (*Picayune*, March 31, 1850).
[70] Clapp, *op. cit.*, p. 174.
[71] See W. B. Sprague, *Annals of the American Pulpit* (New York, 1858), IV, 341-348.

were generally antislavery men was one cause for the failure of this liberal church. But the key to its moribund state below Mason and Dixon's line was that it did not satisfy the emotional needs of a rural people. When Moncure Conway preached a Unitarian sermon in Richmond in 1855, his uncle remarked that Unitarianism tended to cultivate the head more than the heart.[72] In a similar vein wrote Thomas Arnold, a Unitarian physician at Savannah, to his pastor who proposed to do missionary work in the eastern part of the state: "No, no, Georgia is too new a country, in that section of it, for Unitarian Christianity. A few from the land of steady habits may carry it thither with them, but if it were strangled in Augusta, I have no hopes of its reviving and flourishing in Marietta, Cobb Co., which 20 yrs. since was an Indian hunting ground—."[73]

By 1860 the Unitarian churches in the South had collapsed or become inactive. The church at Augusta had been "strangled" as early as 1838. The society at Mobile was disrupted by Unitarian ministers who preached against slavery. The church at Savannah sold its property and disbanded in 1851. Charles Manson Taggart preached at Nashville from 1851 to 1853 to a Unitarian congregation whose average attendance was about twenty persons. Finally he became discouraged and abandoned his charge. With his departure Unitarianism in Nashville faded out. The society at Wheeling was no longer listed in the official register of the Unitarian church after 1858. The church at Washington was split by the antislavery sermons of Moncure D. Conway, who was forced to resign in 1857. Internal dissention in the congregation at Baltimore led to a division of the church and loss of members. In Charleston after the death of the veteran, Samuel Gilman, the church was irregularly supplied with ministers until finally during the Civil War the Methodists took possession of the building.[74]

---

[72] Conway, *Autobiography*, I, 190.

[73] *Historical Papers of the Trinity College Historical Society*, XVIII-XIX, p. 27, quoted by Professor Gohdes.

[74] For a detailed history of each of these Unitarian societies, see the essay by Professor Gohdes previously cited. See also Arthur A. Brooks, *The History of*

Another liberal religious trend in the ante-bellum South arose among the Jews of Charleston. This movement began with a revolt from the severe ritual of the Spanish and Portuguese Jews that was used in the Charleston synagogue prior to 1824.[75] In that year forty-seven members of the Beth Elohim congregation presented a petition to the vestry asking for a reform of the ritual. These liberals then organized the Reformed Society of Israelites, the first in America.[76] A committee consisting of Michael Lazarus, Isaac Harby, D. N. Carvalho, Isaac N. Cardozo, and Abraham Moïse announced a subscription to erect a reformed temple.[77] They declared that the purposes of their group were to free the Hebrew religion from bigotry, to repeat the prayers in English, and to attain a more rational way of worshipping the true God.[78] The Reformed Society, unfortunately, lasted only until 1833. At that date it abandoned its idealistic reforms and returned the money collected for building a new synagogue, *with accrued interest*. Elzas explains the failure of the liberal movement among the Jews of Charleston on the grounds that it was ahead of its time and the majority of the Jews were afraid to experiment.[79]

The Jews of New Orleans seem to have been relatively free from religious bigotry. Out of approximately seven hundred Jewish families in the city in 1842, only four kept a Kosher table, and only two observed Saturday as the Sabbath. The synagogue had accommodations for not more than fifty persons. The former Rabbi was described as a Dutchman, whose Catholic wife "with difficulty was restrained from sending a

Unitarianism in the Southern Churches: Charleston, New Orleans, Louisville, Richmond (Boston: American Unitarian Association, n.d.).

[75] The Charleston radicals were apparently influenced by European example, as shown by a long quotation in their original memorial from the *Frankfurter Journal* (David Philipson, *The Reform Movement in Judaism*, New York, 1931, pp. 329, 333).

[76] Samuel Getman, "Harby's Discourse on the Jewish Synagogue," *North American Review*, XXIII, 67-79 (July, 1826).

[77] L. C. Moïse, *Biography of Isaac Harby with an Account of the Reformed Society of Israelites of Charleston, S. C., 1824-1833* (Columbia, S. C., 1931), pp. 32-45.   [78] *Southern Patriot*, Jan. 6, 1827.

[79] Elzas, *The Jews of South Carolina*, pp. 163-164.

crucifix to his grave at his burial."[80]   Judah P. Benjamin was an example of the worldly urbane Jew, who married a Catholic wife and discontinued his connection with the Hebrew church.[81] Judah Touro, the eccentric philanthropist, furnished a church free of rent to Dr. Theodore Clapp, the liberal Protestant minister of New Orleans.

The tolerance shown to Catholics in the ante-bellum South contrasted favorably with the treatment which they received in the North. Bishop England of Charleston, a genial Irishman, for example, was beloved by the people of this intensely Southern city. The conservative merchant, Richard Lathers, attended services at a Protestant church in the city during which a large audience listened to the Catholic bishop preach.[82] Bishop England founded the pioneer Catholic newspaper in the United States at Charleston, the *United States Catholic Miscellany,* which lasted from 1822 to the Civil War. In North Carolina the distinguished career of Judge William Gaston, a prominent Catholic, demonstrated the tolerance of the people toward his sect. After serving in the state legislature or Congress almost continuously from 1800 to 1832, he was elected Chief Justice by the General Assembly in 1833, and held this high position until his death in 1844. The most striking fact about his career was that he remained a trustee of the University of North Carolina for forty-two years.[83] Jefferson Davis was sent by his Baptist father to the Catholic college (so-called) of St. Thomas in Kentucky, nearly a thousand miles from his home in Mississippi. At this academy, conducted by Dominican friars, the youthful Davis desired to become a Catholic, but was restrained by one of his teachers.[84] Just prior to the Civil War Archbishop Hughes, delivering the baccalaureate sermon before the senior class of the University

[80] M. J. Kohler, "Judah P. Benjamin: Statesman and Jurist," *Publication of the American Jewish Historical Society* (Baltimore, 1904), No. XII, pp. 68-69.

[81] Butler, *Judah P. Benjamin,* p. 46.

[82] A. F. Sanborn (ed.), *Reminiscences of Richard Lathers* (New York, 1908), p. 15.

[83] *Dictionary of American Biography,* VII, 180-181.

[84] See Mrs. Jefferson Davis, *A Memoir of Jefferson Davis* (New York, 1890), I, chap. ii.

at Chapel Hill, advised his youthful hearers not to endanger their souls by reading the works of infidels. Charles Manly, a trustee, described the interest evoked by the invitation of the Catholic prelate as amazing: "From appearances there will be as great a rush to see the animal as if he were the big bull of Bashan or Pope of Rome."[85] In Texas toleration for the Catholics was shown by allowing parochial schools to participate in the common school fund, although similar proposals in Louisiana and Alabama were rejected.[86] The courage and humanity of the priests in Louisiana during the yellow fever epidemics tended to make the Protestants more tolerant of Catholicism.

The Know-Nothing movement in the South was much freer from anti-Catholic feeling than was the case in New England, and the Middle States, where a number of mobs against Catholics took place. In fact, many of the Know-Nothings of Louisiana and Maryland were faithful Catholics, disgusted at the political evils arising from immigration. Also, thousands of conservative Southern Whigs entered the party after the passage of the Kansas-Nebraska Bill, hoping to silence the agitation of slavery and preserve the Union. In June, 1855, six delegates from the Know-Nothing party of Louisiana attended a meeting of the national council in Philadelphia. One of these delegates was the historian, Charles Gayarré, who was refused admittance because he was a Catholic. Thereupon, the other delegates declined to participate in the deliberations of the council, and the Know-Nothing party in Louisiana rapidly declined.[87] The greatest fight against the Know-Nothings below Mason and Dixon's line was waged in Virginia by Henry Wise during the gubernatorial campaign of 1855. His opponent, Thomas S. Flournoy, made the mistake of advocating the exclusion of Catholics from office by the independent

[85] Charles Manly to President David Swain, Sept. 23, 1860 (David L. Swain MSS in archives of North Carolina Historical Commission).

[86] Thomas O'Gorman, *A History of the Roman Catholic Church in the United States* (New York, 1895), p. 445; J. G. Shea, *A History of the Catholic Church within the Limits of the United States, 1844-1866* (New York, 1892), pp. 667, 685.

[87] Charles Gayarré, *A History of Louisiana* (New York, 1866), IV, 678-679.

exercise of the suffrage and of the appointing power, although he was not so rash as to recommend a legal exclusion.[88] In the exciting campaign that followed, Wise attacked the Know-Nothing party for its platform of religious intolerance and for its alliance with abolitionists.[89] He won a surprising victory over his opponent by a ten-thousand majority. Principally in Maryland and in Louisville, Kentucky, on the circumference of the South, strong feeling against the Catholics developed.[90]

In Maryland the anti-Catholic flame burned more intensely than in any other Southern state. During the Know-Nothing crusade (1856), the Catholic jurist, Roger B. Taney, wrote: "There is no state in which the clerical influence has been so generally and strenuously exerted to inform the Protestant mind against those who belong to the Catholic Church as in Maryland. In the eyes of the clergymen I am Mordecai the Jew sitting at the King's gate, and their zeal will hardly flag while I remain there."[91]

A survey of the copious anti-Catholic propaganda published in the United States between 1800 and 1860 shows that only a small proportion of such literature originated below the Potomac. In a bibliography of anti-Catholic propaganda published in the United States during this period, prepared by Professor Billington, twenty-five newspapers were listed, of which only three were published for brief intervals in the South: the New Orleans *Protestant,* the Jackson (Tennessee) *Protestant,* and the Baltimore *Weekly Pilot,* owned by Duff Green.[92] The chief anti-Catholic magazine of the South was the *Baltimore Literary and Religious Magazine,* edited by Robert J. Breckinridge. When it was discontinued in 1841, he edited another anti-Catholic monthly entitled the *Spirit of the*

[88] Letters of Acceptance, in the Richmond *Enquirer,* March 26, 1855.

[89] James P. Hambleton, *A Biographical Sketch of Henry A. Wise with a History of the Political Campaign in Virginia in 1855* (Richmond, 1856), pp. 9, 108.

[90] See L. F. Schmeckebier, *History of the Know Nothing Party in Maryland* (Baltimore, 1899), and *The Catholic Encyclopedia* (New York, 1913), VIII, 679.

[91] Swisher, *Roger B. Taney,* p. 473.

[92] R. A. Billington, "Tentative Bibliography of Anti-Catholic Propaganda in the United States, 1800-1860," *Catholic Historical Review,* XVIII, 492-513 (Jan., 1933).

XIX Century, which lasted only a few years. Both of these publications were financial failures. Of the lurid and prurient novels of the period that maligned the Catholic Church, very few were written by Southerners.[93]

Robert J. Breckinridge was the outstanding Southern protagonist of No-Popery. Moving from Kentucky to Baltimore, he became pastor of a Presbyterian church there and editor of anti-Catholic magazines. His attacks upon the Catholic priesthood were so violent that some of his friends feared for his life. Finally, in 1840 suit was brought against him by Catholics for libel and slander. During the trial, in which he came out victorious, he received many letters of praise from sympathizers in the South. His brother, Rev. John Breckinridge, wrote: "You have made the Vatican to tremble by your blows and the earth to stink with the disclosures of Popery."[94] One Southern correspondent described Breckinridge as the victim of Popish cruelty, whose persecution would open the eyes of many lukewarm Christians to the enormities of Popery.[95] Another admirer in a remote Virginia village reported that Breckinridge's magazine containing the melodramatic story of Olivia Neal had stirred up the people of his neighborhood.[96] These numerous anti-Catholic letters from Southerners in the Breckinridge Papers indicate that considerable latent intolerance toward Catholics existed in the South. Yet Catholics were so few in most Southern communities that the crusade against them could gain little headway.

A factor explaining the bitter anti-Catholic feeling in the Northeast was the alarming growth of the Catholic Church in that section, due to immigration. But the spread of Roman Catholicism below the Potomac was not accelerated to the extent that it was in the great seaports of the North by a steady flow of immigrants. During the Know-Nothing campaign in Virginia, Henry A. Wise and others pointed out the ab-

[93] R. A. Billington, *The Protestant Crusade, 1800-1860* (New York, 1938).
[94] John Breckinridge to Robert, Feb. 5, 1840 (Papers of the Breckinridge Family, 1752-1904, Vol. 84, MSS in Library of Congress).
[95] John G. Morris, Lexington, Ky., March 3, 1840, to Breckinridge *(ibid.).*
[96] Robert Bell, Front Royal, Va., Feb. 17, 1840, to Breckinridge *(ibid.).*

surdity of fearing the Catholic vote, since the number of
Catholics in the state was less than eight thousand.[97] In
Louisiana there were only fifty-five Catholic churches in 1850
as compared with one hundred and twenty-five Methodist
churches and seventy-seven Baptist churches. During the next
ten years the Catholic churches in Louisiana increased eighty
per cent while the Methodist and Baptist churches expanded
seventy-three per cent. But in Massachusetts during the same
period the growth of the Roman Church was over one hundred and fourteen per cent, and in New York nearly one hundred and five per cent.[98]

Protestant orthodoxy, indeed, was relatively safe from
Catholicism at this time. It also could boast of having emerged
victorious from the contest with the deists and skeptics of
the eighteenth century. But toward the end of the ante-bellum
period a new source of danger arose from the startling discoveries in the realm of science. The new geology which Sir
Charles Lyell advanced in 1830, indeed cast a disturbing light
on the Mosaic account of the origin of the world. The average
Southerner, nevertheless, was little affected by the struggle between science and religion that it evoked. The newspapers of
the period and the legislators scarcely deigned to notice it. Only
the college communities and isolated intellectuals were affected
by the disintegrating influence of science upon the traditional
religion.

At the University of Virginia a series of lectures were given
on the evidences of Christianity to counteract the tide of infidelity threatened by the new scientific investigations.[99] The
lecture of Dr. Green on "The Relation of Physical Science to
Revealed Religion" was published in the college magazine,
February, 1851.[100] It sought to grapple with the skepticism

[97] Hambleton, op. cit., 9; see also an article entitled "Absurdity of Know Noth-
ingism in this State," in the Richmond Daily Enquirer, Feb. 1, 1855.

[98] These figures are derived from The Census of 1850, pp. 488-491, 62, 131,
and The Census of 1860, Mortality and Miscellaneous Statistics, pp. 401-403, 409,
433.

[99] The radical scientific ideas of the age were popularized by Vestiges of the
Natural History of Creation (London, 1844), attributed to Robert Chambers.

[100] The Jefferson Monument Magazine, II, 142-144 (Feb., 1851), in the Library
of the University of Virginia.

produced by the recent discoveries of geology. Dr. Green declared that geology simply confirmed the truth of the Bible; it added proof to the Biblical account of the Deluge; it confirmed the probability of the earth's being destroyed by fire; and it supported the Biblical record that the age of man was not more than five or six thousand years. Geology, he maintained, showed that miracles had been performed in the past, and that nothing could be found in science to cast discredit on the first chapter of Genesis.[101]

The reaction of Southern society to the new geology was reflected in the fear that young men would be driven from their religious faith. Accordingly, when orators were invited to address college students, they almost invariably tried to slay the dragon of skepticism. In June, 1853, Dr. J. H. Dickson delivered an address at the University of North Carolina in which he dealt with the conflict between science and religion. Geology, he declared, furnished no clue by which the sublime mysteries of Creation could be unraveled. He would allow this science to justify itself by "a conformity, either symbolical or literal, to the written record."[102] Speculation on the origin of the world and man could lead only to negative results and foster infidelity. The commencement speaker at the University of Virginia in 1854, B. J. Barbour, likewise pointed out the perils of infidelity. Citing the awful example of Shelley, who made a wreck of his life by his skepticism, he advised young men to take warning and not to attempt to unravel the mysteries which God meant to conceal from men. Especially he admonished them not to be misled by geology, for if they waited but a few months new theories would arise to make geology inconsistent with itself.[103]

One of the most gifted scientists the Old South produced,

[101] *Ibid.*

[102] J. H. Dickson, *Address before the Alumni Association of the University of North Carolina* (June, 1853). A pamphlet.

[103] *Southern Literary Messenger*, XX, 526 (Sept., 1854). It is interesting to note that William Fitzhugh Gordon, who was influential in founding the University of Virginia, ordered his son to take a copy of Shelley out of his house on account of its infidelity and immorality (Armistead Gordon, *William Fitzhugh Gordon*, p. 267.)

Matthew Fontaine Maury, took up the cudgels in behalf of orthodox religion in an address before the students of the University of Virginia (1855). In his address, entitled "Science and Religion," he clung tenaciously to the literal interpretation of the Bible. He maintained that the Mosaic account of creation was correct, and that Job was a learned book of science. He smoothed out the inconsistencies between the findings of science and the account of revelation by the following process of reasoning. "If the two cannot be reconciled, the fault is ours, and is because, in our blindness and weakness, we have not been able to interpret aright either the one or the other."[104] In a speech he made on Sewanee Mountain at the laying of the cornerstone of the University of the South, he said: "I have been blamed by men of science both in this country and in England for quoting the Bible in confirmation of the doctrines of Physical Geography. The Bible, they say was not written for scientific purposes and is therefore no authority in matters of science. I beg pardon: the Bible is authority for everything it touches."[105]

A similar point of view was held by Henry W. Ravenel, the South Carolina scientist. In a lecture delivered at Pineville in 1850 he pointed out that the great antiquity of the earth established by geology did not conflict with the Mosaic account. To substantiate his position, he quoted both from theologians and eminent geologists who held that the Mosaic account and the facts of geology were compatible. Ravenel accepted the interpretation of "in the beginning" to mean a long period of geological time, and that the six days were not the ordinary calendar days. He held that there was a sublimity in the long geological period which raised the conception of the omnipotence of God.[106]

The new study of geology and the cosmic system had nat-

[104] Diana Fontaine Corbin, *Life of Matthew Fontaine Maury* (London, 1888), p. 160.

[105] Letter Book of M. F. Maury, Speech of Oct. 10, 1860, pp. 44-45 (MS in Library of Congress).

[106] H. W. Ravenel MSS in possession of Professor W. C. Coker, University of North Carolina, Chapel Hill, N. C.

urally turned men's thoughts to the origin of man himself. In 1845 the *Southern Literary Messenger* contained a notice of Lamarck's theory of the transmutation of the species. "Grant to Lamarck the slightest possible 'transmutation of the species,'" the reviewer declared, "and you have no good reason to deny that a monkey was your forefather."[107] Joseph Le-Conte relates in his autobiography a conversation that he had with Langdon Cheves of South Carolina, in which before the publication of Darwin's book Cheves advanced the theory of the origin of the species by transmutation and the survival of the fittest. LeConte, at that time a disciple of Agassiz, strongly combatted Cheves's views.[108] On the eve of the Civil War the editors of the *University of North Carolina Magazine* noted the reception of copies of the *Westminster Review* and the *London Quarterly Review,* containing articles on Darwin's *The Origin of Species* but they did not comment on the startling hypothesis of evolution.[109] The absorbing questions of politics and secession overshadowed any interest of the South in a bizarre theory.

Closely associated with the question of evolution was the problem of the unity of the race. In 1854 Josiah C. Nott, a professor at the University of New Orleans, published his *Types of Mankind,* which attempted to establish a thesis denying that all men came from a common ancestor. In the North the great authority of Agassiz gave support to the theory. The hypothesis was advanced in the South that the *negro,* not the lordly white man, may have descended from a chimpanzee or orang-outang.[110] Despite the fact that such a doctrine of racial inequality strengthened the Southern argument for slavery, it found few followers in the South. Nott wrote to Professor Lewis R. Gibbes of the College of Charleston: "The Diversity of the Races was as clear to my mind as the Sun at noonday

---

[107] *Southern Literary Messenger,* VI, 334 (June, 1845).

[108] William Dallas Armes (ed.), *The Autobiography of Joseph LeConte* (New York, 1903), p. 174.

[109] *University of North Carolina Magazine* (Second Series), X, 123 (Sept., 1860).

[110] See a review of Nott's *Types of Mankind* by W. A. Cocke in *Southern Literary Messenger,* XX, 661 (Nov., 1854).

& I was willing to face the storm. . . . The parsons have gored me into controversies for which I have no taste. I have fought back at them not because I was attacked, but because I thought it best to agitate and keep the subject before the world—the more they abuse me, the better the people would *read*."[111] The reviewer of Nott and Gliddon's book in the *Southern Quarterly Review* condemned the authors for their cavalier treatment of the Bible and controverted them by arguments from Dr. John Bachman of Charleston supporting the unity of the race.[112] An article in the *Southern Literary Messenger* placed those who held to the diversity of the human race in the same category with Tom Paine and Voltaire in destroying the Bible and advancing the cause of infidelity.[113]

Although Southern students do not appear to have been exercised greatly over the struggle between science and religion, there were individuals who expressed a liberal attitude toward the modern discoveries of science. In 1856 a student at the University of North Carolina made a speech at commencement, in which he declared: "Nothing can be more unwise or do greater injury to the cause of Religion than the foolish opposition which is sometimes made to the recent developments of natural science. Religion and Philosophy can never conflict if both are based on the truth."[114] A student writing in the University of Virginia magazine sought to awaken the church to a realization of the need of an enlightened attitude toward science. He described the state of mind prevailing in his home community with regard to science as follows: "We find a secret silent abhorrence and dread in

[111] J. C. Nott to Lewis R. Gibbes, Nov. 21, 1850 (L. R. Gibbes Papers, IV, MSS in Library of Congress).

[112] *Southern Quarterly Review*, X, 281 (Oct., 1854).

[113] *Southern Literary Messenger*, XXI, 30 (Jan., 1855). One of the most distinguished reviewers of the South, George Frederick Holmes, also opposed the rationalistic trend of the scientists. Although he introduced the philosophy of Auguste Comte to Americans, he held that the only way to reconcile the conflict between science and religion was to accept the validity of knowledge by faith, namely revelation; "beyond the horizon of science I recognize the domain of faith" (R. L. Hawkins, *Auguste Comte and the United States*, Cambridge, Mass., 1936, pp. 108, 120-121).

[114] Speech on "The Pre-Adamite World" by John S. Hines in a volume of *Senior Speeches*, 1856 (Library of University of North Carolina).

many minds of everything which partakes of a geological nature."[115] The preachers, he observed, had a powerful influence in controlling thought in the South, but they would not discuss the consequences of the new scientific discoveries on religion. Some maintained silence out of deference to the opinions of the more ignorant of their congregations, while others feared to avow that their views had undergone modification caused by "the legitimate conclusions deduced from studying nature's works." Impressed by the delinquency of the ministry, the writer exhorted the ministers to come out fearlessly and enlighten their congregations. One of the fruits of cultivating an acquaintance with natural science, he suggested, was freedom of thought.[116]

If the South was wedded to orthodoxy, and resisted the advance of geological science, the North was scarcely more tolerant or liberal in its views. Benjamin Silliman, professor of geology at Yale, in editing the second American edition (1833) of *Bakewell's Geology* for college students, tried to make the facts of geology accord with the book of Genesis. He drew up a table of coincidences between the book of Genesis and the investigations of geology. But Silliman was not alone in this attitude. Amos Eaton, a prominent geologist of New York, was also restrained by the Biblical account of creation and of the deluge in expounding the principles of geology in his *Geological Text-book* (Second Edition, 1832).[117] When Darwin's theories were introduced into New England after the Civil War, Professors Louis Agassiz at Harvard and James Dwight Dana at Yale opposed them—partly because of the influence of religious feeling.[118]

[115] *The Jefferson Monument Magazine*, I, 106 (Jan., 1850).

[116] *Ibid.*, I, 108. On the other hand, a student writing on "Religious Reforms," declared, should science disagree with the Bible, "away with science and cling to our Bible" (*Virginia University Magazine*, IV, 161-166, Jan., 1860).

[117] G. P. Merrill, *The First One Hundred Years of American Geology* (New Haven, 1924), p. 131.

[118] B. J. Loewenberg, "The Reaction of American Scientists to Darwinism," *American Historical Review*, XXXVIII, 687-701 (July, 1933). Agassiz continued violently to oppose Darwinism until his death, but Dana was later converted to the new views.

In contrast to these eminent Northern scientists, two Southern professors, Dr. Thomas Cooper and James Woodrow, stand out as men ahead of their time. Dr. Cooper found it almost necessary to use Silliman's edition of *Bakewell's Geology* as a text in his class. Nevertheless, he felt it his duty to point out the errors of the Yale scientist in warping the facts of geology to harmonize with the Mosaic account. Accordingly, he published a pamphlet in which he referred to Silliman's "absolute unconditional surrender of his common sense to clerical orthodoxy."[119] In this counterblast Cooper asserted that the Pentateuch was not written by Moses or by anyone else under the influence of divine inspiration. Genesis, he roundly declared, was a collection of "absurd and frivolous tales" and concluded with the warning that it was high time to resist the intermeddling of the clergy and their blind adherents in matters of science.[120] James Woodrow was a professor of science at Oglethorpe College, whose mind had been liberated by a splendid scientific training at Harvard under Agassiz and two years of study in Germany. He had a profound influence on the young poet, Sidney Lanier, one of his students. Later, in the 1880's, Woodrow championed the cause of evolution against its clerical foes and was condemned by the Southern Presbyterian Church.[121]

The discoveries in geology and natural science which were at variance with the account in the book of Genesis excited the intolerance of the relatively few Southerners who were acquainted with them. But the excitement was almost negligible as compared with the storm of the eighties and even in recent times. No professors were driven from their positions, and no laws opposing the march of science were placed on the statute books. Far more opposition was experienced in

[119] Merrill, *op. cit.*, p. 157.
[120] *On the Connection between Geology and the Pentateuch: In a Letter to Benjamin Silliman from Thomas Cooper M.D.; to Which Is Added the Defence of Dr. Cooper before the Trustees of South Carolina College* (Columbia, S. C., 1833), pp. 18, 55, 63.
[121] Edwin Mims, *Sidney Lanier* (Boston, 1905), pp. 28-30.

England, where Sir Charles Lyell was for a time ostracized.[122] Even after the lapse of years the English statesman, Gladstone, engaged in a controversy (in 1885) to save the literal word of Genesis from the attacks of geologists.

A glance at the treatment of skeptics above Mason and Dixon's line will serve to give a truer perspective of conditions in the South. Tolerance is indeed a relative thing. In 1834 one of the most incredible trials in American legal history took place in the city of Boston. Abner Kneeland, editor of the *Investigator,* the first rationalist newspaper in the United States, was on trial for the crime of blasphemy. He was sentenced to jail for certain atheistical statements he had made in his newspaper, and the Supreme Court of Massachusetts upheld the sentence.[123] Nineteen years later a Bible convention was held at Hartford, Connecticut, by the abolitionists. In this assembly Garrison introduced resolutions denying that the Bible was the literal word of God and declaring that the Scriptures "are to be as freely examined, and as readily accepted or rejected, as any other books, according as they were found worthless or valuable."[124] The students of Trinity College tried to break up this gathering of radicals by stamping, groaning, cursing, and derisive laughter. A popular textbook written by Francis Wayland, President of Brown University, also gives a good insight into the rigid orthodoxy inculcated in many Northern schools and colleges. Says Wayland, "It is as much a profanation of the Sabbath to spend it in visiting, journeying, riding, sailing, or in any form of amusement, as in labor. One of the first indications that a person is becoming vicious is his disregard of the Sabbath and his neglect of religious worship."[125] In the North there were violent protests from the conservative classes against the running of trains on

[122] A. D. White, *A History of the Warfare of Science with Theology* (New York, 1898), I, 233.

[123] H. S. Commager, "The Blasphemy of Abner Kneeland," *New England Quarterly,* VIII, 29-41 (March, 1935).

[124] W. P. and F. J. Garrison, *op. cit.,* III, 386.

[125] Francis Wayland, *Elements of Moral Science, Abridged and Adapted to the Use of Schools and Academies* (Boston, 1850), p. 92.

Sunday; there was much hostility directed against the theaters as sinful places; and the Revival of 1858 that swept the North compared favorably with the Great Revival that had agitated the South over fifty years before.[126]   Although the majority of the Northern people would have sympathized with the devotion of the South to orthodoxy, the difference between the two sections was that the Northern States nourished an important minority of skeptics and religious liberals.

[126] For conditions in New York and Ohio in the 1820's and 1830's, consider the revival led by Finney's Holy Band (Barnes, *The Antislavery Impulse,* chap. i).

CHAPTER XIII

THE INTELLECTUAL BLOCKADE

IN THE WINTER of 1828 young Henry Rogers, the son of a professor of William and Mary College, listened entranced to a lecture by Frances Wright in the Belvedere Theater, Baltimore. This tall, stately woman, "with her short hair unbound and in ringlets on a head which would have graced Minerva," was engaged in a dramatic attack on the priestcraft and the theology that shackled the human mind.[1] By her eloquence, her prodigious learning, and her bold spirit of inquiry, she made a profound impression on the young scientist fresh from Virginia, and he sought an interview with her. This Scotch reformer was shocking all staid and respectable people by daring to depart from woman's sphere to lecture on the public platform. Moreover, she was an ardent advocate of all those "pernicious isms" which the Southern people heartily loathed and feared. Unblushingly she advocated birth control, easy divorce laws, the equal education of women with men; she urged the gradual emancipation of the slaves; and she was a disciple of Robert Owen, the founder of the communistic society of New Harmony, Indiana.[2]

Henry Rogers's enthusiasm for Frances Wright continued to grow, although he found it necessary to be guarded in his expressions of it. Eventually he joined the reformers and accompanied Robert Dale Owen, the son of Robert Owen, to Europe. Here his interest in geology was awakened, and he gave up his pursuit of the isms to become one of the pioneers in American geology. But the spectacle of a Southerner even dallying with the isms in his youth was a rare phenomenon. At a period when the rest of the United States was effer-

[1] *Life and Letters of William Barton Rogers Edited by His Wife* (Boston, 1896), I, 70.

[2] See Robert Dale Owen, "An Earnest Sowing of Wild Oats," *Atlantic Monthly,* XXXIV, 71-76 (July, 1874).

vescing with experiments of utopias and efforts to eradicate "the evils" of society, the South was strikingly free from reformers. Thornton Stringfellow, a Virginia minister who wrote an able defense of slavery, pointed out that, although isms flourished in New England like Jonah's gourd, one might travel through the Southern States and not find a single ism with an *organized* existence.[3] The Southern press, as well as the powerful influence of the clergy, was almost uniformly opposed to social experimentation or to radical reform movements. W. W. Holden, editor of the Raleigh *Standard,* and later reconstruction governor of North Carolina, described this unity of the ante-bellum press as follows: "It has uniformly rejected the isms which infest Europe and the Eastern and Western States of this country. Newspapers devoted to socialism, or to social equality, nihilism, communism or to infidelity in any of its shapes or shades, could not live in the atmosphere of North Carolina."[4] Against such foes of the established order the Southern people set up an intellectual blockade, a *cordon sanitaire.*

What were these ideas which seemed dangerous to the shepherds of Southern minds? "Parson" Brownlow answered the question by proposing an organization called "the Missionary Society of the South, for the Conversion of the Freedom Shriekers, Spiritualists, Free-lovers, Fourierites, and Infidel Reformers of the North."[5] His catalogue of the pernicious ideas beyond the Potomac, however, was far from complete. In the Chardon Street Convention of the Friends of Universal Reform at Boston (1840), the "lunatic fringe" of the reform movement held high carnival. Here was gathered, according to Emerson, a pandemonium of the Northern isms, Muggletonians, Dunkers, come-outers, Seventh-Day Adventists, strident feminists, abolitionists, Unitarians, philosophers, and

---

[3] Thornton Stringfellow, *Scriptural and Statistical View of Slavery* (Richmond, 1856), pp. 119-120.

[4] W. W. Holden, *Address on the History of Journalism in North Carolina,* p. 21.

[5] W. G. Brownlow, *Ought American Slavery to be Perpetuated?*, a debate between Brownlow and Prynne (Philadelphia, 1858), p. 167.

many persons whose church was a church of one member only.[6] The North had become a germinating center for feverish reform movements and strange cults. Boston was regarded in the Southern States as the capital city of the isms, although western New York was almost as pre-eminent in radicalism.[7]

The South confronted the various extravagances of the reforming zeal of the North with aristocratic detachment, regarding them as middle-class enthusiasms. Both sections were deeply touched by the romantic movement of the time. In the North, romanticism manifested itself in a passion for making over society according to the dreams of perfectionists, Fourierites, feminists, abolitionists, and transcendentalists. In the South, on the other hand, the romantic movement looked to the past for its inspiration, to the dream of a Greek democracy, or to the feudal charm of Sir Walter Scott's novels.[8] Consequently, the Oneida Free Love Colony, the Village of Modern Times on Long Island, and Trialville in Ohio were unthinkable below the Potomac. They furnished a happy label, indeed, for use against the Republicans in 1856, "Free Love and Frémont."[9] When the Fox sisters began to give their séances in New York about 1850, they were irreverently referred to in the South as the "Knocking Girls of Rochester."[10] The spiritualist craze in the North, leading to numerous spiritualist circles and the establishment of the *Spiritual Telegraph,* found hardly an echo of credulity in the South.[11] The planters and the yeoman farmers were content to enjoy

[6] R. W. Emerson, *Lectures and Biographical Sketches* (Boston, 1887), pp. 351-354.

[7] Governor Henry A. Wise of Virginia, who had never stepped upon the soil of New England, wrote to his cousin in Boston, a son-in-law of Edward Everett: "Why don't he [Everett] and such as he in New England wield such pens against the wild 'isms' of Massachusetts. Their moral influence would overthrow the monster. Boston seems to be a center of 'isms'" (Wise to Lieutenant Wise, Sept. 11, 1855, Henry A. Wise MSS in Library of Congress).

[8] Parrington, *The Romantic Revolution in America*, pp. 99-108, 317-434.

[9] Richmond *Enquirer*, Sept. 13, 1856.

[10] *Southern Literary Messenger*, XVII, 1-7 (Jan., 1851), a review, "The Night-Side of Nature."

[11] *Ibid.*, XIX, 385-394 (July, 1853), an article, "Spiritual Manifestations"; *ibid.*, XX, 343-344 (June, 1854), an article, "The Credulity of the Times."

its rural simplicity, almost wholly free from disturbing social adventures.

The woman's rights movement that was developing in the North struck an almost impenetrable barrier when it attempted to gain converts in the South. There were at least five good reasons why the Southern people would have nothing to do with this Yankee fad. In the first place, the feminist movement in the North had grown up in close alliance with the abolitionist movement. Many of the most odious abolitionists were also aggressive champions of the rights of women. In the second place, Pauline theology, which had a tenacious hold on the Southern churches, was hostile to feminine assertiveness. Moreover, the prevailing romanticism of the South was incompatible with the attempt of the feminists to equalize the sexes. Although the first woman's college in the United States, Wesleyan Methodist College, was founded in the South at Macon, Georgia, Southern women as a class were not sufficiently educated to demand equality of rights with men. Finally, the energies of so many Southern women who might have grown restive under masculine rule were used up in childbearing. Take, for example, Mrs. Calhoun with her nine children, Mrs. Henry Clay with her eleven children, and Mrs. Robert E. Lee, who presented her husband with a new baby at frequent intervals. These women, typical Southern matrons of the upper class, could hardly have had much leisure or desire to crusade for woman's rights. There is probably a genuine correlation between the spread of the practice of birth control and the growth of woman's rights. Those Southern women who were childless or unburdened by large families, such as Mrs. Chesnut, Mrs. Clement C. Clay, Mrs. Pryor, Octavia LeVert, Julia LeGrand, Mrs. Jefferson Davis, found an outlet in the glamour of social life, in the absorption of religious duties, or in writing *belles-lettres*.[12]

[12] See especially Mrs. Chesnut, *op. cit.*; Eron Rowland, *Varina Howell, Wife of Jefferson Davis* (New York, 1927); Schlesinger, "The Role of Women in American History," *New Viewpoints in American History*, chap. vi; and Elizabeth Cady Stanton, Susan B. Anthony, and Matilda Joslyn Gage, *History of Woman Suffrage* (New York, 1881), I, 39-406, "Angelina Grimké."

The few organized groups of radicals in the South, such as
Frances Wright's colony of negroes and whites at Nashoba,
Tennessee, the Spiritualist community at Mountain Cove, Fay-
ette County, (now West) Virginia, the Icarians, and the Free
German Societies, were all sporadic adventures of foreign
radicalism on Southern soil.

Like William Lloyd Garrison, Frances Wright was a universal reformer, cherishing an exquisite dream of a world ren-
ovated and swept clean of all impurities and injustices. One
of the visions which she sought to realize was the banishing of
slavery and the elevation of the Negro to the plane of his white
master.[13] Buying a large plantation in Tennessee in 1826, she
proposed to purchase some slaves and allow them to work out
their emancipation. The white members of the colony were
to teach the slaves and live on a basis of communism with
them. Those left in charge of the experiment eventually
avowed the doctrines of free love and shocked their Southern
neighbors by the unabashed iniquity of their conduct with
the Negroes and mulattoes. These slaves of yesterday were
treated as though they were highly refined white persons. The
indolent darkies, accordingly, loafed and malingered on the
plantation until the experiment was an economic failure.[14]

On the fringe of the South, in Fayette County, Virginia, a
group of more than a hundred Spiritualists settled in 1852, to
await the second coming of Christ. One of the leaders of this
strange cult was Rev. Thomas Lake Harris, a brilliant poet with
a Dr. Jekyl and Mr. Hyde personality.[15] The community published a journal entitled the *Mountain Cove Journal and
Spiritual Harbinger,* which claimed to be "dictated by Spirits
out of the flesh, and by them edited, superintended, and controlled."[16] The colony was abandoned in 1853, when the

[13] Trollope, *Domestic Manners of the Americans,* pp. 33-42; see also Robert
Dale Owen, *Threading My Way* (New York, 1874), pp. 298-302.

[14] W. R. Waterman, *Frances Wright* (New York, 1924), pp. 92-133. See James
Madison's letter to Frances Wright, expressing sympathy for her desire to abolish
slavery but disparaging the Nashoba plan (Hunt, ed., *Writings of James Madison,*
IX, 224-229).

[15] *Dictionary of American Biography,* VIII, 322.

[16] Mott, *A History of American Magazines, 1850-1865,* p. 210.

neophytes realized that they had been dupes to their autocratic leaders.[17]

Another abortive attempt of foreign radicals to secure a lodgment in the South was the settlement of the Icarians in Fannin County, Texas. The Icarians were chiefly natives of France who had been deluded by the impractical visions of Etienne Cabet. This reformer had written a book entitled *Voyage en Icaria* (1839), in which he described his magnificent dreams of utopian communism. In 1848 a part of his followers emigrated to an undeveloped section of Texas, where they had bought a million acres of land. The colony lasted no longer than a few months in its unfriendly environment, the survivors moving to Nauvoo, Illinois.[18]

After the ill-fated revolution of 1848 some German settlers who held very radical ideas entered the South. In 1850 a certain Mr. Steinmetz came to Richmond to organize a Free Germany Society. But the society he founded, numbered only twenty-two persons and was regarded with hostility even by the majority of the German residents. Being threatened with disagreeable consequences if he remained in Richmond, he left the following year. The platform of the Free German Society of Richmond included such revolutionary ideas as the right of the people to change the Constitution when they liked, the abolition of the Presidency, the right of the people to recall their representatives at their pleasure, compulsory education, abolition of capital punishment, repeal of the laws enforcing the observance of the Sabbath, and the support of the program of Cassius Clay for the abolition of slavery.[19] The Free Germans of Louisville, Kentucky, advocated government ownership of railroads, abolition of land monopoly, the rights of woman, complete religious freedom, and the adop-

[17] Sir Arthur Conan Doyle, *The History of Spiritualism* (New York, 1926), I, 119-120.

[18] For an account of these communistic societies see J. H. Noyes, *History of American Socialisms* (Philadelphia, 1870); W. A. Hinds, *American Communities; Brief Sketches of Economy, Zoar, Bethel, Amora, Amana, Icaria, the Shakers, Oneida, Wallingford, and the Brotherhood of the New Life* (Oneida, N. Y., 1878); and Charles Nordhoff, *The Communistic Societies of the United States* (New York, 1875).   [19] Schuricht, *op. cit.*, II, 36.

tion of the program of Cassius M. Clay in regard to slavery.[20]
Likewise the Germans of western Texas harbored some vigorous radicals. Olmsted observed that among the faults of the
Germans of Texas were a tendency to freethinking and a
devotion to reason which were often carried to the verge of
bigotry.[21]

A very few native Southerners displayed an active interest
in the isms. The Grimké family of Charleston, belonging
to the aristocratic circle of that city, presented an interesting
group of radicals. Angelina and Sarah were converted to the
Quaker faith as a result of a visit to Philadelphia. They abandoned Charleston to live in the North, where they could advance their antislavery and feminist enthusiasms unmolested.[22]
After Angelina had published her antislavery pamphlet, *Appeal to the Christian Women of the South* (1836), the mayor
of Charleston notified her family that she would not be allowed to return to her native city. Thomas S. Grimké, brother
of Sarah and Angelina, remained in Charleston and continued
to hold slaves, but he was a leader in the temperance and peace
movements. Senator Hammond of South Carolina, whose father was a New Englander, also was lured by some of the
radical movements in the North. Hammond had a curious
interest in spiritualism and became a convert to its doctrines.
He wrote William Gilmore Simms that he intended to give
a lot in Aiken to the first congregation of Spiritualists who
would erect a church on it.[23] Not only did he read books on
occult science, but he gave Simms ten dollars with which to
consult some mediums in New York and obtain answers to
a set of questions that he had prepared.[24] The Virginia liberal,

[20] M. W. Cluskey, *The Political Text-Book, or Encyclopedia* (Washington, D. C., 1857), pp. 253-254.

[21] Olmsted, *A Journey Through Texas*, p. 430.

[22] Nevertheless, Northern public opinion was shocked when Sarah and Angelina stepped out of the bounds of female propriety to lecture to mixed audiences. Angelina humorously observed that her audiences literally sat with "mouths agape and eyes astare" (*Weld-Grimké Letters*, I, 414).

[23] Hammond to Simms, Dec. 27, 1853 (James H. Hammond Papers, MSS in Library of Congress).

[24] Hammond to Simms, Oct. 2, 1856 (*ibid.*).

Nicholas Trist, was sympathetic to the radical ideas of Robert Dale Owen, whom he consulted about the education of his children.[25]

One of the most extreme of these isolated Southern radicals was a Jewish youth named Marx Lazarus, who eventually joined the North American Phalanx at Red Bank, New Jersey. The disapproval of his family was voiced in an ironic letter of Sam Mordecai to Marx's guardian, George Washington Mordecai. "Marx is enjoying the delights of a sort of Fourier association," Sam wrote, "they have made him a menial and a drudge, but as it is according to the principles of the association, he enjoys it, cleans cow stables, waits on the table, takes orders from the cook, ploughs, helps the Ladies iron clothes, etc."[26] At the same time the enthusiastic reformer was writing an article on capital. Later he was practicing homeopathy and translating Fourier's works. Another member of the Mordecai family, Ellen, became a member of Edger's Village of Modern Times.[27]

The pacifist movement, which attained a respectable following in the North, made little headway in the South. As early as 1819 there was a peace society at Raleigh, North Carolina, whose president, Calvin Jones, had resigned from his position as commander of the state militia on account of his convictions. The Georgia Peace Society, at Augusta, was for a while an auxiliary of the Pennsylvania Peace Society. The outstanding advocate of pacifism in the South was Thomas S. Grimké, who became a member of the American Peace Society, and a contributor to the society's journal, *Calumet*. Grimké was converted to a belief that all war, even defensive war, was incompatible with Christianity. He prepared an American edition of *Inquiry into the Accordancy of War with the Principles of Christianity,* by the British Quaker, Jonathan Dymond. Grimké even boldly challenged the rightfulness of

[25] Robert Dale Owen to Trist, Feb. 12 and March 24, 1832 (Nicholas Trist Papers, MSS in Library of Congress). See also L. M. Sears, "Nicholas P. Trist, a Diplomat with Ideals," *Mississippi Valley Historical Review,* XI, 90 (June, 1924).

[26] Sam Mordecai to G. W. Mordecai, Oct. 17, 1849 (Mordecai Papers).

[27] E. L. Allen to George Mordecai, Jan. 15, 1860 *(ibid.).*

the American Revolution.[28] Although the organized peace movement received little support below Mason and Dixon's line, individual Southerners, like Alexander Stephens and Calhoun, stood courageously against the war fever that swept the nation into the Mexican War.

There was one ism that attained a wide popularity in the South, the temperance movement. It harmonized with the religious and puritanical feeling of many Southern people. Such ardent fire-eaters as Robert Barnwell Rhett and Governor Henry A. Wise, whose mouth was frequently stained with tobacco juice, drank only cold water and were prominent as temperance advocates. Rhett was vice-president of the Young Men's Temperance Society of Charleston.[29] In 1839 the state of Georgia was the dramatic scene of a prohibition movement led by a wealthy planter, named Josiah Flournoy. With indomitable zeal he drove from county to county in his buggy to secure signatures to a monster petition that was presented to the legislature in 1839—a petition which proposed that the legislature should prohibit the retailing of liquor within the state. The movement became involved in a bitter political struggle that resulted in the defeat of a prohibition law by a vote of ninety-eight to fifty-four. During the excited campaign for its adoption Flournoy was subjected to many indignities and died a martyr to the cause.[30] In 1851 the Sons of Temperance in Georgia had reached a maximum growth of over thirteen thousand members, but by the close of the antebellum period the membership had declined to fifteen hundred. The outstanding advocate of temperance in the Upper South was General John Cocke of Bremo, Virginia, who was elected president of the American Temperance Union in 1836. A cavalier Puritan, he abhorred the use of both tobacco and liquor. He symbolized his devotion to the cause of temper-

[28] Merle Curti, *The American Peace Crusade, 1815-1860* (Durham, N. C., 1929), pp. 32, 61, 69-72.

[29] Laura A. White, *Robert Barnwell Rhett: Father of Secession* (New York, 1931), p. 32.

[30] H. A. Scomp, *King Alcohol in the Realm of King Cotton* (New York, 1888), pp. 330-331.

ance by erecting a small stone building in the form of a Greek temple on his plantation with the superscription, "Dedicated to the Sons of Temperance."[31] The Washington revival of the 1840's, based on a pledge of total abstinence, was started by six reformed drunkards of Baltimore.[32]

Many complex factors explain the momentum of the ante-bellum South toward conservatism during the time that New England was becoming a center of radicalism. D. R. Hundley, educated at the University of Virginia and at Harvard, suggested an explanation in his *Social Relations in Our Southern States:* the Southern planter lived out of doors, riding and hunting, and thus developed a sanity of outlook which made him immune to the fanaticism of the North.[33] In a land where it is so pleasant to be out-of-doors a large part of the year both literature and wild theories are not likely to find favorable soil. The predominantly rural condition of the South undoubtedly contributed to the resistance to Northern radicalism. Yet this point should not be overstressed, for in colonial days and during the Revolutionary period, when the South was even more bucolic, the leaders of liberalism were Southerners.

In New England and the Middle States lyceums were an important instrument in disseminating radical doctrines. The lyceum movement in the South, on the other hand, attained comparatively a feeble foothold. In 1838 a lyceum was started at Richmond modeled on the Franklin Institute of Philadelphia.[34] The Fredericksburg lyceum founded for mutual improvement in 1837 secured a special column in the *Southern Literary Messenger* for the literary productions of its members.[35] Lexington had a Franklin Society in 1847 before which John Letcher debated the proposition, "Should the people of western Virginia delay any longer in taking steps to bring about a division of the state?"[36] Charleston, although a city

[31] *William and Mary College Quarterly* (Second Series), XIII, 143-154 (July, 1933).
[32] See J. L. Krout, *The Origins of Prohibition* (New York, 1935), chap. ix.
[33] Hundley, *Social Relations in Our Southern States,* pp. 40-41.
[34] *Southern Literary Messenger,* IV, 8 (Jan., 1838).
[35] *Ibid.,* III, 461 (July, 1837).
[36] Prettyman, "John Letcher," III, 314.

of only twelve thousand white people in 1842, had sixty-three different societies, most of them religious in nature, but including such organizations as a Young Men's Debating Society and a Literary and Philosophical Society.[37] An attempt was made to establish a lyceum in Augusta, Georgia, for regular lectures, but it failed.[38] In the little college community of Washington, Mississippi, a lyceum existed between 1835 and 1838, of which the amateur scientist, Benjamin L. C. Wailes, was an active member.[39] The lyceum movement in the South affected only a few people in the cities. It did not serve, as in the North, as a means of adult education and of popularizing the novel ideas and reforms from Europe.

Indeed, many of the radical movements that agitated the North originated across the Atlantic. The South of 1850, however, shared only slightly in this importation of foreign ideas. Not only did European immigrants avoid the South, but Southerners who went abroad were chiefly interested in recreation or in the more romantic aspects of European culture. There was no movement in the South to correspond with the transcendental school of New England, which was stimulated in part by German thought and Oriental literatures.[40] Southern importations, whether of ideas or of goods, came largely by way of the North. It is a significant cultural fact that the principal railroads in the Upper South ran north and south, rather than east and west to Southern seaports. The unceasing efforts of Southern commercial conventions to change these trends of commerce, by establishing direct steamship lines with Europe, were realized only in pipe dreams and the imagination of orators.[41] Furthermore, European nations considered Southern slavery as a repellent anachronism, a fact which tended to preclude any sympathetic consideration of foreign radical ideas by Southerners.

[37] Buckingham, *Slave States of America*, I, 80.

[38] *Ibid.*, p. 167.

[39] C. S. Sydnor, *A Gentleman of the Old Natchez Region: Benjamin L. C. Wailes* (Durham, N. C., 1938), pp. 144-148.

[40] See W. P. Trent and others (eds.), *The Cambridge History of American Literature* (New York, 1917), Vol. I, chaps. viii and ix.

[41] Wender, *Southern Commercial Conventions*, chaps. ii and vii.

One of the appeals to Southern prejudice which the Know-Nothing party adopted was the assertion that foreign immigrants brought dangerous ideas into the country. Said Alexander H. H. Stuart, a leader of the party in Virginia: "Many of the educated foreigners bring with them the most distorted views of the ends and aims of social organization. Many of them are infidels, atheists, socialists, and agrarians, and by their wild and demoralizing ideas corrupt the very fountains of liberty."[42] Since the Southern States received only a small percentage of these immigrants, its prevailing conservatism of thought was relatively unaffected.

In New England the way was prepared for radical movements by the breakdown of Puritanism. The land of Dixie, on the other hand, remained the great stronghold of puritanical feeling in nineteenth-century America. In general, the Southern yeomanry had puritanical prejudices, frowning upon the indulgent society of the aristocrats. "Parson" Brownlow summed up the narrow creed of these unsophisticated country people: "I have never been arraigned in the church for any immorality. I never played a card. I never was a profane swearer. I never drank a dram of liquor until within a few years—when it was taken as a medicine. I never had a cigar or a chew of tobacco in my mouth. I never was in attendance at a theatre. I never attended a horse-race, and never witnessed their running save on the fair-grounds of my county. I never courted but one woman; and her I married."[43] Men like "Parson" Brownlow or Stonewall Jackson were as militant Puritans as John Endicott ever was.

Even the well-to-do planter, despite the myth of the gay cavalier, was frequently affected by this mood of puritanism. Colonel Richard Malcolm Johnston has related how his father, after his conversion, gave up dancing and card playing, and, above all, denied to himself his former luxury of a delicious

---

[42] Robertson, *Alexander Hugh Holmes Stuart*, p. 120.

[43] W. G. Brownlow, *Sketches of the Rise, Progress and Decline of Secession; with a Narrative of Personal Adventures Among the Rebels* (Philadelphia, 1862), p. 19.

bowl of toddy.[44] When the correct Senator Clement C. Clay of Alabama visited the Creole country, he revealed his puritanical prejudices in a letter to his daughter: "The Creoles—especially French and English—are the most unchristian, ungodly, devilish, pleasure-seeking people I have yet seen. The stores, drinking saloons, workshops, etc., are kept open on Sunday, as on any other day; and everybody who can spare time from business goes fishing or hunting or to play billiards or ten pins. Sunday is the chief day for circus, theatre, and other shows."[45] Such a strict attitude toward morals was not conducive to an open mind in regard to the new social propositions that were fermenting Northern society.

The fact that abolitionists were the most prominent advocates of the isms constituted a strong motive for repelling such vagaries from the South. The Richmond *Examiner* in an editorial, "Our Enemies, the Isms and their Purposes," pointed out the close alliance between the abolitionists and the advocates of free love and infidelity. Horace Greeley was described as the leader of the abolitionists and also "the autocrat and prophet of the northern isms."[46] The career of Garrison undoubtedly lent support to this view, for he gradually made the *Liberator* an organ of universal reform, championing abolition of the Sabbath, woman's rights, temperance, the peace movement, and so on. Harriet Beecher Stowe, the author of *Uncle Tom's Cabin,* was often cited as typical of the alliance between feminism and abolitionism.[47] The Northern reformers seemed to the Southern clergy to be fanatics because they would not wait for the slow action of Providence. Said Rev. Benjamin Palmer in an ironic allusion to these immediatists: "the sun must be stricken from the heavens if a spot be found

[44] *Autobiography of Col. Richard Malcolm Johnston* (Washington, D. C., 1900), p. 13.

[45] Clay to Celeste, New Iberia, La., Dec. 5, 1860 (C. C. Clay Papers, MSS in Duke University Library). For a Northerner's equally severe condemnation of Creole laxity see Whipple, *Southern Diary,* p. 119.

[46] Richmond *Examiner,* Sept. 5 and 9, 1856.

[47] See G. F. Holmes's review of Mrs. Stowe's famous novel in *Southern Literary Messenger,* XVIII, 631 (Oct., 1852).

upon his disk and the stars swept from the skies if their courses be erratic."[48]

The Southerners greatly exaggerated the numbers and importance of the Northern radicals. The *Free Enquirer,* edited by Frances Wright and Robert Dale Owen, had a subscription list of only one thousand names.[49] The *Liberator* had less than four hundred white subscribers in 1833 and was sustained largely by the Negroes of Philadelphia, New York, and Boston.[50] The aversion toward the isms among the overwhelming majority of Northern people was expressed by B. D. Silliman, of New York City, who had been asked by the Jewish lawyer, Mordecai, to investigate the Village of Modern Times. He wrote: "I am sorry to learn that 'Modern Times' is a rendezvous of 'isms.' Whether Fourierism, Transcendentalism, communism, or which of the crazy isms predominate I am uncertain. The accounts which I hear of it are in every way unfavorable, and I fear Mrs. Allen will not find it a desirable residence."[51] When Judge John W. Edmonds of the New York Supreme Court became prominent in the advocacy of spiritualism, he was pointed at on the street as a crazy spiritualist and was forced to resign from his judicial position.[52] The distorted idea that Southerners entertained of the Northern radicals and of their number was an important cause of the intellectual blockade.[53]

George Fitzhugh, a brilliant and trenchant writer of Virginia, published two volumes in which he tried to rationalize and justify the conservative prejudices of his section. These two works, *Sociology for the South* and *Cannibals All,* however, must not be taken as representative of Southern thought,

---

[48] Thomas, *The Carolina Tribute to Calhoun,* pp. 250-251.

[49] Owen, "An Earnest Sowing of Wild Oats," p. 73.

[50] Barnes, *The Antislavery Impulse,* p. 50.

[51] B. D. Silliman to G. W. Mordecai, April 25, 1860 (Mordecai MSS).

[52] Doyle, *op. cit.,* pp. 130, 141.

[53] Governor Wise revealed a typical Southern viewpoint: "We can't be made to comprehend here how it is that the Sumners and Wilsons and Burlingames of Massts. should not be in a majority of the masses when they are so strong in the offices and in the influence of the North" (Wise to Lt. Wise, Oct. 6, 1856, Wise MSS).

except that of the extreme right wing. Fitzhugh advanced the idea that slavery had saved the South from the unhealthy radicalism of the North. Southern civilization, he maintained, was founded on Aristotelian principles, by which the inequality of man was recognized. Consequently, Southern society was well ordered and serene, while the North was constantly in turmoil. "Mormons and Oneida Perfectionists," he said, "would no sooner be tolerated in Virginia than Pyrrhic dances and human sacrifices to Moloch."[54] With characteristic exaggeration, he affirmed: "In the whole South there is not one Socialist, not one man, rich or poor, proposing to subvert and reconstruct society."[55] Likewise, in articles for *De Bow's Review* and in his books, he praised the South for its freedom from skepticism in religion and for its resistance to the Woman's Rights Movement which sought to drive women from their sphere (the angelic).[56] Rejoicing in this conservatism of his section, Fitzhugh transmuted the *status quo* of Southern society into an extremely brittle philosophy.

In a chapter on "The Philosophy of Isms," Fitzhugh offered an ingenious theory to explain why the North was the home of radical ideas and social experiments. Free society, he contended, had proved a failure. This was due to excessive individualism, which had led to cutthroat competition and exploitation. A result of this unhealthy condition was the emergence of the phenomena of strikes, trade unions, phalansteries, communistic establishments, Mormonism, and other excrescences. Isms arose to redress the evils of excessive individualism. "Man's nature is social," said Fitzhugh, "not selfish, and he longs and yearns to return to parental, fraternal, and associative relations. All the isms concur in promising closer and more associative relations, in establishing at least a qualified community of property, and in insuring the weak and unfortunate the necessaries and comforts of life."[57] Examine the

[54] George Fitzhugh, *Sociology for the South* (Richmond, 1854), p. 110.
[55] *Ibid.*, p. 306.
[56] *De Bow's Review*, XXVIII, 7 (Jan., 1860).
[57] George Fitzhugh, *Cannibals All* (Richmond, 1857), p. 332.

communism of the Mormons, the socialism of Fourier and Owen, the free love villages of Trialville and Modern Zion, he declared, and you will find this trend toward closer and more organic association. Fitzhugh cleverly pointed out the evils of Northern industrialism in exploiting the lower classes and reducing them to wage slaves. Despite his bitter condemnation of Yankee industrialism, he advocated the South's developing manufactures. The inconsistency of this program with the maintenance of slavery was pointed out in the *Southern Literary Messenger* in an able, and on the whole favorable, review of Fitzhugh's *Sociology for the South.*[58]

Henry W. Ravenel, a South Carolina scientist, also attempted to explain the causes that gave the South immunity from "the isms." In an address before the Black Oak Agricultural Society, he observed that the Southern people were dominated by a spirit of conservatism, which saved them from excesses on the one hand, and at the same time caused them to uphold law and order. The South, he declared, was "the breakwater which is to stay that furious tide of social and political heresies now setting toward us from the shores of the old world." The rural life of the Southerners gave an attachment to the soil, a serene habit of mind, and an indisposition to excesses. The institution of African slavery and the relative freedom from foreign immigrants contributed to this end. "We should shrink intuitively," he warned, "from all the novel and revolutionary notions which are infecting the masses in Europe and the free states of the North."[59]

The Southerners of the ante-bellum period preferred the old patterns of life, the path of conservatism. This preference was the natural choice of an agrarian society. But sectionalism, lack of European contacts, a puritanical religious background, the influence of slavery, intensified the distaste for radicalism

[58] *Southern Literary Messenger,* XXI, 137 (March, 1855). Nevertheless, the Tredegar Iron Works, some tobacco factories in Richmond, and some cotton factories in Georgia successfully employed slaves.

[59] "Address of Henry W. Ravenel delivered before the Black Oak Agricultural Society, April, 1852" (H. W. Ravenel MSS in possession of Professor W. C. Coker, University of North Carolina, Chapel Hill, N. C.).

or utopian experiments. Calhoun pointed out that this conservatism of the South was the salvation of the nation, acting in the capacity of a makeweight against radicalism. "The balance of this system is in the slaveholding States," he declared. "They are the conservative portion—always have been the conservative portion—always will be the conservative portion; and with a due balance on their part may, for generations to come, uphold this glorious Union of ours."[60] The ripe experiences of mankind, what the race had learned by innumerable trials and errors, was not to be lightly set aside. The Southern planters had learned this lesson, which made them cautious of disturbing old social moulds.

Only an atmosphere of good will and understanding could have led to an interchange of ideas and fruitful reforms between the radical North and the conservative South. The Virginia liberal, William Alexander Caruthers, pointed out a method of cultivating intersectional comity and the open mind. "Every southern should visit New-York," he wrote in *The Kentuckian in New-York*. "It would allay provincial prejudices and calm excitement against his northern countrymen."[61] Lucian Minor after his trip through New England was also convinced that great benefit would result to Southern farmers, planters, and their wives if they would follow his example. He traveled with an open mind and reported that New England was as far above the South in the achievement of comfort, as the latter section was above the Hottentots or Esquimaux.[62] But the bitter feeling of sectionalism continued to grow, exacerbated by politicians, fire-eaters, and antislavery crusaders, until an intellectual blockade was set up by the South not only against abolitionism, but also against many associated isms that were destined to triumph in the future.[63] Aversion to things Northern even precluded the development of a lively interest among the book readers of the South in the

[60] Crallé, *Works of John C. Calhoun*, IV, 343-344.

[61] Parrington, *The Romantic Revolution in America*, p. 42.

[62] *Atlantic Monthly*, XXVII, 684 (June, 1871).

[63] See Clement Eaton, "The Resistance of the South to Northern Radicalism," *New England Quarterly*, VIII, 215-231 (June, 1935).

contemporary literature of New England. Emerson's works, representing the best thought of the country, were scarcely read below the Potomac.[64] At the height of the excitement against the North during the resistance movement of 1850, R. S. Holt wrote to Joseph Holt that it had become a question "Whether Southern chivalry will hereafter condescend to cool its Mint Juleps with Northern ice?"[65] Instead of following the advice of Caruthers, Southerners of the prewar years listened to the admonition of Calhoun to meet the pernicious ideas "on the frontier." The dynamics of Southern thought moved, after the death of Jefferson, in the direction of defense, a trend which explains much in the cultural history of the Old South.

[64] Fredrika Bremer wrote: "It is remarkable how very little, or not at all, the authors of the Northern States, even the best of them, are known in the South. They are afraid of admitting their liberal opinions into the Slave States." She found that Joel Poinsett, one of the most cultivated of Southerners, was unacquainted with Emerson's philosophy, which he condemned as "unpractical" when Fredrika discussed it with him (*The Homes of the New World*, I, 298).

[65] R. S. Holt to Joseph Holt, Benton, Miss., Oct. 27, 1850 (Joseph Holt Papers, MSS in Library of Congress).

CHAPTER XIV

FREEDOM OF CONSCIENCE IN POLITICS

ALEXIS DE TOCQUEVILLE wrote of a visit to America during the Jacksonian period: "I know of no country in which there is so little true independence of mind and freedom of discussion as in America."[1] The tyranny of majority opinion in the United States, he noted, contrasted with the free political institutions of the Americans. One of these institutions which increased the awesome power of the majority was the doctrine of the right of state legislatures to instruct their Senators and Representatives in Congress how to vote. Were such instructions binding on them, or were they free to cast their votes as their judgment and conscience dictated? The principle involved in this question was considered by Edmund Burke in 1774 in a speech before the citizens of Bristol, who had just elected him to Parliament. Burke maintained that the representative should deliberate for the nation and ought not to sacrifice "his unbiased opinion, his mature judgment, his enlightened conscience" to the will of his constituents or to any set of men. The coercive authority of instructions he rejected as utterly unknown to the laws of England.[2]

This question was also debated at length in the first Congress when Thomas Tudor Tucker of South Carolina proposed to incorporate the right of instruction in the first amendments of the Constitution. Four states, North Carolina, Pennsylvania, Massachusetts, and Vermont, had included in their original constitutions the right of the people to instruct their representatives.[3] During the debate on Tucker's proposal the Federalist

[1] Alexis de Tocqueville, *Democracy in America,* translated by Henry Reeve (New York, 1900), I, 267.
[2] *The Writings and Speeches of the Right Honourable Edmund Burke* (New York, 1901), II, 95-97; see also Carl Cone, *Edmund Burke and the Nature of Politics* (Lexington, Ky.), 274-275.
[3] F. N. Thorpe (ed.), *The Federal and State Constitutions* . . . (7 vols., Washington, 1909), III, 1892; V, 2802, 3084; VI, 3764.

senators clearly presented the evils that would flow from the practice of this doctrine. Thomas Hartley of Pennsylvania observed that the exercise of the right of instruction had been attended with bad consequences both in England and America. "When the passions of the people are excited," he warned, "instructions have been resorted to and obtained to answer party purposes; and although public opinion is generally respectable, yet at such moments it has been known to be often wrong; and happy is the Government composed of men of firmness and wisdom to discover and resist popular error."[4] Instructions, he maintained, would embarrass representatives in consultation and in the compromise of differences and would substitute the rule of the partial or local view for the broad view in considering proper legislation for the country. James Madison, who had once violated instructions as a delegate of Virginia in the Continental Congress, also opposed binding the representative by a constitutional amendment to vote according to instructions. Consequently, Tucker's amendment was defeated by a vote of 41 to 10.

Nevertheless, the doctrine of the right of instruction was frequently used in states controlled by the early Republican party. For six years, from 1789 to 1795, the Senate, in contrast to the House of Representatives, sat behind closed doors, and not until 1802 did it permit a record of its debates to be published. Finally, it was compelled to abandon this aristocratic policy as a result of the protests of southern states. The instrument that opened the doors of the Senate to the American public was the exercise of the doctrine of instruction, for in 1789-1791 the southern states forced the issue by instructing their senators to use "their utmost endeavors" to obtain free admission of the American people to the Senate.[5] Perhaps the staunchest upholder of the right of instruction in the Senate was William Maclay of Pennsylvania, who expressed the Republican doctrine that senators, being serv-

[4] *Annals of Congress,* 1 Cong., 1 Sess., 761 (August 15, 1789).
[5] Elizabeth G. McPherson, "The Southern States and the Reporting of the Senate Debates, 1789-1802," in *Journal of Southern History* (Baton Rouge, 1935-   ), XII (1946), 228-33.

ants of the people, were responsible to the will of their states and therefore in voting should follow the instructions of their legislatures.[6]

The doctrine of instruction was elaborated by the legislature of Virginia in 1812 during the course of a controversy with the state's senators over instructions for them to vote against the recharter of the Bank of the United States. One of the Virginia senators, Richard Brent, refused to obey this order; the other, William Branch Giles, acquiesced although he denied the right of mandatory legislative instruction. Thereupon, the legislature adopted a set of resolutions written by Benjamin Watkins Leigh, a young representative from Petersburg, which censured the conduct of both senators. This able document, after reviewing the history of the practice of instruction in England, asserted that it was the indubitable right of the legislature to instruct the state's senators in Congress on all points, either constitutional or political, and that the senators were bound to obey or resign.[7] Likewise, John Taylor of Caroline vigorously affirmed the right of instruction in the sixth section of his *An Inquiry into the Principles and Policy of the Government of the United States* (1814). In approving this work Jefferson wrote to Taylor that "it settles unanswerably the right of instructing representatives, and their duty to obey."[8]

During the decade of the 1830's a violent struggle arose between Whigs and the Jackson party over the question of the legislative instruction of senators. The exultantly victorious Jacksonians were disposed to use their power ruthlessly, without a sense of responsibility, and they found the doctrine of instruction a ready instrument at hand for their purposes. The conservative Whigs, on the other hand, were cast in the role of defender of minority rights and upholders of the federal Con-

---

[6] E. S. Maclay (ed.), *Journal of William Maclay, United States Senator from Pennsylvania, 1789-1791* (New York, 1890), 193, 220, 399-400.

[7] "The Right of Instruction. Preamble and Resolutions," February 20, 1812, in Virginia General Assembly, *House Journal*, 1834-1835, Doc. No. 9, p. 6.

[8] P. L. Ford (ed.), *The Works of Thomas Jefferson* (12 vols., New York, 1904-1905), XI, 528. John Taylor argued in favor of instruction of representatives by districts. See John Taylor, *An Inquiry into the Principles and Policy of the Government of the United States,* ed. by Roy F. Nichols (New Haven, 1950), 364-70.

stitution, which they thought were threatened by the practice of instruction. The dramatic struggle which occurred over this issue provided the backdrop for a remarkable display of moral courage and independence of thought by certain southern senators, notably Willie P. Mangum, John Tyler, and Benjamin Watkins Leigh. It illustrated the fact that strong conservatives do at times advance the cause of liberalism.

The immediate occasion for the great debate over the right of senatorial instruction in the decade of the 1830's was the bitter controversy between the Jacksonians and the Whigs over the removal of the deposits from the Second Bank of the United States and over the expunging of the censure of the President by the Senate for this action. On February 10, 1834, the Whig majority in the Virginia legislature instructed the senators and requested the representatives from the state to use their best exertions to obtain the restoration of the deposits.[9] John Tyler favored this policy and obeyed orders, but William Cabell Rives, an ardent administration supporter, resigned rather than violate his convictions.[10] Promptly his place was filled by the election of Benjamin Watkins Leigh, a strong opponent of Jackson.[11]

On March 28 the Senate by a vote of 26 to 20 passed Henry Clay's resolution of censure of Jackson for ordering the removal of the deposits. Shortly after the passage of this rebuke of the

[9] *Congressional Debates,* 23 Cong., 2 Sess., 2840 (February 27, 1834). The Virginia instructions were presented to the United States House of Representatives by William Fitzhugh Gordon.

[10] Draft of letter of resignation to the General Assembly, February 22, 1834, in William Cabell Rives Papers (Division of Manuscripts, Library of Congress). In a letter to John T. Brown, December 5, 1834, Rives wrote that he did not resign to make up an issue before the people and the legislature but because the resolutions had instructed him to vote, not for a specific law, but for *"abstract declarations of principles or opinions"* which were contrary to his convictions. *Ibid.*

[11] John W. Murdaugh, a member of the Virginia legislature, described Leigh's hostility to Jackson as follows: "I met Mr. Leigh & Jno. Robertson yesterday, they are unceremonious in the use of their terms when speaking of his Majesty." Murdaugh also reveals the practice in this period of the instruction of state legislators by their constituents. He wrote to John N. Tazewell to oppose all attempts "to instruct me & my colleague to vote approval of the Proclamation or condemnation of nullification —I'll be D———d if I'll do either." Murdaugh to Tazewell, January 16, 1833, in Littleton W. Tazewell Papers (Southern Collection, University of North Carolina Library).

President, Senator Thomas Hart Benton announced that he would introduce a resolution to expunge the censure from the Senate journal. Furthermore, a bitter Jacksonian protagonist, Senator Isaac Hill of New Hampshire, on June 23 presented resolutions from his state legislature approving Jackson's course in the bank controversy, instructing the senators to vote for an expunging resolution, and requesting Senator Samuel Bell to resign since he misrepresented the opinions of a majority of his constituents.[12] It was a day when partisanship knew no bounds. Jackson's personality, his program, and his methods were as effective in polarizing men into Jackson haters and Jackson enthusiasts as were Franklin Roosevelt and the New Deal a hundred years later.

This violence of faction was demonstrated in North Carolina during the struggle to instruct the senators to vote for expunging. The chief Jackson foe in North Carolina was Senator Willie P. Mangum, who until the emergence of the nullification and bank controversies had been a supporter of the President. On December 22, 1833, he wrote to Governor David L. Swain: "The only check to an absolute power as that in Russia is found in the Senate. The policy of the man in power is to destroy that body in public opinion. Every other branch of the Govt. is unquestionably and almost unqualifiedly subservient to the will and passions of one man—or to speak more truly to the will and passions of a cabal that gives a decided direction to the Executive."[13] This "man worship" of Jackson infuriated the Whigs. James Whitaker of Franklin County, North Carolina, wrote to Mangum that there were many people in his county "who seem to think that Andrew Jackson can do no rong [sic]."[14] Much of Jackson's power, Mangum observed, was due to the belief that he was invincible. Judge William Gaston, one of the greatest of the North Carolina Whigs, wrote gloomily to Mangum deploring "our thralldom to corrupt and factious misrule,"

[12] Cong. Debates, 23 Cong., 1 Sess., 1813 (March 28, 1834), 2061-62 (June 23, 1834).
[13] Willie P. Mangum to David L. Swain, December 22, 1833, in Willie P. Mangum Papers (Division of Manuscripts, Library of Congress).
[14] James Whitaker to Mangum, June 13, 1834, ibid.

which he attributed to a combination of popular infatuation, the discipline of party, and the bribes of office.[15]

On November 28, 1834, Dr. John Potts threw a firebrand into the legislature by introducing resolutions asserting the right of instruction and instructing the senators to vote for expunging. In the rough and tumble of debate which followed, some Whigs maintained that the legislature did not possess the right of instruction but that this power belonged only to the people in their sovereign capacity, acting through a specially elected convention. Hugh McQueen of Chatham County introduced a resolution that the people "possess the right of instructing our Senators on questions of national policy connected with their own immediate interest and not upon questions of constitutional law."[16] Senators, he held, should be allowed discretion in deciding on the constitutionality of bills before Congress.

The strongest speech made against the resolutions for instructing the senators to expunge was delivered on December 17 by William A. Graham. Graham was an outstanding leader of the North Carolina Whigs, later to be United States senator, Secretary of the Navy, and vice-presidential candidate of the Whig party. At no point in the speech did he challenge the right of instruction, but he argued against its expediency and justice. His main contentions were that the alarming exercise of executive power by Jackson threatened the independence of the Senate, that Congress had a constitutional right to censure the President, and that it would be futile to mutilate the journal of the Senate. He opposed the instruction of Senator Mangum, for it would make him violate his conscience in revoking his honest opinion as to the preservation of the Constitution.[17]

Notwithstanding, the resolutions to instruct Mangum (the

[15] William Gaston to Mangum, December 3, 1834, *ibid*. At this same period the Virginia Whigs were expressing similar sentiments. Hugh Mercer of Fredericksburg condemned "the glaring usurpations of the Federal Executive over laws & Constitutions" and declared that "this baneful spirit of party will soon or later dissolve the union unless put down." Hugh Mercer to Littleton W. Tazewell, January 20, 1834, in Tazewell Papers.

[16] North Carolina General Assembly, *Senate and House Journals*, 1834–1835, p. 83.

[17] Raleigh *Register and North Carolina Gazette*, January 27, 1835.

other senator, Bedford Brown, was a Jacksonian and needed no instruction) passed the House of Commons December 11 and the Senate December 27. The vote in the House of Commons asserting the right of instruction was 99 to 28, but the resolution instructing Mangum was carried by the narrow margin of 69 to 57 votes.[18] Graham declared that the Jacksonian majority were first inspired to begin the move for instruction by their success in re-electing Bedford Brown over the Whig candidate, Governor David L. Swain, which gave them full confidence.[19] The Whig newspapers, the Raleigh *Register* and the Raleigh *Star,* printed speeches of Graham, John Branch, and Mr. Fleming of Burke County against the resolutions of instruction and protested against the man-worship of Jackson by the party representing King Numbers.[20] After the Whigs were defeated on the instruction issue they tried to discredit the instructions by maintaining that the state senators who voted for the resolutions came from counties containing a minority of the population of the state by the federal ratio. The Jacksonian *North-Carolina Standard,* on the other hand, maintained that this Whig calculation was insulting to the people of the state, for it placed white freemen in the same scale with Negroes.[21] It strongly supported the right of instruction and accused Mangum and the Whigs of being aristocrats.

Mangum now had to make a decision whether to obey, resign, or refuse to heed the instructions. In the Mangum correspondence in the Library of Congress there are numerous manuscript resolutions from various meetings in the state urging him to disregard the instructions. Michael Holt, the pioneer textile manufacturer, wrote, "I hope you will not be drove so easily."[22] Only one prominent man, Burton Craige of Rowan County, advised him to resign, on the ground that public

[18] North Carolina General Assembly, *Senate and House Journals,* 1834-1835, pp. 188, 189.
[19] William A. Graham to Mangum, December 8, 1834, in William A. Graham Papers (North Carolina Department of Archives and History).
[20] Raleigh *Register and North Carolina Gazette,* December 2, 16, 23, 1834, January 27, 1835.
[21] Raleigh *North-Carolina Standard,* January 9, 1835.
[22] Michael Holt to Mangum, December 13, 1834, in Mangum Papers.

opinion sanctioned the right of instruction and that it would be politically expedient to take such a course and seek to change the composition of the legislature in the summer election, which he predicted would result in his re-election.[23] Among his correspondents was John Chavis, a free Negro, who had taught Mangum in a white private school. Chavis bitterly opposed both expunging and the abolitionists.[24]

In two letters to William A. Graham, December 16 and 17, Mangum revealed the inner conflict of his mind over the dilemma presented by the instructions. He declared that were he to consult his pride or his desire to recover his wrecked popularity he would resign instantly. However, regarding the Senate as the only barrier to the virtually absolute power of the Executive, he believed that if he resigned he would give countenance to the perversion of the spirit of the Constitution. The doctrine of instruction, he pointed out, was being used to reduce office in the Senate to a mere tenancy at will and by mining and sapping to convert the Senate to a less stable branch of the legislature than the House of Representatives. If he yielded to the popular infatuation, he would be lacking in moral courage. Therefore, he announced that he had no intention to resign to the present legislature.[25]

In addition to this high moral ground he gave a political reason for refusing to resign: "If I resign Jackson will be able to command the Senate in the *next* Congress—if I stand firmly the opposition will continue in the ascendancy in the *next* Congress."[26] He observed that Senators Gabriel Moore of Alabama and John Black of Mississippi would probably be placed in the same predicament in which he was and that his course would be decisive of their action. They had declared to him that it would be impossible for them to withstand the storm if he yielded. On March 3, 1835, in presenting the instructions of the North Carolina legislature to the Senate, he announced that he

[23] Burton Craige to Mangum, January 21, 1835, *ibid.*
[24] John Chavis to Mangum, April 4, 1836, February 1, 1837, *ibid.*
[25] Mangum to Graham, December 16, 17, 1834, in Graham Papers.
[26] *Id.* to *id.*, December 17, 1834, *ibid.*

would disregard them. He maintained that the legislature had no right to require him to become the instrument of his own degradation.[27]

The Alabama resolutions instructing the senators to vote for expunging, presented by Senator William R. King on January 28, 1835, touched off an acrimonious debate in the Senate on the subject. A month previously Mangum had written: "Gov. [Senator] Moore of Ala. has this morning recd intelligence of the resolutions having passed the Ala. legislature by so large a majority that the firmness of his friends at home is much shaken; & he in turn is so deeply shaken in his purpose that I think his resignation at the close of this session exceedingly probable."[28] Mangum expressed the gloomy thought that if there should be a general yielding by the Whig senators, "the power of resistance in the Senate would be lost and it will settle practically the Constitution in the South." When Senator King, a Jacksonian, introduced the resolutions of his state in the Senate, and announced that he felt bound to obey them, his colleague, Gabriel Moore, refused to obey. Although Moore acknowledged the right of instruction by the legislature on all questions of policy and the obligation of the senator to obey, he declared that on subjects involving constitutional questions he felt himself not bound by instructions but "by higher and paramount obligations due to his conscience."[29] King yielded to Benton the honor of introducing the expunging resolution, which the latter did on February 18.[30] Calhoun, Clay, George Poindexter of Mississippi, Leigh, and Alexander Porter of Louisiana made bitter attacks on these resolutions which they regarded as stultifying the Senate.

In Virginia the storm center in the fight over instruction and expunging was Benjamin Watkins Leigh. The Virginia legislature was scheduled to choose a senator for the regular term of six years early in 1835, and Leigh was the candidate of the

[27] *Cong. Debates,* 23 Cong., 2 Sess., 722 (March 3, 1835).
[28] Mangum to Graham, December 28, 1834, in Graham Papers.
[29] *Cong. Debates,* 23 Cong., 2 Sess., 256 (January 28, 1835).
[30] Thomas Hart Benton, *Thirty Years' View . . . from 1820 to 1850* (2 vols., New York, 1854), I, 524-50.

Whigs. The Democrats, under the lead of the veteran editor, Thomas Ritchie of the Richmond *Enquirer,* engaged in a feverish campaign to defeat Leigh and restore Rives by starting a movement in the counties to instruct their representatives in the legislature to defeat the aristocrat, Leigh.[31] Leigh won by the narrow margin of 85 to 81 votes in a joint ballot of both houses of the legislature. The administration Democrats claimed that Rives had been defeated by the flagrant violation of instructions. Some representatives, they charged, ignored the mandate of a majority of signatures of voters in the county by "swelling" the number of voters and then claiming that the list of signatures did not represent a majority.[32]

It is surprising that a man of Leigh's haughty personality could win high office in Virginia, for he was never popular, particularly in western Virginia.[33] Small in stature, "of striking manly beauty, with hair of silky, soft, chestnut brown, floating in curls," and gray eyes, he was distinctly a patrician in appearance. His voice was "soft, clear, flute-like . . . a murmuring music," and his mannerisms, according to Henry A. Wise, always excited sympathy for his infirmity, a short leg, for which he compensated by wearing a cork on the sole of his shoe.[34] Leigh was a man of commanding intellect, a very able lawyer, cultivated, and master of a style "equal to that of the Elizabethan age of English literature."[35] In the Virginia constitutional convention of 1829-1830 he had been one of the leaders of the conservatives. Working for the selfish economic interests of the

[31] State Senator Thomas P. Atkinson resigned December 26, 1834, because he could not conscientiously obey instructions of the people of Mecklenburg and Halifax counties to aid in the elevation to the United States Senate of Rives, "an avowed advocate of the Proclamation and Protest." Virginia General Assembly, *Senate Journal,* 1834-1835, p. 39. See also H. H. Simms, *The Rise of the Whigs in Virginia, 1824-1840* (Richmond, 1929), 94.

[32] Alex. Brown to Rives, January 9, 1835; Jno. L. Anderson to Rives, January 30, 1835; A. B. Davies to Rives, February 6, 1835, in Rives Papers.

[33] For a brief biographical account of Leigh, published two years after his death, see *Southern Literary Messenger* (Richmond, 1838-1864), XVII (1851), 123-27, 148-49.

[34] Henry A. Wise, *Seven Decades of the Union* (Philadelphia, 1876), 139-42.

[35] Quoted by Claude G. Bowers, *The Party Battles of the Jackson Period* (Boston, 1922), 321.

eastern slaveholders, he had opposed granting fair representation in the legislature to the West and the expansion of the suffrage. During the convention he had made a statement which caused him to be burned in effigy in the West and which plagued him in his later political career. He compared the farmers beyond the Blue Ridge to peasantry who occupied the same position in Virginia's economy as the slaves of the East, and he boldly asserted that those who depended on their daily labor for subsistence could never enter into political affairs.[36] Indeed, he looked with disdain upon the Jackson rabble, its electioneering methods, its elevation of mediocre men into office, and its disregard of constitutions.

The Democrats ardently wished to retire this exponent of aristocratic doctrines from his office as senator. Their victory in the spring elections of 1835 gave them control of the legislature. In the following February they used their recently acquired majority to force through the legislature resolutions instructing the senators, Tyler and Leigh, to vote for Benton's expunging measure. Declaring that it was the solemn duty of the legislature "to re-assert" the right of instruction, they passed the resolution declaratory of the principle of instruction by a vote of 114 to 14 in the House of Delegates.[37] Governor Littleton W. Tazewell, however, refused to forward the instructions to Virginia's senators on the ground that they were "a palpable violation of the Constitution."[38]

Both Tyler and Leigh were uncompromisingly opposed to carrying out the instructions of the legislature, which were really designed to vacate their offices and make way for the election of Jackson men. Most Whigs desired that the two senators should act in unity, but Tyler and Leigh chose different courses in responding to the legislative mandate. According to Leigh, Senator William C. Preston of South Carolina, a native Virginian,

[36] Charles H. Ambler, *Sectionalism in Virginia from 1776 to 1861* (Chicago, 1910), Chap. V; Simms, *Rise of the Whigs in Virginia,* 38-39.

[37] Virginia General Assembly, *House Journal,* 1835-1836, p. 111.

[38] Rebecca S. Luttrell, "The Campaign to Expunge the Resolution of Censure, 1834-1842" (M.A. thesis, University of North Carolina). See also Charles H. Ambler, *Thomas Ritchie: A Study in Virginia Politics* (Richmond, 1913), 178.

jealous because of "a notion he has that there is some rivalry between us as to reputation for oratory," began an intrigue to persuade Tyler to resign and thus discredit Leigh, who had no intention of resigning.[39] In this crisis the Whig leaders gave him conflicting advice. John Hampden Pleasants, powerful editor of the Richmond *Whig,* urged him to resign for political expediency.[40] The Washington *Globe,* spokesman for Jackson, insinuated that a motive for Tyler's resignation was to offer "a small oblation in order to be candidate for Vice President."[41]

Tyler was so devoted to consistency of political conduct that at times he turned a virtue into a vice.[42] The fact that he had in 1811 introduced a motion to censure the Virginia senators for their cavalier attitude to legislative instructions had great weight with him on this occasion. On February 19, 1836, he sent his resignation to the legislature. His letter reaffirmed his belief in the right of legislative instruction. Since he could not obey the instruction to vote for expunging without in his opinion violating the Constitution, he felt obliged to offer his resignation. He declared that he would not resign for every difference of opinion between himself and the legislature but that he would not hold office for an hour against the settled wishes of his constituents. He observed, however, that the right of instruction might degenerate into an engine of faction, an instrument of the outs to get in office.[43] Tyler's resignation gave the Jackson men in the legislature the opportunity to return Rives to the Senate on March 3, 1836.

Seven months before the legislature had passed the resolutions of instruction, Leigh had anticipated the event and had determined neither to obey nor resign. "I will not be instructed

[39] Leigh to Littleton W. Tazewell, February 18, 1836, in Tazewell Papers. Henry A. Wise offered another explanation for the refusal of Leigh to resign, namely that Leigh had earlier advised Mangum not to resign. Wise, *Seven Decades,* 140.

[40] Lyon G. Tyler, *The Letters and Times of the Tylers* (2 vols., Richmond, 1884-1885), I, 525-27.

[41] Washington *Globe,* March 1, 1836.

[42] Oliver P. Chitwood, *John Tyler, Champion of the Old South* (New York, 1939), Chap. X.

[43] Virginia General Assembly, *House Journal,* 1835-1836, pp. 171-75; and Doc. No. 49.

out of my seat," he wrote Tyler. "I will not obey instructions which shall require me to vote for a gross violation of the Constitution."[44] After the instructions arrived, he wrote to Tazewell: "I have refrained from all correspondence with the members of our Assembly; because I was resolved that no man should be committed, in any way, to share my fate and sacrifice their [sic] political hopes by sustaining me."[45] The Richmond Enquirer taunted the political-minded Whigs for changing their opinions in regard to obeying instructions. The editor of the Richmond Whig, it observed, belonged to the Resigning School now; with an eye on the polls in April, he was eager for Leigh to resign.[46]

On March 2 Leigh wrote a letter to the legislature explaining his recalcitrant position on obeying instructions. He announced that although he adhered to the right of instruction as stated by the Virginia resolutions of 1812 of which he himself had been the author, he had stipulated in those resolutions that a senator was not bound to obey instructions which required him to violate the Constitution or commit an act of moral turpitude. He could not vote for the expunging resolution, for he regarded it as a clear violation of the Constitution. At the same time he believed that his duty forbade him to resign. The real motive, he observed, behind the instructions was to instruct him out of his seat in the Senate. If he yielded, he would aid in the establishment of a pernicious practice by which the tenure of the senatorial term of office would be changed from six years to tenure at the pleasure of the legislature. The doctrine which the Jacksonian party wished to impose, he declared, was that the senator "has no right to exercise his own judgment at all, or consult his own conscience; he is not in this case a moral agent."[47] The abuse of the right of instruction, he also pointed out, would give a President who was checked by senatorial opposition an incentive to intervene in state politics and by

[44] Tyler, Letters and Times of the Tylers, I, 523.

[45] Leigh to Littleton W. Tazewell, February 18, 1836, in Tazewell Papers.

[46] Richmond Enquirer, March 3, 1836.

[47] Virginia General Assembly, House Journal, 1835-1836, pp. 186-94; and Doc. No. 50.

using the patronage to secure the removal of his opponents in the Senate.

Leigh realized that it would be expedient for him to resign since most Virginians believed in the right of instruction. Nevertheless, he felt that he must "signalize his resistance to unconstitutional instructions" by remaining at his post in the Senate.[48] Thus he deliberately sacrificed his political career to maintain his principles inviolate. On April 4 he made a powerful speech in the Senate against the adoption of the expunging resolution and the surrender to party spirit. Three months later he resigned for personal reasons but reaffirmed his views on instruction. On December 31 the legislature condemned Leigh's letter of March 2 as "sophistical and unsatisfactory" and reasserted that it was the duty of a senator to obey instruction or resign.[49] After Leigh's defiance of popular opinion on this occasion, he never afterwards held political office except from 1839 to 1841 when he served as reporter of the Supreme Court of Appeals in Virginia.

The fate of the Whig senators in the South who opposed Jackson in the expunging controversy was far from happy. Senator Willie P. Mangum resigned his seat in November, 1836, after North Carolina had elected another Democratic legislature.[50] Alexander Porter, Whig senator from Louisiana, who had delivered a long speech against expunging, followed a somewhat similar course by resigning voluntarily in 1836 after a Democratic legislature had been elected.[51] The bitter, vituperative George Poindexter of Mississippi was defeated for reelection by Robert J. Walker. The legislature of Alabama tried to recall Gabriel Moore by passing resolutions requesting him to resign because of his opposition to Jackson policies, but he refused to do so, filling out his term until 1837.[52]

[48] *Ibid.*, Doc. No 50, pp. 8-9.

[49] *Ibid.*, 256-57.

[50] For Mangum's career as a Whig leader, see Joseph G. deR. Hamilton, *Party Politics in North Carolina, 1835-1860* (Durham, 1916), 32-33, 41-42.

[51] Wendell H. Stephenson, *Alexander Porter, Whig Planter of Old Louisiana* (Baton Rouge, 1934), 97-100.

[52] *Niles' Weekly Register* (Baltimore, 1811-1849), XLVII (January 10, 1835), 317.

The fight of the anti-Jackson senators against legislative instruction to expunge the censure of the President was a powerful force in the growth of the Whig party in the South.[53]

The use of the doctrine of legislative instruction was not confined to the southern states. Both New Jersey and Ohio instructed their senators to support Jacksonian policies, but Senators Samuel L. Southard and Thomas Ewing from those states proved "recreant" to the doctrine of obedience to instruction. The legislature of New York on January 26, 1835, ordered the senators from that state to vote for expunging the censure of Jackson in the manner indicated by the Virginia legislature, namely, "by causing black lines to be drawn around the resolution in the original manuscript journal, and these words plainly written across the face of the said resolution and entry: 'Expunged by order of the senate of the United States.'"[54] The Vermont legislature two years later instructed the senators and requested the representatives from the state to present antislavery resolutions to Congress and to work toward their fulfillment.[55]

The practice of instructions in the 1830's constituted a standing invitation to the President to intervene in state politics and purge his opponents, as was illustrated in the history of instruction in Tennessee. Senator Hugh Lawson White was conscientiously opposed to expunging although he was willing to vote to repeal or rescind the Senate vote of censure without mutilating the Senate journal. Accordingly, when a Jackson supporter, Joseph C. Guild, introduced a resolution to instruct the senators to vote to expunge, the friends of Judge White, regarding this resolution as an effort to expunge Judge White

[53] Professor A. C. Cole in his study of *The Whig Party in the South* (Washington, 1913) devotes little attention to the significance of the expunging controversy in developing the Whig party in the South; for recent studies, see Paul Murray, *The Whig Party in Georgia, 1825-1853* (Chapel Hill, 1948), and Clement Eaton, *A History of the Old South* (New York, 1949), Chap. XIII.

[54] J. M. Mathews and C. A. Berdahl, *Documents and Readings in American Government* (New York, 1930), 324.

[55] United States Congress, *Senate Journal*, 25 Cong., 2 Sess., 144.

from his seat in the Senate, bitterly opposed it.[56] President Jackson urged his lieutenants in the state to promote meetings in the counties for the purpose of instructing the representatives to the legislature to vote for instructions to the senators to expunge. The "Old Hero" did not scruple to draft resolutions instructing the Tennessee senators to vote for expunging and to send them to Governor William Carroll to present to the legislature.[57] Thus he hoped to prevent the re-election of Senator White, who had become independent of executive dictation. But the legislature tabled the instructing resolutions and later re-elected White.[58]

The practice of instructions proved to be a double-edged sword. In January, 1838, the Whig majority in the Tennessee legislature, for example, tried to drive the old Jackson warhorse, Felix Grundy, from his seat in the Senate by instructing him to vote against the Sub-Treasury scheme of Van Buren.[59] Grundy turned the tables on his opponents, however, by obeying instructions and throwing the responsibility of his act upon the legislature.[60] In a delightful letter of irony, written February 6, 1838, he observed "You, by your instructions, have taken upon yourselves the responsibility of the vote I am required to give, and I am relieved from it. The people will look to you as the principal and to me merely as the agent, in performing an act expressly required by those in whom I recognize the right to instruct."[61] During the next year the Democrats won control of the legislature and instructed the Whig senators, Hugh Lawson White and Ephraim H. Foster (Grundy had in the meantime resigned

[56] The Nashville *Republican*, February 25, 1836, declared that Jackson used his frank freely to influence the adoption of expunging resolutions. The Nashville *Union*, September 18, 30, and November 24, 1835, on the other hand, urged the legislature to pass the instructing resolutions. See also J. C. Guild, *Old Times in Tennessee* (Nashville, 1878), 145-54.

[57] Andrew Jackson to James K. Polk, August 13, 1835, in John Spencer Bassett (ed.), *Correspondence of Andrew Jackson* (6 vols., Washington, 1926-1935), V, 18.

[58] Joseph H. Parks, *John Bell of Tennessee* (Baton Rouge, 1950), 109-11.

[59] Tennessee General Assembly, *House Journal*, 1837-1838, pp. 402-403, 515-18; the resolution passed January 23 by a vote of 39 to 19.

[60] Joseph H. Parks, *Felix Grundy, Champion of Democracy* (University, La., 1940), 309-17.

[61] *Niles' Weekly Register*, LIV (March 10, 1838), 20-21.

to become Attorney General of the United States), to vote for Van Buren's Sub-Treasury bill, in effect forcing them to resign. Foster resigned almost immediately after the passage of the instructing resolutions, and Grundy was re-elected to fill the vacancy. White, however, postponed his resignation until January 14, 1840, when the Sub-Treasury bill was introduced in the Senate. Thus, the doctrine of legislative instruction developed virtually into a form of recall of senators, anticipating the Progressive Movement for the recall in the early twentieth century.

The driving of such a venerable and eminent senator as Hugh Lawson White from his office by the instrument of instructions undoubtedly contributed toward discrediting its use in Tennessee. White was a republican of the old school, noted for his independence of mind and his incorruptible virtue. Although he sincerely believed in the right of the legislature to instruct and the obligation of a senator to obey or resign, he felt keenly that by the abuse of instructions he had been sacrificed on the altar of his principles. In the Senate he gave his "swan song" reaffirming his principles, and at a farewell dinner he bitterly condemned "that monster, party spirit," which had banished him from the service of his country because he would not recant his principles.[62] For thirty-eight years White had been in public service, and now his abrupt dismissal by the partisan use of instruction was shocking to many people in Tennessee who loved and respected him.

In the same year of White's instruction the Whig majority in the North Carolina legislature passed some resolutions hostile to Van Buren's administration and condemning the expunging resolution of 1837. The Democratic senators of the state, Bedford Brown and Robert Strange, refused either to carry out the

[62] The instructing resolutions were not presented by White until January 13, 1840; the resolutions and a brief summary of his farewell remarks are found in *Cong. Globe,* 26 Cong., 1 Sess., 116-17 (January 16, 1840); N. N. Scott (ed.), *A Memoir of Hugh Lawson White* (Philadelphia, 1856), 397; and L. P. Gresham, *The Public Career of Hugh Lawson White* (Nashville, 1945). See also Powell Moore, "James K. Polk: Tennessee Politician," in *Journal of Southern History,* XVII (1951), 502-503; C. G. Sellers, *James K. Polk, Jacksonian* (Princeton, 1957), 382-5.

will of the legislature or to resign. They declared that they regarded resolutions of the legislature which did not explicitly instruct them as advisory only.[63] Senator Henry Clay, on the other hand, maintained that the North Carolina senators should carry out the intent of the legislature without quibbling over technical terms. As for his own position, he stated that he supported the doctrine of instruction "as it stood in 1798," namely that the representative should vote in matters of expediency but not on questions of constitutionality in accordance with the will of his constituents.[64] Yet Clay's record on instructions was variable and inconsistent; he had advised the Kentucky representatives in Congress in 1825 to disregard their instructions and vote for John Quincy Adams for President. In 1842, shortly before he retired from the Senate, the House of Representatives of Kentucky instructed the Senators to vote for the repeal of the General Bankruptcy Law which had been recently enacted. Instead of following instructions, the great Whig Senator took the opposite course, making a speech in favor of retaining the law; but Congress repealed it, nevertheless.[65]

One of the most independent Senators from the slave states who defied legislative instructions was Thomas Hart Benton, Senator from Missouri from 1821 to 1851. Benton had many objectionable traits—he was egotistic, bombastic, and given to long and boring speeches in the Senate—but he was courageous, devoted to the interests of the West and the common man, and opposed to the extension of slavery into the free territory of the West.[66] In 1834-7 he led the fight in Congress to expunge the censure of President Jackson from the Senate Journal, during which he upheld the right of instruction.[67] Yet when the two-edged sword of instruction was turned against him, as in 1849 after the legislature had passed the "Jackson Resolutions"

[63] *Cong. Globe*, 25 Cong., 3 Sess., 109-12 (January 14, 1839).

[64] Calvin Colton, *The Life, Correspondence, and Speeches of Henry Clay* (6 vols., New York, 1864), VI, 134-38.

[65] *Journal of the House of Representatives of the Commonwealth of Kentucky*, 1841-2 (Frankfort, 1841), 61-63; "On a General Bankrupt Law," in Senate Jan. 17, 1842; Colton, *Clay*, VI, 296-300; Clement Eaton, *Henry Clay and the Art of American Politics* (Boston, 1957), 151.

[66] See William N. Chambers, *Old Bullion Benton* (Boston, 1956).

[67] Benton, *Thirty Years' View*, I, 524, 529, 531.

ordering the Missouri Senators to support the extreme pro-
Southern position of Calhoun on the extension of slavery into
the territories, he refused to obey.[68] A free-soiler by conviction,
he could not obey these instructions without violating his conscience. Instead, he appealed to the people of Missouri to
support his position. In a strenuous campaign across Missouri,
he denounced the "Jackson Resolutions" and the pro-slavery
group headed by Claiborne F. Jackson and Senator David
Atchison, who he believed were trying to instruct him out of
his seat in the Senate. His defiance of instruction and his brave
fight against slavery extension, however, was not only in vain,
but the legislature also selected a pro-slavery Whig to take his
place in the Senate.

Mandatory legislative instruction was practised most frequently in the Southern states, but it was also exercised on
occasions by Northern legislatures. In 1834 James Buchanan
expressed a view of the binding nature of legislative instruction
in a letter to a committee of the Pennsylvania legislature in
which he said that in voting contrary to his judgment, "I act
merely as their [the legislature's] agent. The responsibility is
theirs, not mine."[69] Four years later the Pennsylvania legislature instructed him as Senator to vote against the Sub-Treasury
Bill, which he had previously sponsored. He could not disobey,
for he had publicly stated that the right of instruction was a
fundamental article in the creed of the Democratic Party to
which he belonged. To those friends who urged him to disregard these instructions on the ground that they did not represent popular opinion, he replied that if a Senator should look
behind his instructions and act according to his own opinion of
the popular will, the right of instruction would at once be
abandoned.[70] But he temporized by securing a postponement
of a decision on the bill.

[68] *Congressional Globe*, 31 Cong. 1 Sess. Vol. XXI, Part I, 97-98. Jan. 8, 1850,
Resolutions of Instruction presented by Senator David Atchison. Benton replied that
they did not represent the will of the people.

[69] Buchanan to Jacob Kern *et al.*, Dec. 22, 1834, George T. Curtis, *Life of James
Buchanan* (New York, 1883), I, 229-31; Philip S. Klein, *President James Buchanan,
a Biography* (University Park, Pa., 1962), 102.

[70] John Bassett Moore (ed.), *The Works of James Buchanan* (New York, 1960),
III, 380-385.

Another significant instance of legislative instruction by a Northern state was the instruction of Senator Lewis Cass by the Michigan legislature in 1849 to support a Wilmot Proviso law. Cass was widely known as the champion of popular sovereignty and in 1848 he had been the candidate of the Democratic party for president. He strongly protested against this instruction, which if he obeyed would cause him to violate his principles. He believed in obeying instructions, notwithstanding, if they were fairly administered; accordingly, he offered to resign if he could not reconcile his duty to follow his conscientious scruples with obeying instructions.[71] Shortly afterwards, he was released from this dilemma by the legislature's rescinding its instructions and leaving him free to vote for the Compromise of 1850. Five years later, the problem again arose when the legislature under the dominance of the Republicans issued a peremptory set of instructions ordering the Michigan Senators to vote for any bill prohibiting slavery in the federal territories or repealing the Fugitive Slave Act.[72] This time, declaring that the passage of such laws would lead to "the dissolution of the Confederacy," Cass defied the instructions of a Republican majority in the legislature.[73]

The doctrine of the right of instruction was subjected to a devastating criticism by John Bell of Tennessee in a speech before the Senate, February 23, 1858. Bell had just received instructions from the Tennessee legislature disapproving of his vote four years before against the Kansas-Nebraska Bill (he and Sam Houston were the only Southern Senators who had voted against the bill), virtually requesting him to resign, and instructing the Tennessee Senators to vote for the admission of Kansas under the Lecompton Constitution. Bell refused to obey instructions and maintained that such a practice had long ago been discarded by the Whig party. He traced the origin of the practice of instruction to the period of the Confederation, when delegates to

[71] *Appendix to the Congressional Globe,* XXII, Part I, 74 (Jan., 1850).

[72] Resolutions of Michigan legislature, presented by Senator Stuart, Feb. 5, 1855. *Congressional Globe.* 33 Cong. 2 Sess., XXX, 555-556.

[73] See Andrew C. McLaughlin, *Lewis Cass* (Boston, 1899); Frank B. Woodford, *Lewis Cass, the Last Jeffersonian* (New Brunswick, 1950).

Congress were regarded as ambassadors. He declared that legislative instruction had no warrant in the Constitution and that it was resorted to chiefly as "an engine of party and to promote party ends." Senators, he argued, did not represent the legislatures but the people, and therefore they were no more responsible to the fluctuating opinions of factions in control of legislatures than was the President to the electoral college.[74]

After the Civil War the doctrine of mandatory legislative instruction became obsolete. The last notable practice of it occurred in 1878 when the Mississippi legislature instructed the Senators from that state to vote for the Bland Silver Act. On February 15 of that year Lucius Quintus Cincinnatus Lamar, a man of imposing presence, darkly handsome, eloquent, and aristocratic, arose in the Senate and had the chief clerk read the Mississippi resolutions of instruction, which he announced he should disregard.[75] While he was a professor at the University of Mississippi, he explained, he had taught his students to respect truth and courage; he himself must abide by these precepts and not shrink from his duty. The Silver Bill created a dishonest dollar and he must vote against it as a matter of preserving "unsullied the spotless legacy of Southern honor." To his wife he wrote: "The Legislature has instructed me to vote for the Silver Bill. I cannot do it; I had rather quit politics forever."[76] If he followed the instructions of the legislature against his judgment, he maintained, he would be throwing away the fruit of his previous preparation and study of the subject and and become merely an echo of current opinion.[77]

Jefferson Davis, whom Lamar admired and whose leadership he had followed for so many years, took a different view of the doctrine of legislative instruction. In a letter published in

[74] *Congressional Globe,* 35 Cong., 1 Sess. 804-806, Feb. 23, 1858.

[75] *Congressional Record,* 45 Cong. 2 Sess. Vol. VII, 1061 Senate, Feb. 15, 1878.

[76] Edward Mayes, *Lucius Q. C. Lamar, His Life, Times, and Speeches. 1825-1893* (Nashville, 1896); 347; 333; see also W. A. Cate, *Lucius Q. C. Lamar, Secession and Reunion* (Chapel Hill, 1935).

[77] The then Senator John F. Kennedy in *Profiles in Courage* (New York, 1956), 142–150, cited Lamar's act in disobeying instructions as a distinguished example of political courage.

the Jackson (Miss.) *Clarion,* January 15, 1879, the former Confederate president stated his belief that legislative instructions
were mandatory on representatives. No representative of the
people, he held, "should assume that he had more wisdom than
the aggregate of his neighbors."[78] Here was an expression of
Jeffersonian faith in the judgment of the democratic majority
that was almost mystic in nature. Lamar and the old Whigs,
on the other hand, believed that the majority was subject to
transient passions and that the statesman should take the high
ground of acting for the permanent interests of the people
(yet in this instance he was probably wrong on the silver issue),
trusting that they would later recognize his action to have been
wise and just. In the case of Lamar, the people did vindicate his
courageous devotion to his principles in opposing the popular
will and through the legislature re-elected him to his seat in the
Senate.

The doctrine of mandatory legislative instruction, which had
arisen in the early republic, matured during the Jacksonian
period when the sovereignty of the people and state rights were
at their height. The concept of public office held by the Jacksonians regarded the representative as largely a transmitter of
the will of the people, a theory that was vigorously expressed
by Peter V. Daniel of Richmond in a letter to Van Buren, Sept.,
25, 1835. He criticized both Senators Tyler and Leigh for being
"upstart gentry who have dared to place themselves above the
people." He had only scorn for "the impudence of Leigh's
pretension of referring every thing to *his own sense of right
exclusively* whatever his constituents may order, or his statement
that altho he may *now* be condemned *futurity* will approve and
commend his acts."[79] Although in theory the doctrine of instruction seemed to be a noble expression of representative
government, in actual practice it was subject to dangerous abuses
which thoroughly discredited it. Hezekiah Niles in 1834 pointed
out that the frequent use of instruction would render the

[78] Mayes, *Lamar,* 363-364.
[79] Peter V. Daniel to Martin Van Buren, Sept. 25, 1835. Van Buren Papers, MSS,
Library of Congress.

legislation of the country uncertain and would unsettle business and commerce.[80] Indeed, the partisan use of instruction in the 1830's caused thoughtful men to reflect upon the dangers of an unrestrained and irresponsible majority in a democracy. Later, Calhoun was to incorporate this distrust of a partisan majority in his theory of government.

Like the duel and virtually at the same time, the practice of legislative instruction disappeared from the political mores of the American people. One explanation of the passing of this highly democratic doctrine, Professor William E. Dodd has suggested, was the prevalence after the Civil War of the idea that election to office gave a property right in the office which a legislature could not take away by the exercise of repugnant instructions.[81] The adoption of the Seventeenth Amendment in 1913 gave a final blow to the venerable doctrine of instructions which had been transplanted from England. Nevertheless, long before that date the development of the Solid South rendered the practice of instructions below the Potomac an act of supererogation. With the passing of this political practice one of the serious threats to independent thought on the part of legislators was removed. The record of those Southern representatives who disobeyed instructions and followed their consciences forms a sober annotation to the history of freedom of thought in the Old South, a rubric written, not by liberals, but by conservatives who withstood the storm of unpopularity rather than sacrifice their political principles.

[80] *Niles' Weekly Register*, XLVII (Nov. 15, 1834), 61.
[81] William E. Dodd, "The Principle of Instructing United States Senators," *South Atlantic Quarterly*, I (October, 1902), 326-332; see also William S. Hoffman, "Willie P. Mangum and the Whig Revival of the Doctrine of Instructions," *Journal of Southern History*, XXII (August, 1956), 338-354, and Holman Hamilton, "Democratic Senate Leadership and the Compromise of 1850," *Mississippi Valley Historical Review*, XLI (December, 1954), 410.

CHAPTER XV

MEN OF INDEPENDENCE, 1860–1861

THE APOTHEOSIS of the will of the majority was never higher in the South than in the years between 1828 and 1861. A frontier fervor animated the axiom of Jacksonian democracy in this region that the people's will was sovereign and must prevail over all dissenters and all minorities. Only South Carolina under Calhoun's leadership denied it. Instead of trying to lead public opinion, the politicians sought to discover what was popular with the voters and then to follow it. Nevertheless, the Southern states produced a group of public men who put devotion to principle above their own private welfare.[1]

The tyranny of the majority in the American republic (which De Tocqueville had observed) was intensified in the South by the vigilante tradition.[2] This violation of civil liberties was institutionalized by the vigilance committee, which arose to deal with abolitionists lurking in the Southern states, persons who had committed atrocious crimes, and especially, suspected instigators of servile revolts. It flourished in the South not only because this region was much closer to the frontier than the Northeast, but because of the streak of violence in the regional character of the Southern people of this time. Governor Sam Houston aptly described this proneness to violence in a speech in 1860 when he was seeking to calm the secession fever in Texas; the Southerners, he said, were different from the Northerners, for they were "a fiery, impulsive people."[3] This was not a glib phrase, for the Southerners, individually and collectively, were inclined to violence, easily stirred to reach for the bowie knife or the dueling pistol and very susceptible to the oratory

---

[1] The politician, however, occupies a different position from that of the private citizen (Thoreau for example), and should be judged in the context of political reality.

[2] Clement Eaton, "Mob Violence in the Old South," *Mississippi Valley Historical Review*, XIX (Dec. 1942), 351-370.

[3] Marquis James, *The Raven, a Biography* (Indianapolis, 1929), 410.

of agitators and the fervid exhortations of fundamentalist preachers.

Because of the vigilante tradition the price of non-conformity in the Old South was often high. The men of independence of 1860-61 spoke against an ominous background, a legacy of the suppression of civil liberties. Furthermore, in 1860 public opinion in the slave states had recently been inflamed by the John Brown Raid. In the very year of the secession crisis the poise of the Southern people had been overthrown by alarming rumors of slave insurrections. Sam Houston discounted these rumors but he recognized their powerful impact upon Southern public opinion. "Terrible stories," he said, "are put afloat of arms discovered, your capital in flames, kegs of powder under houses, thousands of negroes engaged in insurrectionary plots, wells poisoned, and hundreds of bottles of strychnine found. Town after town has been reported in ashes, and by the time the report has been found to be false, some new story to keep up the public excitement has been invented. The people of the South have been filled with horror by these accounts. . . ."[4]

Accordingly, mob violence and vigilance committees sprang up at the slightest provocation below the Mason-Dixon line. Their flagrant disregard of civil liberties was sanctioned by the educated upper classes of Southern society and even by the constituted legal authorities who were sworn to uphold the orderly processes of law. Daniel R. Hundley, author of *Social Relations in Our Southern States,* educated at Harvard and the University of Virginia, was a prime example of upper class support of violence. In May 1861, he accepted membership on a Vigilance Committee of Triana in North Alabama that "elicited" testimony from frightened slaves of a "hellish insurrectionary plot" by severely whipping them. The committee hanged several Negroes, including a Negro preacher named Peter Mud, whose owner vainly tried to save him; it was more lenient with two white men suspected of tampering with the slaves, "an old English abolitionist, who, for lack of evidence, was sent to jail

[4] A. W. Williams and E. C. Baker (eds.), *The Writings of Sam Houston* (Austin, 1943), VIII, 156.

in Huntsville to await the future action of the committee," and Bob Williams, who was given until Christmas to settle up his affairs and leave the county.[5]

Men in high station were not exempt from the dictates of these illegal tribunals. Justice John Catron of the Supreme Court of the United States, a native of Tennessee, was driven from Nashville in 1861 by a Vigilance Committee because of his strong Union sentiments.[6] Certainly many judicious-minded Southerners condemned lynch law, but in a time of crisis or great public danger, a decided majority seemed to have approved of its use. The dormant, ever-present threat of mob action was undoubtedly an important force in suppressing independent minds who differed from the majority on emotional issues.

A potent economic force, the overwhelmingly agrarian nature of Southern society, also influenced Southerners toward a uniformity of mind. Horace Holley, commenting on the differences between the people of his native New England and those of the South, wrote home to his father: "The people of Tennessee are much like the Kentuckians, showing the same influences of slavery and of an agricultural interior. Commerce makes a different sort of population from agriculture."[7] Not only did the ways of agriculture tend to promote a homogeneity of thought on economic interests and of politics, but it strengthened the folk mores and the hold of tradition upon the Southern mind. Moreover, the economy of the South, with its lack of large cities and its use of slave labor, discouraged immigrants from coming into the region, bringing new ideas and a conflict of cultures.

Locality and social environment subtly sway the minds of most people to conformity. The great Southern liberal Thomas Jefferson, for example, from whom, of all his contemporaries, one might have expected philosophic detachment from local

[5] Diary of D. R. Hundley, May 18, 20, 21, 25, 1861. MS in Southern Collection, University of North Carolina; for an account of Hundley, see Blanche H. Weaver, "D. R. Hundley; Subjective Sociologist," *Georgia Review,* X (Summer, 1956), 222-234.

[6] *Dictionary of American Biography,* III, 577.

[7] Horace Holley to Luther Holley, Aug. 14, 1823. Horace Holley Letters, MSS, Transylvania College Library.

prejudices, became more and more "Southern" as he neared the end of his life. His attitude toward the expansion of slavery at the time of the Missouri Compromise was warped from his earlier liberalism by his distrust of the Northern politicians, who he thought were motivated by a drive for power.[8] In his old age he also became very prejudiced against Northern institutions of learning. To Joseph C. Cabell, who was associated with him in founding the University of Virginia, he lamented that the South was sending so many of its sons to the North for education, there "learning the lessons of anti-Missourianism." "These will return home, no doubt," he sarcastically observed, "deeply impressed with the sacred principles of our Holy Alliance of restrictionists." To another Virginian he wrote in the same year that the South was sending hundreds of its sons to Northern schools where they were "imbibing opinions and principles in discord with those of their own country [presumably the South]. This canker is eating on the vitals of our existence, and if not arrested at once, will be beyond remedy."[9] He was therefore concerned that the University of Virginia should open its doors as soon as possible.

New England had been stimulated to the development of new ways of thought and clashing ideas not only by a diversity of industry, but by the disintegration of Calvinism in that region. From the thralldom of Puritanism, Emerson, Thoreau, and the Transcendentalists in general had emerged in the 1830's to preach the doctrine of extreme individualism. In the Southern states, on the other hand, fundamentalism in religion grew firmer as the slavery controversy drove the region to a narrow Biblical defense of the peculiar institution. It also contributed powerfully to a wave of anti-intellectualism (not confined, however, to the Southern states) which the rise of Jacksonianism promoted in the political sphere. A striking manifestation of such anti-intellectualism was a suspicion of uni-

---

[8] Glover Moore, *The Missouri Controversy, 1819-1821* (Lexington, Ky., 1953), 253-256.

[9] Jefferson to Joseph C. Cabell, Jan. 31, 1821; to James Breckinridge, Feb, 15, 1821. Lipscomb, *Writings of Thomas Jefferson*, XV, 311, 315; see also Leonard W. Levy, *Jefferson and Civil Liberties, the Darker Side* (Cambridge, Mass., 1963), chap. 7.

380 FREEDOM OF THOUGHT IN THE OLD SOUTH

versities and of intellectual men among the devout. Dr. John Bolton of Baltimore expressed this feeling in a letter to a relative protesting against sending a young man to the University of Virginia. "I do believe," he wrote to Ann Harrison on July 16, 1838 (letter in the Brock Collection, Huntington Library), "Charlottesville to be the worst place he could be sent. That institution has always been tinctured with the immoral, irreligious opinions of its founder, who though a great statesman, was fearfully in error regarding these highest of all subjects and will have a dreadful account to settle with his maker for the destruction of his own Soul and of those who by going to this institution have been in a measure committed to his charge."

Moreover, the Romantic movement, which swept all America during this period, failed to have the effect in the South of developing individuality and independence of mind, as it did in Europe and the intellectual centers of the North. In the North it underlay the reform and humanitarian movements; below the Mason and Dixon line it took a different course, glorifying the slave-based society and the *status quo,* strengthening the cult of chivalry, exalting florid oratory that evaded reality, and limiting the natural freedom of women by idealizing them.[10]

The Romantic Movement in the South, far from encouraging unconventionality or variety in thought and taste, imposed a uniform taste for sentimental literature and for romantic styles of dress. Mrs. Chesnut's *Diary from Dixie* affords abundant evidence of the reign of sentimentality in the Confederacy. "Maggie Howell [sister of Mrs. Jefferson Davis]," she wrote, "says there is a girl in large hoops and a calico frock at every piano between Richmond and the Mississippi, banging on the out-of-tune thing and looking up into a man's face, singing that song [the sentimental "Lorena"]."[11] In Lamar County,

[10] See Rollin G. Osterweis, *Romanticism and Nationalism in the Old South* (New Haven, 1949), and William R. Taylor, *Cavalier and Yankee, the Old South and American National Character* (New York, 1961).

[11] Ben Ames Williams (ed.), *A Diary from Dixie by Mary Boykin Chesnut* (Boston, 1949), 304.

Texas, while Kate Stone and her family were refugeeing, Kate observed how all the women, even the cracker women, attempted to follow the romantic fashion of hoop skirts. "Nothing," she commented in her journal, "looks funnier than a woman walking around with an immense hoop, barefooted."[12]

The Southern sense of values, which emphasized the code of the gentleman, was also a force strengthening conformity of mind and conduct. "The southerner, himself," wrote Henry Benjamin Whipple in his journal "is different from the northerner in many striking particulars. He is more chivalrous, that is to say, he has more of that old English feeling common in the day of the feudal system and crusades."[13] Despite the artificiality of some of the provisions of the chivalric code, strong individuals such as Benjamin F. Perry of South Carolina and Henry Clay bowed to its dictates. A sophisticated society does not ordinarily condemn contradiction of opinion in conversation if it is not done dogmatically; but in the South one had to be cautious in contradicting a person or even in being too frank in criticism—such were regarded as the vices of New Englanders. To contradict a high-mettled Southerner was often to risk a duel—and death.

One of the most imperative compulsions to conformity in any society is the desire of people to be liked by their neighbors and associates; ostracism is a force that few people can withstand. The case of the Minor family in the Old South is an illustration of the terrible penalty incurred by holding to a different loyalty from that of one's neighbors. The Minors were a wealthy and aristocratic sugar and cotton planting family of Natchez. They not only opposed secession, but practised passive resistance against the Confederate government, refusing to buy Confederate bonds, volunteer for the Southern army, or co-operate with the Confederate government in burning their cotton when it seemed likely that it would fall into Federal hands. The chief of the clan was William J. Minor, an old-line

---

[12] John Q. Anderson (ed.), *Brockenburn, the Journal of Kate Stone, 1861-1868* (Baton Rouge, 1955), 225.

[13] Shippee (ed.), *Bishop Whipple's Southern Diary*, Dec. 12, 1843.

Whig, who ardently opposed the secession of Mississippi; his wife Rebecca was a former Philadelphian; of their three sons one was conscripted; another volunteered after succumbing to public pressure; and the third, John, defied public opinion and with his wife remained a Unionist throughout the war.

John Minor, a graduate of Harvard, had married a rich heiress. A gay pleasure-lover, he lived on his wife's fortune, spending his life in fox hunting, drinking, giving dinner parties, and reading literary works. He avoided military service by hiring the gardener of the estate to go as a substitute and he and his wife further alienated his friends and neighbors by entertaining Federal officers when ever they came into the vicinity. One cannot help but wonder to what extent selfishness and his Northern connections, rather than devotion to principle, played in his intransigent independence. Mrs. Minor testified before the Southern Claims Commission after the war when she was applying for damages to their plantations: "I was always an abolitionist at heart, but I am afraid not a philanthropist. I did not know how to set them [her numerous slaves] free without wretchedness to them, and utter ruin to myself, you know."[14] On account of their Unionism, she and her husband were ostracized; he died a few years after the war, a dissipated and despondent man. When he was urged to go North for medical attention he revealed the depth of his agony because of ostracism by replying that his treatment from his old friends and associates had been such that "he did not care whether he lived or died."[15]

An implement of great effectiveness in 1861 to force individuals to conform to the Southern consensus was the argument that the South must present a united front to its foe. When Stanislas Wrotnowski, who was to be elected Secretary of State in the restored government of Louisiana under Lincoln's ten per cent plan, was living in Baton Rouge, he came under the

---

[14] Catherine Minor claimed damages $64,155 but was allowed only $13,072. Frank W. Klingberg, *The Southern Claims Commission* (Berkeley, 1955), 112.

[15] Frank W. Klingberg, "The Case of the Minors: A Unionist Family within the Confederacy," *Journal of Southern History*, XIII (Feb. 1947), 29, 33.

suspicion of his neighbors and the townspeople because he did not employ slaves in his sugar refinery and on his plantation. This scholarly Pole, who had fought in the Polish Revolution of 1830 before emigrating to Louisiana, took the unpopular side of the Union during the secession crisis, with the result that his property was destroyed and his two sons had to flee to the woods.[16] Non-conformity to Southern views on slavery and to the secession cause was regarded as evidence of being a traitor to the section. Before the shooting war for Southern Independence began, a "cold war" against Northern "fanaticism" existed, somewhat like the situation that bred McCarthyism in the United States in the 1950's, both being stimulated by popular fear, the one of abolitionism, the other of communism. The pressure for a united front in 1861 was powerful enough to cause many original Unionists and Cooperationists to change their votes in the secession conventions.

In the secession crisis of 1860-61 many devices were used to intimidate or to pressure people into supporting the cause of Southern Independence. The Unionists were stigmatized as traitors to the South, "Submissionists," without a sense of honor, "Abolitionists," "Tories," and "Lincolnites." In South Carolina the blue cockade was worn by the young men to designate that they were secessionists, and those who did not wear this emblem were looked upon askance. In Memphis after Lincoln's election the Minute Men were organized, who paraded wearing black glazed caps painted "M.M." in red letters and carrying a flambeau; they pledged themselves to sustain the equality of Tennessee, or in case of failure to attain that objective, to unite with the Southern states to resist "the fanatical aggressive power of the North."[17] While the conventions were considering the question of secession, eloquent orators were dispatched as commissioners or ambassadors from state to state to urge that secession ordinances be adopted, and sensational telegrams were sent to influence wavering sentiment.

[16] *New York Times,* April 26, 1864. Reports from its New Orleans correspondent.
[17] *Constitution and By-Laws of the Minute Men of Memphis* (Memphis 1860), a pamphlet.

It is difficult to-day to comprehend the psychosis of the Southern mind that developed after the election of Lincoln, the Black Republican candidate, to the Presidency. James Louis Petigru, the Charleston Unionist, wrote to Edward Everett on October 28, 1860 that the people of South Carolina were "distempered to a degree that makes them to a calm and impartial observer real objects of pity—they are credulous to every whisper or suspicion about insurgents or incendiaries."[18] The contagion of the popular delusion, he observed, affected sober men such as Governor R. F. W. Allston and Dr. Francis Y. Porcher, the friend of Henry Clay.

Outstanding among the few independent individuals of consequence in the state who opposed the popular hysteria was Benjamin F. Perry of Greenville. The son of a New England merchant who had settled in the up country of South Carolina, he was disassociated from the plantation aristocracy of the lowlands. Though not college educated, he constantly sought to improve his mind; his diary is filled with accounts of his reading; in 1842, for example, he bought a fine edition of the novels of Scott and described *Ivanhoe* as "perhaps the Prince of novels;" in the same year he purchased $200 worth of books from Dr. Thomas Cooper's library at an auction.[19] In many respects he conformed to typical Southern attitudes and ideas, such as supporting slavery, opposing the protective tariff, accepting the code duello, and being very religious. On the other hand, as editor of the Greenville *Mountaineer* and *The Southern Patriot,* he displayed an independent mind and a courageous spirit by stoutly opposing the nullification movement and the disunion movement of 1850.

Perry's most courageous political act was his refusal to follow the South Carolina delegation in bolting from the Charleston Convention on April 30, 1861. On the following day he arose, an impressive, virile figure, well over six feet in height, to speak in behalf of preserving the unity of the Democratic party in

[18] James Petigru Carson, *Life, Letters, and Speeches of James Louis Petigru* (Washington, D. C., 1920), 360, 363.
[19] Journal of Benjamin F. Perry, June 5, July 24, 1835; Feb. 18, 1842.

order to save the Union. According to the report of the *Charleston Daily Courier,* he was greeted from the gallery by "a storm of hisses."[20] When the chairman ordered the galleries to be cleared, Perry insisted that the spectators be allowed to remain, for he wished them to hear what he had to say. He declared that he respected and admired the gallant Democrats of the North who had been fighting the South's battles and he hoped that the convention would give them a viable platform. He observed that the quarrel over the expansion of slavery in the territories was over an abstraction, a statement that was regarded as heresy in the Cotton Kingdom. Two weeks later he published a letter in the Columbia *South Carolinian* and the Charleston *Courier* in which he wrote of "the contagion of political excitement" and of "outside pressure" that was hard for men to resist, but he predicted that "the time may come when my creed and opinions will be found to savor more of truth and wisdom than they are now supposed to do."[21]

After Lincoln's election Perry braved the popular hysteria that followed in South Carolina to declare publicly that this event was no proper cause for secession. There was not a single Unionist newspaper in South Carolina in 1860, but Perry was able to get the Charleston *Courier,* owned by the Northerner Aaron Willington, to publish his article "Disunion", reasoning with the people of his state against disunion. He also spoke earnestly in his Congressional district against secession, but when he sought election as a delegate to the secession convention he was overwhelmingly defeated. After the fateful ordinance of secession was passed, however, he accepted the decision of the majority and became a loyal Confederate.[22]

There were a few other prominent Unionists in the state, notably Chief Justice John B. O'Neall, Colonel Lemuel Boozer, and James L. Petigru, but they did not arouse strong popular disapprobation by making public speeches and writing articles

---

[20] *Charleston Daily Courier,* May 2, 1860.

[21] *Ibid.,* May 19, 1860.

[22] Lilian Kibler, *Benjamin F. Perry, South Carolina Unionist* (Durham, 1946), chaps. 18 and 19.

for the newspapers against secession as did Perry.[23] Probably they felt that such speaking and writing would have no effect on the course of events in the state. They were, like Perry, conformists to the general views of their society except in respect to nationalism.

Petigru occupied a unique position in Carolina society; he was a lovable, witty man of such high standing in the legal profession that Lincoln considered appointing him to the Supreme Court. A realist who thought that his fellow South Carolinians had gone mad in breaking up the glorious Union, he wrote to President Swain of the University of North Carolina on March 4, 1861: "The most deplorable part of our case here [in South Carolina] is the total absence of a minority and the general contempt for consequences—what hope is there for the human race when there is no minority?"[24]

Unambitious for political honors, he was South Carolina's preeminent private citizen. Accordingly, though he remained a staunch Unionist until his death in 1863, the Charlestonians tolerated him, whereas another man of less stature and less popularity would have been ostracized. In the "very fury of secession," wrote his biographer James Petigru Carson, he was chosen by the legislature at the high salary of $5,000 to codify the laws of the state and the appointment was renewed annually during his lifetime.[25] The correspondent of the London *Times*, William H. Russell, who was in Charleston shortly after the secession of South Carolina, explained this tolerance. In describing a dinner party he attended, he wrote: "Only one of the company, a most lively, quaint, witty old lawyer named Petigru, dissented from the doctrines of Secession; but he seems to be treated as an aimable, harmless person, who has a weakness of intellect or 'a bee in his bonnet' on this particular matter."[26]

[23] O'Neall refused to be a candidate for the secession convention, but he wrote a letter earlier, April 28, 1860, protesting against the whiskey-drinking, ignorant, irresponsible politicians in the state and the infatuation of the people with secession, *Charleston Daily Courier*, May 11, 1860.

[24] Petigru to David L. Swain, March 4, 1861. David L. Swain Papers, MSS, Southern Collection, Chapel Hill, N. C.

[25] Carson, *Life, Letters and Speeches*, 358.

[26] William H. Russell, *My Diary North and South* (Boston, 1863), 117.

In Georgia there was far more diversity of thought on politics than in South Carolina, as was demonstrated during the secession crisis. Alexander H. Stephens was the most nationally prominent of the Georgia leaders to fight for the preservation of the Union, but more active and important than he in marshalling the Union forces in the state was Herschel V. Johnson, who had twice been governor of Georgia and in 1860 was the vice presidential candidate on the Douglas ticket. Many of the Southern Unionists such as Stephens had been old-line Whigs, but Johnson was an ardent Democrat. He had strongly opposed the Compromise of 1850 and had acted with the Southern Rights party. Nevertheless, Johnson was a very independent man with a realistic mind, capable of changing his views to meet a practical situation.[27] He had shown his freedom from religious orthodoxy by becoming a Swedenborgian. Although a large slaveholder, he was not a fanatical advocate of the expansion of the "peculiar institution" ("after California was surrendered," he declared, "there was nothing left worth struggling for"). When he accepted the nomination of vice president as the running mate of Douglas, he wrote in his autobiography (1867), that he "was deserted by life long friends, abused by the almost entire Southern press, denounced by men of talent and high position from the hustings, and maligned by the entire crew of small politicians that followed the banner of Breckenridge [sic] and Lane."[28]

After Stephens's famous Union speech of November 14 before the Georgia legislature the frail little statesman was strangely inactive in opposing secession. Apparently because of his pessimistic nature he thought it useless to resist the rush of secession sentiment, and so it was left to Johnson to take the leadership of the Unionists in the convention. Accordingly, it was Johnson who introduced a resolution, strongly supported by the prominent Whig and American politician, Benjamin H. Hill, to reject the secession ordinance and substitute an

[27] See Percy S. Flippin, *Herschel V. Johnson of Georgia, State Rights Unionist* (Richmond, 1931).

[28] Percy S. Flippin (ed.), "From the Autobiography of Herschel V. Johnson," *American Historical Review, XXX* (Jan. 1925), 317.

ultimatum to the Northern states.[29] His proposal was to seek
guarantees that Southern rights would be protected as a condition of the South's remaining in the Union. The vote on this
measure was a test of the strength of Unionist and Cooperative
semtiment; it was defeated by a vote of 164 to 133. Johnson
was typical of the Unionist leaders of the lower South in that
after his state had adopted the policy of disunion he followed
it loyally into the Confederacy.

Quite unlike the Georgia leader, both in personality and
probably in motivation, was the great Unionist planter of Mississippi, James Lusk Alcorn. In contrast to Herschel Johnson,
who was an unselfish patriot of his section, Alcorn displayed
an ambivalent attitude toward the South. Reared in Kentucky
and educated at Cumberland College in Tennessee, he was an
ardent Whig and a devoted admirer of Henry Clay. At the age
of twenty-eight he emigrated to Mississippi, where he practised
law, operated a plantation, participated in politics, and grew
rich. A delegate from the fertile delta county of Coahoma, he
was defeated as the candidate of the anti-secessionists for president of the Mississippi convention. When the resolution of J.
Shall Yerger for "the final adjustment of all difficulties between
the free and slave states by securing further Constitutional
guarantees within the present Union," was defeated, he introduced a proposal for cooperative action of the cotton states and
he voted to submit the secession ordinance to ratification by
the people.[30] He was not, however, among the fifteen hard-
core Unionists in the convention who voted against the secession
ordinance.[31] Too practical for such quixotic action, he finally
cast his vote for secession. Shortly thereafter he became a briga-
dier general of Mississippi troops, but his service was short, for
he was captured early in the war.

[29] See Benjamin H. Hill, Jr., *Senator Benjamin H. Hill of Georgia: His Life,
Speeches, and Writings* (Atlanta, 1893), and Haywood J. Pearce, Jr., *Benjamin H.
Hill, Secession and Reconstruction* (Chicago, 1928).

[30] *Journal of the [Mississippi] State Convention and Ordinance and Resolutions
Adopted in January 1861* (Jackson, 1861), 14-16.

[31] H. S. Fulkerson, *A Civilian's Recollections of the War Between the States*
(Baton Rouge, La., 1939), 6-9, gives Alcorn's explanation to him of his course in
the secession convention.

His subsequent career was far from patriotic; he retired to his plantation, cultivated Federal officers, and became an extensive trader of cotton through the Confederate lines. His acquisitive nature is revealed in letters to his wife during the war, in one of which he wrote, December 18, 1862, "I wish, however, to fill my pocket—and should the war continue, we will spend our summer in New York—and leave them to fight who made the fight."[32] His independent stand in the secession crisis seems to have been motivated both by his shrewd sense of realism (possibly his anticipation that secession would be followed by war and invasion of the exposed delta country) and by his strong Whig partisanship. After the war he and numerous other old-line Whigs turned scalawags, and he became the first Republican governor of Mississippi.[33]

The neighboring state of Louisiana, containing the metropolis of New Orleans and a considerable number of Northern-born business men, might have been expected to produce more critics of secession than Mississippi. But in the convention of January 1861, consisting of one hundred and twenty-nine delegates, only seventeen voted against the secession ordinance. Although the convention permitted these dissenters to speak in the assembly, it refused to allow their remarks to be entered on its minutes. The protest against the secession of the state by one of these delegates, which was thus suppressed, was published in the New Orleans *Daily Crescent* on January 31, 1861. This intransigent individual was James G. Taliaferro, representative of the parish of Catahoula, one of the poor parishes of the state. He was sixty-two years old, a native of Virginia and a graduate of Transylvania University. During the 1830's he had moved to Louisiana, established a law practice, and at this time was a judge. Part, at least, of his animus against secession must have been derived from his strong support of the Whig party and Whig principles. In his protest he declared that secession was

[32] Percy L. Rainwater (ed.), "Letters of James Lusk Alcorn," *Journal of Southern History*, III (May, 1937), 202.

[33] David H. Donald, "The Scalawag in Mississippi Reconstruction," *Journal of Southern History*, X (Nov. 1944), 447-460.

unconstitutional and that the grievances of the South could be redressed within the Union. The interests of Louisiana, he maintained, lay with the border states and not with the other states of the lower South, and secession would lead to adverse economic consequences, including the impairment of slavery. Finally he observed that the prospective evils anticipated from Lincoln's administration might never materialize.[34]

Two of the most prominent Unionists in New Orleans were Christian Roselius, born near Bremen, Germany, and Michael Hahn, a Bavarian. Roselius emigrated to New Orleans under indenture to pay for his passage across the ocean. A prodigious worker, he educated himself in the classics and the civil law so thoroughly that he became a leader of the New Orleans bar and a professor of law in Louisiana University.[35] His protégé, Michael Hahn, a graduate of Louisiana University, also became a prominent lawyer as well as president of the New Orleans School Board. A strong opponent of slavery, this eloquent German campaigned earnestly against the secession of Louisiana. During the Civil War he became the editor of the Republican *Daily True Delta* and in 1864 was elected governor of the state under Lincoln's ten per cent plan.

The influence of birth and rearing outside of the slave states may have caused some Unionists to take a detached position in regard to a movement directed at least in part toward saving the institution of slavery. Of the seven state officers who had opposed secession and later served in the administration of Governor Hahn, only the lieutenant governor, James Madison Wells, was a native-born Louisianan. Wells had been a prominent planter and slaveholder in Rapides parish. The secretary of state was Stanislas Wrotnowski, who has previously been mentioned. The attorney general was Bartholomew Leahy Lynch, a native of Limerick, Ireland, who had emigrated to America in 1851, taught school, and had become a lawyer in

[34] Roger W. Shugg, "A Suppressed Cooperationist Protest Against Secession," *Louisiana Historical Quarterly*, XIX (Jan.- Oct., 1936), 199-203.

[35] *Dictionary of American Biography* XVI, 164-65; *see also* W. M. Caskey, *Secession and Restoration of Louisiana* (Baton Rouge, 1938).

the state; in 1860-61 he was an unconditional Unionist. The treasurer was Dr. James Belden of New York, nephew of Noah Webster, who had settled in Louisiana and, though a slave holder, opposed the secession of the state. Both the superintendent of public education and the auditor of public accounts were also born in New York. John McNair, the superintendent, had received only a meager common school education in the backwoods of New York but had taught in the public schools of New Orleans. Dr. A. P. Dostie was somewhat of an adventurer, a roving dentist who had practised his profession both in Texas and New Orleans before the Civil War. An impulsive talker, he had frankly and freely avowed his Unionist views during the secession crisis and was compelled to leave the state. After Federal control had been established he returned, but he forsook his calling of dentistry for the much more exciting occupation of politician.[36]

Some of the Northerners in the South, such as Frederick A. P. Barnard, president of the University of Mississippi, and Dr. George Junkin, president of Washington College in Lexington, Virginia, strongly opposed disunion, but pursued the prudent course of returning to the North after the adoption of secession. In contrast to this action, Isaac Murphy of Arkansas, a former Northerner, courageously stood his ground in the South and continued to oppose disunion. Murphy was born near Pittsburgh in 1802 but as a young man had emigrated to Tennessee, where he taught school for four years before settling in Fayetteville, Arkansas. Here he studied law and was elected to the legislature. Though a Democrat, he vigorously opposed some of the policies of the Democratic machine in the state, headed by the powerful Johnson family who dominated Arkansas for many years. After living in California from 1849 to 1854, he returned to Arkansas to conduct the Huntsville Female Academy. Not at all distinguished either in appearance or ability, he possessed the rare virtue of moral courage. He was elected a delegate to the May 1861 Convention from the north-

[36] *New York Times*, April 22, 1864. Report of New Orleans correspondent.

ern section of the state which held few slaves.[37] When the convention passed the secession ordinance he was one of the five men who cast dissenting votes. The president of the convention asked these dissenters to change their votes in order to secure unanimity. All except Murphy acceded to the request; he replied, "I have cast my vote after mature reflection, and have duly considered the consequences, and I cannot conscientiously change it. I therefore vote 'No' ".[38] For his independence he paid the penalty; he and his family were so persecuted thereafter that he fled to the Union lines. In 1864 he was elected provisional governor of the restored state.

In opposing secession in Texas, Governor Sam Houston displayed even greater moral courage than Murphy had shown in Arkansas. Houston was built on a heroic mould.[39] In 1857 he had been defeated in his candidacy for governor largely because he, alone among the Southern Senators with the exception of Bell, had voted against the Kansas-Nebraska bill; but two years later he regained his popularity and was triumphantly re-elected governor. When South Carolina seceded, great pressure was put on him to summon the legislature in extra session in order that it might call a convention. He resisted this step toward disunion until the end of January; in the meanwhile, ardent secession leaders had summoned an unofficial people's convention, which on February 1 passed a secession ordinance, to be submitted, however, to the people for ratification. Houston, though seventy years old, now made a strenuous campaign of stump speaking in appealing to the people to vote for the Union. Often he was in danger of mob violence and

[37] Murphy represented the area of northwest Arkansas where secret peace societies arose in 1861. See T. R. Worley, "The Arkansas Peace Society of 1861; A Study in Mountain Unionism," *Journal of Southern History*, XXIV (Nov. 1958), 445-456.

[38] There are two versions of Murphy's defiant speech in the convention; one in A. W. Bishop, *Loyalty on the Frontier, or Sketches of Union Men of the Southwest* (St. Louis, 1863) and another, the *Dictionary of American Biography*, XIII, 352; see also Thomas S. Staples, *Reconstruction in Arkansas, 1862-1874* (New York, 1923), 45-47, and D. Y. Thomas, *Arkansas in War and Reconstruction* (Little Rock, 1926).

[39] For accounts of Houston's enigmatic personality, see Llerena Friend, *Sam Houston, the Great Designer* (Austin, 1954) and W. K. Wishart, *Sam Houston, Texas Giant* (Washington, D. C., 1962).

his life was threatened. His noble effort to preserve the Union was in vain, for the people ratified the secession ordinance by a vote of 39,415 in favor to 13,898 negative votes. So firm was he in loyalty to the Union that he refused to take the oath of loyalty to the Confederate government and was deposed from his office.[40] Houston was a belated Jacksonian nationalist in the South, as was Richard Keith Call of Florida, an aristocratic political leader who also strenuously opposed the secession of his state.[41]

A comparison of Houston with John Bell of Tennessee, both candidates in 1860 for the nomination for president by the Constitutional Union Party, points the contrast between the rugged independence and fighting spirit of Houston and the yielding nature of the Tennessee statesman. Though Bell was strongly devoted to the Union, he was a cautious, conservative politician.[42] After Lincoln's requisition for troops he and some of the Whig leaders of Tennessee recommended the calling of a border state conference and the arming of the state for any emergency. By the end of April he despaired of any concessions to the South from Lincoln's administration and decided to support the Confederacy. Concerning this reversal of opinion, Oliver Temple, a Unionist lawyer of Knoxville and a friend of Bell, wrote: "Physically he was regarded as a man of courage, but he seemed to be powerless to resist a counter current of popular opinion in times of high excitement."[43] Some men exhibit a fluctuating courage and Bell seems to have been one of these.

The independent man is frequently a self-contained person who resists being swept along with the temporary passions of the populace. He is likely to be at one end of the spectrum of human character and thought—either a conservative such as John Pendleton Kennedy of Maryland or an idealistic reformer

[40] President Kennedy selected Houston as one of his examples of political courage in *Profiles in Courage* (New York, 1956), chap. 5; see Donald Day and H. H. Ullom, *The Autobiography of Sam Houston* (Norman, 1954), chap. 20.

[41] See Herbert J. Doherty, *Richard Keith Call, Southern Unionist* (Gainesville, 1961), chap. 10.

[42] Joseph H. Parks, *John Bell of Tennessee* (Baton Rouge, 1950), 396-7.

[43] Oliver Temple, *East Tennessee and the Civil War* (Cincinnati, 1899), 231.

such as William Lloyd Garrison. Kennedy, out of his conservatism, sought to hold the border states and especially Maryland in the Union. Born into a business family in Baltimore, Kennedy had strong connections at the same time with the plantation aristocracy of Virginia through his Pendleton relatives on his mother's side. In his novels, particularly *Swallow Barn,* he romanticized the Southern plantation and slavery. Nevertheless, as he developed into a young lawyer and politician and married into a wealthy manufacturing family he acquired the point of view of the conservative business class of the North. He became a prominent Whig politician, a strong advocate of the Compromise of 1850, and Secretary of the Navy in Fillmore's administration.

Kennedy's home, Baltimore, and its leading newspaper, *The Sun,* were pro-Southern, while the western part of the state was loyal to the Union. In eastern Maryland tremendous feeling was generated against the federal government when a Baltimore mob on April 19 attacked troops from the North apparently on their way to coerce the seceded states. So pro-Southern was the Maryland legislature that the federal government arrested nineteen of its members, closed its meeting place in Frederick, and imprisoned hundreds of Maryland Confederate sympathizers. Against this background Kennedy wrote his appeal to the people of his native state to stand firm for the Union, entitled "The Great Drama" (May 9, 1861). Instead of criticizing the federal government for its ruthless suppression of civil liberties, he condemned the wave of pro-Confederate sentiment—"the heated utterances of passionate and thoughtless youth, of impressible women and girls, of infuriated politicians, of all that multitude of excitable, rash, unreasoning persons who fly to conclusions under the impulse of prejudice, desire, or interest; and lastly and more significantly, of wily, unscrupulous partisan leaders who are moved by premeditated design to accomplish a selfish party triumph."[44] He warned against "the domineering ascendency of these agencies over the public

[44] Frank Moore (ed.), *The Rebellion Record; a Diary of American Events* (New York, 1861), I, 368.

mind," which repressed the quiet and reflective citizens, over-awed and silenced the timid, and misled the credulous in the community.

Kennedy found that there existed in Maryland much snob-bery among the Confederate sympathizers, who regarded them-selves as the "Chivalry" and the Unionists as the plebeians. His outspoken Unionism caused some of his friends to ostracize him and he became almost an outcast in his native city.[45] In their minds he was a traitor to the South, to be classed with the odious Henry Winter Davis, the Maryland Congressman who had attacked slavery and joined the Republican party.

Until the firing on Fort Sumter, it took much less courage to be a Unionist in the Upper South, where the decided majority of the people were opposed to secession, than it did in the cotton states. Virginia had some notable Unionist leaders at this time from the eastern part of the state and the Valley, the areas of slave concentration, such as William C. Rives who was promi-nent in the Washington Peace Conference, John B. Baldwin, with whom Lincoln conferred, the Quaker John Janney, Presi-dent of the Convention, R. Y. Conrad, chairman of the Federal Relations Committee, and ex-President John Tyler.[46] Never-theless, as soon as Lincoln called upon the state for troops to coerce the lower South these men quickly abandoned their Unionism. The delegates from western Virginia, where there were relatively few slaves, notably Waitman T. Willey, George Summers, and John S. Carlisle were unconditional Unionists and, as soon as the state seceded (April 17), they returned to their homes, soon to begin a movement to separate the western part of the state from the Old Dominion.[47] They did not dis-play any remarkable independence, for they represented the majority sentiment of their section of the state.

The individual who stands out as a courageous and bellig-erent Unionist in eastern Virginia was John Minor Botts, former

[45] Charles H. Bohner, *John Pendleton Kennedy, Gentleman from Baltimore* (Baltimore, 1961), 228-230.

[46] William C. Rives Papers, Feb.-April 1861, MSS Library of Congress.

[47] See James C. McGregor, *The Disruption of Virginia* (New York, 1922), and Henry T. Shanks, *The Secession Movement in Virginia* (Richmond, 1934).

Whig congressman from the Richmond district. Botts had a long record of opposing typical Southern projects, such as the gag rule in Congress, the annexation of Texas, the Mexican War, and the Kansas-Nebraska Bill. After the election of Lincoln he made earnest Union speeches and wrote letters to the *Alexandria Gazette* opposing secession. He was defeated in his candidacy to be a delegate to the Virginia Convention. In early April he had an interview in Washington with Lincoln for the purpose of preventing the outbreak of hostilities.[48] Botts has given a racy but prejudiced account of his activities during the secession crisis, entitled *The Great Rebellion,* in which he develops the conspiracy theory of the secession movement. Because of his bold attacks on the secessionists, he was warned that he was risking his life in walking the streets of Richmond, but he disregarded the warnings.

Passion and intolerance were aroused among the citizens of Virginia especially during the vote on the secession ordinance which was submitted to them in the election of May 23rd. Botts himself failed to vote because he feared violence. As he reports it: "I finally suffered myself to be dissuaded from exercising my right as a citizen of Virginia, which I regretted and have been ashamed of to this day. The truth is, the vote throughout the state, with the exception of a few counties bordering on the Potomac and in the Northwest, was a perfect farce."[49] The voting was *viva voce,* and Botts was undoubtedly right in maintaining that intimidation played an important role in the result of the vote. He cited as a suspicious circumstance that only two votes were cast against the ordinance in Richmond. After the referendum on the secession ordinance Botts retired to his plantation, where he continued to speak freely against the secessionists and the Confederate government until he was arrested on March 2, 1862 and thrown into "a filthy negro jail," from which he was later released after giving his parole.

[48] John Minor Botts, *The Great Rebellion; its Secret History, Rise, Progress, and Disastrous Failure* (New York, 1866), 194-200.

[49] *Ibid.,* 211-212.

Both the secessionists and the Unionists practised intimidation in the regions where each was dominant. In the executive papers of Governor Letcher, for example, there is strong evidence of intimidation of secessionist voters. G. Huddleston of Springdale, near Grafton, for example, wrote to the governor on May 13, 1861, "We are in a deplorable political position . . . We the 'true Virginians' are largely in the minority and the Black Republicans & submissionists are daily growing more presumptious. They are organizing on every side of us marauding companies under the *nickname* of Home Guards for the avowed purpose of controlling the coming election—can our Good old Mother forsake us in this our day of trial. Many true & loyal subjects are terror stricken and are afraid to come to the Polls—."[50]

On the other hand, the papers of Governor Francis H. Pierpont of the loyal government at Alexandria contain letters showing the intimidation of Unionists. The editor of the *Richmond Whig* at the time of secession, Robert Ridgway, wrote to him shortly after the war, protesting the suppression of his newspaper by General Terry. He cited his pre-war record: "As you are aware, Sir, my position was one of resolute and determined opposition to secession, and that I sustained the Union when it required some moral courage and personal sacrifice to do so."[51] The son of a former mathematics professor at Hampden-Sydney College wrote to the governor that his father and other members of the family "were compelled by the force of public opinion as well as by the threats of personal violence to leave Virginia, from whence we succeeded in escaping to the North in December, 1861."[52]

Instances of independence of mind and courageous defiance

[50] J. Huddleston to Governor John Letcher, May 13, 1861. Executive Papers of Virginia, MSS in Virginia State Library.

[51] Robert Ridgway to Governor Francis H. Pierpont, July 13, 1865. Francis H. Pierpont Papers, MSS. Virginia State Library.

[52] Charles J. Snyder to Francis H. Pierpont, June 27, 1865, *ibid*. Another Virginian, B. B. Fitzgerald, wrote, July 19, 1865, "I left my home on account of the Rebellion. I had made myself obnoxious to the rebels by having openly published in the newspapers my abomination of slavery—"

of public opinion are usually recorded only of prominent men; similar acts of unimportant men, the little people, pass into oblivion unless they themselves leave accounts. Such an account has been preserved by R. S. Tharin in *Arbitrary Arrests in the South, or Scenes from the Experience of an Alabama Unionist.* Tharin was a graduate of the College of Charleston, who settled as a lawyer in Wetumpka, Alabama. He took unpopular cases, such as defending a poor white who sold liquor to slaves or an illiterate jeweler in Wetumpka who had been punished by a mob for being a "Lincolnite." Furthermore, he formed an organization among the non-slaveholders called "True Southern Rights Club" and announced the publication in Montgomery of a newspaper, *The Non-Slaveholder.* For such defiance of public opinion, he was brought before a vigilance committee, sentenced to thirty-nine lashes, and banished.[53]

Two editors of small-town newspapers who strongly supported the Union cause found that they could not survive as independent editors. One of these, A. B. Hendren of Athens, Alabama, who edited the *Union Banner,* described his precarious position in a letter to Governor Letcher of Virginia dated February 18, 1861: "Situated in the midst of a small community of Union loving men, to whom I flatter myself the 'Banner' has been mainly instrumental in giving tone and character," he wrote, "I would with pleasure be willing to continue an unrelenting warfare against the spirit of secession if my subsequent labors could promise the least encouragement to our cause, but being *the only press* now in Alabama that 'shows its hand' in that particular, I cannot of course expect to survive the mighty powers brought against me."[54]

The other editor, James W. Hunnicutt, who published *The Christian Banner* in Fredericksburg, Virginia, has left an account of his persecution for Unionist views in a volume entitled *The Conspiracy Unveiled. The South Sacrificed; or The Hor-*

[53] R. S. Tharin, *Arbitary Arrests in the South, or Scenes from the Experience of an Alabama Unionist* (New York, 1863), 64-86.

[54] A. B. Hendren to Governor John Letcher, Feb. 18, 1861. Executive Papers of Virginia.

rors of Secession. Born in the Pendleton District of South Carolina in 1814 of "pious and respectable" parents, he studied at Randolph-Macon College and became a strenuous preacher and an outspoken editor. He wrote violent editorials against secession, maintaining that it would bring Canada to the very doors of the South and thereby result in the destruction of slavery. Secession, he held, was being promoted by a conspiracy of politicians such as Henry A. Wise. When Hunnicutt expressed such views in a speech before a court house crowd, "some cowardly unprincipled scoundrel, a sinner against God, and a traitor to his country, threw an egg at us from the extreme part of the house." After the Virginia Convention had passed the secession ordinance but before it had been ratified by the people, Hunnicutt wrote concerning the publication of his paper: "We saw and felt that the liberty of the press, the liberty of speech, and the rights of freemen were all wrested from us, and that the withdrawal of patronage would ultimately force us to discontinue the publication of the 'Banner' and we determined after the publication of the number of May 9, 1861 to close our office."[55] Hunnicutt became a scalawag after the war and prominent as a radical Republican leader of the Negroes and a candidate in 1868 for governor of Virginia.[56]

Very much like Hunnicutt in his championship of the underdog was Andrew Johnson of Tennessee. Johnson's independence at times passed the boundary of a virtue into the vice of stubbornness and inability to compromise. Outwardly arrogant and bold, he was different from Lincoln or Jackson—both men of humble background like himself—in being an insecure man, constantly aware of the lowly class from which he had sprung. This sense of inferiority probably explains the violence of his language in denouncing his opponents and social superiors. Of the citizens of Greeneville, Tennessee, where he had begun his climb to political power as a humble tailor, he wrote in a

[55] James W. Hunnicutt, *The Conspiracy Unveiled. The South Sacrificed; or The Horrors of Secession* (Phila. 1863), 171, 297.

[56] H. J. Eckenrode, *The Political History of Virginia during the Reconstruction* (Baltimore, 1904), 49, 68-69, 88.

letter to a friend in 1847: "the God forsaken and hell deserving, money loving, back biting Sunday praying Scoundrels—. Send me some new fangled oaths that I can more effectually dam some of the brood in the town." He did not need any aid in this respect, for when he expressed his feelings about the aristocracy of the mountain town he exceeded all bounds: "I never want to own a foot of dirt in the *damned* town while I live—the God damned Murrell gang may take it, and make a perfect 'pandemonium' of it and headquarters for all the infernal spirits that are now out of hell, for I know of no place more suitable."[57]

This politician of violent temperament was one of the most independent of Southerners. He had scathingly denounced the Whigs in his campaigns for governor in 1853 and 1855, but during the secession crisis he united with them in trying to preserve the Union. In January, after he had made a strong Union speech in the Senate, the secessionists in Memphis and Nashville hanged and burned him in effigy. On March 2 he made another bold speech in the Senate, denouncing secessionists as traitors. He declared that he would treat secessionists as Jefferson did Burr in 1806, have them arrested and tried, and if convicted, "by the Eternal God I would execute them."[58]

When he returned to Tennessee, he himself was regarded as a traitor to the Democratic party and the South, and was in deadly peril as he travelled on the railroad cars. No longer "dominated by his usual love of office and power," wrote Oliver Temple, Johnson strove earnestly to keep Tennessee in the Union. Though he displayed cool bravery on all occasions, he confined his campaigning against secession to East Tennessee, where the majority of the people were already in accord with his views. He told Temple that the reason he did not go into Middle Tennessee was that the people there would not allow him to speak. "That was probably true," Temple commented.[59]

[57] Andrew Johnson to B. B. McDonnel, Jan. 10, 1847. Andrew Johnson Papers, Vol. I (1831-1859), MSS Library of Congress.

[58] *Congressional Globe,* 36th Cong. 2nd Sess. Vol. 30, Part 2, p. 1354 March 2, 1861.

[59] Oliver P. Temple, *Notable Men of Tennessee from 1833 to 1875* (New York, 1912), 400; see also *East Tennessee and the Civil War,* 560.

After the firing on Fort Sumter, it became unsafe for any man publicly to oppose the secessionists in Middle and West Tennessee. Robert Johnson, son of Andrew, wrote to his father on April 29, 1861 from Nashville, where he was attending the legislature: "I find a pretty strong Union feeling existing here but it is silenced by the mob and dare not express their Sentiments—I have had a great many Union men to call on me but they are all alarmed and afraid to say anything on the street.

"[Emerson] Etheridge [Unionist Congressmen from West Tennessee] made a speech at Trenton last Monday, which is said to be the most bitter speech ever heard fall from the lips of man—he was not permitted to speak at Paris."[60]

The source of Andrew Johnson's independence lay only partly in a high patriotism; he was also, as Eric McKitrick has pointed out, a slave of abstractions (the only exception being his strenuous fight for free homesteads). This weakness made him inflexible in his opinions, unable to yield to pragmatic considerations or to compromise.[61] He was not a party man as Lincoln was, but displayed the psychology of a person who is always an outsider, a maverick. His independence therefore was as often a weakness as a virtue.

Some individuals take an independent stand against the crowd because there is a touch of the martyr in their make-up. "Parson" (William G.) Brownlow, for instance, developed a martyr complex during his unremitting fight against secession in East Tennessee. Oliver Temple, who knew the Union men of East Tennessee better than any other writer, gave Brownlow the credit of having the greatest influence of any individual of this area in keeping East Tennessee loyal to the Union.[62] This man of varied occupations—carpenter, Methodist circuit-rider, editor, and bigoted Whig politician—was the antithesis of aristocracy; he looked like a bright peasant, with a "hard favored" face, and possessed of a voice which he boasted to be as

---

[60] Robert Johnson to Andrew Johnson, April 29, 1861. Johnson Papers, XI.

[61] Eric L. McKitrick, *Andrew Johnson and Reconstruction* (Chicago, 1960), chap. IV, "Andrew Johnson, Outsider," and Robert W. Winston, *Andrew Johnson, Plebeian and Patriot* (New York, 1928).

[62] Temple, *Notable Men of Tennessee,* 41, 47.

strong as that of any man in East Tennessee; he declared that he had no desire to be polite.

As editor of the *Knoxville Whig,* he was absolutely fearless in attacking the secessionists and upholding the Union. He continued to fly the American flag over his house in defiance of the secessionists. On June 1, 1861 he noted in his newspaper that a vigilance committee in Memphis, headed by the president of the Bank of Tennessee, had ruled that the *Louisville Journal* and the *Knoxville Whig* were incendiary newspapers and therefore could not circulate in the city.[63] For seven months after the actual secession of Tennessee, Brownlow continued his bold editorials of opposition to the Confederacy, claiming that a reign of terror existed in the state, and awaiting the suppression of his paper. The Confederate government, however, was unwilling to follow the example of the Federal government in suppressing the *Louisville Courier* and the New York *Day Book.* Finally Brownlow voluntarily stopped publication of the *Whig* on October 24, 1861, announcing that he was about to be arrested and portraying himself as a martyr to his principles.[64] The burning of vital railroad bridges in East Tennessee, attributed to his instigations, aroused the civil authorities in East Tennessee to arrest him, but after several weeks of imprisonment he was released and expelled from the Confederacy. Subsequently he traveled in the North lecturing, and after Burnside captured Knoxville, he returned to re-establish his newspaper (November 11, 1863), renamed the *Knoxville Whig and Rebel Ventilator.*[65]

Parson Brownlow's career illustrates well the role that intrastate sectionalism played in the development of the Unionist point of view. The loyalty of the mountaineers to the Union was motivated in part by strong prejudices against the lowlanders who controlled the state governments—rather than by any deep attachment to the Union. The inhabitants of the Appalachian highlands and the mountainous country of Ar-

[63] *Brownlow's Knoxville Whig,* June 1, 1861.

[64] William G. Brownlow, *Sketches of the Rise, Progress, and Decline of Secession* (Philadelphia, 1862), 249-254.

[65] E. M. Coulter, *William G. Brownlow, Fighting Parson of the Southern Highlands* (Chapel Hill, 1937), chaps. IX-XI.

kansas were isolated and parochial-minded; a large majority were ignorant, unlettered men who wished to be let alone. Owning few slaves and disassociated from the cotton economy, they saw no reason to vote for secession or later to muster, as one of the Arkansas Unionists phrased it, under "the d—d nigger flag."[66] Consequently, most of the thirty-nine delegates out of the hundred members of the Alabama convention who voted against secession came from the hill counties, and in Georgia over half of the delegates who voted against the secession ordinance were from the red hills of the northern part of the state. In East Tennessee the vote on ratifying the secession ordinance in the June referendum was over two to one against secession; so aroused were the mountain people that they met in the Greeneville Convention (June 17) and issued a manifesto declaring that the Unionist voters had been intimidated in the election and requesting that the eastern part of Tennessee be erected into a separate state; Brownlow had suggested the name of "Frankland" for the proposed new state.[67]

The motives that influenced the Unionists such as Brownlow as well as the secessionists cannot adequately be explained by a simple economic interpretation. There were other powerful springs of action that affected both the independent men and the majority, notably race prejudice, inveterate party feelings, intrastate sectionalism, the fear of what the future might bring with the Republicans in power, regional pride, and an antique sense of honor. These commingled in an inextricable fashion with economic considerations in influencing the alignments. Ralph A. Wooster, using the manuscript census of 1860 for information on the economic interests of 1200 individuals who composed the secession conventions, has found a close correlation between the ownership of slave property and sentiment for secession.[68] Nevertheless, could it not be that the people of the black belts, slaveholders and non-slaveholders alike, favored

---

[66] Worley, "The Arkansas Peace Society of 1861," 454.

[67] U.S. War Department, *The War of the Rebellion; Official Records of the Union and Confederate Armies* (Washington, 1880-1901), Ser. I Vol. LII, Part I, p. 148.

[68] Ralph A. Wooster, *The Secession Conventions of the South* (Princeton, 1962), chap. 16.

secession more strongly than the yeomen of Appalachia because they had greater reason to fear the social consequences of freeing the Negroes than the latter had?

A selfish economic motive may explain the position of some of the wealthy Unionists of Mississippi, as Percy Rainwater thought in his analysis of the secession movement in that state.[69] They were mostly conservative men of property who feared the consequence of a movement that would likely result in war and endanger their privileged status. They preferred not to take a leap in the dark but wait and see whether Lincoln's administration actually threatened the loss of their slave property. These conservative men who were opposed to hasty action on the secession issue lived mainly in the rich delta counties of the Mississippi and the Yazoo; they as well as the poor farmers who inhabited the hilly northeast counties had no enthusiasm for secession.

There is a subtle connection between the ownership of land and the expression of independent opinions. Anton Chekov in his short story "Gooseberries" tells of a poor clerk in Russia who was too timid to have opinions in his lowly condition, but after he had by heroic saving acquired money to buy a small estate his personality changed, and he became a man of decided views. In the Old South the small farmers by 1860 had come to own the land they tilled. Professor Frank L. Owsley has estimated from the manuscript census records of 1860 that eighty per cent of the farmers of the lower South owned their farms; thus they had the economic basis to be independent in the expression of their convictions (which did not include, however, hostility to slavery).[70] Accordingly, the independent spirit shown by the Unionists was seldom derived from the tradition of the gentry, with the notable exception of some of the delta planters, but arose principally among the yeomanry of the Southern uplands, who in 1860 constituted the freest and most independent class of common people to be found in the world.

[69] Percy L. Rainwater, *Mississippi, Storm Center of Secession, 1856-1861* (Baton Rouge, 1938), chap. X.

[70] Frank L. Owsley, *The Plain Folk of the Old South* (Baton Rouge, 1949), 16.

Relatively few of the independent men of 1860-61, indeed, belonged to the country gentry class. In general, these men of independence were commoners and of a different breed from the individualistic planters of an earlier epoch. A colorful example of the independent yeoman who rose to great power in politics was Governor Zebulon Baird Vance of North Carolina. Vance was a self-made man who had lifted himself from a lazy, unambitious life in Buncombe County by going to the University at Chapel Hill. He arrived there by walking from the mountains, dressed in rustic garb, and without money. After a brief period of study at the University he located in Asheville as a lawyer and politician. He had abundant gifts to succeed in the rough and tumble politics of western Carolina. A large, powerful man, with a bushy mustache, he possessed an earthy and ribald type of humor, shrewd understanding of human nature, and a rude eloquence that captivated the masses. Better than any academic historian, the novelist Thomas Wolfe in *The Hills Beyond* has caught the authentic spirit of this prince of folksy politicians as well as the attraction he had for the people of the state.

Temperamentally a conservative, "Zeb," as he was called, adhered to the Whig party; the Democratic party, he thought, was fostering dangerous sectionalism within the nation. When the Whig party broke up after 1854, instead of following the path of expediency, as did the congressman from the western district, Thomas L. Clingman, by joining the Democratic party, he supported the unpopular American party primarily because it was the representative of conservatism.

This devotion to principle stands out in a letter that he wrote on February 19, 1858 to a former Whig leader: "And though I am completely shut off from advancement by these opinions, which to a young man endowed with considerable ambition is a gloomy enough prospect, yet I can say it with a clear conscience before God & man, that the very fact of my standing almost alone in the defense of what I believe to be the right, in the face of overwhelming odds, affords me a gratification—an internal feeling of moral rectitude—that I would not surrender for a seat in the senate of the United States, were I old enough to be allowed one."[71] Nevertheless, so irresistible was he as a campaigner before the mountain people that in this very year he was elected to represent them in Congress. In 1860–61, though he made impassioned speeches against secession, after Lincoln called for troops he resigned from Congress and raised a company to fight on the Confederate side. While he was still in the army he was elected in 1862 governor of North Carolina, and in this position he displayed both his conservatism and a strong sense of independence in asserting state rights.

The action of the independent man is often determined by personal temperament. Some individuals seem by nature to be rebels against society, against authority; some oppose the community consensus out of perverseness; some are attracted by the challenge of asserting their individuality against the mores of a conservative social organization; others are simply "loners" or mavericks incapable of adjustment to or cooperating with their fellowmen; a very few have an extremely realistic and iconoclastic temperament that makes them scorn the compromises of conventional society. Among the obscure psychological forces that drive men to opposition is frustration of ambition. This motive seems to have contributed powerfully to the enigmatic conduct during the secession crisis of Jeremiah Clemens, the leader of the Alabama Unionists.[72]

The deepest and most admirable well-spring of independence of action is located not in mental reflection but in idealism of character. It is this quality that makes men go against wind and tide in opposing the emotional behavior of the crowd, or statesmen risk their private fate for the public good. Such a motivation seems to have dominated, for example, the actions of Judge Garnett Andrews of Georgia. His daughter Eliza wrote that he "did his best to hold Georgia in the Union, but he might as well have tried to tie up the Northwest wind in the

[71] Frontis W. Johnston (ed.), *The Papers of Zebulon Baird Vance* (Raleigh, 1963), I, 34.
[72] See Clement Eaton, *The Mind of the Old South* (Baton Rouge, 1964), 214-216.

corner of a pocket handkerchief."[73] He could not prevent his own family from succumbing to the emotional stampede of their associates into secession.

The problem of the man of independence involves, in most instances, the possession of moral courage. Such a quality is not absolute, for some individuals fluctuate in their strength and weakness—in the will power to defy public opinion. They are like Conrad's "Lord Jim." Moreover, moral courage is often not enough to make men independent: they must have the power of realization. The great majority of men, through insensitivity or lack of imagination or the critical mind, are blind to long-established social evils that encompass them; they look upon these unjust practices or institutions as being the very order of nature. Thus it was in the society of the Old South in respect to slavery; thus it has been in the modern South until very recently in respect to civil rights for Negroes. Only after a long evolution of social thinking have Americans come to expand the concept of liberalism to include equality of rights for people of all colors. Still, the victory for this ideal lies in the future, and the intolerance exhibited today by large segments of our population is an eloquent reminder that the suppression of freedom of thought and expression in the Old South was only an incident in the timeless struggle between liberal and conservative thought.

[73] Spencer B. King, Jr., (ed.), *The War-Time Journal of a Georgia Girl, 1864-1865* (Macon, 1960), 176.

INDEX

Abolitionists, 97–105, 117–119, 143, 197, 202, 204, 206–208, 281, 313, 333, 378, 380; petitions of, 26, 148–149, 206; stereotype of, 194, 269
Academic freedom, 216–237, 397
Academies, 71–73; female, 392
Acadians, 250
Acton, Lord John E. E. D., 29
Adair, John, 4
Adams, James H., 81, 229
Adams, John Quincy, 204, 282, 370
"Address of the Southern Delegates in Congress" (1849), 153–154, 157
African Church, Richmond, Va., 283
Agassiz, Louis, 219, 329, 331 n., 332
Age of Reason, The, 13, 18
Agriculture, 37, 43–47, 258, 260, 378
Alcorn, James Lusk, 388–389
Alexander, Nathaniel, 168–169
Alexandria, Va., *Gazette,* 168, 188, 255, 395
Aliens, 238–266; *see Foreigners*
Allen, Ethan, 14
Allston, R. F. W., 383–386
American Colonization Society, 175, 278–279
American Party, 387, 404
American Revolution, 12, 18, 25, 31, 52, 342–343
Anderson, Joseph R., 38
Andrews, Garnett, 310, 405
Anti-Catholic feeling, 323–326
Anti-Intellectualism, 80, 82, 380
Anti-Semitic feeling, 253
Antislavery men in the South, 18–22, 133–143, 267–299; publications, 197–199; anti-slavery sentiments in South, 3, 73, 382, 390
Appeal to the Christian Women of the South (1836), 341
"Appomattox," pamphlet of, 109, 170–171
Architecture, Georgian, 7; Greek Revival, 34–35, 57
Aristocrats, colonial and early republic, 3–31; of the ante-bellum period, 35,

38, 57, 60–61, 84–85, 271, 276, 346, 362, 381–382, 404
Aristotle, 144, 349
Asbury, Francis, 301
Atchison, David, 371
Athens, Ala. *Union Banner,* 398

Bachman, Dr. John, 219, 330
Bacon, Jarvis, 133–135
Badger, George, 95, 193
Bailey, William, 191
Baldwin, John B., 395
Baldwin, Joseph G., 45
Baltimore, Md., 243 n., 248, 310, 317, 324, 393–394
Baltimore *Literary and Religious Magazine,* 324
Baltimore *Saturday Visitor,* 209
Baltimore *Sun,* 159, 184–185, 393
Baptist Church, 30, 302, 311, 322, 326
Barbour, B. J., 327
Barnard, Frederick A. P., 219, 233, 262, 391
Barnard, Henry, 69
Barrett, Lysander, 133
Bascom, H. B., 268, 310, 313
Belden, Dr. James, 390
Bell, John, 193, 250, 271, 372–373, 392–394
Benjamin, Judah P., 229, 251, 253
Benton, Thomas Hart, 146, 150, 204–205, 274, 357, 361, 370–371
Berea College, Ky., 234–236
Berryville, Va. *Clarke Journal,* 181–182
Birdseye, Ezekiel, 274–275
Birney, James G., 175–177, 221, 249, 292–293, 313
Black Belt, 57, 86, 104, 198, 298, 388, 403–404
Blair, Francis P., 247
Bledsoe, A. T., 225, 267
Bluegrass region, 14, 20, 34
Boozer, Lemuel, 385
Botts, John Minor, 281–282, 395–396
Bradford, John, 21
Braun, Johannes, 239

harper ☦ torchbooks

HUMANITIES AND SOCIAL SCIENCES

American Studies

JOHN R. ALDEN: The American Revolution, 1775-1783.† *Illus.*   TB/3011

BERNARD BAILYN: The New England Merchants in the Seventeenth Century   TB/1149

RAY STANNARD BAKER: Following the Color Line: *American Negro Citizenship in the Progressive Era.‡ Illus. Edited by Dewey W. Grantham, Jr.*   TB/3053

RAY A. BILLINGTON: The Far Western Frontier, 1830-1860.† *Illus.*   TB/3012

JOSEPH L. BLAU, Ed.: Cornerstones of Religious Freedom in America. *Selected Basic Documents, Court Decisions and Public Statements. Revised and Enlarged Edition*   TB/118

RANDOLPH S. BOURNE: War and the Intellectuals: *Collected Essays, 1915-1919.‡ Edited by Carl Resek*   TB/3043

A. RUSSELL BUCHANAN: The United States and World War II. † *Illus.*   Vol. I TB/3044
                                                       Vol. II TB/3045

ABRAHAM CAHAN: The Rise of David Levinsky: *a novel. Introduction by John Higham*   TB/1028

JOSEPH CHARLES: The Origins of the American Party System   TB/1049

THOMAS C. COCHRAN: The Inner Revolution: *Essays on the Social Sciences in History*   TB/1140

T. C. COCHRAN & WILLIAM MILLER: The Age of Enterprise: *A Social History of Industrial America*   TB/1054

EDWARD S. CORWIN: American Constitutional History: *Essays edited by Alpheus T. Mason and Gerald Garvey*   TB/1136

FOSTER RHEA DULLES: America's Rise to World Power, 1898-1954.† *Illus.*   TB/3021

W. A. DUNNING: Reconstruction, Political and Economic, 1865-1877   TB/1073

A. HUNTER DUPREE: Science in the Federal Government: *A History of Policies and Activities to 1940*   TB/573

CLEMENT EATON: The Freedom-of-Thought Struggle in the Old South. *Revised Edition. Illus.* TB/1150

CLEMENT EATON: The Growth of Southern Civilization, 1790-1860.† *Illus.*   TB/3040

HAROLD U. FAULKNER: Politics, Reform and Expansion, 1890-1900.† *Illus.*   TB/3020

LOUIS FILLER: The Crusade against Slavery, 1830-1860.† *Illus.*   TB/3029

EDITORS OF FORTUNE: America in the Sixties: *the Economy and the Society. 72 two-color charts*   TB/1015

DIXON RYAN FOX: The Decline of Aristocracy in the Politics of New York.‡ *Edited by Robert V. Remini*   TB/3064

LAWRENCE HENRY GIPSON: The Coming of the Revolution, 1763-1775.† *Illus.*   TB/3007

FRANCIS J. GRUND: Aristocracy in America: *Jacksonian Democracy*   TB/1001

ALEXANDER HAMILTON: The Reports of Alexander Hamilton.‡ *Edited by Jacob E. Cooke*   TB/3060

OSCAR HANDLIN, Editor: This Was America: *As Recorded by European Travelers to the Western Shore in the Eighteenth, Nineteenth, and Twentieth Centuries. Illus.*   TB/1119

MARCUS LEE HANSEN: The Atlantic Migration: 1607-1860. *Edited by Arthur M. Schlesinger, Sr.; Introduction by Oscar Handlin*   TB/1052

MARCUS LEE HANSEN: The Immigrant in American History. *Edited with a Foreword by Arthur M. Schlesinger, Sr.*   TB/1120

JOHN D. HICKS: Republican Ascendancy, 1921-1933.† *Illus.*   TB/3041

JOHN HIGHAM, Ed.: The Reconstruction of American History   TB/1068

† The New American Nation Series, edited by Henry Steele Commager and Richard B. Morris.

‡ American Perspectives series, edited by Bernard Wishy and William E. Leuchtenburg.

* The Rise of Modern Europe series, edited by William L. Langer.

‖ Researches in the Social, Cultural, and Behavioral Sciences, edited by Benjamin Nelson.

§ The Library of Religion and Culture, edited by Benjamin Nelson.

Σ Harper Modern Science Series, edited by James R. Newman.

º Not for sale in Canada.

DANIEL H. HUNDLEY: Social Relations in our Southern States.‡ *Edited by William R. Taylor*　TB/3058

HELEN HUNT JACKSON: A Century of Dishonor: *The Early Crusade for Indian Reform.*‡ *Edited by Andrew F. Rolle*　TB/3063

ROBERT H. JACKSON: The Supreme Court in the American System of Government　TB/1106

THOMAS JEFFERSON: Notes on the State of Virginia.‡ *Edited by Thomas Perkins Abernethy*　TB/3052

JOHN F. KENNEDY: A Nation of Immigrants. *Revised and Enlarged Edition. Illus.*　TB/1118

WILLIAM L. LANGER & S. EVERETT GLEASON: The Challenge to Isolation: *The World Crisis of 1937-1940 and American Foreign Policy*　Vol. I　TB/3054
Vol. II　TB/3055

WILLIAM E. LEUCHTENBURG: Franklin D. Roosevelt and the New Deal, 1932-1940.† *Illus.*　TB/3025

LEONARD W. LEVY: Freedom of Speech and Press in Early American History: *Legacy of Suppression*
TB/1109

ARTHUR S. LINK: Woodrow Wilson and the Progressive Era, 1910-1917.† *Illus.*　TB/3023

ROBERT GREEN McCLOSKEY: American Conservatism in the Age of Enterprise, 1865-1910　TB/1137

BERNARD MAYO: Myths and Men: *Patrick Henry, George Washington, Thomas Jefferson*　TB/1108

JOHN C. MILLER: Alexander Hamilton and the Growth of the New Nation　TB/3057

JOHN C. MILLER: The Federalist Era, 1789-1801.† *Illus.*　TB/3027

PERRY MILLER: Errand into the Wilderness　TB/1139

PERRY MILLER & T. H. JOHNSON, Editors: The Puritans: *A Sourcebook of Their Writings*
Vol. I　TB/1093
Vol. II　TB/1094

GEORGE E. MOWRY: The Era of Theodore Roosevelt and the Birth of Modern America, 1900-1912.† *Illus.*
TB/3022

WALLACE NOTESTEIN: The English People on the Eve of Colonization, 1603-1630.† *Illus.*　TB/3006

RUSSEL BLAINE NYE: The Cultural Life of the New Nation, 1776-1801.† *Illus.*　TB/3026

RALPH BARTON PERRY: Puritanism and Democracy
TB/1138

RALPH BARTON PERRY: The Thought and Character of William James: *Briefer Version*　TB/1156

GEORGE E. PROBST, Ed.: The Happy Republic: *A Reader in Tocqueville's America*　TB/1060

WALTER RAUSCHENBUSCH: Christianity and the Social Crisis.‡ *Edited by Robert D. Cross*　TB/3059

HEINRICH STRAUMANN: American Literature in the Twentieth Century. *Revised Edition*　TB/1168

FRANK THISTLETHWAITE: America and the Atlantic Community: *Anglo-American Aspects, 1790-1850*
TB/1107

TWELVE SOUTHERNERS: I'll Take My Stand: *The South and the Agrarian Tradition. Introduction by Louis D. Rubin, Jr.; Biographical Essays by Virginia Rock*　TB/1072

A. F. TYLER: Freedom's Ferment: *Phases of American Social History from the Revolution to the Outbreak of the Civil War. Illus.*　TB/1074

GLYNDON G. VAN DEUSEN: The Jacksonian Era, 1828-1848.† *Illus.*　TB/3028

WALTER E. WEYL: The New Democracy: *An Essay on Certain Political and Economic Tendencies in the United States.*‡ *Edited by Charles Forcey*　TB/3042

LOUIS B. WRIGHT: The Cultural Life of the American Colonies, 1607-1763.† *Illus.*　TB/3005

LOUIS B. WRIGHT: Culture on the Moving Frontier
TB/1053

Anthropology & Sociology

BERNARD BERELSON, Ed.: The Behavioral Sciences Today　TB/1127

JOSEPH B. CASAGRANDE, Ed.: In the Company of Man: *20 Portraits of Anthropological Informants. Illus.*　TB/3047

W. E. LE GROS CLARK: The Antecedents of Man: *An Introduction to the Evolution of the Primates.*° *Illus.*
TB/559

THOMAS C. COCHRAN: The Inner Revolution: *Essays on the Social Sciences in History*　TB/1140

ALLISON DAVIS & JOHN DOLLARD: Children of Bondage: *The Personality Development of Negro Youth in the Urban South* ‖　TB/3049

ST. CLAIR DRAKE & HORACE R. CAYTON: Black Metropolis: *A Study of Negro Life in a Northern City*　Vol. I　TB/1086; Vol. II　TB/1087

CORA DU BOIS: The People of Alor. *New Preface by the author. Illus.*　Vol. I　TB/1042; Vol. II　TB/1043

EMILE DURKHEIM et al.: Essays on Sociology and Philosophy: *With Analyses of Durkheim's Life and Work.* ‖ *Edited by Kurt H. Wolff*　TB/1151

LEON FESTINGER, HENRY W. RIECKEN & STANLEY SCHACHTER: When Prophecy Fails: *A Social and Psychological Account of a Modern Group that Predicted the Destruction of the World* ‖　TB/1132

RAYMOND FIRTH, Ed.: Man and Culture: *An Evaluation of the Work of Bronislaw Malinowski* ‖ °
TB/1133

L. S. B. LEAKEY: Adam's Ancestors: *The Evolution of Man and his Culture. Illus.*　TB/1019

KURT LEWIN: Field Theory in Social Science: *Selected Theoretical Papers.* ‖ *Edited with a Foreword by Dorwin Cartwright*　TB/1135

ROBERT H. LOWIE: Primitive Society. *Introduction by Fred Eggan*　TB/1056

R. M. MacIVER: Social Causation　TB/1153

BENJAMIN NELSON: Religious Traditions and the Spirit of Capitalism: *From the Church Fathers to Jeremy Bentham*　TB/1130

TALCOTT PARSONS & EDWARD A. SHILS, Editors: Toward a General Theory of Action: *Theoretical Foundations for the Social Sciences*　TB/1083

JOHN H. ROHRER & MUNRO S. EDMONSON, Eds.: The Eighth Generation Grows Up: *Cultures and Personalities of New Orleans Negroes* ‖　TB/3050

ARNOLD ROSE: The Negro in America: *The Condensed Version of Gunnar Myrdal's* An American Dilemma　TB/3048

HENRI DE SAINT-SIMON: Social Organization, The Science of Man, and Other Writings. ‖ *Edited and translated by Felix Markham*　TB/1152

KURT SAMUELSSON: Religion and Economic Action: *A Critique of Max Weber's* The Protestant Ethic and the Spirit of Capitalism. ‖ ° *Trans. by E. G. French; Ed. with Intro. by D. C. Coleman*　TB/1131

PITIRIM SOROKIN: Contemporary Sociological Theories. *Through the First Quarter of the Twentieth Century*   TB/3046

MAURICE R. STEIN: The Eclipse of Community: *An Interpretation of American Studies*   TB/1128

SIR EDWARD TYLOR: The Origins of Culture. *Part I of "Primitive Culture."*§ *Introduction by Paul Radin*   TB/33

SIR EDWARD TYLOR: Religion in Primitive Culture. *Part II of "Primitive Culture."*§ *Introduction by Paul Radin*   TB/34

W. LLOYD WARNER & Associates: Democracy· in Jonesville: *A Study in Quality and Inequality*   TB/1129

W. LLOYD WARNER: A Black Civilization: *A Study of an Australian Tribe.* | *Illus.*   TB/3056

W. LLOYD WARNER: Social Class in America: *The Evaluation of Status*   TB/1013

Art and Art History

WALTER LOWRIE: Art in the Early Church. *Illus. Revised Edition*   TB/124

EMILE MÂLE: The Gothic Image: *Religious Art in France of the Thirteenth Century.*§ *190 illus.*   TB/44

MILLARD MEISS: Painting in Florence and Siena after the Black Death: *The Arts, Religion and Society in the Mid-Fourteenth Century. 169 illus.*   TB/1148

ERICH NEUMANN: The Archetypal World of Henry Moore. *107 illus.*   TB/2020

ERWIN PANOFSKY: Studies in Iconology: *Humanistic Themes in the Art of the Renaissance. 180 illustrations*   TB/1077

ALEXANDRE PIANKOFF: The Shrines of Tut-Ankh-Amon. *Edited by N. Rambova. 117 illus.*   TB/2011

JEAN SEZNEC: The Survival of the Pagan Gods: *The Mythological Tradition and Its Place in Renaissance Humanism and Art. 108 illustrations*   TB/2004

OTTO VON SIMSON: The Gothic Cathedral: *Origins of Gothic Architecture and the Medieval Concept of Order. 58 illus.*   TB/2018

HEINRICH ZIMMER: Myths and Symbols in Indian Art and Civilization. *70 illustrations*   TB/2005

Business, Economics & Economic History

REINHARD BENDIX: Work and Authority in Industry: *Ideologies of Management in the Course of Industrialization*   TB/3035

THOMAS C. COCHRAN: The American Business System: *A Historical Perspective, 1900-1955*   TB/1080

ROBERT DAHL & CHARLES E. LINDBLOM: Politics, Economics, and Welfare: *Planning and Politico-Economic Systems Resolved into Basic Social Processes*   TB/3037

PETER F. DRUCKER: The New Society: *The Anatomy of Industrial Order*   TB/1082

ROBERT L. HEILBRONER: The Great Ascent: *The Struggle for Economic Development in Our Time*   TB/3030

ABBA P. LERNER: Everybody's Business: *Current Assumptions in Economics and Public Policy*   TB/3051

ROBERT GREEN McCLOSKEY: American Conservatism in the Age of Enterprise, 1865-1910   TB/1137

PAUL MANTOUX: The Industrial Revolution in the Eighteenth Century: *The Beginnings of the Modern Factory System in England* °   TB/1079

WILLIAM MILLER, Ed.: Men in Business: *Essays on the Historical Role of the Entrepreneur*   TB/1081

PERRIN STRYKER: The Character of the Executive: *Eleven Studies in Managerial Qualities*   TB/1041

PIERRE URI: Partnership for Progress: *A Program for Transatlantic Action*   TB/3036

Contemporary Culture

JACQUES BARZUN: The House of Intellect   TB/1051

JOHN U. NEF: Cultural Foundations of Industrial Civilization   TB/1024

NATHAN M. PUSEY: The Age of the Scholar: *Observations on Education in a Troubled Decade*   TB/1157

PAUL VALÉRY: The Outlook for Intelligence TB/2016

History: General

L. CARRINGTON GOODRICH: A Short History of the Chinese People. *Illus.*   TB/3015

BERNARD LEWIS: The Arabs in History   TB/1029

SIR PERCY SYKES: A History of Exploration.° *Introduction by John K. Wright*   TB/1046

History: Ancient and Medieval

A. ANDREWES: The Greek Tyrants   TB/1103

P. BOISSONNADE: Life and Work in Medieval Europe: *The Evolution of the Medieval Economy, the Fifth to the Fifteenth Centuries.°* *Preface by Lynn White, Jr.*   TB/1141

HELEN CAM: England before Elizabeth   TB/1026

G. G. COULTON: Medieval Village, Manor, and Monastery   TB/1022

HEINRICH FICHTENAU: The Carolingian Empire: *The Age of Charlemagne*   TB/1142

F. L. GANSHOF: Feudalism   TB/1058

J. M. HUSSEY: The Byzantine World   TB/1057

SAMUEL NOAH KRAMER: Sumerian Mythology   TB/1055

FERDINAND LOT: The End of the Ancient World and the Beginnings of the Middle Ages. *Introduction by Glanville Downey*   TB/1044

CHARLES PETIT-DUTAILLIS: The Feudal Monarchy in France and England: *From the Tenth to the Thirteenth Century* °   TB/1165

STEVEN RUNCIMAN: A History of the Crusades. Volume I: *The First Crusade and the Foundation of the Kingdom of Jerusalem. Illus.*   TB/1143

FERDINAND SCHEVILL: Siena: *The History of a Medieval Commune. Introduction by William M. Bowsky*   TB/1164

HENRY OSBORN TAYLOR: The Classical Heritage of the Middle Ages. *Foreword and Biblio. by Kenneth M. Setton* [Formerly listed as TB/48 under the title *The Emergence of Christian Culture in the West*]   TB/1117

J. M. WALLACE-HADRILL: The Barbarian West: *The Early Middle Ages, A.D. 400-1000*   TB/1061

4

RELIGION

Ancient & Classical

Biblical Thought & Literature

Judaic Thought & Literature

Christianity: Origins & Early Development

7

8

```
Code to Torchbook Libraries:

TB/1+      : The Cloister Library
TB/301+    : The Cathedral Library
TB/501+    : The Science Library
TB/1001+   : The Academy Library
TB/2001+   : The Bollingen Library
TB/3001+   : The University Library
```